The Westminster Handbook
to Theologies
of the Reformation

Other books in The Westminster Handbooks to Christian Theology series

THE WESTMINSTER HANDBOOKS
TO CHRISTIAN THEOLOGY

The Westminster Handbook to Theologies of the Reformation

Edited by R. WARD HOLDER

WESTMINSTER
JOHN KNOX PRESS
LOUISVILLE · KENTUCKY

For Penelope, Samuel, and Harley
Joshua 24:15

"Ego autem et domus mea serviemus Domino"

© 2010 Westminster John Knox Press

First edition
Published by Westminster John Knox Press
Louisville, Kentucky

10 11 12 13 14 15 16 17 18 19—10 9 8 7 6 5 4 3 2 1

Scripture quotations from the New Revised Standard Version of the Bible are copyright © 1989 by the Division of Christian Education of the National Council of the Churches of Christ in the U.S.A. and are used by permission.

Book design by Sharon Adams
Cover design by Cynthia Dunne
Cover art: Monks Copying Manuscripts
(Corbis/© Archivo Iconografico)

Library of Congress Cataloging-in-Publication Data
The Westminster handbook to theologies of the Reformation / R. Ward Holder, editor. — 1st ed.
    p. cm. — (The Westminster handbooks to Christian theology)
  Includes bibliographical references.
  ISBN 978-0-664-22398-4 (alk. paper)
  1. Reformation. 2. Theology, Doctrinal—History—16th century. I. Holder, R. Ward. II. Title: Handbook to theologies of the Reformation.
  BR305.3.W47 2010
  230'.04409031—dc22

2010017888

PRINTED IN THE UNITED STATES OF AMERICA

∞ The paper used in this publication meets the minimum requirements of the American National Standard for Information Sciences—Permanence of Paper for Printed Library Materials, ANSI Z39.48-1992

Westminster John Knox Press advocates the responsible use of our natural resources. The text paper of this book is made from 30% post-consumer waste.

Contents

Series Introduction

The Westminster Handbooks to Christian Theology series provides a set of resources for the study of historical and contemporary theological movements and Christian theologians. These books are intended to assist scholars and students in finding concise and accurate treatments of important theological terms. The entries for the handbooks are arranged in alphabetical format to provide easy access to each term. The works are written by scholars with special expertise in these fields.

We hope this series will be of great help as readers explore the riches of Christian theology as it has been expressed in the past and as it will be formulated in the future.

The Publisher

Acknowledgments

All scholarship represents the fruit of collaboration; the deepest monograph has been watered with the rain of innumerable conversations. When the book is an edited volume, that collaboration expands exponentially. That truth makes the first task in recognizing debts of gratitude a simple one: I owe a tremendous amount to the team of scholars assembled here. They have served as my collegium for this project—my sounding board, my advisers, and my colleagues. I find myself particularly blessed to have come to know these individuals through my academic work, acquaintances that have so often turned into friendships. It is a rich privilege to work with people whom I admire, and I appreciate them more than my words can express.

Beyond that first joyful responsibility, there are a few more people whom I would be remiss if I did not thank by name. Randall C. Zachman began this project as the author of the book, but family issues made it impossible for him to continue. I am indebted to him for his notes, his contributions, and his blessing on taking over the project and pointing it in a new direction. Don McKim approached me with this project, and I am grateful to work with an editor of his talent and experience. On the production side of the book, the efforts of Dilu Nicholas and Julie Tonini have kept the volume on track; and they have been there to answer every question. Finally, I wish to give thanks to my family, who frequently sacrificed husband or father, or at least good humor as deadlines approached. They are my anchor that reminds me of the difference between those things that truly are of primary concern and the rest of my task list.

Contributors

Brian C. Brewer
Assistant Professor of Christian
  Theology
George W. Truett Theological Semi-
  nary, Baylor University
Waco, Texas

Amy Nelson Burnett
Professor of History
University of Nebraska
Lincoln, Nebraska

Stephen G. Burnett
Associate Professor of Religious Studies
  and History
University of Nebraska
Lincoln, Nebraska

J. Laurel Carrington
Professor of History
St. Olaf College
Northfield, Minnesota

Esther Chung-Kim
Assistant Professor of the History
  of Christianity
Claremont School of Theology
Claremont, California

Geoffrey Dipple
Professor of History
Augustana College
Sioux Falls, South Dakota

John Patrick Donnelly, S.J.
Professor of History
Marquette University
Milwaukee, Wisconsin

Kathryn A. Edwards
Associate Professor of History
University of South Carolina
Columbia, South Carolina

Daniel Eppley
Associate Professor of Religion
Thiel College
Greenville, Pennsylvania

Jill R. Fehleison
Associate Professor of History
Quinnipiac University
Hamden, Connecticut

Bruce Gordon
Titus Street Professor of Ecclesiastical
  History
Yale Divinity School
New Haven, Connecticut

Gary Neal Hansen
Assistant Professor of Church History
University of Dubuque Theological
  Seminary
Dubuque, Iowa

R. Ward Holder
Associate Professor of Theology
Saint Anselm College
Manchester, New Hampshire

Beth Kreitzer
Instructor, Departments of History
  and Theology
Belmont Abbey College
Belmont, North Carolina

Greta Grace Kroeker
Assistant Professor of History
University of Waterloo
Waterloo, Ontario

Amy E. Leonard
Associate Professor of History
Georgetown University
Washington, D.C.

R. Emmet McLaughlin
Professor of Early Modern History
Villanova University
Villanova, Pennsylvania

Jennifer Powell McNutt
Assistant Professor of Theology
    and History of Christianity
Wheaton College
Wheaton, Illinois

Peter Marshall
Professor of History
University of Warwick
Coventry, West Midlands, United
    Kingdom

Mickey L. Mattox
Associate Professor of Theology
Marquette University
Milwaukee, Wisconsin

Gregory J. Miller
Professor of History
Malone University
Canton, Ohio

G. Sujin Pak
Assistant Professor in the History
    of Christianity
Duke University Divinity School
Durham, North Carolina

Charles Parker
Professor of History
St. Louis University
St. Louis, Missouri

Sean T. Perrone
Professor of History
Saint Anselm College
Manchester, New Hampshire

Ronald K. Rittgers
Erich Markel Chair of German
    Reformation Studies
Valparaiso University
Valparaiso, Indiana

Rady Roldan-Figueroa
Assistant Professor of Religion
Baylor University
Waco, Texas

Alec Ryrie
Professor of the History
    of Christianity
Durham University
Durham, United Kingdom

William Bradford Smith
Professor of History
Oglethorpe University
Atlanta, Georgia

Karen E. Spierling
Associate Professor of History
Denison University
Granville, Ohio

Edwin Woodruff Tait
Assistant Professor of Bible
    and Religion
Huntington University
Huntington, Indiana

Kristen Post Walton
Associate Professor of History
Salisbury University
Salisbury, Maryland

David M. Whitford
Professor of the History
    of Christianity
United Theological Seminary
Dayton, Ohio

Hans Wiersma
Assistant Professor of Religion
Augsburg College
Minneapolis, Minnesota

Randall C. Zachman
Professor of Reformation Studies
University of Notre Dame
Notre Dame, Indiana

Pathways and Possibilities: Using the *Westminster Handbook to Theologies of the Reformation*

At the end of many lectures on Reformation theology, there is a gaping chasm between what the professor wants the students to be pondering, and those things they are actually wondering. The professor generally wants the students to have questions about the big picture and the majestic themes. He or she hopes the students are walking away, their heads filled with eternal questions: "Does God's grace impact human freedom?" or "What if the Holy Roman Empire had not been in a state of transition during the early years of the Luther affair?" or "Is English Protestantism Calvinistic, or does it really achieve some middle way between evangelicalism and Catholicism?" Students, however, frequently walk out of class wondering: "Who was Beatus Rhenanus?" or "What is an elector?" or "Is anything that Heinrich Bullinger wrote available in English?"

This *Handbook* seeks to give students a place to start on finding the answers to those questions. It is not meant as a replacement to deeper studies, but rather a quick reference to give students a guide as they begin to orient themselves to the study of the Reformation. The articles are brief, averaging between one hundred fifty and four hundred fifty words. They are written by experts in the field, scholars who have spent their careers explaining the arcana of the Reformation to undergraduates and seminarians.

A few words may be helpful on the possible ways to use the *Handbook*. First, the articles themselves should suffice to give the novice a place to start. Further, each entry has a very brief bibliography of secondary sources at its conclusion; these sources are a good place to begin further study. The full citations are given in the bibliography of secondary sources at the end of the book. If the reader also wants to find works by the Reformation-era authors, these are collected in the primary bibliography, also found at the end of the volume. The principal criterion of selection was availability in translation. Occasionally, this was not possible, but in most cases a great wealth of the thought of the Reformation has been made available in translation over the intervening centuries.

The *Handbook* makes some assumptions that are useful to acknowledge. First, there is not a large divide between "history" and "theology" in this guide to Reformation theology. This editorial choice reflects the facts on the ground during the period of the Reformations, roughly from 1500 to 1650. Early modern people did not draw sharp divisions between their mental concepts—popes were spiritual and temporal lords. Some Reformers argued that this should not be the case, but that should not blind us to what circumstances actually prevailed. Further, the historical-political figures frequently acted in the religious sphere. One can hardly imagine the sixteenth-century English church without the influence of Elizabeth I. The Church of England may never have existed without Henry VIII! Second, the *Handbook* assumes that it will be a desk reference, or guide, not the endpoint of the student's examination of any particular topic. The Reformation is endlessly fascinating—as demonstrated by the forest of trees that are consumed by books and monographs on the period every decade. The editor and contributors hope that this guide will be helpful as a beginning and invitation to further understanding. Finally, the *Handbook* assumes that the proper way to study the period of the Reformation is to study the various theologies of the time. One may have preferences, even favorites. But it is crucial to realize that all theological and religious decisions were made against a backdrop of possible alternatives. When a person, clergy or lay, made a positive religious decision, he or she also denied other possible options.

So we offer this brief guide to the commencement of answering those questions. Whether of eternal significance or of momentary concern to the student, the thoughts and realities of the Reformation remain a source of wonder and fascination. I offer this to those who would question, and wish them well on their searching.

R. Ward Holder
Manchester, New Hampshire

Abbreviations

a.k.a.	also known as		Ger.	German
b.	born		Gr.	Greek
ca.	circa, about		*Inst.*	John Calvin, *Institutes of the Christian Religion*
d.	died			
diss.	dissertation		Lat.	Latin
Eng.	English		r.	reigned
fl.	flourished		LW	Luther's Works
Fr.	French		WA	Weimarer Ausgabe

List of Articles

Articles

Absolution According to the medieval Roman Church, the word of absolution is to be spoken to the penitent by the priest after the penitent has confessed her sins. The *sin* of the penitent is not removed by the word of absolution, but rather by the *contrition* for sin that should be exhibited in confession itself. The word of absolution, "I absolve thee" (*ego te absolvo*), is therefore a judgment made by the priest that the sin has been removed by contrition. Moreover, the "loosing" of the eternal guilt of sin in absolution is always to be accompanied by the "binding" of sin by means of the imposition of penitential satisfactions, such as fasting, praying, and/or almsgiving. Such satisfactions serve three purposes: they pay the debt of temporal guilt from the sin, are punishments for the sin, and help to ward off future sin by instilling the opposing virtues. *Martin Luther*'s understanding of the *gospel* was shaped by his new understanding of the word of absolution. Luther believed the word of absolution is not a judgment by the priest evaluating the penitent's contrition, but is a promise spoken by Christ himself, wherein he offers the forgiveness of sins won by his death on the cross. This stance contributed greatly to Protestants denying the sacramental character of penitence. The *Council of Trent* reaffirmed the prior Roman understanding of absolution as a judgment made by the priest, and denied that anyone other than a priest or bishop could forgive sin. Trent also denied that absolution could be found anywhere other than the *sacrament* of private *penance*.

Forde et al. (2007); Osborne (1990)
RANDALL C. ZACHMAN

Accommodation The idea of accommodation comes from the teaching of the classical rhetoricians, who describe the effective speaker as one who accommodates his message to the capacities of his intended audience. Among the church fathers, Chrysostom in particular makes accommodation central to his understanding of divine and human pedagogy. The idea of accommodation emerges in the sixteenth century in the theology of *Desiderius Erasmus* and *John Calvin*. Calvin in particular insists that God always accommodates God's teaching to the capacity of the most unlearned person, not only in the theater of God's glory in creation, but also in *Scripture*, making Scripture, and not human images, the "books of the unlearned." Since Scripture is adapted to the capacities of the unlearned, Calvin is not at all surprised that its descriptions of the world differ from those provided by the philosophers, who were the "scientists" of Calvin's day.

Battles (1977); Benin (1993); D. Wright (1997).

RANDALL C. ZACHMAN

Act of Supremacy (1534)

Act of Supremacy (1534) From the very beginning of his divorce campaign in 1527, the English king *Henry VIII* raised the threat that he might settle the matter by taking his kingdom into schism, as some German and Scandinavian territories already had. This threat was eventually fulfilled by stages through a series of parliamentary statutes between 1532 and 1536. The 1534 Act of Supremacy is normally seen as the decisive break, asserting that Henry VIII was "the only Supreme Head on earth of the Church in England"—a title the statute recognized but did not bestow. All adult males were required to swear to accept this title; refusal was construed as treason and several dozen executions resulted. As well as abolishing papal jurisdiction, the act subordinated the English church to statute law. It was the model for the similar act passed by *Elizabeth I* in 1559, which altered the royal title to supreme governor.

Elton (1973); Eppley (2007); Lehmberg (1970).

ALEC RYRIE

Adiaphora The Stoics used *adiaphora* to describe morally neutral actions. *Martin Luther* distinguished between ecclesiastical laws that are divine and bind the conscience, and those that are human and hence indifferent. Problems arose because confessions and theologians disagreed on what *was* indifferent. In Luther's absence from Wittenberg in 1521, *Andreas Bodenstein von Karlstadt* introduced changes in worship, arguing one should never be slow to reform abuses. Luther returned in 1522 and preached sermons that rolled back Karlstadt's reforms, arguing he had harmed those weak in faith. Luther insisted that the law forbidding images was adiaphora, over against the iconoclastically minded Karlstadt and *Huldrych Zwingli*, and later *John Calvin*. After the defeat of the Schmalkaldic League in 1547, the emperor attempted to reintroduce Roman ceremonies into *evangelical* territories. In response, *Philip Melanchthon* distinguished between those matters that are necessary for faith and those that are indifferent. Other Lutheran theologians, led by Matthias Flacius Illyricus, claimed the reimposition of Roman ceremonies by threat of force made these matters necessary—in such a situation, there could be no adiaphora. This position was later formalized in the Formula of Concord of 1580.

Eire (1986); Gritsch and Jenson (1976); Verkamp (1977).

RANDALL C. ZACHMAN

Adoration The Fourth *Lateran Council* of 1215 taught that body and blood of Christ were substantially present in the Eucharist. Since the body and blood are one with Christ's soul, and Christ's soul is hypostatically united to Christ's divinity, the practice arose of adoring the Son in the reserved host of the Eucharist, especially on the Feast of Corpus Christi. *Martin Luther* and *Philip Melanchthon* argued that the body and blood of Christ were present only during the use of the *sacrament*. Christ's command was to eat and drink, not to adore. *Huldrych Zwingli* and *Johannes Oecolampadius* believed this to be idolatry, since it led people to worship a creature instead of the Creator. The *Council of Trent* responded to the Wittenberg and Swiss reformers by insisting that the faithful are to "give to this most holy sacrament in veneration the worship of latria, which is due to the true God," thereby making adoration a distinguishing mark of Roman Catholic worship.

————

T. Davis (2008); Goldberg (1999); Rubin (1991).
                              RANDALL C. ZACHMAN

Agricola, Johann (1492?–1560)

Agricola came to the University of Wittenberg in 1515/16. Associated with *Martin Luther*'s reform movement in Wittenberg, participating in the *Leipzig Disputation* of 1519 and the burning of *Exsurge Domini* in 1520, Agricola lectured on *Scripture* in Wittenberg from 1523 through 1525, after which he became pastor and educator in Eisleben. Agricola was critical of the Articles of Visitation drafted by *Philip Melanchthon* in 1527, especially the teaching that the Law brings the knowledge of sin. For Agricola, the Law is abolished in the life of the Christian, and thus the Gospel, not the Law, brings the knowledge of sin. Luther did not respond to this teaching until Agricola returned to Wittenberg in 1536, after which Luther directed a series of theses against Agricola's teaching, which he termed "*antinomian*." Agricola left Wittenberg for Berlin in 1540, where he spent the rest of his life as court chaplain to Elector Joachim II Hektor of Brandenberg.

————

Spitz (1963); Wengert (1997).
                              RANDALL C. ZACHMAN

Alcala, University of

The University of Alcala was founded by Cardinal Francisco Jiménez de Cisneros (1436–1517) in 1499. It soon rivaled the University of Salamanca as the leading university in Spain. It continued to cultivate scholastic theology but it became the preeminent center of humanist scholarship. Many of the leading Catholic reformers and religious innovators of the period made their way through Alcala, including *Juan de Valdés, Igna-* *tius of Loyola*, and Juan de Ávila. Characteristic of the humanist leaning of the university was the other great achievement associated with Cardinal Jiménez de Cisneros, the *Complutensian Polyglot* Bible, the first Bible of its kind to appear in print (1514–17, 1522). With the coming of the *Council of Trent*, however, a major shift took place in the direction of Spanish religious life. A concomitant change in attitudes toward *humanism* meant that the university experienced a sudden decline.

————

J. Edwards (2000); Pellistrandi (1991); Rummel (1999).
                              RADY ROLDAN-FIGUEROA

Aleander, Girolamo (1480–1542)

Bishop of Brindisi and later cardinal, Aleander was a humanist scholar and active opponent of *Martin Luther* in the early years of the *Reformation*. Aleander was among the critics of *Desiderius Erasmus*'s *Novum Instrumentum* of 1516. After the election of *Charles V*, Aleander was named papal nuncio. He was able to convince Charles to publish the bull *Exsurge Domine* in the Netherlands and arranged the burning of Luther's books at Liège, Louvain, and Cologne (in the last case with the support of the Cologne city fathers). At the *Diet of Worms*, Aleander was primarily responsible for drawing up the questions directed against Luther. He also wrote the edict condemning Luther, but was unable to convince Charles to publish the edict prior to the conclusion of the diet and Luther's flight. In his later years, Aleander was among the leading figures laying the foundation for the *Counter-Reformation*. At the request of *Pope Paul III*, Aleander, along with *Gasparo Contarini*, wrote a manual for the instruction of priests that remained in use into the eighteenth century.

————

Bagchi (1991); Daniel-Rops (1964).
                      WILLIAM BRADFORD SMITH

Allegorical Interpretation The
locus classicus of allegorical interpretation is in the Epistle to the Galatians, where Paul describes the relationship of Hagar to Sarah as an allegory about the children of slavery and the children of promise. The allegorical method claimed that there are narratives of *Scripture* whose true meaning is to be found at the spiritual level. This method of interpretation was popularized by Origen in the third century, and had developed throughout the medieval period into sophisticated systems of signification with multiple levels. Through its use, interpreters could find positive meaning in otherwise morally and spiritually offensive passages of Scripture. Though *Martin Luther* was trained in allegorical interpretation, he insisted that articles of faith could only be grounded on clear and certain texts of Scripture, and not on allegory. *John Calvin* was even more suspicious of allegory, preferring instead what he termed the genuine and natural meaning of Scripture.

De Lubac (1998–2009); Smalley (1964); D. Turner (1995).

RANDALL C. ZACHMAN

Alumbrados This Spanish religious movement flourished in the area of Toledo between 1519 and 1529. The term *alumbrado(s)* does not lend itself to easy translation. It could be rendered as "illuminated" or "enlightened," yet both English terms would be misleading as both have been used in English to refer to other historical religious movements. The *alumbrados* of Toledo were condemned by the Spanish *Inquisition* in an edict of 1525. The edict was followed by an *auto de fe* in 1529. The leading figures of the *alumbrados* were Pedro Ruiz de Alcaraz and María de Cazalla. Their central tenet was the assertion that union with God could be achieved by anyone through the practice of a form of silent prayer, known as *dejamiento*.

They tended to reject the need for the *sacraments* and of any other form of mediation between God and the faithful believer. Accordingly, over time the term *alumbrado* became Spanish shorthand for heresy.

Hamilton (1992); Homza (2000); Kinder (1994).

RADY ROLDAN-FIGUEROA

Alveldt, Augustin (ca. 1480–1535)
Alveldt was a *Franciscan* friar who became one of the first polemical opponents of *Martin Luther*. Alveldt thought Luther represented a serious heretical threat to the church, and wrote a spirited defense of papal primacy in 1520. Luther's colleague Johannes Lonicer wrote a refutation of Alveldt, provoking Alveldt to write yet another defense of the *papacy*, as well as a defense of the withholding of the chalice from communicants in the Eucharist. These writings provoked two of Luther's most important treatises of 1520, *On the Papacy in Rome* and *A Prelude concerning the Babylonian Captivity of the Church*. Luther and Lonicer expressed contempt for Alveldt's abilities as a theologian, but he clearly identified one of the central issues of the *Reformation*—the *authority* of the *church*.

Hammann (1989).

RANDALL C. ZACHMAN

Amsdorf, Nikolaus von (1483–1565) A theologian and pastor, Amsdorf was one of the earliest of the Wittenberg faculty to associate himself with *Martin Luther*, and became one of Luther's closest friends. Amsdorf accompanied Luther to Leipzig in 1519 and to Worms in 1521, and helped to lead the Wittenberg movement during Luther's absence in 1521–22. Believing that the *papacy* was the *antichrist*, and that he was living in the final days,

Amsdorf argued in 1523 for the right of lesser magistrates to resist those above them. He initiated the **Reformation** in Magdeburg in 1524, opposing the influence of **Anabaptists**. Installed as bishop of Naumburg-Zeitz by **Elector John Frederick I,** he faced intense opposition from Catholics, and went into exile after the defeat of the Schmalkaldic League in 1547. After his return to Magdeburg in 1548, Amsdorf opposed a collaborating response to the Augsburg Interim. He also opposed **Philip Melanchthon**'s concession that *good works* are necessary for salvation, claiming that this undermined the *gospel*. Amsdorf became one of the leaders of the Gnesio-Lutherans, and helped to shape the subsequent reception of Luther's theology, editing one of the early editions of Luther's works.

Kolb (1987); Rummel (2000); Steinmetz (2001b).

RANDALL C. ZACHMAN

Anabaptists   These Radical Reformers in the German- and Dutch-speaking areas of central Europe practiced adult believer's *baptism*. Anabaptist groups sprang up in different regions, but by the end of the sixteenth century the movement developed a fairly uniform confessional stance. Their opponents branded them Anabaptists (= rebaptizers) since early **Reformation** Christians were already baptized as infants. Anabaptists sought to reconstitute the New Testament church described in the Acts of the Apostles and Paul's Epistles. For the Hutterites in Moravia this included common ownership of all property. Anabaptists practiced strict discipline, including *excommunication* and expulsion of manifest sinners. While Anabaptists agreed that salvation was a free gift of God through *faith,* they also insisted that it could be lost if not followed by the new life of holiness made possible by the Holy Spirit. They retained the two *sacraments* of the **Lord's Supper**

and baptism, but they denied the real presence. By baptism individuals confessed their faith and declared their commitment to a life of Christian discipleship. Considering the rest of society as outside the pale of *grace,* most Anabaptists refused to serve in government. The example and command of Christ barred them from bearing arms or otherwise supporting violence. Dutch Anabaptists also professed a "heavenly flesh" **Christology**.

The earliest Anabaptists began as followers of **Huldrych Zwingli** in Zurich. Convinced that Zwingli was conceding too much to the secular authority in religious reform and proceeding too slowly, **Conrad Grebel** and others separated from the state church (1525) and were driven from the city. The *Schleitheim Confession* (1527) is the classic statement of their beliefs. By contrast, **Balthasar Hubmaier** eschewed separatism and reformed Waldshut, just north of the Swiss border, as an Anabaptist city before fleeing the Catholic Habsburgs. The protection he and other Anabaptists received in Moravia soon made that the home of a sizable Anabaptist population. In Augsburg, **Hans Hut,** a follower of **Thomas Müntzer,** rebaptized believers in anticipation of the second coming of Christ. In north Germany **Melchior Hoffmann** also combined Anabaptism with the expectation of Christ's imminent return. Moved by Hoffmann's apocalyptic message, Dutch Anabaptists seized the city of Münster, where they established the infamous Anabaptist Kingdom (1534–35). In the years that followed, **Menno Simons** turned Dutch Anabaptism toward the *pacifism* for which Mennonites are still well known. Swiss Anabaptists and most Moravian Anabaptists also embraced pacifism. Nonetheless, given the debacle of Münster and the divisiveness that adult baptism brought in both church and state, governments throughout Germany and the Low Countries persecuted Anabaptists. Rebaptism had been a capital crime since antiquity, and more than fifty thousand Anabaptists were executed in the sixteenth and early seventeenth centuries.

Snyder (2003); Stayer (1994); G. H. Williams (1992).

R. EMMET MCLAUGHLIN

Anagogy   Anagogy is a method, frequently exegetical, by which one elevates from the temporal and earthly to the spiritual and eternal significance of a reality. Anagogy is usually applied in the interpretation of symbols or types. For instance, David can be seen as a type of Christ, but by anagogy, he rises from the earthly king in Jerusalem to the spiritual king in heaven. In the Gospel of John, Jesus uses anagogy to speak about the meaning of his person and work, beginning with the earthly meaning of a reality such as bread or water, in order to lead his listeners to the spiritual meaning of his work. Some reformers who rejected allegory accepted anagogy as part of the literal sense of *Scripture*. *John Calvin* claimed that the allegory in Galatians 4:24 was technically an example of anagogy, and was part of the genuine and literal meaning of the scriptural text.

De Lubac (1998–2009, 2007); Smalley (1964).

RANDALL C. ZACHMAN

Analogy   Analogy follows the similarity amid difference between two realities, so that when one sees one reality, one is referred to the other. Reformed theologians such as *Huldrych Zwingli*, *Heinrich Bullinger*, and *John Calvin* made the analogy between the sign of bread and wine and the reality of the body and blood of Christ central to their understanding of the *Lord's Supper*, using the sixth chapter of John to specify the nature of the analogy. Just as bread and wine nourish and delight our

bodies, so the body and blood of Christ nourish and delight our souls. Calvin applied this principle to all of the signs used by God in the *Law* and the *Gospel*, insisting that one must always hold to the analogy between the sign and the thing signified.

New Catholic Encyclopedia, s.v. (2003); Santoni (1968); Smith and Olthuis (2005).

RANDALL C. ZACHMAN

Anathema   An anathema is a person or thing rejected by God, and therefore accursed. The term came to refer to people who pervert the preaching of the *gospel* by their teaching, following Paul's threat, "if anyone proclaims to you a gospel contrary to what you received, let that one be accursed [anathema]" (Gal. 1:9). It became customary in the ecumenical councils to condemn *heresy* by canons that set forth the teaching that made one anathema, and this practice was carried into the controversies of the sixteenth century. *Martin Luther* claimed that the teaching of *Huldrych Zwingli* on the *Lord's Supper* made him anathema, and both Luther and Zwingli concluded that the teaching of the *Anabaptists* made them anathema as well. The most extensive set of anathemas ever promulgated at a council took place at the *Council of Trent*, which pronounced over thirty anathemas in the canons on *justification* alone.

Jedin (1957–61); *New Catholic Encyclopedia*, s.v. (2003).

RANDALL C. ZACHMAN

Ancient Church   The writings of the early church fathers were made much more available to the theologians of the *Reformation* due to the editorial work of *Desiderius Erasmus*, and the publication of new critical editions of the fathers by Froben, his publishing house in Basel. The fathers were always seen as a crucial part of the teaching office of the church, and they quickly became central to the polemics regarding the legitimacy of *evangelical* theology. Roman opponents of *Martin Luther, Huldrych Zwingli*, and others claimed that their teaching could not be supported by the fathers and councils of the church, whereas Luther, *Philip Melanchthon, Martin Bucer*, and others claimed that the Roman Church had broken the continuity with the fathers that they were seeking to restore. *John Calvin* indicated the importance of the ancient church by describing his own theology as evangelical and orthodox, and Melanchthon came to highlight the centrality of the ancient church by speaking of the consensus of the prophets, apostles, and fathers in the 1543 *Loci Communes*. Many theologians came to identify with the teaching of Luther by finding it to be more in line with the teaching of the ancient church than that of Rome, most notably *Thomas Cranmer* and *Heinrich Bullinger*. However, the evangelicals also credited the ancient church with introducing innovations that would later develop into serious abuses, most notably the tendency to describe the Eucharist as a sacrifice.

Backus (1997); Dipple (2005); Lane (1999).
RANDALL C. ZACHMAN

Ancient Heresies A common polemical strategy was to describe an opponent's position as the reappearance of a *heresy* already condemned by the church, especially in the venerable ecumenical councils. Thus *Martin Luther* described the teaching of *John Duns Scotus* and *Gabriel Biel* on *merit* and *grace* as Pelagian, whereas *Johann Eck* claimed that Luther's teachings on the *papacy* were Hussite, and had already been condemned by the *Council of Constance* of 1415. Luther thought that *Huldrych Zwingli*'s distinction between the divinity of Christ, which is everywhere, and the humanity of Christ, which is in

heaven, was Nestorian, in that it denied the hypostatic union of the two natures of Christ. *John Calvin*, on the other hand, claimed that the Lutheran teaching that the humanity of Christ is to be found wherever the divinity of Christ is present recapitulated the denial of the genuine humanity of Christ by Marcion. Such claims are less an argument against the merit of one's opponent's position than they are guilt by association. Roman opponents of the Reformers claimed that the appearance of so many ancient heresies in their own day, including the Donatist heresy of the *Anabaptists* and the Arian heresy of the *anti-Trinitarians*, proved that Luther had opened a Pandora's box of heresy in his teaching. *Evangelical* theologians, on the other hand, saw the appearance of ancient heresies in their own day as a sign that they were in fact retrieving the true doctrine of the ancient church, since the same heresies were appearing in their own day as had appeared then.

Dipple (2005); Fenlon (1972); Frend (1984).
RANDALL C. ZACHMAN

Anfechtung (Lat. *tentatio*) *Martin Luther* used *Anfechtung* to convey his combined sense of dread, misery, and fear when he was confronted by the realities of sin, *death*, the devil, and damnation. It has been variously translated as "trial," "temptation," "tribulation," though perhaps the best translation is "affliction." He used the word throughout his life. Generally, Luther experienced *Anfechtungen* when he confronted the reality of his own sinfulness and contemplated the righteousness of God, who sits in judgment of all sinners. In his *Explanations of the Ninety-Five Theses*, he describes the feeling of *Anfechtung* vividly, "Yet they were so great and so much like hell that no tongue could adequately express them, no pen could describe them, and one who had not himself experienced them could not believe them. . . . At such a time God seems terribly angry, and with him the whole creation. At such a time there is no flight, no comfort, within or without, but all things accuse. . . . All that remains is the stark-naked desire for help and a terrible groaning, but it does not know where to turn for help" (LW 31:129; WA 1:557–58). *Anfechtung* is for Luther the harsh light of the *Law* of God upon the soul of a sinner. Though he originally felt that he did "not know where to turn," he eventually argued that *Anfechtung* and the judgment of Law leave sinners no other choice but to throw themselves upon the *mercy* and *grace* of God. Luther believed that the dependence upon God's grace alone after the experience of *Anfechtung* was an essential aspect, a touchstone, of a truly Christian theologian: "[finally], there is *tentatio, Anfechtung*. This is the touchstone which teaches you not only to know and understand, but also to experience how right, how true, how sweet, how lovely, how mighty, how comforting God's Word is, wisdom beyond all wisdom" (LW 34:286; WA 50:660).

Lohse (1999).

DAVID M. WHITFORD

Antichrist   The Letters of John speak of the coming of the antichrist, who will appear in the last hour. The antichrist is one who denies the truth of God and Christ under the guise of the truth, and is hence a deceiver. "Who is the liar but the one who denies that Jesus is the Christ? This is the antichrist, the one who denies the Father and the Son" (1 John 2:22). The identity of the antichrist was therefore filled out by turning to other passages that speak of the way the faithful are deceived, in particular the description in 2 Thessalonians of "the lawless one" who will appear before the final day of judgment. "He opposes and exalts himself above every so-called god or object of worship, so that he takes

his seat in the temple of God, declaring himself to be God" (2 Thess. 2:4). To this was added the description of deceitful spirits with "seared consciences" in 1 Timothy. "They forbid marriage and demand abstinence from foods, which God created to be received with thanksgiving by those who believe and know the truth" (1 Tim. 4:3). By 1520 *Martin Luther* agreed with *John Wyclif* before him that the pope was in fact the antichrist described by John and Paul, due to the way the *papacy* claimed to impose human commandments as divine law binding on consciences, thereby usurping the authority of God. The emergence of the *gospel*, with which Luther identified himself, was therefore the beginning of the return of Christ, who would appear to destroy the works of the antichrist. "And then the lawless one will be revealed, whom the Lord Jesus will destroy with the breath of his mouth, annihilating him by the manifestation of his coming" (2 Thess. 2:8). Luther therefore did not see himself as a reformer of the institution of the church, but rather as the one called to save Christians from the power of the antichrist before Christ returned to destroy him. *Huldrych Zwingli, Philip Melanchthon,* and *John Calvin,* among others, came to agree with Luther that the pope was the antichrist, though it may not have had the same eschatological significance for them as it did for Luther. They agreed with Luther, however, that as the antichrist the pope would be categorically opposed to the preaching of the gospel, for it would pose a direct threat to the entirety of his kingdom.

Bostick (1998); Lake and Questier (2002); McGinn (1994).

RANDALL C. ZACHMAN

Anticlericalism   The division of the church into the *clergy* and laity was codified by Gratian in his *Decretum* of 1150. The clergy were described as being endowed with an indelible character by means of their ordination, allowing them to bind and loose sins in confession, and to offer the sacrifice of the *Mass*, as well as to consecrate the Eucharist. As a consequence, clergy were freed from judgment by civil law, and did not have to serve in the military, as they were of a more perfect order of Christian life, following the counsels of perfection of Christ rather than the commandments of Moses. Clergy did not have to pay taxes, but were instead supported by tithes exacted from the laity. By the end of the fifteenth century, widespread resentment of the clergy emerged throughout Europe, due in large part to the failure of priests and *bishops* to embody the *counsels of perfection* in their own lives, in spite of repeated calls to "reform the church in its head and members." Those who should live as servants were seen as exercising lordship over others; those who should embody love and mercy were seen as imposing heavy burdens on their flocks; those who should live in apostolic poverty were seen as greedily devouring the incomes of their flock, often excommunicating those with whom they had financial disagreements.

At the beginning of the sixteenth century, *Desiderius Erasmus* popularized such criticisms of the clergy and monks in his *Enchiridion*, which went through several editions after 1518. *Martin Luther* intensified such criticism in his writings of 1520, especially his *Appeal to the German Nobility*, in which he accused the papacy of robbing the German nation and taking all its wealth to Italy. Luther also attacked the ontological distinction between clergy and laity in several of his writings of 1520. According to Luther, all faithful Christians are priests, and hence there is no spiritual difference between "clergy" and "laity." All Christians are called to the perfection of *faith* and love, and no Christian should be free of obedience and accountability to temporal rulers and the rule of law. These ideas were immediately and widely received, and

only served to intensify the anticlericalism that was created by the perceived moral failures of the clergy.

Thomas Müntzer and *Andreas Bodenstein von Karlstadt* further attacked the divide between "clergy" and "laity" by identifying themselves with ordinary, unlearned believers over against the learned elites of university theologians and powerful rulers. The iconoclastic riots and violent disruptions of masses during the 1520s should be seen as expressions of this more powerful kind of anticlericalism, as should the dissolution of monasteries and the refusal to pay tithes. The *Anabaptist* movements of the latter 1520s effectively tapped into this anticlerical resentment, as did the *Peasants' War* of 1525.

One of the major social contributions of the reformation movements was the complete removal of Gratian's description of the clergy as ontologically superior to the laity. Even though all of the movements emerging from the sixteenth century had pastors, they differed from their congregations only with regard to their office, not with regard to their spiritual level of perfection. On the other hand, one of the major contributions of the *Council of Trent* was its attempt to reform the *education* and morals of the Roman Catholic clergy. Indeed, the *Jesuits* quickly emerged to a role of prominence in the latter part of the sixteenth century precisely because of their ability to develop forms of ministry that were spiritually and morally compelling.

Dykema and Oberman (1993); Goertz (1996); Shagan (2003).
RANDALL C. ZACHMAN

Antinomianism
Although antinomianism can describe any position that denies the validity of the *Law* in the Christian life, it is most closely associated with two sets of controversies that took place within the Wittenberg reform movement. By 1520 *Martin Luther* made

a sharp dialectical distinction between the Law and the *Gospel* that was to last throughout his career. According to Luther, the Law does not have the power to remove *sin*, as he accused Rome of teaching, but rather it only has the power to reveal sin. Luther's colleague *Johann Agricola* disagreed with Luther's description of repentance as beginning with the preaching of the Law prior to *faith*, echoing the criticism of Roman theologians such as *Johann Eck* that only those who have faith in God's mercy will acknowledge their sin to God. The controversy erupted in 1527 and 1537. After a series of disputations about this question in Wittenberg, Luther wrote his treatise against Agricola, *Against the Antinomians*, in 1539 reasserting his claim that the Law alone reveals sin, and therefore plays an essential role in bringing people to faith. Agricola fled to Berlin, where he retracted his understanding of the Law. After Luther's death in 1546 and the 1547 defeat of the Schmalkaldic League, another controversy erupted regarding *Philip Melanchthon*'s statement in the Leipzig Interim that "good works are necessary for salvation." Melanchthon's opponents asserted that *good works* are harmful to salvation, and that the Law can only bring about a coerced obedience, as opposed to the spontaneous works brought about by faith in the *Gospel*. The Formula of Concord of 1580 ended this dispute by affirming the role of the Law in its "third use" in the life of the Christian, along with the necessity of good works, even if those works do not justify or bring about our inheritance of eternal life.

Mann (2000); Wengert (1997).

RANDALL C. ZACHMAN

Anti-Trinitarianism

Anti-Trinitarianism describes a complex movement in the sixteenth century that called into question the legitimacy of the doctrine of the *Trinity* as an expression of the biblical descriptions of God and Christ. Early Reformers had insisted that nothing could be made into an article of faith that was not to be found in the clear and unambiguous statements of *Scripture*. This interpretive model was soon used by some thinkers to call into question the doctrine of *homoousios* set forth in Nicaea (325), Constantinople (381), and Chalcedon (451). Though the *Anabaptist* Ludwig Haetzer (d. 1529) and the spiritualist Johannes Campanus (d. 1574) questioned the doctrine of the Trinity, the major impetus for anti-Trinitarian thought came from the controversial writings of *Michael Servetus*, especially his works *On the Errors of the Trinity* (1531), *Dialogues concerning the Trinity* (1532), and *The Restitution of Christianity* (1553). Servetus examined the biblical passages usually adduced to support the doctrine of the Trinity in an attempt to demonstrate that they did not allow for that interpretation, based on his claim that there is a strong line of continuity between the Old and New Testaments. After he was executed in Geneva for *heresy* in 1553, his writings were transmitted by the Italian followers of *Juan de Valdés* who emigrated from Italy to the Swiss territories, especially the physician *Giorgio Biandrata*, the jurist Mateo Gribaldi, and the philologist Valentino Gentile. Facing increasing opposition from the Swiss Reformed churches, the Italian anti-Trinitarians moved to Poland. With the arrival of Genile in 1562, Biandrata set up the "minor church" of Reformed anti-Trinitarians. The arrival of Fausto Sozzini in 1579 helped to consolidate the doctrinal position of the "minor church." The anti-Trinitarians were acknowledged to be one of four legitimate churches in Transylvania, along with the Roman Catholic, Lutheran, and Reformed.

Dán and Pirnát (1982); Lubieniecki and Williams (1995); Mulsow and Rohls (2005).

RANDALL C. ZACHMAN

Apocalypticism   The Christian movement was decisively shaped by the eschatological and apocalyptic views that developed in the Second Temple period, most notably in the book of Daniel, which finds a loud echo in the predictions of Jesus about the fall of the temple and the signs of the end, and in the Epistles of Paul, culminating in the Revelation of John. Although such expectations tended to diminish by the time Christianity became the religion of the Roman Empire, the theology of Joachim of Fiore (1135–1202) gave a strong impetus to apocalyptic expectation, with its description of the three stages of history. The latter medieval period saw increasing interest in Daniel and Revelation, as the faithful attempted to discern their place in what was taken to be the final cosmic drama of history before the return of Christ, accentuated by the spread of the plague and the emergence of three popes, in Rome, Avignon, and Pisa, at the dawn of the fifteenth century. Apocalyptic expectation was especially strong in German territories at the dawn of the *Reformation*. *Martin Luther* fully shared this expectation. Luther became convinced that the *papacy* was the *antichrist*, a sign of the last days before the return of Christ. Luther's colleague in Wittenberg, *Philip Melanchthon*, a serious student of both history and *astrology*, shared with Luther his reading of the times, confirming their sense that the world was approaching the last days.

Luther's Roman opponents, on the other hand, took the emergence of Luther, *Huldrych Zwingli*, and the *Anabaptists* as the unleashing of satanic deception in their day, and saw the cessation of the *Mass* in *evangelical* territories as the "desolating sacrilege" of the last days. Radicals took up this theme as well. *Thomas Müntzer* also shared in Luther's apocalyptic view of the world, but he saw himself as the prophet sent by God to guide the rulers, and then the peasants, in the violent purgation of the ungodly from the earth, in preparation for the return of Christ. *Melchior Hoffmann* looked toward a temporal and spiritual fulfillment of prophecy, and thus helped to create the circumstances that led to the establishment of the earthly Davidic kingdom in the city of *Münster*, which would herald the return of Christ. The Reformers of south Germany and the Swiss cities did not share this apocalyptic outlook, though they shared Luther's view that the pope was the antichrist.

Barnes (1988); Baylor (1991); G. H. Williams (1992).
RANDALL C. ZACHMAN

Apostles' Creed   The church *fathers* asserted that there was a harmony between the Old and New Testaments, the rule of faith, and the preaching of the bishops. Although the "rule of faith" varied by time and place in the first centuries of the church, it eventually came to be codified in what was called the Apostles' Creed. *Martin Luther* profoundly challenged the assumption of this harmony of teaching by asserting that the preaching of the *bishops*, both in the *papacy* and in councils, was directly contrary to the clear teaching of *Scripture* and the Creed. The Apostles' Creed therefore came to be seen as a true summary of the teaching of Scripture by many in the sixteenth century. One of *Desiderius Erasmus*'s dialogues featured Luther being tested on Christian *faith* by his adherence to the teachings of the Apostles' Creed. *John Calvin* admitted that the Creed may not have been written by the apostles, but he insisted that it contained "the certain truth of the Holy Spirit." However, the assumed harmony between Scripture and the Creed also could divide the *evangelical* community, as *Huldrych Zwingli* appealed to the Creed to argue against Luther that Christ is at the right hand of the Father, and therefore cannot be bodily present in the *Lord's Supper*. The Apostles' Creed was also a central element in the renewed interest in catechesis, as it formed the sum of the teaching of faith that all Christians should know, in conjunction with the Ten Commandments, the Lord's Prayer, and the *sacraments* of *Baptism* and the Lord's Supper. At the *Council of Trent*, Rome chose to center on another creed, the Nicene Creed of 381, as the symbol of faith.

Cochrane (2003); Dyk and Koop (2006); Leith (1982); Young (1991).

RANDALL C. ZACHMAN

Apostolic Succession

The legitimacy and necessity of episcopal ordination was defended in the early church by theologians such as Hippolytus of Rome by means of the claim that such ordination takes place within the apostolic succession of the church, which also undergirds the *apostolicity* of the teaching of the *bishops*. That succession was a theoretical chain leading from a contemporary bishop back finally to an apostle. Many of the early Reformers, such as *Martin Luther*, were themselves ordained by bishops. However, the question of future ordinations arose when no Roman bishops converted to the *evangelical* movement, meaning that those ordained in subsequent generations would not stand in the apostolic succession of the church. Luther responded by insisting that apostolic succession takes place by means of the *gospel*, and not by the laying on of hands by bishops. However, even *John Calvin* was aware of the extraordinary nature of evangelical ordinations, which were out of continuity with the ordinary ministry of the church. The Roman opponents of the evangelicals pointed to apostolic succession as one of the criteria undermining the legitimacy of evangelical forms of ministry.

Campenhausen (1969); Pettegree (1993).

RANDALL C. ZACHMAN

Apostolic Tradition

The early church claimed that the apostles handed on their teaching not only in the writings of the New Testament, and in summaries such as the *Apostles' Creed*, but also in the oral traditions handed down by the *bishops* in communion and succession with one another. The practice of infant *baptism* was described as an apostolic *tradition* by Origen, and was received as such by the later Greek and Latin churches. *Martin Luther* affirmed that articles of faith could not be established on the basis of unwritten traditions, but instead only on the basis of the clear words of *Scripture* and the Creed. Protestants argued that other practices of the church, such as private masses, clerical *celibacy*, and binding monastic vows, were of much later origin than the apostolic age, and hence had to be abandoned. The *Council of Trent* responded to this challenge and asserted that all saving truths and rules of conduct are contained in the written books and in the unwritten traditions, which either came from Christ himself through the apostles, or came from the apostles themselves under the dictation of the Holy Spirit, being handed on to the present day.

Campenhausen (1969); Pettegree (1993).

RANDALL C. ZACHMAN

Apostolicity

The controversy with the Gnostics in the first centuries of the church brought to the fore the importance of determining the apostolic status of the doctrine taught in the church. According to Irenaeus, apostolic doctrine is found in the harmony between the preaching of the apostles and the economy of redemption foretold by the prophets, which is confirmed by the rule of faith handed on to the faithful in *baptism*, and expounded by the teaching of *bishops* in communion with one another. The teaching of the bishops was itself seen to constitute a *tradition* going back to the apostles. Thus

Irenaeus claimed to teach the doctrine handed on to him by Polycarp, who himself handed on what he received from John. The decisions of bishops meeting in council, such as the councils of Nicaea or Constantinople, were seen as apostolic in nature, given the consensus of the bishops, and the agreement of their doctrine with the rule of faith and the Old and New Testaments.

Though subsequent theologians such as *John Wyclif* and *Jan Hus* questioned the authority of the pope, *Martin Luther* was the first to call into question the assumed harmony between *Scripture*, the rule of faith, and the decisions of bishops in council, either under papal authority or under their own authority. Luther asserted first that the pope could err, and then, at Leipzig, that councils could err, including the *Council of Constance*, which claimed its authority directly from the Holy Spirit, and not from the pope. Luther reduced the criteria of apostolicity to Scripture and the Creed, and insisted that only these are certain, whereas bishops could go wrong either individually or in council. This stance opened the question of all the authenticity of all dogmas, and various confessions and theologians began to question orthodox views with ancient standing, such as the *Trinity* and the *incarnation*. The dissolution of the *evangelical* movement into mutually exclusive communities of interpretation and practice appeared to confirm the charge of Luther's earliest opponents, that Scripture and Creed need to be interpreted by the decisions of the bishops over the past fifteen centuries of the history of the church, and could not be left to an individual theologian. Protestant theologians responded to this accusation by demonstrating their fundamental continuity with the fathers of the church, and accused Rome of introducing novel innovations that departed from the apostolic teaching of the church. The *Council of Trent* reasserted the prior understanding of apostolicity against the evangelical movements,

claiming that it taught nothing that is not attested by the Holy Scriptures, the apostolic traditions, the holy fathers, the most approved councils, and the judgment and unanimity of the church herself. It would not be until the First Vatican Council that a council would assert papal authority as the guarantor of apostolicity.

Durnbaugh (1985); Dvornik (1958); Stephens (2004).

RANDALL C. ZACHMAN

Aristotle (384–322 BCE)

Among Greek philosophers, Aristotle and *Plato* have had the most lasting influence. The larger corpus of Aristotle was reintroduced to the Latin West from the Muslim world, together with Arabic commentaries. Though it was not clear that the writings of Aristotle were harmonious with Christianity, Albertus Magnus and Thomas Aquinas were convinced of their utility, and established Aristotle as one of the great sources of scholastic theology (*see Scholasticism*). There were pronounced reactions to the influence of Aristotle on Christian theology in the sixteenth century. *Desiderius Erasmus* claimed that the influence of Aristotle's logic, and especially its use of dialectical thinking, made scholastic theologians highly argumentative. He believed that Aristotle's physics and metaphysics led scholastics to speculate about matters, in contrast to the simple and transformative *philosophy of Christ*. *Martin Luther* was trained in Aristotelianism, but he soon became convinced that Aristotle was the source of the increasing Pelagianism of later scholastic theologians. Luther removed Aristotle and the scholastic theologians from the theology curriculum at Wittenberg, replacing them with the study of *Scripture* in its original Greek and Hebrew. *John Calvin* was more impressed by Plato, but *Theodore de Beza* was trained in Aristotelian philosophy, and constructed his own theology in terms of an argument from effect to cause, after the manner of Aquinas. Through the influence of **Philip Melanchthon** and Beza, Aristotle returned to the theological curriculum, and became an important resource in the development of Lutheran and Reformed scholastic theology.

Donnelly (1976); Rummel (1998); Schmitt (1983).
RANDALL C. ZACHMAN

Arminius, Jacobus (1560–1609)
Arminius was born in Oudewater, Holland, and became one of the first students to matriculate at the recently established university in Leiden. He then went to Geneva to study theology under **Theodore de Beza**, and returned to Amsterdam in 1587, where he was ordained. Arminius criticized the doctrine of predestination taught by **John Calvin** and Beza, and as it was represented in the **Belgic Confession** of 1561. Arminius attempted to show the lack of scriptural support for this doctrine in his expositions on Romans, and continued this criticism in his teaching at the University of Leiden. According to Arminius, the **Holy Spirit** is not an irresistible force given only to the elect, but rather the sufficient aid to those who do not resist. God's predestining act is foresight of those who will and will not respond. Arminius's position was ultimately rejected by the **Synod of Dort** of 1618–19.

Bangs (1971); Muller (1991); Stanglin (2007).
RANDALL C. ZACHMAN

Assurance   Latin Christianity was decisively shaped by the theology of **Augustine** of Hippo, who thought that the Christian life was best exemplified by humility. Augustine wanted to avoid both self-satisfied presumption and despair. Christian life is lived in tension between hope and despair.

Martin Luther's experience of a terrified *conscience* made the Augustinian field of tension no longer tolerable. Luther wanted certainty of divine *love*. He found this assurance in the *gospel*, which proclaimed to him that Christ died for the forgiveness of his sins. Luther's desire for assurance, which he found satisfied only in the gospel, struck a chord in others, especially **Philip Melanchthon**, as well as **Martin Bucer** and **John Calvin**. Rome, however, maintained the tension, and rejected what it termed the "vain confidence of heretics" that they are loved and forgiven by God, insisting to the contrary that "no one can know with the certainty of faith, which cannot be subject to error, that he has obtained the grace of God."

Beeke (1991); Zachman (1993).
RANDALL C. ZACHMAN

Astrology   Based on the ancient belief that the heavens influenced everything on earth, astrology was indebted to the theories of **Aristotle** and Ptolemy, and was influenced by Arabic, Hebrew, and apocryphal works. It was integrated into many aspects of daily life: medical treatment, scientific studies, and personality assessments. The most common types of astrology involved casting individual horoscopes (genethliacal), interpreting the stars' influence at the time of a particular event (horary), predicting astronomical events (natural), and determining the stars' influence on an event (judicial). Many leading scholars supported astrology, including Cornelius Agrippa, **Philip Melanchthon**, Marsilio Ficino, and Girolamo Cardano, but judicial astrology strayed into dangerous territory: if an event could be predicted, humans could conceivably intervene to change its course. Such actions came dangerously close to challenging God's will and led to astrology's condemnation by theologians such as **John Calvin**. Despite such opposition, the debate over astrology's accuracy and spiritual legitimacy continued throughout the early modern period.

Curry (1989); Newman and Grafton (2001); Williams and Gunnoe (2002).
KATHRYN A. EDWARDS

Atonement   Atonement   concerns the way the death and resurrection of Christ reconciles the sinful world to God. In the Latin West, the reconciling power of the death of Christ was seen to lie in his sinlessness. Anselm taught that only the God-human could pay a debt that he did not owe, as he laid his life down to make *satisfaction* to the justice of God for sinners. *Martin Luther* developed a distinctive understanding of the death of Christ, influenced in large part by *Johannes von Staupitz*, which was predicated not on the innocence of Christ, but on Christ's willingness to burden himself with our sin and curse. According to Luther, Christ engages in a "joyous" or "happy exchange" with sinners: he freely takes upon himself sin, guilt, *death*, and curse, bearing them away in his body in order to give his divine righteousness, innocence, life, and blessing. *John Calvin* accepted this "wonderful exchange," and went beyond Luther by insisting that Christ bore human sin in his body, but experienced the full wrath of God against sin in his soul, as revealed in his cry that God had forsaken him, representing for Calvin the descent of Christ into hell. Luther and Calvin's understanding of the atonement as a "happy" or "wonderful exchange" therefore marks a decisive contribution to the Western understanding of the death of Christ, as it assumes the innocence of Christ, but also shows Christ's identification with sinners under God's wrath.

Aulén (1969); Bromiley (1978); Davies and Leftow (2004).
RANDALL C. ZACHMAN

Augsburg Confession   The Augsburg Confession (a.k.a. *Confessio Augustana*) is a fundamental document containing the central articles of belief of the Lutheran branch of church reform. The document was the result of Emperor *Charles V*'s demand that the *Wittenberg* reformers present a confession of faith at an Imperial convention (diet) in Augsburg, Germany, in 1530. In preparation for just such a summons, *Martin Luther, Philip Melanchthon*, and other Wittenbergers had met in the towns of Schwabach and Torgau to draft articles for an official confession. However, when it came time to travel to Augsburg, Luther was persuaded to remain behind. The task of writing a final version of the "Lutheran" party's official Confession of Faith was therefore left mainly to Melanchthon. On June 25, 1530, both a Latin and a German edition of the Augsburg Confession were read aloud and then presented to the emperor.

The Augsburg Confession comprises twenty-eight articles. In the first twenty-one articles, Melanchthon outlined the "Chief Articles of Faith" of the Wittenberg theologians. These articles were organized according to subject matter, including *original sin, justification*, the *church, baptism*, the *Lord's Supper, free will*, and *good works*. The remaining seven articles review certain ecclesiastical "abuses which have been corrected," including "The Marriage of Priests," "The Mass," and "Ecclesiastical Power." Generally speaking, the twenty-one articles of faith demonstrate concise theological formulations and an implied insistence that the Wittenberg theological method was not a departure from catholic teaching. Notable among the many noteworthy statements in the Augsburg Confession is the assertion (in article 7) that it is enough to base Christian unity upon doctrinal agreement, rather than upon uniform practices. On the other hand, the reproving tone of the seven articles addressing perceived church abuses indicates that even if doctrinal consensus was achieved, the reform of ecclesiastical practice and oversight would remain a core concern for the *evangelical* Reformers.

Despite initial hopes, the Augsburg Confession did not result in doctrinal consensus with the *papacy* or in political harmony with the emperor. A "Confutation of the Augsburg Confession" was drafted by a committee—which included *Johann Eck* and *Johannes Cochlaeus*—representing the papacy. Melanchthon's response to the Roman Confutation is preserved in his Apology of the Augsburg Confession (1531). Luther, for his part, was publicly appreciative of Melanchthon's efforts.

After 1530, Melanchthon's interest in conciliation between conflicting theological parties would inspire, in part, his ongoing efforts to amend the language of the first edition of the confession. His rewording of article 10 (On the Lord's Supper) in 1540 led to a backlash of sorts. Ever since, Lutheran church bodies have given the original, "Unaltered Augsburg Confession" (rather than Melanchthon's later altered versions) the distinction of being the preferred, confessionally accurate edition.

———
Burgess (1980); Gassman and Hendrix (1999); Grane (1987).

HANS WIERSMA

Augsburg, Religious Peace of
(1555)   The treaty that marked the end of the Schmalkaldic War also granted limited toleration to Lutherans in Germany. Since 1529 and the Protestation of Speyer, tensions had increased between the emperor *Charles V* and the Lutheran princes. In 1531 a defensive alliance of princes was established, the Schmalkaldic League, under the leadership of Landgrave *Philipp of Hesse* and Elector *John Frederick I* of Saxony. In the early 1540s the league expanded, forging diplomatic ties with *England*, France, and Denmark. Following the conclusion of a peace treaty with France and the death of the English king, Charles V took to

the field against the Lutheran princes, who were defeated at the battle of Mühlberg (April 24, 1547). Philipp of Hesse and John Frederick of Saxony were imprisoned; meanwhile the electoral title was transferred to Maurice of Saxony, who had supported the emperor in the Schmalkaldic War. Charles also attempted to force a solution to the religious crisis through the Interim of Augsburg (1548).

Charles's actions met with resistance from Lutherans throughout the empire. The emperor's attempts to unite his Burgundian and Spanish holdings to the empire, along with his extralegal actions following the battle of Mühlberg, constituted a violation of the terms of his electoral capitulation in the view of a number of princes and jurists. Charles found himself at odds with his erstwhile supporters, including Maurice of Saxony and the rulers of Hesse and Brandenburg. With financial and military support from Henry II of France, the princes were able to force Charles to back down. The Peace of Passau (August 2, 1552) required the release of the imprisoned princes, the lifting of the interim, and restoration of church properties reclaimed by the Catholics since 1548. Section 9 insisted that "adherents of the Augsburg Confession" be allowed to practice their religion unmolested.

The negotiations at Passau were understood as a preliminary to a future *Reichstag*, which finally met in Augsburg in August 1555. The final decree of the Diet of Augsburg (September 25, 1555) dealt generally with matters regarding the end of hostilities in the empire as well as a range of other secular matters (including the administration of justice) that had been disputed between the emperor and the princes. Sections 7–30 dealt specifically with the matter of religion. Sections 15–16 gave official recognition to the religion of the Augsburg Confession (Lutheranism) within those territories ruled by Lutheran princes, following the language from the Peace of Passau. This provision allowed the prince to choose the confession of the lands he ruled (*Jus Reformandi*). The Lutheran jurist Joachim Stephani later summarized this principle with the Latin phrase *cuius regio, eius religio* (whose realm, his religion) in a treatise published in 1576. The principle had its limits. Sections 18–20 contain what is known as the "Ecclesiastical Reservation," prohibiting any Catholic ecclesiastical states from being transformed into Protestant states. Should a prelate convert, he must abdicate and surrender his territories. Section 27 stipulated that in the Imperial cities there had to be parity between Catholic and Lutheran members of the town council. Insofar as most cities were dominated by Protestants, this provision clearly favored the Catholic minorities. Finally, section 17 prohibited any other confession than Lutheranism or Catholicism; not until the *Peace of Westphalia* (1648) did Calvinism receive official recognition in the empire.

Fuchs (1970); Grimm (1973); Holborn (1959).

WILLIAM BRADFORD SMITH

Augustine (354–430)
Augustine of Hippo was the most influential of the *fathers* in the Latin West, and the Augustinian legacy was enormously important throughout the sixteenth century. In the struggle over the possession of the legacy of the fathers, Augustine was the prize. Augustine was especially influential for the views on the *grace* of God he developed during the controversy with the Pelagians, which dominated the last years of his life. According to Augustine, the fall of Adam took place by the mysterious and inexplicable turning of the wills of Adam and Eve from the *love* of God for the sake of God, to the love of self for its own sake. The sin of Adam is inherited by all, making it impossible to fulfill the commandment to love God for God's own sake, and one's neighbor for the sake of

God. The *law* was given not to reveal what we can do, as Pelagius thought, but rather to show us what we can no longer do, so that we seek the aid of the grace of God in Jesus Christ. *Faith* seeks the ability to love God from Christ, who pours such love into our hearts by the *Holy Spirit*, thereby justifying or making right the *will*. Since both faith and love are gifts of God, and not objects of human boasting, Augustine concluded that both were given only to the elect, through God's *mercy*, while the rest of humanity was allowed to perish, through God's justice.

Martin Luther read the later writings of Augustine and began to see that the teaching of later scholastic doctors such as *John Duns Scotus* and *Gabriel Biel* echoed the teaching of the Pelagians. They claimed that the sinner could follow the injunction of both the law and reason to love God above all things, thereby meriting in a congruent way the grace of God. Luther found by experience that the more he tried to merit the grace of God by doing works, the more his *conscience* became terrified by the power of *sin*. Luther came to agree that the law is given to show our inability, but he went beyond Augustine by insisting that it also has the power to reveal sin, *death*, and wrath, in order to humble the self-righteous by their terrors of conscience. Luther also agreed with Augustine that faith seeks the love of God from Christ, but Luther did not primarily seek the ability to love God for God's sake, but rather the love of God for the terrified sinner.

Augustine also influenced *Huldrych Zwingli* in his description of faith as the true eating of the flesh of Christ. This led to a rupture between the *evangelical* movements in Zurich and Wittenberg. *John Calvin* retrieved Augustine's understanding of election to demonstrate that all good things are given freely by God, though his teaching on reprobation goes further than Augustine. Roman theologians denied that Protestant thinkers had fully understood

Augustine, or that they took his thought out of context.

P. Brown (2000); Kaufman (1982); Oberman, James, and Saak (1991).

RANDALL C. ZACHMAN

Authority   In the *Reformation* the issue of authority is central. Traditionally, authority is the power to make doctrinal and disciplinary decisions. Prior to the sixteenth century, the greatest question of authority was the divide between temporal and sacred authority. Thinkers as varied as Dante, Marsilius of Padua, and *John Wyclif* had argued about the proper place of ecclesiastical authority. Reformation arguments about the nature of authority brought previously less-discussed questions to the fore, including the sources of authority, who could hold authority, and what actions might cause a loss of authority. Protestants tended to link authority to right order and the carrying out of scriptural injunctions. Roman theologians tended to see the sources of authority as twofold, *Scripture* and *tradition*; this position was formally defined at the *Council of Trent*. Further, Protestants tended to see authority attached to performance of divinely sanctioned acts, while Roman theologians connected authority to properly ordained *offices*.

M. Edwards (1994); G. Evans (1992); Rittgers (2004).

R. WARD HOLDER

Auto de fe   Auto de fe (act of faith) was a public ceremony at which the *Inquisition* sentenced the accused. The ceremony consisted of a procession, a mass, a sermon, the reconciliation of penitents, the denunciation of heretics, and the handing down of sentences. Most accused were reconciled with the church and for their punishment had to wear sanbenitos (i.e., penitential garments), pay fines, face exile, or go to the galleys. Only unrepentant and relapsed heretics were condemned to burn at the stake and handed over to secular officials for execution. Gruesome burnings epitomize the auto de fe in popular imagination, but an execution was not an essential part of the ceremony.

Autos de fe were public events and attracted large crowds. Early modern Spaniards considered these acts of faith as a representation of the judgment awaiting all humanity, and many spectators perceived the act of faith as a morally edifying experience.

Flynn (1991); Kamen (1999); Rawlings (2006).

SEAN T. PERRONE

Ban   In the medieval Catholic Church the ban or *excommunication* had two forms: minor excommunication excluded from the *sacraments* while major excommunication could require social shunning. Excommunication was designed to reform the sinner, to deter sin, and to prevent the profanation of the sacraments. Abusive imposition of excommunication, however, was one of the most consistent complaints of the late medieval laity and church reformers.

Biblical warrant (e.g., Matt. 18:15–18; 1 Cor. 5:5; 1 Tim. 1:20) ensured the continuance of the ban among Protestants. *Martin Luther*'s pastoral focus upon the promise of the *gospel* and his pessimistic view of the continued sinfulness of believers meant that ecclesial discipline, including the ban, played little role in his teaching. The ban remained available to Lutheran consistories, but held little prominence. For *John Calvin* and the Reformed, church discipline— including the ban—was a distinguishing mark of the true church. In *Huldrych Zwingli*'s Zurich, the city council administered the ban, which reinforced late medieval municipal morals legislation. In Calvin's *Geneva* the ban was part of the discipline imposed by a consistory composed of ministers and lay elders (presbyters) drawn from the city council. The Geneva model was imitated by the Reformed throughout Europe, even in regions where they were not the established church.

The *Anabaptists* laid even greater emphasis upon the ban, including it with *baptism* and the *Lord's Supper* as one of the three ordinances of the church. By contrast with the Reformed, who normally imposed only the minor ban, relying on further secular sanctions for the recalcitrant, Anabaptists often used the major ban as well. In the first generation of Anabaptism in southern Germany and Moravia, doctrinal disagreements, perfectionist behavioral expectations, and competition among charismatic leaders resulted in frequent, often mutual, banning that splintered the entire movement. In the second generation, the Anabaptists of the Middle and Lower Rhine moderated its application and limited it to the minor ban. In Lower Germany and Holland, however, rigorists like Leonard Bouwens (1515–82) and, more hesitantly, *Menno Simons* (1496–1561), insisted upon the full major ban (including the separation of spouses from "bed and board"). They went further by forgoing the biblically witnessed (Matt. 18:15–18) three preliminary warnings. The stringent new standard caused a definitive break with the Anabaptists to the south (1557) and divided the Dutch themselves, with many withdrawing from rigorist communities to found congregations (Waterlander, later *Doopsgezinden* [baptism-favorers]) that were more moderate on the ban. They also avoided the authoritarian leadership characteristic of more rigorist congregations and cultivated a less suspicious attitude to the larger society.

Modern Mennonites are sparing in their use of the ban, but the Old Order Amish and the Hutterites continue the rigorist *tradition*.

E. Vodola (1986); G. H. Williams (1992).
R. EMMET MCLAUGHLIN

Báñez, Domingo (1528–1604)

Báñez was a *Dominican* theologian of the school of Salamanca and confessor of *Teresa of Avila*. He studied in Salamanca under the guidance of leading Dominican theologians such as Melchor Cano (1509–60). He joined the Order of Preachers in 1547 and finalized his doctoral studies at the University of Sigüenza in 1565. Báñez joined the faculty of Salamanca in 1577, later becoming the successor of Bartolomé de Medina (1527–80) in 1581. In 1582 he confronted the Jesuit Prudencio de Montemayor and the Augustinian Fray Luis de León (1527–91) in a heated scholastic debate as they inquired if Christ died freely. Later, in 1588, he confronted the teachings of the Jesuit Luis de Molina (1535–1600). Molinism asserted that the efficacy of *grace* is founded on God's foreknowledge of free human cooperation with the gift of grace (*ab extrinseco*). Báñez retorted by affirming the intrinsic efficacy of grace (*gratia efficax ab intrinseco*).

McGrath (2005); Nichols (1991); K. White (1997).
RADY ROLDAN-FIGUEROA

Baptism
Protestant reformers recognized two *sacraments*: the *Lord's Supper* and baptism. As in all aspects of worship, Protestants privileged the Word of God in baptism, but varied in their interpretations of the precise significance and correct form of the sacrament. *Martin Luther* believed that God enacted a change in the individual during baptism, gracing the baptized infant with the seed of *faith*. The image of washing was also important for Luther, but he rejected the Roman Catholic belief that baptism was necessary for salvation as well as the notion that the souls of unbaptized children were consigned to *limbo*. Luther maintained some traditional practices, including one rite of exorcism, and he continued to permit emergency baptism by midwives, although Lutheran

authorities imposed their authority over midwives by providing them with specific instruction manuals for baptisms.

In contrast, *Huldrych Zwingli* dismissed exorcism and other Roman practices as entirely superfluous, insisting that baptism was a symbolic act of initiation into the Christian community. *John Calvin* also omitted all "superstitious" rituals, rejected baptism as essential to salvation, and emphasized the rite as a mark of entrance into the Christian community. But Calvin also argued that baptism was a visible sign of God's *grace* working in the participants during the ceremony; in contrast to Luther, Calvin emphasized the faith of the parents, godparents, and other participants, rather than the incipient faith of the child. As a result, he rejected emergency baptism and insisted that all baptisms be performed publicly, in church, at the time of a sermon. Calvin and *Heinrich Bullinger* each developed a covenantal defense of infant baptism, arguing that it replaced circumcision as the mark of God's covenant with God's people. Later, the Anglican Church attempted to blend Reformed baptismal theology with the continuation of more traditional baptismal practices.

Baptism was a major point of divide between mainstream Reformers and Anabaptists, who practiced adult, or believers', baptism. Anabaptists insisted that a valid baptism had to be preceded by a public statement of faith, arguing that infant baptism was not scriptural. During the decade between the *Peasants' War* of 1524–25 and the takeover of *Münster* by apocalyptic Anabaptists in 1534–35, adult baptism became the main mark by which mainstream Reformers and secular governments identified the Radical Reformers they believed were a threat to a stable Christian society.

Protestant changes to baptism challenged social customs and traditional religious beliefs. The Reformed rejection of emergency baptism, for example, led some parents of sickly newborns to have their children baptized secretly, and then to arrange for a later public baptism. Controversies involving the role of godparents and the naming of children at baptism also arose as the Reformers tried to enact their ideas.

The *Council of Trent* defended all seven sacraments as valid and affirmed the belief that baptism washed away *original sin* and was necessary for salvation.

Cressy (1997); Karant-Nunn (1997); Old (1992); Spierling (2005); Spinks (2006); Trigg (1994).

KAREN E. SPIERLING

Basel A city on both banks of the Rhine River in northwest Switzerland, Basel is today at the exact junction of Germany, France, and Switzerland. In the sixteenth century Basel was one of the most important cities in the Swiss Confederation (joined 1501), a wealthy university town, and an important center of the Protestant *Reformation*. Basel was also a significant printing center and long-time home of *Desiderius Erasmus*. The triumph of the reform was established through an iconoclastic riot in February 1529 that forced the abolition of the *Mass*, the dismissal of Catholics from the council, and the removal of all images. The most important Protestant leaders in Basel were *Johannes Oecolampadius* and his successor, *Oswald Myconius*. The Reformation in Basel underwent several distinct phases over the course of the sixteenth century from Zwinglian to Lutheran to Calvinist and provides an important illustration of the varying relationships between city government and the Protestant Reformation.

Guggisberg (1982); Rupp (1969); Tracy (1996); Wandel (1995).

GREGORY J. MILLER

Beda, Noël (1470?–1537) From his position as the leader of the Paris Faculty of Theology (1520–34), Beda was the most important figure in the university's opposition to the Protestant *Reformation*. Using the reestablished office of "syndic," he staunchly defended church *tradition* with a strong emphasis on censorship. He opposed any hint of humanistic or Reformed views. He considered the humanists to be responsible for Protestantism and spearheaded the university's formal condemnation of *Desiderius Erasmus* in 1528. Beda's downfall began in 1530 when against the explicit wishes of Francis I he publicly opposed *Henry VIII*'s annulment proceedings. In 1534 he accused the regius professors of the Collège de France of humanist sympathies before the Parlement of Paris and subsequently was arrested and thereafter exiled to Mont-Saint-Michel. As civil tensions escalated in France around the mid-century, however, Beda's positions and policies became the established guidelines for the conservative defense in France against the Protestant Reformation.

Farge (1985); Rummel (1989).

GREGORY J. MILLER

Belgic Confession   First published in 1561, the Belgic Confession of Faith (*Confessio Belgica*) became the basic statement of faith and doctrine of the Reformed Church throughout the *Low Countries* (Netherlands). Guy de Brès, Reformed pastor in the southern Netherlands (present-day Belgium), drafted the document, with assistance from colleagues, to demonstrate the biblical character of Reformed Protestantism to Spanish authorities who governed the region. A student of *John Calvin* in Geneva, de Brès was influenced heavily by the French Reformed movement and followed the 1559 Gallican Confession of Faith. Written in French, the Belgic Confession circulated widely in Reformed circles and subsequently was translated into Dutch, German, and Latin. Dutch reformers adopted the confession with minor revisions at every national synod:

Emden (1571), Dordrecht (1574), and Middelburg (1581). The Belgic Confession received ultimate affirmation at the 1618–1619 *Synod of Dort* (Dordrecht), which established the theological form of the Dutch Reformed Church.

Gootjes (2007); Rohls (1998); Van Halsema (1961).

CHARLES PARKER

Bellarmino, Roberto (1542–1621)
Jesuit, cardinal, archbishop, and theologian, Bellarmino was the leading Roman Catholic controversialist during the late 1500s and early 1600s in the doctrinal disputes raised by Protestant challenges. He also participated in the condemnation of Galileo Galilei (1564–1642), prohibiting him from advocating Copernican heliocentricism.

Bellarmino was born in Montepulciano in Tuscany and entered the Society of Jesus at Rome in 1560. With a prodigious intellect and indefatigable stamina, he studied first in Rome, Mondovì (Piedmont), and Padua, but was transferred after nine years in his theological formation to the University of Leuven (Louvain) in the southern Low Countries so that he could focus his study on the heresies of his day. He was ordained in 1570. After completing his studies and teaching at Leuven, Bellarmino returned to the Roman (*Jesuit*) College in Italy in 1576, where he took residence as the chief controversialist. He was made a cardinal in 1599 and archbishop of Capua in 1602.

Bellarmino's erudition and personal *piety* made him an effective preacher and even more capable polemicist. From 1586 to 1593, he published his most influential work, the multivolume *Disputationes de controversiis Christianae fidei adversus huius temporis haereticos* (Disputations on the Controversies of the Christian Faith Against the Heretics of This Time). In it, he thoroughly scrutinized and roundly rejected all Protestant positions and unequivocally defended the *authority* of the church under papal governance. Bellarmino also contended with Gallicans and other parties in the Roman Church that sought to restrict the authority of the pope. To that end, he wrote *De Potestate Summi Pontificis in Rebus Temporalibus* (*On the Power of the Supreme Pontiff in Temporal Affairs*), which championed ultramontanism, a strict understanding of papal authority. Among his other works, Bellarmino produced a catechism in 1597 and contributed to the revision of the Vulgate in 1592. The corpus of his works, published collectively between 1870 and 1874, runs to twelve volumes.

Though a brilliant scholar and able defender of the Roman Church, Bellarmino's polemical work did not lead to any significant Protestant defections. Rather, the significance of his work lay in the renewed confidence it gave to Catholic apologists and churchmen as the *Counter-Reformation* got underway.

Bellarmino is also known for his role in the early stages of Galileo's conflict with the Holy Office. Galileo's writings intrigued Bellarmino, who carried on a correspondence with the Florentine astronomer. Bellarmino, along with other theologians, examined Copernicanism at the instigation of the Holy Office, and condemned the theory as heretical. In 1616 Bellarmino held an audience with Galileo, ordering him not to teach or defend Copernican astronomy.

Bellarmino was canonized in 1930 and proclaimed a Doctor of the Church in 1931.

Blackwell (1991); Brodrick (1961); E. Ryan (1936).

CHARLES PARKER

Beza, Theodore de (1519–1605)

Beza was a Reformed pastor and theologian. Born in Vezelay to a family of the lesser nobility, Beza was educated in humanism and the law. He served as professor at the academies of Lausanne (1550–58) and Geneva (1559–99), as rector of the Academy of Geneva (1559–63), as a pastor in Geneva (1559–1605), and as moderator of the Genevan *Company of Pastors* (1564–80). He conducted an extensive correspondence and was an influential participant in colloquies with Catholics and Lutherans. His theological contributions primarily constituted a defense and development of *John Calvin*'s theological legacy. Beza is particularly important for his articulation of the right of subjects to resist a tyrannical ruler, his defense of presbyterian church *polity*, and his supralapsarian doctrine of *predestination*, but he also contributed to eucharistic theology and the Reformed doctrine of *justification*, besides defending Genevan church discipline and the execution of heretics. He has been seen as a transitional figure pointing toward Reformed *orthodoxy*, but the nature of this transition and Beza's role in it is a subject of controversy.

Bray (1975); Manetsch (2000); Muller (1988).

EDWIN WOODRUFF TAIT

Biandrata, Giorgio (ca. 1515–88/90)

Biandrata was an Italian physician and Unitarian reformer. He graduated in arts and medicine from Montpellier in 1533, whereupon he became a specialist in women's disorders and physician to the royal courts of Poland and Hungary. In 1557 he moved to Geneva, where he discussed theology with *John Calvin* and began to espouse anti-Trinitarian beliefs. However, following the execution of *Michael Servetus*, Biandrata retreated ultimately to Poland, the birthplace of Unitarianism, in 1560. In Kraków Biandrata became the physician to the queen, Bona Sforza, and also a significant leader of the Unitarian party at the synods of Pinczów and Ksiaz. Later moving to Transylvania and working in close association with the royal court there, Biandrata continued to maintain a moderate Unitarian view within the Reformed church that sought to venerate Jesus despite the belief that Jesus was created by God. Biandrata worked to mitigate the more radical forms of Unitarianism.

G. Brown (1933); Church (1932); DeWind (1952); Tylenda (1977).

BRIAN C. BREWER

Bible   From the Greek, meaning literally "the book," the Bible is a collection of primarily Hebrew and Greek writings understood as "Holy Scripture," inspired by God and therefore authoritative for *faith* and practice.

The sixteenth century was a time of epoch-making controversy over faith and practice, much of it centered on the Bible and its interpretation. Exegetical trends with roots in the Middle Ages led many (Catholics and Protestants) away from allegorizing methods toward a new focus on the literal sense. Scholars like *Faber Stapulensis* (Jacques Lefèvre d'Étaples) and *Martin Luther* also experimented with christological readings of *Scripture*, particularly the Psalms. With the assistance of enterprising printers and the advantages provided by the recovery of the biblical languages, they took biblical commentary beyond its medieval limits and moved it to center stage.

Reformers and humanists alike sought to bring out the authentic meaning of Scripture for the edification of the individual, church, and society. Often these purposes were intertwined. In Zurich, for example, *Huldrych Zwingli* instituted the *Prophezei*, public readings of Scripture in the original languages followed by a Latin translation and sermon/lecture. The result, in Zurich and elsewhere, was the intensification of the religious aspect of public life, that is, the further christianization of society. From Wittenberg to Geneva, the Bible, *exegesis*, and preaching were closely connected to both personal and civic reform.

The words of Scripture, too, became the subject of controversy. New texts became available, including the Bible in the original languages. Intense controversy followed *Desiderius Erasmus*'s 1516 publication of an annotated edition of the Greek New Testament, because it cast doubt on doctrines and practices based on the traditional Latin translation. Scholars quickly seized on Erasmus's work as the basis for new vernacular translation, where once again the impact of the *Reformation* was felt in church and society alike. Men like Luther and *William Tyndale* (who translated the Bible into German and English, respectively, though they were hardly the first to try) made lasting contributions not just to theology but also to the development of language, literature, and culture. Literary monuments to such contributions include the Luther Bible (1534) and the *Geneva Bible* (1560).

Although they ignored neither the Vulgate nor the patristic and medieval commentaries, over time Protestant interpreters looked increasingly to study of the Bible in the original languages to support their doctrinal formulations. Catholic theologians did so as well, but at the *Council of Trent* (1546) the church—keenly aware of deficiencies in the available Greek and Hebrew manuscripts, and determined to defend their faith against Protestant criticism—opted to make the revised Vulgate edition its authoritative text, which eventually resulted in the Sixto-Clementine Vulgate of 1592. Outstanding Catholic biblical scholars of the era include Santes Pagnini, *Thomas de Vio Cardinal Cajetan*, and Sixtus of Siena.

Muller and Thompson (1996); Pelikan (1996); J. Preus (1969).

MICKEY L. MATTOX

Biel, Gabriel (ca. 1420 or 1425–95)

A scholastic and professor of theology at the new University of Tübingen,

Germany, Biel's theology emerged out of what came to be known as the *via moderna* (modern way), which espoused that all *philosophy* and theology should be tested by reason and was. Biel's thought was greatly influenced by *William of Ockham* and nominalism and played an important role in the development of the theology of *Martin Luther*, who studied at the University of Erfurt under one of Biel's students. In particular, Biel's understanding of *justification* based on the reliability of God's pact with humanity and the importance of pastoral concerns are also present in Luther's theology, though Luther rejected many of Biel's works that he felt expressed semi-Pelagian views.

Cameron (1991); McGrath (2005); Oberman (1963); Ozment (1980).
GRETA GRACE KROEKER

Bishops   The role of bishops (ordained members of the secular *clergy* usually in charge of a diocese) came under attack by Protestants on both theological and pragmatic grounds. Reformers claimed bishops had overstepped their traditional role as guides and accused them of worldliness, corruption, dereliction of duty, and luxurious living, especially within the *Holy Roman Empire*, where bishops were also powerful territorial princes. Most Protestant churches dispensed with the episcopacy, with the notable exceptions of Lutheran Sweden and Anglican *England*, where bishops were more closely allied with the state. Other offices arose in Protestant churches that took over some of their duties, such as church superintendents, but without the idea of apostolic succession or the power of traditional bishops. The *Council of Trent* debated the role of bishops and their relationship to the laity, other ordained offices, and the popes but decided to leave the role vague, although the council increased the power and authority of bishops to spread reform and correct abuses.

Bergin (1999); Jedin (1967); Kingdon (1987); Kirk (1989).
AMY E. LEONARD

Blaurock (Cajacob), Georg (ca. 1492–1529)   In 1524 the former pastor Jörg vom Hause Jakob (Georg from the house of Jacob) traveled to Zurich to consult with *Huldrych Zwingli* but eventually joined the Swiss Brethren led by *Conrad Grebel* and Felix Manz. On January 18, 1525, the day after the Zurich town council ruled in favor of continuing the practice of infant *baptism*, a meeting was held among the Brethren where Blaurock requested baptism by the hand of Grebel, thus becoming the first *Anabaptist*. He received the surname "Blaurock" from the *blauer rock* (blue coat) he wore during this meeting. Blaurock's baptism is seen as the initial event of the Anabaptist movement. Blaurock fled to Austrian Tyrol but was arrested and burned at the stake near Klausen in 1529. Blaurock's only extant writings are a letter and two hymns. Among his converts was *Jakob Hutter*, whose followers, known as "Hutterites," eventually spread to Russia and the United States.

Estep (1996); J. Moore (1984); G. H. Williams (1992).
BRIAN C. BREWER

Blessed Exchange (Wonderful Exchange)   Based on a number of New Testament verses such as 2 Corinthians 5:21, the blessed exchange is a theological concept that seeks to explain the gracious foundation of a sinner's *justification*. Explaining the blessed exchange, *Martin Luther* writes, "this is the confidence that Christians have and our real joy of conscience, that by means of faith our sins become no longer ours but Christ's upon whom God placed the sins of all of us. He took upon himself our sins. Christ himself is 'the Lamb of God who takes away the sins of the world.' All the righteousness of Christ becomes ours" (LW 31:189; WA 1:593). *John Calvin*, likewise, noted that a sinner's guilt, through the power of grace, "has been transferred" to Christ (*Inst.* 2.16.5). Through the power of this exchange the sinner and Christ are united.

Zachman (1993).

DAVID M. WHITFORD

Bolsec, Jerome (Hieronymus) (d. 1584) A former Parisian Carmelite monk, Bolsec converted to Protestantism around 1545. Having gained protection from the Duchess of Ferrara, he married and studied medicine. In 1550 Bolsec settled as a physician in the outskirts of Geneva. Though an advocate of Reformed teaching, Bolsec publicly rejected *John Calvin*'s doctrine of double *predestination* on October 16, 1551, at one of the Bible study meetings held in Geneva every Friday. He was arrested and permanently exiled from Geneva on December 23, 1551; however, the controversy revealed that many of the Swiss Reformed churches of Basel, Zurich, and Bern supported Calvin's doctrine of double predestination only with great reserve. After being unable to settle successfully in Thonon, Paris, and Lausanne because of his insufficient *orthodoxy*, Bolsec eventually recanted his Protestant faith and rejoined the Catholic Church. Thereafter, he published biographies of Calvin and *Theodore de Beza*, in which he collected a number of the calumnies against them.

Holtrop (1993); Wendel (1997).

G. SUJIN PAK

Book of Common Prayer The official establishment of Protestantism in *England* upon the accession of Edward VI (1547) led to thoroughgoing liturgical reform. Whereas the forms for medieval worship had been spread across a variety of service books, the Reformers replaced them with a single volume, "one uniform order of worship," in the vernacular rather than Latin. Archbishop *Thomas Cranmer* was the principal author of the prayer book that came into use at Whitsun 1549. It contained forms of morning and evening *prayer*, with their "proper" psalms and lessons for the course of the year, along with services for *baptism*, *confirmation*, *marriage*, *visitation* of the sick, burial, the thanksgiving of women after childbirth, and administration of Holy Communion. The last was always the most controversial part, and it provoked rebels in the southwest of England to demand the return of the Latin *Mass*. On the other hand, influential Protestant critics (including *Martin Bucer*, currently exiled in England), felt the service, which billed itself as "the Supper of the Lord and Holy Communion, commonly called the Mass," did not go far enough. A second prayer book in 1552 made clear that this was no mere vernacularization of the old service: priests' vestments were simplified, and the Eucharist celebrated at a wooden table rather than an east-end stone altar, with ordinary bread rather than wafers. The 1549 "words of administration" spoken by the minister as he gave Communion were: "the body of our Lord Jesus Christ which was given for thee preserve thy body and soul unto everlasting life." This was replaced with: "take and eat this, in remembrance that Christ died for thee, and feed on him in thy heart by faith"—a "memorialist" formula leaving little scope for belief in the real presence.

After the interlude of Mary's reign, a revised version of the 1552 prayer book was restored by *Elizabeth I* in 1559. This combined the words of administration from the two previous versions, most likely a response to how Protestant theology of the Eucharist had been developing on the Continent, rather than an attempt to conciliate Catholics. Nonetheless, there was much in the prayer book to which Elizabethan *Puritans* objected: its prescribed readings from the Apocrypha; its insistence on the use of the sign of the cross in baptism, and on wedding rings; the burial service's emphasis on "sure and certain hope" of the resurrection (implicitly denying *predestination*). In response, the bishops made the prayer book an instrument of conformity, requiring ministers to subscribe to articles stating it contained "nothing contrary to the word of God." In the seventeenth century, devotion to the prayer book came to symbolize the disunity of Protestants: nonconformists despised its "prescript service"; Anglicans valued its order and solemnity.

Booty (1976); Collinson (1967); MacCulloch (1999).

PETER MARSHALL

Book of Concord   Also called *Concordia*, the Book of Concord is a collection of core Lutheran documents representing the "unanimous confession" of its signatories. Published in 1580, the Book of Concord is formed by the three ecumenical creeds (the *Apostles' Creed,* the Nicene Creed, and the Athanasian Creed), the *Augsburg Confession* (1530), the Apology of the Augsburg Confession (1531), the *Schmalkald Articles* (1537), the "Treatise on the Power and Primacy of the Pope" (1537), the Small Catechism (1529), the Large Catechism (1529), and the Formula of Concord (1577). The last document is presented in two formats: the "Solid Declaration" and the "Epitome" (i.e., summary). Together, these documents comprise the doctrinal "symbols" of the Lutheran Confession of Faith.

Intra-Lutheran conflicts that began after *Martin Luther*'s death (1546) and continued after the death of *Philip Melanchthon* (1560) gave rise to the efforts that produced the Book of Concord.

These efforts, primarily led by "second-generation" Lutheran theologians *Martin Chemnitz* and Jakob Andreae, were encouraged and sponsored by German political leaders who desired religious concord in their territories. Chemnitz, Andreae, and others spent many years building consensus and support for what would become the Book of Concord.

Published on June 25, 1580 (on the fiftieth anniversary of the presentation of the Augsburg Confession), the Book of Concord was not the first attempt to produce a collection of defining and confessionally binding Lutheran documents (or "symbols"). Previous attempts, such as *Corpus doctrinae Philippicum* (1560), consisted in the publication of collections of doctrinal writings that usually included the Unaltered Augsburg Confession and other works by Melanchthon and/or Luther. The Book of Concord, however, represents the most successful attempt—and the most enduring.

The publication of the Book of Concord brought to a close a thirty-year period of conflict between warring Lutheran parties—the "Gnesio-Lutheran" and "Philippist" parties in particular. It has been observed that the compilers of the Book of Concord leaned toward the "Gnesio" side of the debate. Indeed, the last document in the Book of Concord (i.e., the Formula of Concord, authored by Chemnitz, Andreae, and two others) clearly favors Luther as "the most eminent teacher of the churches which adhere to the Augsburg Confession" who "more than all others . . . understood the true, correct interpretation of the Augsburg Confession." On the other hand, it is worth noting that the Book of Concord contains three works authored by Melanchthon (the Augsburg Confession, its apologia, and the treatise on papal authority) and three by Luther (the two catechisms and the Schmalkald Articles).

Approximately two-thirds of Protestant Germany ratified and implemented the Book of Concord in the wake of its release. Its publication marked a turning point in a period of growing *"confessionalization"*—a period in which Europe found itself increasingly partitioned into territories demarcated by their confessions of faith, whether Lutheran, Reformed, or Roman Catholic. The Book of Concord continues to be esteemed as a faithful interpretation of *Scripture* and authoritative guide for Lutheran teaching, *preaching*, and *polity*.

Bohlman (1983); Gassman and Hendrix (1999); Kolb (1996).

HANS WIERSMA

Book of Homilies The parish *clergy*'s unreliability as instruments of new Protestant doctrine prompted the government of Edward VI to produce a set of model sermons for parochial use. The Book of Homilies published in July 1547 (which all parishes were ordered to acquire) contained twelve sermons on a range of topics that ministers were to read on Sundays. They were composed by several authors, conservatives as well as evangelicals, and some dealt with uncontroversial moral themes. But the key theological homilies—on salvation, on *faith*, and on *good works*—were the work of Archbishop *Thomas Cranmer* and promoted the doctrine of *justification* by faith. A second book of homilies, containing an additional twenty sermons (mostly the work of Bishop *John Jewel*), was added in 1562–63, and received their final form in 1571 when a homily "against disobedience and wilful rebellion" was added in response to the 1569 rising in the North.

Bond (1987); MacCulloch (1999).

PETER MARSHALL

Brenz, Johannes (1499–1570) Born in Weil der Stadt in the duchy of Württemberg, Brenz became arguably the most important of the south German Lutheran reformers. After earning B.A. and M.A. degrees at the University of Heidelberg, he soon became a partisan of *Martin Luther*. Appointed preacher in the city of Schwäbisch Hall in 1522, he played a leading role in the reform of its churches and schools. In 1525, in opposition to *Huldrych Zwingli* and *Johannes Oecolampadius*, he defended Luther's doctrine of the *Lord's Supper*. He participated in the *Marburg Colloquy* (1529) and the Diet of Augsburg (1530). Afterward he assisted with the *Reformation* in Württemberg, where he developed an evangelical church structure and provided a catechism for religious instruction. Late in his career he defended and further developed Luther's doctrine of the ubiquity of Christ's human body against Reformed opponents of the real presence. His extensive writings include commentaries on twenty books of the Bible.

Ehmer (2002); Estes (2002, 2007); Steinmetz (2001b).

MICKEY L. MATTOX

Briçonnet, Guillaume (1472–1534) Bishop of Meaux, Briçonnet was an early Reformer in France. In 1521 he invited reform-minded preachers from Paris to his diocese, including *Faber Stapulensis* (Jacques Lefèvre d'Étaples), *Guillaume Farel*, and Gérard Roussel, to conduct a preaching circuit. The bishop distributed Lefèvre's Bible translations to the laity in his diocese, and one of the Meaux group's supporters at court, the king's sister *Marguerite* of Angoulême (Navarre after 1527), distributed Briçonnet's letters of spiritual guidance and offered protection to members of the group. Briçonnet's activities angered the local *Franciscans*, and he was put on trial by the Parlement of Paris with other active Reformers for spreading ideas of *Martin Luther*, before the intervention of King Francis I stopped the proceedings. Despite his early support for reform, especially the promise of *humanism* in Christian *education*, Briçonnet stayed Catholic, publicly condemning Lutheran teachings, reaffirming Catholic practices, and preventing Farel and others from preaching in his diocese.

Greengrass (1987); Reid (2000); Taylor (2001).

JILL R. FEHLEISON

Bucer, Martin (1491–1551)   Bucer entered the *Dominican* order in his birthplace, the Alsatian city of Sélestat (Schlettstadt), at the age of 15. He received most of his education within the order, but he was also influenced by *Desiderius Erasmus* and other humanist scholars. He matriculated at *Heidelberg* in 1517, and after attending *Martin Luther*'s disputation there in 1518 he became a convinced "Martinian." In 1521 he obtained release from his monastic vows. After acting as court chaplain to the Count Palatine Frederick for a year, he served briefly as parish pastor in Landstuhl (where he married a former nun), and then as chaplain in Wissembourg. Excommunicated by the bishop of Speyer in May 1523, Bucer fled to *Strasbourg*. He began lecturing on the Bible, first in Latin and then in German, and in early 1524 became pastor of St. Aurelien. Together with his colleague *Wolfgang Capito* he took a leading role in defending evangelical doctrines, and he published a justification of the liturgical changes introduced in Strasbourg at the end of 1524. By that time he had also endorsed *Huldrych Zwingli*'s symbolic understanding of the *Lord's Supper*, and over the next few years he promoted that understanding in his correspondence and in his translations of works by Luther and *Johannes Bugenhagen*. He attended the *Marburg Colloquy* in 1529 and for the next seven years worked tirelessly to reconcile Lutherans and Zwinglians. His efforts met partial success with the signing of the Wittenberg Concord in 1536, which was accepted by the south German churches but rejected by the Swiss.

In 1531 Bucer was appointed pastor of St. Thomas, a larger and more prominent church in Strasbourg. His efforts to combat first Catholic opponents, then *Anabaptist* sectarians, convinced him of the need for an officially recognized creed and a fixed institutional structure for the church, and he was the architect of the Strasbourg synod of 1533, which resulted in the city's first ecclesiastical ordinance. In 1544 his role as leader of the church was officially recognized when he was named president of the Kirchenkonvent, the body of pastors and their assistants that met biweekly to consider the needs of the church. Bucer helped write church ordinances for Ulm and Augsburg as well as for the territory of Hesse, which spread his influence throughout south Germany. Bucer was one of the leading Protestant theologians at the religious colloquies of 1540–41. Together with the Catholic theologian Johannes Gropper he prepared the draft of the *Regensburg* Book that was the basis for discussions at the Regensburg Colloquy. Exiled from Strasbourg in 1549 after the Protestants' defeat by Imperial forces, he accepted a call to Cambridge and taught theology there until his death in 1551.

Greschat (2004); Krieger and Lienhard (1993); D. Wright (1994).

AMY NELSON BURNETT

Budé, Guillaume (1468–1540)   A French humanist interested in classical Greek and Roman philology and culture, Budé studied law at Orléans and supported humanist concerns in the court of Francis I, where he encouraged the foundation of the Collège de France. Budé's most remarkable work was done in the field of legal *humanism*, which focused on the study of the sources and transmission of Roman jurisprudence.

A supporter and correspondent of *Desiderius Erasmus*, Budé encouraged Francis I's interest in humanism, in general, and Erasmus, in particular.

Although Budé remarked on Erasmus's theological work, little information survives about Budé's theological opinions. Nevertheless, scholars have speculated about his sympathies for Protestantism, largely based on surviving correspondence with Erasmus and on his wife's conversion to Protestantism after his death.

Bentley (1983); Nauert (2006).
GRETA GRACE KROEKER

Bugenhagen, Johannes (1485–1558)

Born in the city of Wollin in Pomerania (today a part of Poland), Bugenhagen was educated at Greifswald and ordained to the priesthood in 1509. After some correspondence with *Martin Luther*, he came to *Wittenberg* in 1521. In 1523 he was appointed pastor of the city church (St. Mary's) in Wittenberg, where he became Luther's regular preacher and close spiritual confidant. In 1524 he translated Luther's German New Testament into the "Low German" spoken in northern Germany. His chief contribution to the *Reformation* came in the form of "church orders," the rules and regulations that established Lutheran churches in several north German cities, in Denmark, and in his native Pomerania. He earned his doctorate in theology in Wittenberg in 1533 and afterward became a professor. His writings include a commentary on the Psalms (1544). On account of his origins, he was known affectionately to Luther and his colleagues as "Pomeranus."

Hendel (2004); Steinmetz (2001a).
MICKEY L. MATTOX

Bullinger, Heinrich (1504–75)

Bullinger was a Swiss reformer, theologian, and leader of the Zurich church from 1531 until his death. His influence extended across Europe through his publications, correspondence, and networks of contacts. His best-known work was the *Decades*, but he wrote biblical commentaries, histories, and pastoral tracts, all of which were widely translated. On the whole he remained faithful to the theology of *Huldrych Zwingli*, though significant modifications arose from polemical battles with *Anabaptists*, Lutherans, and Catholics, his relations with other Reformers and reform movements, and his pastoral work as head of a large territorial church. He did not write a definitive theological work: his *Decades* were never intended as a treatise of systematic theology, but without doubt they reflect his principal concerns and ideas. Bullinger's early theology was deeply influenced by Zwingli, *Martin Luther*, and *Philip Melanchthon*, particularly his 1521 *Loci Communes*.

Bullinger emerged as a reformer in the years following the outbreak of the controversy between Wittenberg and Zurich over the *Lord's Supper*, and the hostilities dominated his life. From Zwingli he took up the importance of the covenant (*De Testamento*, 1534), but there was movement in his thought. From the later 1530s, following his extensive biblical commentaries, a shift toward pneumatology (*De origine erroris*, 1539) is detectable. This found full expression in the *Decades* of 1549, where it is placed alongside other key aspects of Bullinger's theology, including the covenantal continuity of the Old and New Testaments and the Bible as the unified witness to God's revelation.

Following Zwingli, Bullinger was particularly interested in *sanctification* and the ethical and communal nature of Christianity. He followed Zwingli in his conception of society as a *corpus Christianum* in which magistrates exercised *authority* over the church, whose authority resided in its prophetic witness to God's Word. He moved beyond Zwingli in his willingness to speak of a spiritual presence in the *sacraments*, though he rejected any contention, against *John Calvin*, that the outward forms of the sacraments were instruments by which God conveyed *grace*. Bullinger's reformation emphasis on grace alone was always accompanied with the exhortation to the Christian life.

In Bullinger's mature theology the Spirit and its actions of sanctification, vivification, and communion with Christ are powerful and recurring themes. He emphasized the commandment to *love*, and in his extensive vernacular, pastoral literature enjoined the faithful to *good works* in the service of the community. Bullinger was a profound writer on the Christian life, continuously exploring the ways in which Christians should imitate Christ through humility, suffering, and self-negating love.

Biel (1991); Campi and Opitz (2007); Gordon (2002); Gordon and Campi (2002).
BRUCE GORDON

Burial   Protestants rejected the Roman Catholic concept of *purgatory*, believing instead that God granted salvation to faithful Christians immediately upon *death*, severing all connections to the living human community. Protestant reformers criticized elaborate Roman Catholic burial practices, viewing them as superstitious and unnecessary. Lutheran churches maintained limited rituals, including processions, focused on celebrating the resurrection and honoring the dead person. Calvinist churches required austere burials, emphasizing that the dead body was simply an empty vessel. They forbid all "superstitious" practices like burial in churches or church cemeteries considered to be "sacred grounds." Protestant changes challenged social customs and family traditions, so funeral and burial rituals were often a point of conflict between Protestants and Roman Catholics. Even faithful Protestants were often reluctant to dispense with burial traditions connected to social status; as a result, many churches in France, the Netherlands, and Scotland tolerated more elaborate rites than strict Calvinist teachings permitted.

Cressy (1997); Gordon and Marshall (2000); Koslofsky (2000); Luria (2005).
KAREN E. SPIERLING

Cajetan, Thomas de Vio Cardinal (1468/69?–1534)   A *Dominican* theologian and biblical exegete, he was called Cajetanus after his birthplace, the city of Gaeta in Naples. He entered the Order of Preachers in 1484, and received his training at the universities of Bologna and Padua. He lectured at Padua in 1494 and at Rome from 1501 to 1508. From 1508 to 1518 he served as master general of the Dominicans. He was an ardent defender of papal authority against the remnants of fifteenth-century *conciliarism*, and an exponent of the doctrine of papal infallibility. The legitimacy of the Council of Pisa of 1511 became a point of contention for the Roman curia, as it counted with the support of several disaffected cardinals. Cajetan was an outspoken critic of the schismatic council, and later helped convince Pope Julius II (r. 1503–1513) to call *Lateran Council* V (1512–17). He was rewarded by *Pope Leo X* (r. 1513–21), who created him a cardinal in 1517. He played an important role as part of the papal response to the *Martin Luther* affair. As papal legate, he was commissioned by Leo X to examine Luther. He met with Luther in Augsburg in 1518. As a result of this interview and the examination of Luther's writings, Cajetan concluded that the views of the Wittenberg reformer not only posed a threat to actual papal *authority*, but also questioned the doctrine of papal authority itself.

On November 9, 1518, Leo X addressed to Cajetan his decree "Cum postquam," sustaining the authority of the pope to grant *indulgences*. One of the foundations of this authority was the notion of the *"treasury of merit,"* first articulated in a papal decree by Pope Clement VI (r. 1342–52) in "Unigenitus

Dei Filius" (January 25, 1343). Cajetan's opinions, alongside those of *Johann Eck*, shaped the content of the bull *Exsurge Domine* (1520), which condemned the teachings of Luther. Yet scholars have argued that Cajetan had much agreement with Luther in other points apart from papal authority (see Wicks 1992).

While his intervention in the Luther affair certainly secured for him a place in posterity, his historical significance is far from limited to this episode. Cajetan was in his time the chief interpreter of Thomas Aquinas, to the extent that his contemporaries referred to him as "quasi vivens Aquinatis" ("almost the living Aquinas"), and "alter Thomas" ("the other Thomas"). He was a prolific writer, credited with over a hundred different works. His commentaries on the *Summa theologiae* were first published at Lyons in 1540–41, and they remained influential until very recently. Toward the end of his life he wrote commentaries on almost all the books of the Bible, including Psalms (Venice, 1530), the Gospels (Venice, 1530), and the Pauline Epistles (Paris, 1532).

Cessario (2005); Janz (1983); Wicks (1977, 1992).

RADY ROLDAN-FIGUEROA

Calling   Prior to the *Reformation*, the theological term "calling" (*vocatio*) referred specifically to an activity of divine *grace* leading to *monasticism*. *Martin Luther* explicitly rejected the previous meaning of the term and taught that all of the Christian's responsibilities in the world are "callings" (Ger. *Berufe*) with no special benefit or value attributed to "spiritual" as opposed to "secular" callings. Luther's understanding of calling thus included all legitimate "occupations," but went beyond occupation to include all responsibilities in the world in which God has placed the Christian. Of critical importance for Luther were callings such as husband or wife, father or mother, son or daughter. Luther's position should be considered an embracing of Christian participation in the secular world and entailed a radical restructuring of traditional Christian social values. Calvinist theologians also came to utilize the term *vocatio* for the divine act by which those destined for salvation received the *gospel*.

See also **Vocation**

Althaus (1972); Froehlich (2004); Kendall (1981); Wingren (1957).

GREGORY J. MILLER

Calvin, John (a.k.a. Jean Cauvin; 1509–64)   Humanist and reformer of the church, Calvin was born in Picardy to a family of modest means. His father sent him to Paris to prepare for the priesthood, but at some point during his study of the liberal arts it was decided that he should become a lawyer. At Bourges and Orléans he was exposed to the leading legal minds of his generation. Calvin experienced a conversion to the evangelical faith, possibly in the autumn of 1533, and from that point was in some danger in France. He fled Paris following the *Nicolas Cop* address in that year, living in the south of France, and in 1534 after the Placards Affair he left his native country. He settled first in Basel before coming to Geneva in 1536. He was expelled in 1538 and spent most of his time in *Strasbourg* with *Martin Bucer*. In 1541 he returned to Geneva, where he remained until his death.

Although many of Calvin's principal theological ideas are evident in his first edition of the *Institutes of the Christian Religion* (1536), his thought continued to develop over the course of his life as he studied the Bible, the church fathers, medieval doctors, contemporary writers, and classical *philosophy*. Much of his writing arose from the numerous theological disputes in which he found himself enmeshed. His purpose, however, was constant. He sought to explain sacred *Scripture* to the church and to prepare ministers to teach the Word of God. His commentaries on almost all the books of the Bible were intended to be read alongside his *Institutes*.

Calvin famously wrote of humanity's twofold knowledge of God: as creator and redeemer. According to the first, God's self-revelation is the basis of our natural knowledge of the Divine. The second concerns the work of Jesus Christ and the twofold forms of *grace*, repentance and *justification*. The life of *faith* is sustained by the church, which through *preaching*, the administration of *sacraments*, and *discipline* sustains, feeds, and corrects the faithful in this world. Through the inner guidance of the *Holy Spirit* each person is conformed to Christ, who is the image of the living God.

A prolific writer, Calvin's works were widely translated and disseminated across Europe, and many were drawn to Geneva from afar to study under him. He devoted himself to the *Reformation* in his native France, to the plight of religious refugees, and to resolving the enduring doctrinal conflicts between the Lutherans and Zwinglians.

Gordon (2009); R. Holder (2006); Muller (2000); Partee (2008); Pitkin (1999); Zachman (2007).

BRUCE GORDON

Canisius, Peter (1521–97)   Saint and Doctor of the Church (1925), Canisius was the first Dutch *Jesuit* (1543) and is largely credited with restoring Catholicism in Germany after the Protestant *Reformation*. He established eighteen Jesuit colleges, as well as a number of missions, novitiates, and residences, and traveled extensively throughout the *Holy Roman Empire*, teaching and preaching the Catholic *Counter-Reformation*. His most important contributions were his three extremely popular catechisms—Large (1555), Smallest (1556), and Small (1558)—which were trans-

lated into twenty-eight languages and went through hundreds of editions in the sixteenth century alone; they became the foundation of Catholic teaching in Germany. His teaching of the faith was based in persuasion rather than attack and he pushed for more flexibility from Rome when dealing with Protestants. His ability to explain complex doctrine simply and coherently was instrumental in stemming the spread of Protestantism across the empire and earned him the title Second Apostle of Germany (the first being Boniface).

Begheyn (2006); Brodrick (1998); Donnelly (1981); O'Malley (1993).

AMY E. LEONARD

Canon Law   The body of rules and regulations of the Catholic Church established through *Scripture*, councils, papal proclamations, customs, and practices is called canon law. After official recognition by Emperor Constantine in the fourth century, the Christian Church established its own ecclesiastical courts separate from secular courts. In the twelfth century the University of Bologna was the center of legal studies when a faculty member, *Gratian*, offered a systematic treatise on canon law known as the *Decretum* that became the standard textbook for the subject. Gratian's work sparked a renewed interest in the study and professionalization of canon law. During the *Reformation Martin Luther, John Calvin*, and others challenged canon law and separate ecclesiastical courts, claiming that they were based on common practices and papal innovations rather than Scripture and the foundations of the early church. The Reformation sparked a renewed debate over the jurisdiction of and relationship between religious and secular legal systems.

Brundage (1995); Coriden (2004); Helmholz (1990); Tierney (1982).

JILL R. FEHLEISON

Canon of Scripture

From the Greek *kanōn* meaning rule or guide, the "canon" of *Scripture* has since the earliest centuries of the church described the books that are understood as divinely inspired and authoritative. The twenty-seven books of the New Testament were gradually identified as authoritative during the first three centuries CE. In the sixteenth century, the breadth of the Old Testament canon became a matter of sometimes bitter debate. The Latin Vulgate Old Testament of the medieval church contains all of the books in the Hebrew Scriptures. It also contains a number of books from the Septuagint that are not found in the Hebrew Scriptures. Jerome included these books because of their use by diaspora Jews and because he believed they were inspired by God but not strictly speaking canonical. Over the centuries they came to be seen as canonical, however. Following the increasing knowledge of both *Greek* and *Hebrew* in the Renaissance, many Reformers separated these books from the Old Testament. In the 1611 King James Bible, they are placed between the Old and New Testaments.

Pelikan (1996); Steinmetz (1996).
DAVID M. WHITFORD

Capito, Wolfgang (ca. 1478–1541)

Capito was born in Hagenau and studied in Ingolstadt, Heidelberg, and Freiburg. In 1515 he became cathedral preacher in Basel, where he received his doctorate in theology and was closely associated with the circle of humanists around *Desiderius Erasmus*. As an adviser to the archbishop of Mainz, from 1520 he advocated a policy of moderation toward *Martin Luther*. In 1523 he moved to *Strasbourg* and the following year was appointed parish pastor of Young St. Peter. Capito was an accomplished Hebraist who wrote an influential Hebrew grammar as well as commentaries on Hosea and the first six chapters of Genesis. The most prominent of Strasbourg's reformers during the mid-1520s, he gradually lost influence in the city, in part due to his tolerant attitude toward the *Anabaptists*. In 1532 he was called on to help organize the church of Bern, and through the 1530s he supported the efforts of his colleague *Martin Bucer* for eucharistic concord. He died of the plague in 1541.

Kittelson (1975); Rummel (2000); Rummel and Kooistra (2007).
AMY NELSON BURNETT

Cassander, Joris (Georg) (1513–66)

Cassander was a Flemish humanist and Catholic theologian. He graduated from Louvain and came to settle in Cologne. As a scholar, writer, and irenic Catholic reformer, Cassander sought to restore unity between the Catholic and Protestant churches by emphasizing the history of the church as a basis for Christian consensus. Along with Georg Witzel, he advised emperors Ferdinand I and Maximilian II as well as the French court to support efforts toward unity by advocating concessions by Catholics on issues of Communion in both kinds and clerical *celibacy*. Resembling some of *Desiderius Erasmus*'s ideas, Cassander's treatises and letters proposed a peace plan that united a divided church by emphasizing the vitality and harmony of the early church. Although he recognized the need for reform within the Catholic Church and agreed with some Protestant opinions, he never denounced the Roman Catholic Church. His main work offended both sides and his series of liturgical works were placed on the *Index Librorum Prohibitorum*.

Backus (2004); Berkvens-Stevelinck et al. (1997); Rummel (2000).
ESTHER CHUNG-KIM

Castellio, Sebastien (1515–63)

Castellio was born in Savoy, and became a Protestant as a student in Lyon. In

Strasbourg he met *John Calvin*, who made him head of a Latin school. He was later professor of Greek at the University of Basel. He made classical Latin (1551) and French (1555) translations of the Bible, though his most lasting work was *Dialogi sacri* (*Divine Dialogues*, 1542) for teaching biblical history and Latin. He is best known for championing religious toleration, both in annotations to his Latin Bible and in treatises.

Theological differences, including *predestination* and the canonicity of the Song of Solomon, led to a break with Calvin. The execution of *Michael Servetus* in Geneva prompted Castellio to publish *De Haereticis an sint persequendi* (*Concerning Heretics*, 1554). This contained Castellio's views and quotations of ancient and contemporary Christians opposing the death penalty for *heresy*, and prompted a lengthy literary controversy.

Guggisberg (2003); Hirsch (1981); Zweig (1936).

GARY NEAL HANSEN

Casuistry   Casuistry is the science of determining right action or of determining the level of guilt regarding an action already taken, involving the careful consideration of cases of *conscience* within the framework of moral and pastoral theology. The study of casuistry was closely associated with the *sacrament* of *penance*. In the course of the *Counter-Reformation*, casuistry became a major focus of instruction in Catholic seminaries, displacing patristics in the curriculum adopted by Charles Borromeo. Increasing sophistication of the science of casuistry can be noted in the post-Tridentine era. Several manuals on casuistry, mainly by *Jesuits*, were published in the late sixteenth and early seventeenth centuries. Criticism of the Jesuit method arose in both Protestant and Catholic circles for advocating probabilism and even justifying political assassination. At the same time, Protes-

tant political theory could also be seen as casuist, particularly regarding justifications of rebellion and repression.

A. Wright (1982).

WILLIAM BRADFORD SMITH

Catechism   Publications implementing a method of communicating basic doctrinal tenets are called "catechisms" (from Gr. *katechizein*, "to instruct verbally"). Numerous catechisms were drafted by church reformers and broadly implemented during the *Reformation* era. Intended for popular use, catechisms were printed as pamphlets, broadsheets, and manuals. The eventual proliferation of catechisms in the sixteenth century was, in part, both the cause and the result of increasing public literacy.

The use of catechisms can be traced to the early church period and to early church leaders such as Cyril and Augustine. The medieval period saw the development of a basic outline for catechetical learning: the Ten Commandments, the Lord's Prayer, and the *Apostles' Creed*. During the Reformation, most catechisms took the form of lists of doctrinal questions and the answers to those questions. For instance, *Martin Luther's* Small Catechism (1529), based upon the traditional subjects of the Commandments, Creed, and Lord's Prayer, as well as the *sacraments*, is organized around the simple question, "What does this mean?" (*Was ist das?*). *John Calvin's* Catechism of the Church of Geneva (1542) is also arranged in question-and-answer format, beginning with the inquiry: "What is the main purpose of human life?" (Answer: "To know the God who created human beings.")

Judging by the abundance of catechisms penned and published during the early modern period, it is safe to assume that a majority of Reformers understood catechism-based instruction to be the preferred pedagogical device for imparting the basics of the Christian faith to the laity, especially to children. Ideally, catechisms were to be used in the home with the head of the household functioning as the instructor. However, the extent to which catechetical teaching and learning pervaded early modern households is difficult to determine. It was in any case common among Reformers to preach sermons based on the articles of a given catechism, for the purpose of reviewing and reinforcing Christian basics.

Some catechisms came to be included as part of the defining documents of the major branches of Reformation-era churches, including Luther's Small and Large Catechisms (1529), the Anglican Catechism (1549), the Heidelberg Catechism (1563), and the Roman Catechism (1566). The processes by which such catechisms came to possess official confessional standing varied. Fifty years passed between the first publication of Luther's catechisms and their official adoption as defining Lutheran documents in the *Book of Concord* (1580). Similarly, a half century elapsed before the *Heidelberg Catechism* was established, during the *Synod of Dort* (1618–1619), as one of three official statements of belief among Reformed Christians. On the other hand, the brief Anglican Catechism (included in the original and in all subsequent editions of the *Book of Common Prayer*) and the lengthy Roman Catechism (decreed by the *Council of Trent*) possessed official doctrinal authority upon their initial publications.

Bierma (2005); Green (1996), Noll (1991).
HANS WIERSMA

Catholic Reformation   The Catholic Reformation was an age of robust religious reform in Europe pushed by Catholic authorities from the late 1400s to the early 1700s. The term is interlinked with other descriptors of Catholic reform activity, such as *Counter-Reformation*, Tridentine Catholicism, and early modern Catholicism. The church historian

Hubert Jedin offered what became the classic exposition of terminology for this era in Catholic history, despite lingering dissatisfaction from historians seeking more precise vocabulary. Jedin conceived of the Catholic Reformation as the overarching effort to correct abuses, return the church to its institutional heritage, and inspire heartfelt *piety* among laity and *clergy*. Within this framework, the Counter-Reformation arose in the mid-1500s as an aggressive effort to combat Protestantism. The Counter-Reformation, from this viewpoint, formed a component of the Catholic Reformation.

The Catholic Reformation had roots in widespread criticism of the church hierarchy during the Avignon *papacy* (1309–77) and the Great Schism (1378–1417). New religious orders stressing piety and devotion developed, such as the Oratory of Divine Love in 1497, the Capuchins in 1520, the Theatines in 1522, and the Ursuline nuns in 1535. In northern Europe, a spiritual movement known as the *devotio moderna* originated in the Netherlands under the leadership of Geert Groote (1344–84), who formed the Brethren of the Common Life. Christian humanist scholars in northern Europe, particularly *Desiderius Erasmus* and *Thomas More*, also promoted biblical learning and religious devotion. The most influential religious order emerged under the direction of *Ignatius of Loyola*, founder of the Society of Jesus (*Jesuits*) in 1540. Devoted to *education* and overseas evangelism, the Jesuits became a primary agent of revival among Catholic laity and an instrument for combating Protestantism.

Notable popes in the 1500s reversed the state of papal decadence and took forceful leadership in reform. Beginning with *Paul IV* (1555–59) and Pius V (1566–72), popes worked to eliminate nepotism, to compel bishops to assume pastoral duties, and to fight *heresy*. *Paul III* ordered the creation of the Papal *Inquisition* in 1542 and Paul IV issued the *Index Librorum Prohibitorum* (*Index of Prohibited Books*) in 1547. Most importantly, Paul III called a general church council to address problems, which met at Trent in three sessions from 1545 to 1563.

The *Council of Trent* proved to be a driving force behind the Catholic Reformation. The council rejected Protestantism as heresy, upholding the long-standing teachings of the Catholic Church and papal *authority*. In church reform, Trent required bishops to supervise their dioceses, provided for an educated, disciplined clergy, and demanded stringent compliance for all Catholics. Reforms spread slowly and unevenly across Europe, though by the early 1700s a revived Catholic piety manifested itself in Baroque artistic forms, devotional associations, aggressive evangelism, and close alliance between political and religious authorities.

Hsia (2005); Mullett (1999); O'Malley (2000).

CHARLES PARKER

Catholicity Catholicity (from Gr. *katholikos*, "general" or "universal") refers to a claim to be in the church, that is, to participate in the continuous tradition of correct faith and practice held by true believers in all places and at all times. The use of the appellation became one of serious dispute during the *Reformation* as a result of claims and counterclaims concerning which confession maintained the faith of the apostles. These debates came to be centered on such issues as the "signs of the church," the nature of *authority* in the church, and the dialectic between the church visible and the church invisible. During the time of the Reformation and after, those remaining loyal to the *papacy* claimed the term exclusively for themselves on the basis of apostolic succession of the episcopacy and the leadership of the see of Rome. However, all sides used the term self-referentially and confessed that they believed in "one holy catholic

and apostolic church." *Martin Luther*, for example, always claimed to be catholic and vociferously denied that he was schismatic. The critical theological point for Luther was his claim to have discovered that the bishop of Rome was actually the *antichrist*. According to Luther, therefore, the Roman Church was adamantly not the catholic church, although it did contain some true Christians. Luther did not view *apostolic succession* as a sign of catholicity, but rather stressed the proper administration of the *sacraments* and true preaching of the Word of God, especially the *preaching* of salvation by *faith* alone (the *articulus stantis et cadentis ecclesiae*, the doctrine on which the church stands or falls). For Luther, the institutional structure of the church was a matter of historical contingency. Furthermore, the church was invisible in terms of its true membership (that is, participation in a church did not necessarily demonstrate being in the church universal). However, the church was visible through preaching, sacraments, and suffering. Some Lutherans maintained apostolic succession (for example, in Sweden), but the import of this has been a matter of dispute within the worldwide Lutheran fellowship.

While similar to Luther, *John Calvin* understood catholicity to inherently include a presbyterian ecclesiastical structure and administration. Anglican self-understanding of catholicity was based on the maintenance of apostolic succession, despite independence from Rome. Most *Anabaptists* considered the Word of God and a particular lifestyle to be the criteria for catholicity. Anabaptists generally emphasized the voluntary nature of the church, represented by adult believer's *baptism* and the use of discipline (the *ban*) to preserve ecclesial purity. For many Protestants across confessions, suffering and *martyrdom* became in themselves signs of catholicity. There was great hope among the Reformers in the years prior to 1540 that the divisions within the church were only temporary and would be resolved through a widespread general reform of the church and/or through a reforming great council, although political and ecclesiastical events of the 1540s demonstrated that reconciliation was not possible.

McGrath (1999); Oberman (1981); Steinmetz (2002b); G. H. Williams (1992).
GREGORY J. MILLER

Celibacy of the Clergy   While the New Testament does not prohibit *marriage*, Western Christianity witnessed the gradual development of the institution of clerical celibacy. The Synod of Elvira (Spain, 300–303?) ordered all bishops, presbyters, and deacons to "abstain from their wives and not to procreate children." Pope Siricius in his letter "Directa ad decessorem," of February 10, 385, sustained that all priests are constrained from the moment of their ordination to remain chaste. The prohibition, though, remained difficult to enforce, leading to frequent reiteration in papal and conciliar statements. Thus *Lateran Council* I (1123) prohibited that priests, deacons, and subdeacons have the "intimacy of concubines and wives." The Protestant *Reformation* challenged the institution. In his *Babylonian Captivity of the Church* (1520), **Martin Luther** called the "impediment of ordination" a "mere invention of men." The *Augsburg Confession* (1530) laid down the classic Protestant argument against forced clerical celibacy.

Denzinger (2007); Leith (1982).
RADY ROLDAN-FIGUEROA

Ceremonies   To distinguish between biblically sanctioned *sacraments* and human-made ceremonies, Protestant reformers employed "ceremonies" as a polemical term against Roman Catholic rituals and sacramental practices. Thus **Martin Luther** and **John Calvin** argued

that only *baptism* and the *Lord's Supper* are the sacraments ordained by God in *Scripture* and dismissed the five other practices deemed as sacraments by the Roman Catholic Church (*penance, marriage*, confirmation, ordination, extreme *unction*) as mere human ceremonies. Protestant reformers believed that these so-called human ceremonies endangered Christian consciences by promoting a false confidence in human works and even *superstition* and idolatry. Thus they sought to purify and simplify sacramental practices to align with biblical and apostolic models. Radical Reformers, such as the *Anabaptists*, advocated a more absolute biblicism and whole-scale rejection of ceremonies; while they kept an observance of the Lord's Supper and baptism, they denied their sacramental significance.

Karant-Nunn (1997); Muir (2005).
G. SUJIN PAK

Certainty   In the *tradition* of the medieval Western church, affirmed at the *Council of Trent*, the pilgrim Christian, ever aware of her own weakness and *sin*, can have only a "conjectural certitude" of salvation based on the *sure* knowledge that God will be merciful to the elect coupled with one's own *fallible* experience of the signs of *grace*. Until one is holy, one must "work out" salvation "with fear and trembling" (Phil. 2:12). The Protestant reformers opposed this tradition. They held that *faith* in God's Word, given in the *gospel*, brings an internal certainty—the gift of the *Holy Spirit*—that one has God's grace. For example, *John Calvin* says that one experiences a "full assurance" that enables one to "taste" the goodness of God and call on him as "Father." Certitude precedes holiness; it is a gift to the faithful even if they remain "sinners and saints at the same time."

Schreiner (2010); Zachman (1993).
MICKEY L. MATTOX

Charles V (1500–1558) King of Spain (as Charles I, 1516–56) and *Holy Roman Emperor* (1519–56), Charles attempted unsuccessfully to aggrandize Habsburg royal power in Europe, but nevertheless played a leading role in the political struggles of the *Reformation* and thwarted Ottoman ambitions in central Europe. The heir of fortuitous marriage alliances between Habsburgs, Burgundians, and Spanish royal families, Charles acquired the Burgundian Netherlands through his grandfather, Emperor *Maximilian I*, and his grandmother, Mary of Burgundy, as well as the Spanish throne from his father, Philip I, and mother, Joanna of Castile. Charles was elected emperor in 1519. By virtue of Spanish colonization, he also ruled a large American empire.

Charles's central aims focused on augmenting authority over his dominions and checking expansion of the French Valois monarchy in northern Italy. The Habsburg-Valois rivalry flared into several wars from 1521 to 1559 that involved most of the major political powers of western Europe. The efforts to repel the French were hampered by the outbreak of the German Reformation in the 1520s. A dedicated Catholic, Charles presided over the *Diet of Worms* (1521) that condemned *Martin Luther*'s teachings as heretical. From the 1520s until the *Council of Trent* (1545), he worked to forge religious unity among Lutheran and Catholic princes in the empire by convoking diets and colloquies to reach a rapprochement on theological matters and restore political concord. Dialogue ultimately failed, as war between Charles's forces and the Schmalkaldic League, a Lutheran military alliance, erupted in 1546 and concluded with an Imperial victory in 1547.

Beset by French assertiveness in Italy and Protestant revolt in Germany, Charles was also confronted by the aggressive designs of the Ottoman Empire in the eastern Habsburg domains and in the Mediterranean. The *Turks* routed Imperial troops at Mohács (Hungary) in 1526, though imperial forces managed to withstand the Ottoman siege of Vienna in 1529. Ottoman forces under Suleiman the Lawgiver (1494–1566) and subsequent sultans competed for territory in Hungary and eastern Europe throughout the 1500s. Nevertheless, Charles proved instrumental in defending Christendom from the Turks. Despite the influx of wealth from the Spanish Empire, the incessant military campaigning created huge deficits in the Spanish and Imperial treasuries.

In the realm of church history, Charles's significance lies in his staunch support of Catholic reform and his implacable prosecution of *heresy*. He pushed the *papacy* to convene a church council that eventually met at Trent, he worked to bring Lutheran princes back to the Catholic fold, and he vigorously enforced heresy laws. He abdicated his throne in 1556 and retired to the Yuste monastery in Extremadura, where he lived out his final years.

Blockmans (2002); Rodríguez-Salgado (1988); Tracy (2002).

CHARLES PARKER

Chemnitz, Martin (1522–86) A second-generation Lutheran reformer and theologian, Chemnitz is sometimes called the "Second Martin." He was born in Brandenburg and educated in Magdeburg, Frankfurt, Wittenberg, and Königsburg. During his time in Wittenberg, he studied with *Philip Melanchthon* and later would write his own *Loci theologici* patterned on his teacher's *Loci Communes*. During the 1560s and 1570s, he was the superintendent of the church in Brunswick-Wolfenbüttel, ultimately writing the church order for the region. A theological centrist, he was instrumental in healing the theological rifts that developed after *Martin Luther*'s death. In 1577 he ensured broad support for the Formula of Concord and the *Book of Concord*.

Kolb (2002).
DAVID M. WHITFORD

Children   Protestant reformers were concerned with children as members of families, the primary building blocks of a faithful Christian society. Children were burdened with *original sin*, but most Reformers also recognized a particular innocence in them. Sixteenth-century Protestants emphasized children's obligation to obey their parents, but reformers like *John Calvin* added that a child's first obligation was always to God, permitting resistance to ungodly parental demands. Parental obligations included material care, *baptism*, sufficient discipline, and *education* in the Christian faith. *Anabaptists* underlined the role of the whole community in shepherding children toward baptism at the age of discretion (variously defined). While mainstream Reformers initially counted on parents as primary educators, they soon recognized the need for church involvement as well as the establishment of primary schools for both boys and girls. Concerning discipline, Reformers generally taught that corporal punishment was sometimes necessary to help children overcome sinful impulses, but that parents should carry out all discipline with restraint.

Bunge (2001); Ozment (1983); Strauss (1978); Wood (1994).
KAREN E. SPIERLING

Christology   In many ways, the doctrines of the person and work of Christ were at the center of the most urgent and most violent disputes in the Reformation. While most of the magisterial Reformers and Catholics saw an inherent value in explicitly professing the christological formulae of the ortho-dox ecumenical councils, other voices spoke differently, introducing a level of intentional and thoughtful christological *heresy* that had not been seen in Latin Europe for many centuries. Even theologians who might have been seen to be orthodox could be smeared by an opponent if they failed to subscribe to an ancient creed—as *John Calvin* found out when he refused to subscribe to the Athanasian Creed for Pierre Caroli.

Frequently, the manner in which Christology became the focus of theological dispute in the Reformations came through the theological implications of other doctrines. Such was the case with the doctrine(s) of the Eucharist. Both *Martin Luther* and Calvin objected to Roman ideas of the *Mass* as a sacrifice, arguing that if the Mass was a sacrifice, then Christ's sacrifice on the cross was in some manner incomplete. *Huldrych Zwingli* criticized Lutheran ideas of the Eucharist for confusing the sign with the thing signified, and Luther condemned Zwingli as a heretic for not maintaining the bodily local presence in the *Lord's Supper*. Reformed theologians also disparaged both Lutheran and Roman theories of the corporeal local presence in the *sacrament* as denying the true humanity of Christ. While no party "won" these disputes, the reason for their intensity was the centrality of the doctrines concerning Christ to Christianity in early modern Europe.

Of course, sometimes Christology became the focus not implicitly, but explicitly. Such was the case in the anti-Trinitarian controversies. *Michael Servetus* studied the Scriptures and concluded that the divinity of Christ was fictitious, as was the doctrine of the *Trinity*. He published books to that effect, and was eventually captured, tried for heresy, and executed. His ideas did not die with him, but were passed along through his disciples into Poland, where the Stancaro case brought attention to the issue. Eventually, *anti-Trinitarianism* became firmly ensconced in Poland thanks to the leadership of Fausto Sozzini.

The number of christological and Trinitarian controversies that arose at this time demonstrates the unintended consequences possible when the return *ad fontes* (to the sources) begins. Though traditional Christianity persevered, the new range of possible answers fostered a new range of possible orthodoxies.

Edmondson (2004); McGrath (2005); Willis (1966).

R. WARD HOLDER

Church   The subject of the identity of the true church was a central question of the Protestant reformers. Protestant reformers insisted that they aimed not for the creation of a new church but for the restoration of the one, true, apostolic church from which they believed the Roman Church had departed. Lutherans, Reformed, and *Anabaptists* agreed that the Roman Church had deviated from the crucial foundations of Christ and *Scripture*, added many human beliefs and practices, and no longer rightly administered the *sacraments*. Sixteenth-century Protestants contributed to the theological concept of the church through their emphases on its christological center, its establishment by the Word of God, the distinction between the visible and invisible church, and the importance of naming the true marks of the church.

Against the Roman Church of his day, *Martin Luther* emphasized that the church is not constituted by any human action but only by the action of God. For Luther, the church is created by the Word of God that begets *faith* in Christ, whereby he called it a *creatura verbi divini* (creature of the divine word). In his polemical stance against the Roman Church, Luther often emphasized the concept of the invisible church, which is the universal church constituted by the Word of God, in order to criticize the current visible church of his day. In his 1539 *On the Councils and the Church*, however, he named several key marks of the true church by which one may recognize its visibility on earth; these included the Word of God preached, sacraments rightly administered, commissioning of ministers, public worship, and the bearing of the cross of Christ.

Second-generation Reformers such as *Philip Melanchthon* and *John Calvin* articulated a more robust ecclesiology, especially in response to Luther's lack of considering practical aspects of church governance. Though they retained the distinction between the visible and invisible church, their emphasis was clearly upon the former. Both articulated a definition of the church as an assembly of believers where the Word of God and the *gospel* are preached and the sacraments rightly administered, but added the mark of *discipline* appropriately practiced. Like Luther, Melanchthon and Calvin maintained that the church is established by God's action through Christ and the Word. Calvin, however, used the doctrine of *election* more prominently to maintain God's act of constituting the church; the church for Calvin is instituted through God's election.

Radical Reformers like the Anabaptists were much less concerned about the distinction between the visible and invisible church. Their emphasis was decisively upon embodying the visible church in the world by being the gathered church of the regenerate. They agreed with the Lutherans and Reformed that the church is founded upon Christ and constituted by Scripture, but for them the first mark of the true church was regeneration— evidence of a new spiritual birth. The second and third marks were baptism and discipline. Thereby the Anabaptists removed the emphasis on sacraments, instead insisting upon a community that embodied and maintained holiness by setting itself apart from the world.

Avis (2002); Estep (1996); Schwöbel (1989).

G. SUJIN PAK

Clergy In late-medieval Europe *anticlericalism* was prominent in lands such as the *Holy Roman Empire* while less so in others such as *England* and France. The German *Reformation* was largely a revolt against the clergy by the clergy, though attacks on priests and monks in pamphlet literature and sermons did much to garner wider public support. In the Lutheran and Reformed movements an entirely new understanding of the clerical *office* emerged. No longer of sacramental status, the Protestant priesthood was transformed into a vocation to be held by properly qualified men charged with leading worship, preaching, and overseeing the lives of the community. They were to marry and lead exemplary lives in the parish communities. With the removal of *canon law* and separate church courts the clergy were made subjects under the authority of ruling princes and magistrates. The Reformation saw the widespread control of the clergy by civil authorities. The *Council of Trent* repudiated the Protestant reforms of the clergy and reasserted the sacramental nature of the Catholic priesthood.

Dixon and Schorn-Schütte (2003); Janse and Pitkin (2005); Pettegree (1993).
BRUCE GORDON

Cochlaeus, Johannes (a.k.a. Johann Dobneck; 1479–1552) Cochlaeus was a theologian and an early adversary of *Martin Luther* and, later, *Philip Melanchthon*. His early associations included humanists such as Ulrich von Hutten and *Willibald Pirckheimer*. On the one hand, Cochlaeus demonstrated his humanist influences by invoking the writings of the early church fathers in defending the teachings of the Roman Church. On the other hand, Cochlaeus's polemical writing style contradicted the humanist preference for moderation. Cochlaeus attacked the Reformers on a variety of subjects, including *justification*, human

will, and the *Lord's Supper*. Cochlaeus was involved in the proceedings at the *diets of Worms* (1521) and Augsburg (1530). In 1549 the prolific Cochlaeus published two significant works: a lengthy and hostile biography of Luther as well as a twelve-volume history of *Jan Hus* and the Hussites. Cochlaeus is perhaps best remembered for his 1529 publication, *Septiceps Lutherus* (*The Seven-Headed Luther*).

Bäumer (1980); Keen (2002); Samuel-Scheyder (1993); Spahn (1964).
HANS WIERSMA

Colet, John (1467–1519) Educator and, after 1505, dean of St. Paul's Cathedral, Colet is best known as the founder of St. Paul's School in London, as well as for his friendship with *Desiderius Erasmus*, who developed several textbooks for the school. The oldest son of a member of a prestigious London merchant guild, Colet was educated at Oxford and Cambridge, and spent several years in Italy, where he was influenced by the otherworldly focus of Florentine Neoplatonist Marsilio Ficino. Over a period of years he delivered a series of lectures on Paul's Epistles at Oxford. Acclaimed by nineteenth-century scholars as a humanist who served as Erasmus's inspiration, he has more recently been reevaluated as a rigid yet eclectic interpreter of *Scripture*, relying on guidance by the *Holy Spirit* rather than textual scholarship, tendencies that are evident in his 1499 dispute with Erasmus about Christ's agony in the Garden of Gethsemane.

J. Gleason (1989); Kaufman (1982); Lupton (1909).
J. LAUREL CARRINGTON

Colloquies In Latin the term *colloquies* refers to formal written dialogues, and during the age of the *Reformation*, colloquies were either written or oral forums for debate and discussion about religion. These colloquies became important venues in the sixteenth century for disputing political and religious ideas. *Desiderius Erasmus*'s *Colloquies*, dialogues exploring contemporary religious practices published in 1518, laid the groundwork for the sixteenth-century colloquies. Academics, councils, and religious scholars convened throughout the century and debated the particulars of the Roman and Reformed faiths. The *Marburg Colloquy* of 1529 remains one of the most famous of the era, as was the more informal one held the following year at Augsburg to attempt to reconnect Luther's evangelical faith to the *Church of Rome*. The colloquies developed into a venue for the initial organization and later criticism of the Reformed faiths as they allowed for the tighter definition of their beliefs and organization.

Hillerbrand (1984); Nugent (1974); Raitt (1993).

KRISTEN POST WALTON

Commandments   *Reformation* theologians endorsed the Ten Commandments for use in both confession and *catechism*. *Martin Luther* saw the Decalogue as the basis for Christian ethics, continuing the medieval practice of using it as a guide for confession, and emphasizing its role as central to his catechisms. Likewise, *John Calvin* understood the commandments as the "*Law*," which must precede a Christian's acceptance of the *Gospel*. As Law, the commandments serve to accuse sinners of their iniquity and to guide them to all righteousness. Calvin highlighted the Decalogue's importance in his catechisms and stressed its authority in his sermons and commentaries.

The Ten Commandments substantively served as the moral law for Protestant reformers. After the fall, humanity was incapable of observing this ethical code. Thus the Christ event restored humanity's proper response

to the Decalogue. The Reformers, then, linked the Old Testament with the New. Protestantism has continued this tradition of equating the commandments with Christian ethics.

Bockmuehl (1997); Farley (2000); Packer (2008).

BRIAN C. BREWER

Communication of Properties (Lat. *Communicatio Idiomatum*)

This phrase arose in the medieval era as a summary of Pope Leo's *Christology* as expressed in his famous *Tome* (449), where he stated that the properties of divinity and humanity meet in the union of the person of Christ. The doctrine was formalized at the Council of Chalcedon in 451. In the sixteenth century, it was rejected by *Michael Servetus* in his treatise *De Trinitatis Erroribus* (*On the Errors of the Trinity*, 1531). In general, however, most Roman Catholics and Protestants continued to agree on the nature of Christ. Disagreement did arise not over the doctrine itself but over its implications for a proper understanding of the *Lord's Supper* among Lutherans and Calvinists. Lutherans used the doctrine to support their understanding of the real presence, citing ubiquity as a quality of the person of Christ that can be applied to Christ's body. Calvinists rejected this.

Sasse (1959); Wandel (2006).

DAVID M. WHITFORD

Communion   *See* Lord's Supper

Communion of Saints   The communion of saints (Lat. *communio sanctorum*), confessed in the *Apostles' Creed*, is the collective term denoting all who belong to the body of Christ. According to the cosmology that had evolved over the course of Christianity's first fifteen hundred years, the communion of saints circumscribed believers on earth, in *purgatory*, and in heaven. In this cosmology, the collected prayers and merits of

the *communio*—especially of the saints in heaven—could be distributed to aid others still on their path to heaven. In light of the new understanding of the doctrine of *justification*, Protestant theology dismantled this system, removing purgatory, *indulgences*, the *treasury of merit*, the invocation and intercession of the saints, and so on. The outcome was a streamlined cosmology in which one's faith in Christ determined membership in the communion and immediate entrance into heaven for the "departed faithful." The *Council of Trent* (session 25, 1563) upheld the traditional cosmology, emphasizing the communal benefits of the earlier system.

Benko (1964); P. Brown (1981); H. Preus (1948).
HANS WIERSMA

Company of Pastors

The Company of Pastors was the formal organization of ministers in Geneva and its surrounding rural communities. *John Calvin* codified its existence in the "ecclesiastical ordinances" presented to the city in 1541 and moderated its weekly meetings until his death. It served several purposes: a forum for biblical and theological discussion, a place for mutual exhortation, and a place to formulate common positions in relation to the city council. Prominent in its business was the examination and approval of candidates for ministry in Geneva and its vast mission to France. In contrast to previous forms of church government it vested oversight not in a bishop and hierarchy, but in a body of peers. This reflected Reformed ecclesiology, with shared, mutually accountable *authority* as a check against the tyranny of an individual or institution. Under different names and with numerous variations it provided a model for judicatories in the Reformed churches.

Foxgrover (2004); Kingdon (1985a).
GARY NEAL HANSEN

Complutensian Polyglot

Named for the Spanish city of Alcala (*Complutum* in Latin) in which it was created, the Complutensian Polyglot is a multilanguage edition of the Hebrew Bible (Old Testament) and the New Testament, prepared by a team of scholars under the direction of Cardinal Ximénez de Cisneros. The Hebrew Bible portion consists of three parallel columns with the *Hebrew* and Septuagint (*Greek*) texts on the outside and the Vulgate in the center; in addition, the books of the Pentateuch include an Aramaic paraphrase with Latin translation at the bottom. The New Testament incorporates the Greek text and the Vulgate, while a final volume provides Hebrew, Aramaic, and Greek dictionaries. The entire work was published in 1522. Although it reflects the humanist concern for textual scholarship based on original languages, the Complutensian Polyglot remains faithful to the Vulgate, unlike *Desiderius Erasmus*'s New Testament, which offers an alternative Latin translation in place of the Vulgate.

Abad (1999); Bentley (1983); Rummel (1999).
J. LAUREL CARRINGTON

Conciliarism

Conciliarism grew out of the late medieval fervor for *church* reform and apostolic renewal, and it gained prominence with the Great Schism (1378–1415). Advocates of conciliarism, most notably Jean Gerson, argued that an ecumenical council was the highest *authority* in the church and that a council could depose a pope. These arguments guided the general councils of Pisa (1409), Constance (1414–18), Pavia-Siena (1423–24), and Basel-Ferrara-Florence (1431–49), which issued decrees affirming conciliar principles. For fifteenth-century conciliarists, Christian unity depended on strong corporate associations, limits on papal authority, and constitutional governance of the church. Renaissance popes rejected these arguments, asserting that papal superiority was crucial for church unity. Nonetheless, conciliarism remained a viable ecclesiology into the sixteenth century, and French clerics continued to use conciliar theory to defend Gallicanism against Ultramontanism into the nineteenth century. Several twentieth-century scholars have located the origins of modern representative government and democratic political theory in conciliarism.

Black (1979); Burns (1997); Ryan (1998); Tierney (1955).

SEAN T. PERRONE

Concupiscence (Lat. *concupiscentia*; Gr. *epithumêsis*)

Concupiscence is literally an eager or profound desire. In Christian theology it connotes a wicked or lustful desire. It appears in the Latin Vulgate a number of times but most importantly in Romans 7:7, where Paul condemns covetousness. In Christian theology it developed into a technical definition for the lustful desire present during sexual intercourse. This improper desire is then passed to children as the stain of *original sin*. During the *Reformation*, English translations used "lust" as a translation. In general, Reformation theologians maintained the traditional understanding of concupiscence as lustful desire and its effect in transmitting original sin. It is discussed in Article 2 of the *Augsburg Confession* and in book 2 of *John Calvin*'s *Institutes of the Christian Religion*.

Ozment (1969).

DAVID M. WHITFORD

Confession of Faith

A confession of faith is a formal common statement of belief produced by a religious community. The first Lutheran confessions were put forth in the 1520s, leading to the *Augsburg Confession* of 1530 and the subsequent *Tetrapolitan Confession* of *Strasbourg* and three other Swabian cities. The first important Reformed confession was the *Helvetic Confession*

(1536), derived from *Huldrych Zwingli*'s *Ratio Fidei*. A series of Calvinist confessions appeared in the 1560s, modeled on the French Confessio Gallicana of 1559. Among these are the Scots Confession (1560), drafted by *John Knox*, and the *Belgic Confession* (1561), adopted first by Walloonian Calvinists, and later translated into Dutch and Low German. Other confessions were adopted in Scandinavia, Poland, and Hungary. Among the *Anabaptists* there were several confessions, the best known being the *Schleitheim Confession* (1527). In most cases, the drafting of confessions of faith was associated with political crisis, generally a direct threat against the religious community from external forces.

Cameron (1991); Grimm (1973).

WILLIAM BRADFORD SMITH

Confession of Sin

The act of confession is an enumeration of sins described to another believer, usually a priest or pastor. By confessing, the believer recognizes sins and faults, expresses sorrow for past action, and intends to make amends. In the early church, *penance* after *baptism* was allowed only once in a lifetime. During the sixth century, the Celtic system of penance with its private, repeatable confessions became the typical penitential system of medieval Europe. At the Fourth *Lateran Council* (1215), Pope Innocent III made annual confession mandatory as part of the *sacrament* of penance. Penitential manuals outlined lists of questions designed to prompt thorough confession of various sins, as well as the appropriate penances for these sins. Most of the Protestant reformers rejected the moral interrogation typical of late medieval penance and advocated a general confession and absolution of *sin*. This general act of confession followed by a general absolution became the preparatory act for Holy Communion.

Braswell (1983); Coffey (2001); Rittgers (2004).

ESTHER CHUNG-KIM

Confessionalization   This is the process whereby the older unitary Western Catholic Church divided into distinct religious communities (confessions) each with its own theology, organization, and liturgical forms. The term derives from the German *Konfession*, which refers to religious groupings rather than a particular set of beliefs (*Bekenntnis*). The thesis in its present form was developed by Heinz Schilling and Wolfgang Reinhard in the 1980s, based in part on the older work of Ernst Walter Zeeden, Gerhard Oesterreich, and Volker Press. In a more general sense, the confessionalization thesis derives from a reexamination of Max Weber and Ernst Troeltsch's account of the relationship between the *Reformation* and the development of modern society.

Confessionalization in the theological sense describes the development of the three major religious groupings of the sixteenth century: Tridentine Catholicism, Lutheranism, and Calvinism. These confessions took the form of official creeds within particular states. Indeed, unlike "denominations," the emergence of confessions as official churches was closely tied to the development of the state. The connections between confessionalization and state-building are notable on three levels. Confessions provided a mechanism for binding together the political community more closely in the absence of other strong ideological forces. The position of the prince as head of the state church, whether directly as in Protestant lands or indirectly as in Catholic states, greatly added to the prestige and theoretical *authority* of the ruler. Finally, through control of the *church*, the state was able to penetrate much more deeply into society, influencing nearly every aspect of public and private life. The long-term effect was to transform the subjects of the state into a homogeneous, disciplined social group, understood as a necessary precondition for the emergence of modern industrial society.

The confessionalization thesis has been central to studies of the post-Reformation era for nearly a generation. Two criticisms of the thesis have arisen. Some scholars view the thesis as being too "top-down" an approach, noting as well frequent examples of resistance by local communities and individuals to the religious and social disciplinary reforms enacted by the states. A second criticism has to do with chronology. While the thesis in its original form focused on the period between 1550 and 1650, current scholarship has stressed that the process of securing doctrinal orthodoxy in most European states was not completed until the eighteenth century. The starting point of the process is likely a point of controversy. Several scholars have identified similar processes at work in east-central Europe in the fourteenth and fifteenth centuries. There are also questions as to whether the thesis, developed specifically to describe the interconnection between state-building and religious reform in the German states, can be applied to the national monarchies of Western Europe or the Italian states.

Forster (1992); Reinhard (1989); Schilling (1986); W. Smith (2008).
WILLIAM BRADFORD SMITH

Confirmation   In the medieval view confirmation was the second *sacrament*, and consisted of anointing by the bishop to impart the *Holy Spirit*. Protestants argued that sacraments must be instituted by Christ and bear a *Gospel* promise. Therefore both *Martin Luther* and *John Calvin* rejected confirmation as a sacrament for its lack of biblical institution or command with promise and sign. Protestants did see a need for a practice after *baptism* to mark inclusion in the *church*, and they rethought confirmation as examination at the end of catechetical instruction. For *Martin Bucer* in particular this marked commitment to the faith and preparation for admission to the *Lord's Supper*. The *Council* *of Trent* (1545–63) reaffirmed confirmation as a sacrament instituted by Christ, and **Roberto Bellarmino** defended it, finding a command implicit and a sign explicit in the apostles' action of laying on hands, and a promise in Christ's pledge to send the Spirit.

A. Burnett (1995); J. Fisher (1978); P. Turner (1987).

GARY NEAL HANSEN

Confraternities   Confraternities (or sodalities) are voluntary groups that focus on charity and/or *piety*. Although the term was used in the ancient church, confraternities in the modern sense began in the twelfth century. Many of the late medieval confraternities (also sometimes named congregations, companies, or brotherhoods) were dedicated to **Mary**, other saints, or the Eucharist. Membership often focused around a particular trade, social status, or other common interest, and could include both lay and clerical members, with membership in more than one association common. Often wealthier members took some responsibility for poorer members, especially for purposes of burial and memorial masses.

In the sixteenth century, confraternities became an important element in Catholic renewal, as well as a focus for Tridentine reform. Clerical authority was expanded over these organizations, while the pious elements were stressed over the social. Many Marian sodalities and associations devoted to the rosary were established, particularly by the *Jesuits*, and spread throughout Europe.

C. Black (1989); Chatellier (1989); Fanning (1908); Hsia (2005).

BETH KREITZER

Conscience   In the *Reformation* the conscience was seen as a faculty of the soul that rendered judgment on whether an individual had done what

God expected of him or her, especially regarding salvation. Protestants claimed that Catholic theology burdened their consciences because it did not provide enduring assurance of forgiveness; the human conscience could never know if it had appeased divine wrath sufficiently through *good works* and thus was always anxious and fearful. Protestant theology sought to remove this alleged burden by teaching *justification* by *faith*, which directed human beings to trust in God's *grace* for forgiveness rather than in their own works done in cooperation with grace. Protestants thought this soteriology was biblical and thus believed they had provided the troubled conscience with a divine source of instruction and comfort, whereas the Catholic Church had provided only human teaching and solace. Catholics countered that ongoing participation in the sacramental life of the *church* provided sufficient consolation for troubled consciences.

Neal (1972); Rittgers (2004); Zachman (1993).

RONALD K. RITTGERS

Consensus   Consensus of the faithful has been recognized as a standard of *orthodoxy* throughout Christian history. Protestant emphasis on the highly individualistic doctrinal standard of "*Scripture* alone" raised important issues regarding the nature of consensus and its role in the *church*. There was disagreement concerning the authority of consensus relative to the claims of individual conscience, the identity of "the faithful" whose consensus was authoritative, and how their consensus was expressed. The concept of consensus nevertheless retained a great deal of prestige. The formation of denominational identities typically involved statements (such as the *Augsburg Confession*, the decrees of the *Council of Trent*, the Canons of Dort, and many others) that were understood to be in some sense articulating a consensus within each church community. The term "consensus" was also sometimes applied to specific doctrinal statements, notably the Consensus Tigurinus (*Zurich Consensus*) of 1549, a standard of eucharistic doctrine within the Swiss Reformed churches.

Eppley (2007); Pelikan and Hotchkiss (2003); Rorem (1988); J. Simpson (2007).

DANIEL EPPLEY

Consilium de emendanda ecclesia

The "Counsel Concerning the Reform of the Church" was signed in 1537 by a commission of nine Catholic cardinals and prelates. This commission was appointed in July 1536 by *Pope Paul III*, who had recently convoked a general council in Mantua in 1537. The council had to be postponed, but the commission dutifully submitted its report, signed by all nine of its reform-minded members, including notably: *Gasparo Contarini* (as president), Gian Pietro Carafa, *Reginald Pole, Jacopo Sadoleto*, and *Girolamo Aleander*. The report first rejected the claim that the pope, as lord over all the church's properties, had the right to sell them at will and so could not be guilty of simony. It went on to criticize financial abuses and moral failings among the rest of the *clergy* and in the religious orders. The text was soon leaked and published in German translation with a biting commentary from *Martin Luther*.

Jedin (1957–61).

MICKEY L. MATTOX

Consistory

A consistory is a disciplinary body of Reformed churches, sometimes referred to as a "morals court." The Genevan consistory was established in 1541 as a condition of *John Calvin*'s return to Geneva. It was composed of annually elected lay elders and all the ordained pastors of the city, and was presided over by one of the four leading magistrates (syndics) of the city government. As Calvin believed that even faithful Christians were still depraved human beings, the consistory's goal was to enforce Christian *discipline* across the community. Genevan inhabitants could be called before the consistory for myriad reasons, from "misbelief" and suspicion of Catholic practices to causing "scandal" by fighting too publicly with spouses or children. In other parts of Europe, where the Reformed Church was not legal (France) or was not the sole recognized religion (the Netherlands), consistories had varying roles, sometimes having more responsibility for *church* administration, and often having less authority to impose discipline on the community as a whole.

Graham (1996); Kingdon (1994); Mentzer (1994).

KAREN E. SPIERLING

Consubstantiation

Consubstantiation is the doctrine that the body of Christ is materially present with the bread and wine in the Eucharist. It is contrasted with the doctrine of *transubstantiation*, which holds that the substance of the elements is miraculously changed into the actual body and blood of Christ, although the "accidents" (perceptual qualities such as smell and taste) remain. While all Protestant reformers rejected transubstantiation, there was fractious disagreement concerning the appropriate understanding of the Eucharist. *Martin Luther* affirmed a real bodily presence in the Eucharist based on Christ's words of institution: "This is my body." He utilized the combination of prepositions "in, with, and under" to describe the presence of Christ in relationship to the elements. Although Luther's position is commonly designated consubstantiation, Luther himself never used the term; and later Lutherans, while affirming the real presence, denied this involved a mingling of the body and blood of Christ with the elements.

Hall (1985); Macy (1992); Steinmetz (2002a).

GREGORY J. MILLER

Contarini, Gasparo Cardinal (1483–1542)

Contarini, Gasparo Cardinal (1483–1542) Italian cardinal and reformer, Contarini was born in Venice to a prominent family and was educated at the University of Padua, where he was trained in the humanistic style. He returned home and rose to prominence as a diplomat, serving the state of Venice. It was in this capacity that he was made ambassador to the Imperial court, and came to the attention of *Charles V*. Charles requested his presence at the Council of *Regensburg*.

Contarini was also an accomplished lay theologian, who wrote a treatise on the immortality of the soul and a polemic against *Martin Luther*. *Paul III* named him to the college of cardinals in 1535, though he had never been ordained. He was a recognized leading Roman voice for reform of the *Church of Rome*, and he served on the council that prepared the *Consilium de emendanda ecclesia*. Seeing the new order of the Society of Jesus as a helpful implement for reform, he strongly supported its acceptance. At the Council of Regensburg he was one of the leading participants, and a strong proponent of a theology of *justification* called "double justification" that was received negatively by both Roman and Protestant theologians. Though some Roman theologians believed that Contarini had conceded far too much in this effort, Paul III continued to value him and appointed him as legate to Bologna, where he died.

E. Gleason (1993); Matheson (1972); Steinmetz (2001b).

R. WARD HOLDER

Contrition

Contrition Contrition played a key role in the medieval *sacrament* of *penance* according to the formula: contrition, *confession, absolution*, and *satisfaction*. Late medieval theologians understood it to be a more perfect form of sorrow for one's sins and commitment to rectify one's life, imbued with divine *grace* and derived from one's *love* for God, than attrition, which arose from fear of punishment. However, they disagreed about the role of contrition in the forgiveness of sins and its relationship to priestly absolution in the sacrament of penance. Some historians argue that the more stringent demands for complete contrition placed excessive psychological burdens on late medieval Christians. Protestant reformers dissociated contrition from the sacrament of penance, but identified it as passive sorrow for one's sins and as a necessary prelude to *justification*. The *Council of Trent* reaffirmed the validity of the sacrament, but did not resolve the disputes within Catholic teaching about attrition, contrition, and absolution.

Lualdi and Thayer (2000); Myers (1996); Spykman (1955); Tentler (1977).

GEOFFREY DIPPLE

Coornhert, Dirck Volkertszoon (1522–90)

Coornhert, Dirck Volkertszoon (1522–90) Often considered the father of Dutch Renaissance scholarship, Coornhert was a humanist scholar, engraver, and book illustrator who translated Latin classics and a portion of the New Testament into Dutch. During Holland's political struggles with Spain, Coornhert was a staunch supporter of William the Silent, becoming a political agent to the prince while in exile in Cleves. However, Coornhert is known particularly in theological circles for his refutation of orthodox Calvinism upon his return to Holland in 1572. Highly critical of the *Heidelberg Catechism*, Coornhert argued for the freedom of the human *will*, individualism, and the call to Christian *perfection*. He viewed church reform, dogma, and confessions of faith as human inventions and instead argued for inner *piety*. *John Calvin* himself attacked Coornhert's writings. Later, *Jacobus Arminius*, employed to refute Coornhert, became strongly influenced by Coornhert's arguments. Consequently, Coornhert is often viewed as a forebear of Arminianism and Pietism.

Bonger (2004); R. Jones (2005); Voogt (2000).

BRIAN C. BREWER

Cop, Nicolas (ca. 1501–40)

Humanist, physician, and rector of the Sorbonne, Cop is best known for his address opening the fall term of the university on November 1, 1533. This address took the form of a sermon on the Beatitudes and reflected an *evangelical*, reformist *humanism* reminiscent both of *Desiderius Erasmus* and of the early *Martin Luther*. Cop's public endorsement of *justification* by *faith* alone provoked a crackdown on evangelical sympathizers in Paris, forcing both Cop and his friend *John Calvin* to flee to Basel. Cop returned to France in 1536 and devoted the rest of his life to medicine. One of the two extant manuscripts of the address is in Calvin's hand, and Calvin's possible role in the composition of Cop's address is a subject of controversy.

Ganoczy (1987); Tylenda (1976); Wendel (1997).

EDWIN WOODRUFF TAIT

Copernicus, Nicolaus (1473–1543)

A true Renaissance polymath, Copernicus studied *canon law*, medicine, and mathematics; he served as a canon, worked as an administrator and physician, and wrote a treatise on currency. Despite these skills he is best known as the man who overturned the Ptolemaic geocentric view of the universe and replaced it with a heliocentric system in his book *De Revolutionibus orbium coeles-*

tium (*On the Revolutions of the Heavenly Spheres*) published in 1543 after his death, an event that is often seen as marking the beginning of the scientific revolution. Yet Copernicus was far from the modern scientist such designations imply. Disturbed by the complexities and inconsistencies of the Ptolemaic/Aristotelian system, which he felt did not reflect the elegance and intelligence of God's plan, Copernicus followed traditional motivations and mathematical methods in completing his work. Although his work was controversial, many Catholic and Protestant theologians and scientists adopted at least part of his system, especially by the end of the century.

Gingerich (2004); Kuhn (1985); Repcheck (2007); Vollmann (2006).

KATHRYN A. EDWARDS

Corpus Christi

Corpus Christi (the Feast of the Body of Christ) is a feast day in honor of the Eucharist celebrated by Catholics and some Anglican churches. The feast began in Liège in the late twelfth century and was officially added to the liturgical calendar in 1264. It became one of the most popular and important festivals of the later Middle Ages, especially in urban areas, typified by processions, plays, pageants, and public preaching on the Eucharist as the body of Christ. Most Protestants condemned the celebration as showing the errors of *transubstantiation*, and it often became a dividing line in confessionally mixed areas. Both Protestants and Catholics criticized the excesses of feast celebrations in general, which were often accompanied by violence and disorder, and tried to bring them under outside control as part of the social disciplining movement of the Reformation. In some areas the feast day turned into a purely secular celebration.

Burke (2009); Rubin (1991); Walters et al. (2006); Wandel (2006).

AMY E. LEONARD

Corro, Antonio del (1527–91)

A Spanish Protestant theologian, Corro was a member of the observant branch of the Spanish Order of Saint Jerome. At the moment of his conversion he resided in Seville, in the convent of San Isidro. He had unique access to prohibited books, including works by Andreas Osiander. He left Seville in 1557 after the *Inquisition* discovered that San Isidro had become a Protestant conventicle. He attended the Academy of Lausanne (1558–59) and developed a unique irenic spirit. He articulated his ecumenical theology in his *Epistle or Godly Admonition* (Fr., 1567; Eng., 1569), and in his more polemical *Supplication Exhibited to the Most Mighty Prince Philip King of Spain* (Fr., 1567; Eng., 1577). By the end of 1567, Corro had already moved to *England* and remained there to the end of his life. His most important work was his *Theological Dialogue* (Lat., 1574; Eng., 1575).

Hauben (1967); Kinder (1986); Roldan-Figueroa (2009).
RADY ROLDAN-FIGUEROA

Council of Constance (1414–18)

The sixteenth ecumenical church council was held in the Free Imperial City of Constance in the southwestern corner of the *Holy Roman Empire* (now Konstanz, Germany). It was called by Emperor Sigismund (1368–1437; r. 1410) in order to end the Western Schism, bring about needed reforms, and stamp out *heresy*. By the time Sigismund called for the council there were three claimants to the papacy: Benedict XIII of Avignon (Pedro de Luna, 1328–1423; r. 1378–1417), Gregory XII of Rome (Angelo Corrario, ca. 1327–1417; r. 1406–15), and John XXIII of Pisa (Baldassare Cossa, 1370–1419; r. 1410–15). All three were ultimately deposed, and Martin V (Odo Collona, 1368–1431; r. 1417) was elected to replace them as the sole pope. In 1415 the Bohemian reformer *Jan Hus* was guaranteed safe passage to and from the council in order that he might defend his theological convictions and his calls for reform. He was, instead, tried for heresy and condemned by the council. He was burned at the stake on July 6, 1415. A century later, the events of the council would play a significant role in *Martin Luther*'s debate with *Johann Eck* at the *Leipzig Disputation* (1519), where Luther declared that many of Hus's propositions were orthodox and that the council had erred in condemning him.

Izbicki and Rollo-Koster (2009); Mladenovic (1965); Stump (1994).
DAVID M. WHITFORD

Council of Trent (1545–47, 1551–52, 1562–63)

This was the nineteenth ecumenical council of the Roman Catholic Church, held in the alpine Italian city of Trent in three intervals to address doctrinal issues raised by the Protestant *Reformation* and to confront abuses within the *church*. *Martin Luther* had called for a general church council as early as 1518 to reform the church and to consider his theological propositions. Powerful political and ecclesiastical figures professed interest in such a meeting, though the emperor (*Charles V*), French kings (Francis I, Henry II), a succession of popes, as well as churchmen across Europe possessed distinct and conflicting agendas that delayed an actual convention until December 1545. Political powers hoped for a diminution of papal authority, whereas popes battled to overcome lingering conciliarist sentiments that proposed to elevate the power of church councils over popes. The choice of Trent as the location represented a victory for the papal party, which feared the results from any meeting outside of its most influential base in Italy. Close to one hundred delegates, consisting of cardinals, archbishops, bishops, and theologians, descended on Trent in 1545.

Conflicts over protocol and competing priorities plagued the council, particularly during its first interval. Delegates chose to take up the tasks of institutional reform and doctrinal resolution simultaneously, and from 1545 to 1547 they affirmed the *authority* of church *tradition* alongside *Scripture,* upheld the seven *sacraments,* and condemned the doctrine of *justification* by *faith.* Thus the council denied every doctrinal tenet of Protestantism that differed with traditional Catholic teaching. Outbreaks of plague and war necessitated relocation to Bologna in 1547 and then suspension of the council.

A much smaller convocation reconvened in 1551, joined by Protestants who sought review of Trent's previous statements and assertion of conciliar authority over papal prerogative. Delegates rejected both proposals, but accomplished little else other than confirming the doctrine of *transubstantiation.*

The largest contingent of delegates met for the third and final phase, enacting an extensive array of reforms to root out abuses and ensure a trained clerical corps. These included provisions for clerical residence, establishment of seminaries, prohibition of simony, pluralism, and amending the practice of selling *indulgences.* The council also defended long-standing positions on *marriage, purgatory,* clerical *celibacy, intercession of saints,* and the *Mass* as a reenactment of Christ's sacrifice.

Though implemented gradually and unevenly, Trent marked a watershed in Catholic history. It provided a canonical basis for a broad reform movement, articulated an unambiguous repudiation of Protestantism, and enhanced the authority of the *papacy.* In so doing, Trent set the course for Catholicism in both the early modern and modern eras.

Bulman and Parrella (2006); Jedin (1957–61); Pedersen (1991).

CHARLES PARKER

Councils, Authority of The Protestant reformers challenged the *author-*

ity of the *church*—both in the forms of papal authority and the authority of church councils—in favor of the supreme authority of *Scripture. Martin Luther* and *John Calvin* argued that church councils are fallible human enterprises that can be helpful only insofar as they concur with Scripture. They pointed out that past councils not only erred but contradicted one another. Furthermore, they contended that councils could not establish new doctrine, but should only defend and explain that which is already taught in Scripture. Though many Protestant groups continued to address issues by way of church councils, they held skepticism as to their effectiveness and measured the council's success by its concordance with Scripture. The English reformers asserted very similar views in article 21 of the *Thirty-Nine Articles* of Religion, with the addition that a church council may not be gathered without the approval of the civil authority.

Avis (2006); Steinmetz (2002b).

G. SUJIN PAK

Counsels of Perfection In Matthew 19 Jesus was approached by a young man seeking eternal life. When he claimed he already lived in obedience to the *Commandments,* Jesus said that if he wanted to be "perfect," he should sell his possessions, give to the poor, and follow him. In the Middle Ages, this became the foundation of the "evangelical counsels" that bound the "religious" (priests, monks, and nuns) to a life of poverty, chastity, and obedience. These were viewed as *supererogatory works,* above and beyond what is generally required.

The Reformers viewed this with disdain: taking these as "counsels" made *Scripture*'s commands seem optional. Perfection was ruled out by Protestants, both Lutheran and Reformed, for whom all human behavior was tainted by *sin.* They believed faithfulness in these areas is required of all Christians, not just a clerical elite, and objected to supererogation as implying that our works earned merit toward salvation.

Rahner (1967); Steinmetz (1993); Wendebourg (2005).

GARY NEAL HANSEN

Counter-Reformation The term "Counter-Reformation" is often used interchangeably with "Catholic Reformation" to describe the reform efforts of the Catholic Church from the fifteenth to the eighteenth century or used uniquely to refer to Rome's responses to the Protestant *Reformation*. The movement included the Catholic Church's efforts to revitalize itself, with many reforms commencing prior to 1517, as well as Rome's responses to the emergence of *Martin Luther* and other Reformers. The movement produced new religious orders, a general council, lay confraternities, missions, seminaries, and higher expectations of both *clergy* and laity. New religious orders, including the Society of Jesus (*Jesuits*), which was recognized before the first session of the *Council of Trent*, and existing orders spread the ideas through their mission work. First called by *Pope Paul III*, the Council of Trent met intermittently between 1545 and 1563 and established an official program of reform for the Catholic Church. Rome launched missionary programs in Europe and abroad, entering into both the Americas and Asia. New female orders appeared, including traditional ones subject to enclosure like the Ursulines and the Visitandines, and innovative lay orders that ministered to the poor like the Daughters of Charity.

The *papacy* increased centralization and came to resemble a secular state making efforts to enforce a strict clerical hierarchy and employing papal nuncios as Rome's diplomatic representatives across Europe. Catholic monarchs and popes found some common goals in their efforts to centralize and desire for religious hegemony but experienced conflict over who would oversee reform within a country's borders. Catholic princes frequently limited Rome's ability to introduce Tridentine reforms in their kingdoms. The papacy attempted to enforce *orthodoxy* through inquisitorial courts and the *Index Librorum Prohibitorum* (*Index of Forbidden Books*), but its ability to prosecute *heresy* and suppress Protestantism was limited primarily to portions of Italy.

Catholic reform gave new power to bishops. Carlo Borromeo, a model bishop, established the standard for systematic and thorough supervisions of parishes during his tenure as archbishop of Milan (1564–84). The fundamental goal of most reformers was to establish a community that revolved around a clearly delineated parish populated by a laity that practiced Catholicism as defined by Rome. Better-educated and more qualified priests were to be the main agents of reform and renewal within Catholic parishes. Priests were to perform *sacraments*, offer spiritual guidance, but also provide an example to all Christians. There was greater emphasis on *education* of laity through formal schooling by religious orders and catechetical instruction. Officials encouraged lay *piety* through clergy-sanctioned confraternities dedicated to the Eucharist and the rosary as well as parish celebrations such as Jubilees and eucharistic processions. While Catholicism became more uniform, it was never monolithic, and there remained multiple outlets for both lay and clerical devotion.

Bireley (1999); Hsia (2005); O'Malley (2000).

JILL R. FEHLEISON

Covenant The concept of covenant concerns the special relationships between God and God's people throughout biblical history. During the *Reformation*, the doctrine of covenant became the starting point or thread for Reformed theology. Continental as well as later English and New England Puritan reformers developed what came to be called covenant or federal theology based on biblical teachings structured according to the various covenantal arrangements between God and humanity. Covenant theology developed through generations of theologians—first in Zurich with the polemics of *Huldrych Zwingli* against the *Anabaptist* challenge to infant *baptism*; then with *Heinrich Bullinger, Wolfgang Musculus*, and *John Calvin*; and finally at Heidelberg in the theology of Zacharias Ursinus and Caspar Olevianus. They discussed the covenant in the contexts of the *sacraments* and the relationship between the Testaments, which intersected in the doctrine of infant baptism. The covenant of *grace* in the *gospel* revealed the fulfillment of the righteousness demanded by the covenant of *nature* in the *law*.

Baker (1980); Bierma (1996); Strehle (1988).

ESTHER CHUNG-KIM

Coverdale, Miles (ca. 1488–1568)

A humanist, born in Yorkshire, Coverdale received his doctorate from Tübingen, and returned to *England*, where he joined the Augustinians and adopted belief in the doctrine of *grace*. He later became one of the leaders of the English *Reformation* and the bishop of Exeter under Edward VI. Coverdale is most famous for completing the first printed edition of the entire Bible in English. Revising *William Tyndale*'s 1534 translation of the New Testament, the Coverdale Bible was printed originally in 1535 and became the Bible of the early English Reformation in England. He published a second version in 1539 that included both the Latin Vulgate and English translation. Coverdale's life was spent in and out of exile in England, flourishing most during the reign of Edward VI,

when he became chaplain to the young king, and joining the Marian exiles on the continent during the next reign. He died in England in either 1565 or 1568.

Dallman (1925); Guppy (1935); Mozley (1953).

KRISTEN POST WALTON

Cranach the Elder, Lucas (1472–1553)

Official painter of the Saxon Court, 1505–53, Cranach was part of the German renaissance movement that included Albrecht Dürer. Cranach's more famous portrait subjects included *Frederick the Wise*; Albrecht, archbishop of Mainz; Emperor *Charles V*; as well as *Martin Luther*, Katharina von Bora, and *Philip Melanchthon*. That Cranach lived in *Wittenberg* gave him access not only to the local reformers but also to their theological ideas. Some of Cranach's work (such as the woodcut *Law and Grace*, 1530) demonstrates an attempt to render the theology of the Wittenberg school in visual form. In addition to painting the images of his contemporaries, Cranach painted scenes from the Bible as well as from classical literature. Cranach's famous *Wittenberg Altarpiece* (1547) remains on view at Wittenberg's Church of St. Mary. His son, Lucas Cranach the Younger (1515–86), became an accomplished painter in his own right.

Moser (2005); Noble (2009); Schade (1980).

HANS WIERSMA

Cranmer, Thomas (1489–1556)

Cranmer had a routinely successful early career as a theologian and humanist at Jesus College, Cambridge. Although more inclined to stress conciliar than papal authority, through the 1520s he showed no sympathy for Lutheranism. In 1529, however, he was caught up in *Henry VIII*'s divorce campaign when the king was enthused by his suggestion of bypassing the pope and canvassing the opinion of Europe's universities. He swiftly became a close royal adviser.

Cranmer's *evangelical* conversion cannot be dated precisely, but was certainly completed in 1532, when, on a diplomatic mission to the German Lutheran cities, he secretly married the niece of Andreas Osiander, the Lutheran pastor of Nuremberg. During this mission, the aged William Warham, archbishop of Canterbury, died. Determined to find a replacement who would support his divorce unconditionally, Henry VIII nominated the still-obscure Cranmer. Cranmer returned, concealing his new wife and his newfound evangelical convictions, and did his master's bidding, swiftly annulling one royal marriage and solemnizing another.

As primate of *England*, Cranmer pressed the evangelical cause cautiously but tirelessly. With his more ruthless ally *Thomas Cromwell*, he helped drive the partial reforms of the 1530s. After Cromwell's fall in 1540, the prospects for reform dimmed, and Cranmer himself was the target of a dangerous plot in 1543. Yet he retained the king's trust and was able to implement certain liturgical reforms.

Following the boy-king Edward VI's accession in 1547, Cranmer was at the heart of the new regime and was finally able to prosecute a full-scale Protestant reformation. During Edward's reign (1547–53), Cranmer welcomed Protestant fugitives such as *Martin Bucer* to England, wrote *A defence of the true and Catholic doctrine of the sacrament of the body and blood of our saviour Christ* (1550), prepared a comprehensive *canon-law* reform (never implemented), and drew up doctrinal articles for the English church. His most lasting reform was the *Book of Common Prayer* (1549, 1552). His theological convictions by this period were Reformed and broadly Bucerian, with ambitions for pan-Protestant union. Yet he also retained an exceptionally high doctrine of royal authority and a concern for order in church life that lent his liturgy a conservative flavor.

On Edward's death, Cranmer opposed the accession of *Mary I*, who imprisoned him for treason and *heresy*. Kept in isolation, his theological defenses crumbled over the winter of 1555–56 and he seemed ready to forswear his Protestantism. Yet Mary determined to execute him nevertheless, and he recovered his convictions. He was burned in Oxford on March 21, 1556, holding his right hand (which had signed his recantations) in the fire so that it burned first—turning a potential propaganda coup for Mary's regime into an enduring image of Protestant commitment.

MacCulloch (1996, 2001a); Null (2000).

ALEC RYRIE

Creation   Protestant and Catholic theologians during the *Reformation* concurred that God created the world ex nihilo, declared it "good," and sustains and governs the creation. *John Calvin* underscored creation as the work of the *Trinity* and connected it with God's *providence*. Thus God's perpetual involvement in the creation became a form of *creatio continua* to complement *creatio ex nihilo*. Calvin saw creation, "the spectacle of God's glory," as God's general revelation that fallen humanity was blinded from observing. Thus Calvin's post-fall epistemology required of humans the divine special revelation of *faith* to observe God's handiwork in the created order. *Martin Luther* argued that God designed humanity to perceive the privilege of exercising dominion over the creation and live as responsible creatures within it, understanding that God is continually creating, sustaining, and renewing all nature.

Guzman (2009); Kolb and Arand (2008); Wyatt (1996).

BRIAN C. BREWER

Cromwell, Thomas (ca. 1485–1540)

After a colorful early career as a soldier, merchant, and lawyer, Cromwell entered English royal service in 1524. He may already have had *evangelical* sympathies. In the early 1530s Cromwell emerged as the political manager of *Henry VIII*'s divorce campaign. His strategy was to break the English *clergy*'s independence, assert the supremacy of statute law, and use that supremacy to take *England* into schism in 1534. He became lord privy seal and, in 1535, "vicegerent in spirituals," exercising Henry's supremacy over the English church on his behalf (despite being a layman). From 1535 to 1540 Cromwell drove England's *Reformation*, promoting evangelicals, suppressing the monasteries, driving out perceived *superstition*, and patronizing the English *Bible*. An administrative as well as a religious reformer, his political style was as ruthless as his master's. In 1540, for reasons that remain obscure, the king suddenly lost his trust in Cromwell; he was tried and beheaded.

Elton (1972, 1973); MacCulloch (1996).

ALEC RYRIE

Curia

Curia (originally "meeting place") during the Middle Ages meant court, either ecclesiastical or lay. The Curia Romana, broadly the papal court and its representatives, formed the administrative and judicial backbone of the Latin church and evolved from the *clergy* of the city of Rome. The main component of the curia was the college of cardinals (prelates chosen by the pope) whose most important duties were meeting in consistories (technically to give advice but coming close to legislative) and in the papal conclave to choose the new pope. From its establishment in the high Middle Ages the curia was a touchstone for criticism. By the *Reformation* period it was particularly attacked for its secular nature, the worldly living of its members, and financial corruption, such as the widespread selling of offices (simony). Sixtus V (d. 1590) reorganized parts of the curia, creating congregations, which lessened the power of the college as a whole. Other branches of the curia included the Roman *Inquisition*, tribunals, and nunciatures.

Jedin et al. (1993); Signorotto and Visceglia (2002).

AMY E. LEONARD

Death

The Reformation transformed understandings of death, though many important continuities remained. A "good death" remained paramount for people at all levels of society, but the confessions disagreed about what precisely constituted this. The "last rites" of the medieval church, comprising anointing of the body, confession to a priest, and reception of the Eucharist, along with crucifix and lighted candle, were rejected by Reformers as superstitious and unnecessary. No longer was the deathbed a place where salvation could be won or lost. Rather, a "good death" should provide testimony of a virtuous Christian life, and comfort to the bereaved. Calvinist and Lutheran authors wrote treatises on preparation for death, though these often preserved the medieval presumption that the devil would be active around the deathbed. Protestant churches composed orders for the visitation of the sick, and German Lutherans retained the practice of confession and Communion for the dying.

Ariès (1981); Houlbrooke (1998); P. Marshall (2007).

PETER MARSHALL

Denck, Hans (ca. 1500–1527)

During his short life, Denck encountered and assimilated many of the intellectual and spiritual currents of the early *Reformation*: Renaissance *humanism*, the theologies of *Martin Luther* and the

Saxon radicals *Andreas Bodenstein von Karlstadt* and *Thomas Müntzer*, and *Anabaptists*. His reforming activities took him to Nuremberg, *Strasbourg*, Worms, Augsburg, and *Basel*. Denck's thought is marked by a consistent spiritualism, which identified *Scripture* as the greatest treasure given to humanity, but denied it as the living Word of God, and the *sacraments* as valuable external signs of spiritual change in the believer, but as valueless in and of themselves. While accepting the Reformation emphasis on the primacy of *grace* in salvation, he rejected Luther's predestinarianism and put much greater emphasis on *sanctification* than did the Wittenberg reformers. Denck's thought influenced Anabaptism, especially through *Hans Hut*, *Michael Sattler*, and *Melchior Hoffmann*, as well as spiritualism, primarily through Johannes Bünderlin and *Sebastian Franck*.

Bauman (1991); Packull (1977); G. H. Williams (1992).

GEOFFREY DIPPLE

Devotio Moderna (New Devotion or Modern Devotion)   Founded by the Dutch preacher Geert Groote (1340–94), the Devotio Moderna encouraged a life devoted to *prayer, penance*, and service. During Groote's life, the movement became associated with the development of the Brethren of the Common Life, a lay group that encouraged communal living. Some of Groote's followers later founded a monastery of the reformed branch of the Augustinian Canons at Windesheim. Thomas à Kempis (1379–1471), a monk at Windesheim, wrote the *Imitatio Christi* (*The Imitation of Christ*), perhaps the most famous treatise related to the Devotio Moderna.

While scholars have traditionally associated the Devotio Moderna and the Brethren of the Common Life with the spread of *humanism* in northern Europe, it is unlikely that this was the

case. Although the group often attacked *scholasticism*, this was likely the symptom of a general anti-intellectualism rather than a sign of support of humanistic educational reform. Furthermore, although some humanists, most notably *Desiderius Erasmus*, emerged from the schools of the Brethren of the Common Life, the school teachers were rarely members of the order.

Nauert (2006); Tracy (1996).

GRETA GRACE KROEKER

Diaconate   During the *Reformation* the diaconate became associated with pastoral care and poor relief, especially in Reformed churches. *John Calvin* in particular argued that the diaconate should be restored to its apostolic role of social welfare. In his 1541 *Ecclesiastical Ordinances*, Calvin included deacons as the fourth order of church *office*. Although he recognized a role for deaconesses (widows) in social welfare, the Genevan diaconate did not include women during the Reformation period. Genevan deacons were responsible for the administration and daily running of the hospital, the city's center of poor relief. Reformed churches in France, the Netherlands, *England*, and Scotland followed the Genevan model and included deacons, responsible for poor relief (usually restricted to church members), in their church structure. In Lutheran churches, deacons were sometimes connected to poor relief, sometimes simply general assistants to parish rectors. The Roman Catholic Church maintained the office of deacon as a step toward the priesthood, not directly related to social welfare.

Gamble (1992); McKee (1984); Olson (1989); C. Parker (1998); Sunshine (2003).

KAREN E. SPIERLING

Dialectics   The term "dialectics" comes from the Greek word for the

art of conversation, and in ancient and medieval *philosophy* it became associated with logical inquiry. It took its stereotypical form in the disputations of high *scholasticism* where a question was posed, arguments were made for and against, and a position was declared in resolution. This was derided by the early Protestant theologians as a method leading to speculative theological conclusions far from biblical teachings. Before a generation had passed, however, Protestant scholars were writing on dialectic. The Dutch humanist Rudolf Agricola (1443–85) had paved the way, showing that dialectic could be linked with *rhetoric* for textual analysis. *Philip Melanchthon* wrote the textbook that dominated the field in Germany, and Peter Ramus (1515–72) taught the form that shaped Puritan theology. By the last decades of the sixteenth century both biblical commentaries and theological treatises were strongly shaped by methods *Martin Luther* had rejected.

A. Burnett (2004); Ong (1958); Wengert and Graham (1999).

GARY NEAL HANSEN

Diet of Worms The Diet of Worms, which met from January 27 to May 25, 1521, was the first meeting of the newly elected emperor *Charles V* with the Imperial estates of the *Holy Roman Empire*. Its agenda originally included political and constitutional issues only, but the estates added a discussion of religious grievances against Rome. In February *Martin Luther* was granted an Imperial safe conduct to Worms, and he appeared before the delegates on April 17. Told to recant his published views, he asked for a day to consider; the next day he refused to do so. He left Worms secretly on April 26 and disappeared from public view, thanks to a "kidnapping" arranged by Elector *Frederick the Wise*. On May 25 Charles V issued the Edict of Worms, which ordered Luther to be arrested, forbade anyone to shelter

him, and prohibited the printing, sale, or reading of his books as well as those of his supporters. By condemning Luther and his works, the edict provided the legal mechanism for the persecution and suppression of *evangelical* teaching within the empire, but it could not be enforced in many areas because of popular support for Luther.

Brecht (1985); Jensen (1973).

AMY NELSON BURNETT

Discalced Carmelites The order of the Discalced Carmelites began as a reform movement within the Carmelite order seeking to restore the strict observance of the Carmelite rule. The order's name (Discalced, or without shoes) comes from the members' custom of wearing sandals. Discalced Carmelites were known for their *piety*, obedience, and contemplative *prayer*. *Teresa of Avila* began this reform in 1561. She established the first convent of Discalced Carmelite nuns in 1562 and the first monastery of Discalced Carmelite friars in 1568. Between 1562 and 1582, Teresa and *John of the Cross* founded seventeen female and fifteen male Discalced Carmelite communities in Spain and Portugal. Tensions emerged between the Calced or unreformed Carmelites and the Discalced Carmelites over ecclesiastical jurisdiction, exemplified by the eight-month imprisonment of John of the Cross by unreformed Carmelites in 1577. These conflicts were resolved with papal recognition of the Discalced Carmelites as an independent order in 1593.

Ahlgren (1996); Bilinkoff (1989); Weber (2000).

SEAN T. PERRONE

Discipline The early modern period was marked by increased efforts from both *church* and state to supervise beliefs and behavior. Secular governments issued sumptuary laws and morals edicts that regulated dress, set limits on the lavishness of family celebrations, and forbade sexual misconduct, dancing, gambling, and drunkenness. Each of the confessional churches also developed some form of church discipline to oversee and correct the lives of their members. Although they differed in procedures, personnel, and penalties imposed, Lutheran ecclesiastical courts, Reformed consistories, and the Catholic *Inquisition* were all concerned with eliminating beliefs and practices deemed false or superstitious, bringing sinners to repentance and reconciling them with the Christian community, and preserving the purity of eucharistic fellowship. Private *confession* and sacramental *penance* also had a disciplinary function for Lutherans and Catholics, respectively. Within the Reformed tradition, church discipline was considered by some Reformers, although not by *John Calvin*, to be one of the marks of the church.

De Boer (2001); Hsia (1989); Schilling (1987); Thayer and Lualdi (2000).
AMY NELSON BURNETT

Disputation Public theological disputations were a key element in the conversion of cities from Roman Catholic to Protestant Christianity. The disputation was an established form of debate at medieval universities in northern Europe, based on the notion that there was a single truth that could be arrived at through educated debate. *Martin Luther*'s Ninety-Five Theses were intended to prompt such a disputation at the University of Wittenberg in 1517. During the 1520s and 1530s, city councils considering conversion to the *Reformation* frequently called for public disputations between Protestant and Catholic theologians. Such debates were generally arranged to support the stance already favored by the local government. They were often attended by hundreds of people, laity as well as

clergy. Famous Reformation disputations include *Leipzig* (1519), *Zurich* (January and October 1523), Bern (1528), Geneva (1535), and Lausanne (1536). Such disputations were important in providing a legal basis and public justification for governments' decisions to adopt the Reformation.

Backus (1993); G. Evans (1992); Grendler (2004).
KAREN E. SPIERLING

Dissenters The term "dissenters" is used generally to denominate those who refused to accept in full the standards of *orthodoxy* and orthopraxy of an established *church*, often attempting to reform the established church or to form autonomous churches. Depending on circumstances of time, place, and type of dissent, early modern dissenters were tolerated (officially or unofficially) or subject to various forms of persecution up to and including execution. More specifically the term is used to designate Protestants unwilling to conform to the standards of the early modern English state church, especially *clergy* who refused to conform as required by the Act of Uniformity (1662) and their adherents. Later the Toleration Act (1689) allowed the formation of separate dissenting Protestant churches in *England*. Groups commonly identified with dissent in the latter sense include Baptists, Congregationalists, English Presbyterians, and Quakers. In both of the above senses, the terms "nonconformity"/"nonconformist" are sometimes substituted for "dissent"/"dissenter."

Routley (1960); Watts (1978).
DANIEL EPPLEY

Divorce For Roman Catholics seeking to end a *marriage, canon law* recognized only the possibilities of annulment or permanent separation without permission to remarry. Protestant reformers, attacking *celibacy* as a model for faithful Christians, did not want to deprive people of marriage. Instead, they supported divorce and the right to remarry for a few specific causes. Based on Matthew 19:9, Protestants recognized adultery as the primary reason for divorce. Most acknowledged spousal desertion. Some, including *Huldrych Zwingli* as well as *Anabaptist* Reformers, believed people should be permitted to seek divorce from an "unbelieving" spouse. *Martin Bucer* insisted on the importance of companionship in marriage and thus allowed for the widest variety of reasons for divorce. Many Protestant cities permitted both women and men to request divorce, although men instigated the majority of cases. Despite these changes in belief and legislation, the rate of divorce in Protestant areas remained very low in the sixteenth century.

Kingdon (1995); Phillips (1988); Selderhuis (1999); Watt (2001).

KAREN E. SPIERLING

Dominicans   Officially the Order of Preachers, the Dominicans were a mendicant order founded in 1216 by Dominic de Guzman (ca. 1170–1221) primarily to combat the Albigensien and Waldensian heresies. Dominican theologians such as Thomas Aquinas provided the central definition of many tenets of Catholic doctrine. At the beginning of the sixteenth century, the Dominicans were already in the forefront of Catholic reform. The order had been reformed in the 1490s under the influence of Savonarola and the congregation of San Marco in Florence. Since the early thirteenth century, members of the order regularly served the Roman *Inquisition; Pope Paul III* again placed the order in charge of the Inquisition in 1541 after it had been purged of Protestant members. Throughout the sixteenth century, Dominican teachers and theologians figured among the strongest defenders of the old faith and the most bitter opponents of Protestantism. The Dominicans frequently opposed the techniques of evangelism practiced by the *Jesuits*, especially the adaptation of liturgy and doctrine to local traditions.

Auth (2000); Daniel-Rops (1964); Hinnebusch (1966).

WILLIAM BRADFORD SMITH

Dort, Synod of   This international assembly of Reformed delegates convoked by the Dutch States General met in Dordrecht (abbreviated as Dort), Holland, from November 13, 1618, to May 9, 1619, setting forth basic theological positions of the Dutch Reformed Church. Called to address disputes surrounding the doctrine of *predestination,* the synod rejected the teachings of *Jacobus Arminius* and affirmed the *orthodoxy* of unconditional *election.* Arminius, theologian at the University of Leiden, stressed *free will* in responding to divine *grace,* in opposition to the predestinarian views of Franciscus Gomarius, also a Leiden theologian. Fierce debates raged between Arminians, also known as Remonstrants (because of a 1610 Remonstrance), and Gomarians, also called Counter-Remonstrants, in the early 1600s. Dort established central tenets of Calvinism, including total human depravity, unconditional election, limited atonement (Christ died only for the elect), irresistible grace (humans cannot reject divine grace), and preservation of the saints (the elect will persevere to salvation).

Bangs (1971); Nobbs (1938); Venema (1994).

CHARLES PARKER

Douai-Rheims Bible   The Douai-Rheims Bible is an English translation of the Latin Vulgate produced by English

Catholics living in exile at the English College at Douai, Flanders. The translation work is credited primarily to Gregory Martin, formerly a Fellow of St. John's College, Oxford, who with the help of a small group of scholars from the same university produced this version of the *Bible*. In 1582 the New Testament was printed at Rheims, France, where the college had moved temporarily in 1578, while the Old Testament was not published, due to a shortage of funds, until 1609–10 after the college returned to Douai. The translation served as a Catholic response to Protestant versions of the Bible being produced in English, and was used in the creation of the King James translation and later English versions. It is part of a larger group of literature published abroad for use by recusant English Catholics.

Carleton (1902); Corthell (2007); Haigh (1987).

JILL R. FEHLEISON

Eck, Johann (a.k.a. Johann Maier von Eck; 1486–1543)

Eck was a scholastic theologian who countered the teachings of the Wittenberg school beginning in 1518, when he attacked *Martin Luther*'s Ninety-Five Theses. In the famous *Leipzig Disputation* (1519), Eck debated *Andreas Bodenstein von Karlstadt* on the subject of the human *will*, before debating Luther on a number of issues, including *indulgences*, *purgatory*, and church *authority*. Here Eck connected Luther's admission that popes and church councils could err with the position of *Jan Hus* a century earlier. It was through Eck's early efforts that others—including members of the theological faculty at Louvain and, ultimately, *Charles V*—were made aware of the extent of the Lutheran "trouble." Eck tangled with *Philip Melanchthon* at the Diet of Augsburg (1530), and, throughout his career, challenged many other key Reformers, including *Huldrych*

Zwingli, Johannes Oecolampadius, and *Martin Bucer*.

Bagchi (1991); Iserloh (1981); Rischar (1968).

HANS WIERSMA

Economy of Manifestation

The theological term "economy" (Gr. *oikonomia*, "management, organization") refers to how God works out his eternal purposes in the temporal realm. It was widely used in patristic theology to refer to God's self-manifestation in the *Trinity* and the *incarnation*. All Reformers engaged aspects of this topic, however, of critical importance is the economy of manifestation represented in the covenantal theology of *Huldrych Zwingli, Heinrich Bullinger*, and *John Calvin*. In the *Institutes* (2.9–11), for example, Calvin emphasizes the essential unity of God's manifestation to humankind through the ages, while at the same time arguing that the mode of administration (economy) of the *covenant* shows an orderly, progressive development from Adam to Christ. The economy of manifestation as revealed through "covenant history" served Reformed theologians both as a critical hermeneutic tool for the contextual understanding of the Old Testament and as a means of demonstrating the essential unity of all Scripture.

Baker (1980); Lillback (2001).

GREGORY J. MILLER

Edict of Nantes

The Edict of Nantes overturned the persecution waged against French Protestants or *Huguenots* since 1534 under the reign of Francis I. Despite persecution, the number of Huguenots grew in France, and in 1562, the first of eight wars of religion began. Various negotiations of peace proved to be fleeting. In 1572 the *St. Bartholomew's Day Massacre* decimated thousands of Protestants. Despite this setback, the "War of the Three Henries" led to Protestant King Henri of Navarre's succession to the French throne in 1589. As *Henri IV*, he later signed the edict granting Huguenots freedoms in April 1598 that included the right to worship in specified localities and to hold offices, estates, and titles. Huguenot schools and ministers were given financial support from the treasury, and separate tribunals were established for Huguenot legal matters. Not until 1685 was the edict revoked under the rule of Louis XIV with the Edict of Fontainebleau.

Diefendorf (2009); Greengrass (1987); Holt (1995).
                    JENNIFER POWELL MCNUTT

Education

By the late 1400s many Europeans were complaining that priests were uneducated and unable to guide them correctly toward salvation. Mainstream Protestant reformers insisted on well-educated pastors. As the ideas of *sola scriptura* and the "priesthood of all believers" took hold, Reformers also emphasized the importance of educating the laity through catechism services at church, parental guidance at home, and the establishment of primary schools. Protestant educators such as *Johannes Sturm* in *Strasbourg* built on humanist developments of the Renaissance, including an emphasis on learning Latin and on the study of original texts. Among the key universities for training Protestant pastors were Wittenberg, Heidelberg, Cambridge, and Leiden. Strasbourg and Geneva had smaller academies that offered similar theological training. Rome addressed the need for better education in several ways, most importantly in the creation of the *Jesuits* in 1540 and with the *Council of Trent*'s requirement that every diocese establish a seminary to train priests.

Grendler (2004); Luke (1989); Maag (1995); Strauss (1978).
                    KAREN E. SPIERLING

Elders

The term "presbyter," from the Greek word translated "elder," was equivalent to "priest" in Catholic understanding, and those in this role carried out both sacramental and disciplinary functions. In *John Calvin*'s teaching and practice, elders were laypeople charged with moral oversight of the congregation, and were distinguished from "pastors," who exercised the ministry of preaching and the administration of the *sacraments*. In Geneva elders and pastors together made up the *consistory*, which met weekly to exercise discipline by providing Christian counsel to those accused of infractions against Christian practice. Basing his views on his interpretation of New Testament passages, Calvin saw the office of lay elder as necessary to the governance of the church. It became typical, though not universal, in Calvinist Protestant churches. German-speaking Protestants also separated moral discipline from the ministry of Word and Sacrament, but put discipline in the hands of the Christian ruler.

Kingdon (1994); McKee (1988, 1998).
                    GARY NEAL HANSEN

Election

Election refers to God's choice of persons for salvation. It is closely related to the concepts of *predestination* and divine decree. The Pauline theme became prominent in the writings of *Augustine* (354–430) against the Pelagians. Both Lutherans and Reformed emphasized election, though it was not the central doctrine or organizing principle. Teachings varied and controversies abounded between Lutheran and Reformed, as well as within Lutheran and Reformed camps. Variations hinged on several key questions.

First and foremost was whether election was entirely within God's will, or whether it was somehow contingent on human beings. *Martin Luther, Huldrych Zwingli*, and *John Calvin* all affirmed that God was solely responsible for election. This affirmed salvation as a gift of sheer grace, in opposition to the semi-Pelagianism they saw in late medieval theology. However, among Lutherans *Philip Melanchthon* allowed for human cooperation in accepting or rejecting faith, and *Jacobus Arminius* argued that election was based on the foreknowledge of *faith*.

Second was the degree to which the election of some implied God's active choice in the damnation of others. Zwingli strongly emphasized God's decree as double, reprobation being as directly decreed for some as salvation for others. Luther too affirmed double predestination, though very rarely and paradoxically. Calvin presented the double decree as biblical and logical, but shifted the blame: Election to life glorifies God, but reprobation is a just judgment for sin. *Peter Martyr Vermigli* made reprobation more passive, God merely passing over those not elect. *Heinrich Bullinger*, as well as the Lutheran Formula of Concord (1577), only considered the single election to salvation, known in the Word, in Christ, urging no speculation and hope for all.

Third was when, logically, election happened relative to *sin*. The *infralapsarian* view prevailed among the Reformed: God first allowed the fall, and then decreed to save some from just condemnation. The minority view was *supralapsarian*, with election of some and reprobation of others before the fall made reprobation just.

Fourth was where the doctrine fit in theology. Calvin and Bullinger used election pastorally as a way of assuring anxious sinners: Because salvation is fully in Christ's hands, believers rest secure. Thus Calvin resisted discussing election as an implication of God's *providence*, treating it instead subsequent to *justification*. On the other hand Zwingli treated it more philosophically with predestination as part of providence. Similarly the Westminster Confession (1647) included predestination in its initial discussion of God's sovereign decrees.

A fifth question was how one knew one was among the elect. Early Reformers emphasized the reliable promises of Christ to those joined to Christ by faith. *Puritans* came to look for evidence in their spiritual practices and experiences, which came to be known as the *"practical syllogism."*

James (1998); Kolb (2005); Muller (1988).
GARY NEAL HANSEN

Elector "Elector" (Ger. *Kurfürst*) was the title of those German princes given the right to elect the *Holy Roman Emperor*. The first formal election was conducted in 1258; thereafter the form of election was codified in the Golden Bull of Charles IV (1356). The Golden Bull established seven electors: the Archbishops of Mainz, Trier, and Cologne; the King of Bohemia; the Count Palatine on the Rhine; the Margrave of Meissen (Saxony); and the Margrave of Brandenburg. There were several changes in the Electoral College in the *Reformation* era. In 1547, as a consequence of the Schmalkaldic War, the electorate was transferred from the Ernestine Saxon line to the Albertine line (Maurice). One of the main causes of the *Thirty Years' War* was the election of the Calvinist Count Palatine, Frederick V, to the Bohemian throne, an event that would have given Protestants a majority among the electors. After Frederick's defeat, the electorate was transferred to the dukes of Bavaria.

Holborn (1959); Zeumer (1904).
WILLIAM BRADFORD SMITH

Elizabeth I (1533–1603; r. 1558–1603) Elizabeth was queen of *England* and Ireland. The daughter of *Henry VIII* and Anne Boleyn, she ascended the throne on the death of her half sister *Mary I*, despite Catholic allegations of illegitimacy. She restored the Protestant settlement of Edward VI, including a lightly revised *Book of Common Prayer*. Although unambiguously Reformed Protestant, this settlement retained certain ceremonial and conservative features, and Elizabeth (who retained a crucifix in her private chapel) absolutely refused to countenance any changes to these or any other aspects of her religious settlement throughout her reign. Her refusal to be drawn into confessional politics was a dominant feature of the reign's politics. She provided armed assistance to embattled Protestants in Scotland, the Netherlands, and France, but reluctantly, indirectly, and (for her more zealous subjects) too little, too late. Even so, she was at war with Spain from 1585 onward, an unwilling standard-bearer of the international Protestant cause.

Collinson (2007); Doran (2000); MacCulloch (2001b).

ALEC RYRIE

Elizabethan Settlement Queen *Elizabeth I*, daughter of *Henry VIII*, ascended the throne on November 17, 1558, and subsequently restored Protestantism to *England* and Ireland, thereby settling religious divisions in a manner described as the "Elizabethan Settlement." In 1559 Parliament recognized Elizabeth as the "Supreme Governor" of the church by the Act of Supremacy. Reforms previously instituted by King Edward VI and Archbishop *Thomas Cranmer* were reintroduced with revision, such as the Second *Book of Common Prayer* (1552). Similarly, in 1563 the Act of Uniformity advanced the *Thirty-Nine Articles* of Religion, a revision of Cranmer's 1553 articles. These changes precipitated opposition notably by Marian exiles, who came to be known as *Puritans* for seeking total elimination of the vestiges of Catholicism, including the liturgy and vestments of Mary Tudor's reign, bishops, and saints' days. Additional parliamentary sessions sought to advance the *Reformation*

beyond Elizabeth's "middle way," but the church remained "halfly reformed."

Brigden (2000); Haigh (1993); MacCulloch (2001b).

JENNIFER POWELL MCNUTT

Emser, Jerome (Hieronymus; 1478–1527) Emser, a humanist scholar/cleric and secretary to Duke Georg of Saxony, is known primarily as a literary opponent of *Martin Luther*. He studied at Tübingen and Basel, focusing his career on humanist pursuits.

As Duke Georg's secretary, Emser was heavily involved in the cause for canonization of Benno of Meissen, an eleventh-century bishop elevated in 1523. The polemical interchange between Luther and Emser in 1523 was hardly the first. Prior to 1519, Luther and Emser were collegial, but after the Leipzig debate their relationship soured, Luther famously labeling Emser "that goat," from the goat's head on his family crest. Luther burned Emser's writings along with the bull of excommunication and *canon law* in 1520.

In later works, Emser defended the *Mass* and papal *authority*, and critiqued Luther, especially Luther's translation of the New Testament. He published his own translation in 1527, largely copied from Luther, but "corrected" by the Vulgate.

Bagchi (1991); D. Collins (2008); O. Edwards (2004); Kawerau (1903); Strand (1982).

BETH KREITZER

Enclosure Monastic enclosure was the physical separation and cloistering of professed female religious from the outside lay community. Enclosure was both active, meaning no one could leave the cloister, and passive, that is, no one else could enter without specific dispensation; the nuns' spiritual advisers heard confessions through a shuttered window. The church emphasized enclosure as the fundamental aspect of female religious life, dating to the papal bull *Periculoso* (1298). The *Council of Trent* reaffirmed it in 1563 and the bull *Circa pastoralis* (1566) decreed that all female religious communities not practicing enclosure had to be suppressed, including all active orders. There were practical benefits to enclosure, such as protecting nuns' chastity and safeguarding them from disease or attack, although it necessitated a high dowry to support the women within. Enclosure in practice was more flexible than church decrees allowed, and while many religious women fought against it, some convents eagerly welcomed it as a way of cementing elite status.

Evangelisti (2003); Harline (1995); Makowski (1997).

AMY E. LEONARD

England   The English *Reformation* took several peculiar courses, and ended up, by accident, giving birth to a distinct variant of world Christianity: Anglicanism. It began, not with popular protest against the *church*, but with *Henry VIII* declaring independence from Rome to secure a royal divorce. Henry's theological innovation of a "Royal Supremacy" in 1533–34 set the terms for much of what followed. The middle years of the century saw rapid Protestant advance under Henry's son Edward VI (1547–53), Catholic *Counter-Reformation* under his daughter *Mary I* (1553–58), and Protestant restoration under his other daughter *Elizabeth I* (1558–1603). Over the course of the century the English people gradually became culturally Protestant, or at least fervently anti-Catholic. In its theology, the Elizabethan church was strongly Calvinist. But the retention of some medieval Catholic rituals, and of the institutions of bishoprics and cathedrals, allowed a more "ceremonialist" style of Protestant

worship and divinity to emerge in the seventeenth century.

Duffy (2005); Haigh (1993); P. Marshall (2003).

PETER MARSHALL

Enzinas, Francisco de (Dryander; 1520–52)   Enzinas was a Spanish humanist and translator of the New Testament. He was born in Burgos to a merchant family with trade connections to *England* and Flanders. It is uncertain where he did his early university training. It is known for sure, however, that he attended Louvain's Collegium Trilingue in 1539. By late 1541 he was in *Wittenberg*, where he became a disciple of *Philip Melanchthon*. He began work on his Spanish translation of the New Testament while still at Louvain. He continued his work at Wittenberg, and Lutheran theological debates of the period clearly colored his translation. The Spanish New Testament appeared in 1543 in Antwerp. He was imprisoned in Brussels for violating the standing prohibition against the translation of the *Bible* into Spanish. He managed to leave prison and later wrote his attack on the *Inquisition*, *De statu Belgico*, which appeared in print posthumously (Strasbourg, 1558).

Nelson (1999), García Pinilla and Nelson (2001).

RADY ROLDAN-FIGUEROA

Episcopate   The episcopate refers to the form of *church* governance with bishops at the head of the hierarchy. This structure of the Roman Catholic and Orthodox churches was kept by some denominations, including the Anglican Church, after the *Reformation*. The Catholic Church claimed apostolic succession with the bishop of Rome being the chief bishop, but *Martin Luther*'s priesthood of all believers challenged the special status of *clergy* and by progression the hierarchical nature of the Catholic Church. Followers of *John Calvin* rejected the episcopal system and adopted a congregational or presbyterian system that incorporated lay leadership. Calvin asserted that church leadership should be the minister "overseer" along with a group of elders "presbyters" as was the structure of the early church and that bishop as sole leader over church membership disrupted the original vision of church government. The *Council of Trent* reaffirmed the power of bishops and their leadership positions within the Catholic Church.

Benedict (2002); Hsia (2005); Tracy (2006).
                                    JILL R. FEHLEISON

Erasmus, Desiderius (1467–1536)

Erasmus was a humanist, religious reformer, and biblical scholar. He was born in Rotterdam, the illegitimate son of a priest and a physician's daughter. He received a good education, but on the death of his parents in his mid-teens he entered an Augustinian monastery at Steyn, where he remained for five years. He studied theology in Paris but had no affinity for the scholastic curriculum, focusing instead on the community of humanists and poets. In 1499 he traveled to *England*, where he befriended *Thomas More* and *John Colet*. He spent several years in Italy and eventually settled in Basel.

In his early years Erasmus devoted himself to the pagan classics, developing an elegant Latin style, and writing books of Latin pedagogy such as the *Colloquia* (*Colloquies*) and the *Adagia* (*Adages*), collections of dialogues and of literary commonplaces. He believed that a foundation for a well-governed life included an education in good literature and the ability to speak and write well. As a Christian, he endorsed the *philosophia Christi* (*philosophy of Christ*)

in several pietistic works, attaching paramount importance to Christ's teaching in *Scripture* and deploring the popular emphasis on pilgrimages, relics, and elaborate rituals. In 1511 he published the work for which he is best known, the *Moriae Encomium* (*Praise of Folly*). This satirical oration is a reflection on the range of human foolishness, from the relatively benign (the willful blindness of friends to one another's faults), to the more destructive (warmongering, greed), to the transcendent folly of Christ and the cross.

Erasmus's most important work, however, was his biblical scholarship. He undertook the study of *Greek* and prepared a critical edition of the Greek New Testament, to which he appended a collection of annotations and a Latin translation of his own, different from the Vulgate, the text that was standard in the church. He developed expertise in the fields of philology and etymology to gain insight into the meaning of the Greek New Testament in its own linguistic and historical context. Over his lifetime he published five editions, each time expanding the annotations. He also produced paraphrases of the books of the New Testament and scholarly editions of the complete works of a number of the Fathers.

While Erasmus endorsed a moderate, humanist-based reform of the church, he deplored the extent to which the Protestant reformers threatened the unity of Christendom. Beginning with *De libero arbitrio diatribe* (*A Discussion of Freedom of the Will*) in 1524, which *Martin Luther* answered over a year later, he engaged in polemical exchanges with a number of Reformers to distinguish his position from the more radical critique of those who broke with the Roman Church, some of them claiming his work as their inspiration.

Augustijn (1991); Halkin (1993); Rummel (1986); Tracy (1996).
                                    J. LAUREL CARRINGTON

Erfurt   At the start of the sixteenth century Erfurt was a walled city of about twenty thousand inhabitants. It was part of the territory of Electoral Saxony, but was also claimed by the archbishopric of Mainz. Erfurt's university, established in 1392, had become one of northern Germany's most important centers of learning. *Martin Luther* matriculated in Erfurt's law school in 1502. In 1505 he entered Erfurt's Augustinian monastery (est. 1277), was ordained a priest in the monastery's chapel in 1507, and began study at the university's school of theology that same year. Erfurt's theological college was a center for late medieval nominalism as well as biblical *humanism*, before joining the city's churches in adopting Wittenberg's reforms. Johannes Lang, a frequent Luther correspondent, led Erfurt's ecclesiastical reorganization. In 1527 Luther wrote to "all the pious Christians" in Erfurt, commending them for having the "right Christian preaching" on "every corner."

Brecher (1883); Brecht (1985); Freitag (2001).

HANS WIERSMA

Eschatology   Based on the Greek *eschatos* ("last"), "eschatology" refers to the final end of God's creation, including human individuals, history, and the cosmos. It is related to millennialism and *apocalypticism*, and to expectations regarding Christ's second coming. Among the Reformers, eschatology was somewhat overshadowed by varying forms of apocalypticism. Most obviously, some predicted an imminent end. The Radical Reformers *Hans Hut* and *Melchior Hoffmann* predicted Christ's second coming soon: Hut in 1528, and Hoffman in 1534. *Martin Luther* and most "magisterial" reformers, too, discerned signs of the end in the events of their times, as well as in their identification of the pope as the *antichrist*. But they did not see an activist role for the faithful in bringing about the end, as did radicals such as Sebastian Müntzer. Lutherans seem to have tended to expect a final crisis, while the Reformed cultivated an expectation of progress in anticipation of the end.

Backus (2000); Barnes (1988); N. Cohn (1984).

MICKEY L. MATTOX

Estienne, Robert (1503–59)   Estienne, also called Stephanus, was a royal printer, scholar, and lexicographer. Little is known about his childhood or early education, though the connections of his father and his stepfather brought him into contact with many of the best scholars and linguists at the University of Paris. In 1524 he took over responsibility for the family printing business. His first significant publication was a critical edition of the Latin Bible in 1528. It contained glossaries and indexes. In 1532 he published *Thesaurus linguae latinae*, which was a lexicographical masterpiece. In 1539 he was designated a Royal Printer. In 1550 he published the first critical edition of the New Testament in *Greek*, *Novum Iesu Christi*. In 1551 he published another version of that same text, this time with verse numbers. All Bibles now use Estienne's versification. The 1551 version is commonly called the Textus Receptus (or received text); it was used in translating both the *Geneva Bible* and the King James Version. After being accused of harboring Protestant sympathies, he was forced to flee Paris for Geneva in 1550. In Geneva he continued to publish Bibles, commentaries, and dictionaries and added the works of *John Calvin* to his repertoire.

E. Armstrong (1954); Renouard (1843).

DAVID M. WHITFORD

Eucharist   *See* **Lord's Supper**

Evangelical   Early Protestants used "evangelical" to refer to themselves; it means one who believes, preaches, and follows the *evangelium* or *gospel*. They used this term to distinguish themselves from Catholic Christians, who, according to Protestants, had forgotten or even suppressed the gospel. They preferred this term over labels like "Lutheran," "Protestant," or "Calvinist," as the latter terms were usually pejorative in the sixteenth century. As early Protestants fell into doctrinal disagreement, a battle ensued over which of them were the true evangelicals. The battle was never resolved; each group continued to use the term for itself and to deny its (full) applicability to other Protestants. Modern-day evangelical Christians trace their history back to **Reformation** evangelicals, especially to the development of *justification* by *faith*, but there were many intervening historical steps between the two evangelicalisms and thus much that divides them, both theologically and culturally.

Heinze (2005); Hillerbrand (2007).
RONALD K. RITTGERS

Excommunication   Excommunication is the Christian practice of banning that involves the exclusion from the community of the faithful and to varying degrees the imposition of other penalties on members who challenge *orthodoxy* or orthopraxis. Biblical justification for the practice is found in Jesus' statements on how to deal with an errant brother or sister (Matt. 18:15ff.) and the instructions by Paul and John about handling those who deviate from the faith in actions or teachings (1 Cor. 5:3ff; 2 Thess. 3:14; and 2 John 10–11). During the Middle Ages it developed into an elaborate juridical procedure, which became an important weapon in armories of the popes and other ecclesiastical officials. Abuse of excommunication and other spiritual penalties, especially for financial or political reasons, was a frequent concern of late medieval and Renaissance reformers and critics of the *papacy*.

Not surprisingly, such criticism also played an important role in the early years of the **Reformation**. In 1518 **Martin Luther** preached a sermon on excommunication, published shortly thereafter as *Sermo de virtute excommunicationis* (*Sermon on the Power of Excommunication*). In it he insisted that ecclesiastical excommunication excluded one from the **sacraments** and the institutional *church*, but only spiritual excommunication separated one from God and the church as the spiritual communion of the faithful. Nonetheless, he urged his readers to bear unjust sentences of excommunication with patience. He adopted a much sharper tone in *Ein Sermon von dem Bann* (*Sermon on the Ban*) of 1520, which denounced the activities of those tyrants who exploited for their own purposes a practice instituted by Christ merely to admonish the wayward. *Decet Romanum Pontificem* (June 3, 1521), the papal bull excommunicating Luther, reasserted papal *authority* and responsibility to dispense spiritual and temporal punishments as divinely commissioned, and reform decrees at the **Council of Trent** called for an end to abuses in applying spiritual penalties, but again reaffirmed their legitimacy.

In Protestant territories significant disputes arose between civil and religious leaders about where authority to apply the *ban* resided. Reformation Radicals, especially the **Anabaptists**, categorically excluded civil authorities from the application of the ban, but disagreed among themselves about its nature and application. Some Anabaptist leaders, for example **Michael Sattler**, regarded the ban as an extraordinary expedient, applied only infrequently to regenerated believers, while others like **Balthasar Hubmaier** saw it as a more regular means to admonish the faithful. In general, northern Anabaptists tended to vest authority to ban in the hands of leaders of the congregation while southern Anabaptists usually accorded that authority to the community as a whole. Questions about the frequency

68   Exegesis

and severity of the ban played a prominent role in divisions within the Anabaptist tradition in the mid-sixteenth century.

A. Burnett (1994); Mentzer (1994); Roth and Stayer (2007); Vodola (1986).

GEOFFREY DIPPLE

Exegesis   Exegesis is the critical study and explanation of a text, specifically in this case the text of the Bible. Protestant reformers challenged the *authority* of the pope and church tradition in favor of establishing the supreme priority of *Scripture*. *Martin Luther, John Calvin,* and their followers insisted on the primacy of Scripture, but retained the usefulness of church tradition insofar as it complied with Scripture, while *Anabaptists* and other Radical Reformers were the true holders of the *sola scriptura* (Scripture alone) principle. With this profound emphasis on the centrality of Scripture, exegesis became a focal task of the Reformers that was expressed especially in commentaries and sermons. While biblical commentaries and sermons had been around for centuries, Protestant reformers used these vehicles much more acutely for teaching both the lay and ordained the content and message of the *Bible*. Even as they agreed on the utmost importance of biblical exegesis, it became a key venue where doctrinal and methodological differences amongst the Protestant confessions made their stark appearances.

Protestant exegesis retained a fair degree of continuity with Christian medieval exegesis, but it also offered several new developments. With medieval exegetes, sixteenth-century Protestants maintained the beliefs that God is the author of Scripture, Christ is the scope of Scripture, the *Holy Spirit*'s aid is necessary for right *interpretation,* and exegesis should edify the *church*. Protestant reformers also took up several of the prior exegetes' growing concerns, such as a focus on the literal sense and

the importance of philology. On the other hand, they generally rejected the medieval fourfold sense of Scripture (especially allegory) in favor of locating all meaning in the one literal sense. Furthermore, while the medieval commentary was divided into glosses and scholia, sixteenth-century Protestants increasingly opted for the form of the verse-by-verse, running commentary. While prior exegetes read Scripture to uncover doctrine and theological teaching, sixteenth-century Protestants can be seen as drawing an even more concentrated focus on reading Scripture for its theological instruction.

Sixteenth-century Protestants shared an optimism about the perspicuity of Scripture, grounded in their emphasis on the common aid of the Holy Spirit, which soon proved disillusioning. They disagreed upon both the proper exegetical methods to be used and the theological content to be found in Scripture. Exegesis, then, became an important avenue for the expression of separate confessional identities. Lutherans tended to express a more explicit identification of the literal sense with the christological reading of Scripture, while the Reformed tended to prefer the tool of typology and figurative readings of Scripture that preserved a more explicit connection to the historical sense. Anabaptists tended to give the most literal readings of Scripture, with a notable primacy given to the New Testament.

McKim (2006); Muller and Thompson (1996); Pelikan (1996); Steinmetz (1996); Wengert and Graham (1999).

G. SUJIN PAK

Exiles   Exile was an inevitable result of the *Reformation* process, given the almost universal insistence that only one form of Christianity could be tolerated within the state. The earliest exiles were precocious followers of *Martin Luther,* but the establishment of Protestant states, and the outbreak of religious warfare in the mid-sixteenth century, provided substantial incentive for cross-border movement on religious grounds. As the Netherlands split, Catholics moved south, and Protestants moved north. Religious policy swings in *England* caused the departure overseas of hundreds of Protestants under *Mary I*, and thousands of Catholics under *Elizabeth I.* Many of the former went to *John Calvin*'s *Geneva*, where French exiles were a source of moral and logistical support for the native *Huguenot* movement. Some exiles assimilated into their new home, others plotted and awaited their return. One activity in which they excelled was writing: both Catholic and Protestant exiles, for example, made important contributions to the development of political "resistance theory."

Kaplan (2007); Oberman (1992); Pettegree (1986).

PETER MARSHALL

Faith   A central element of the sixteenth-century Protestant interpretation of Christianity was a reassessment of the nature of faith, its definition, and its role in the *justification* and salvation of sinners. In late medieval theology faith was understood as a cognitive assent to objective Christian truths such as belief that only those who die in a state of justified *grace* attain salvation. By itself, such "unformed" faith was merely the beginning of the process of salvation; faith led to salvation only when "formed" by *love*, the decisive principle in uniting the believer to God. Consequently, a tenuous confidence that one was in a state of grace and progressing toward salvation could be gained only through seeking signs that God's love was present in one's heart and humbly hoping in God's mercy.

Protestant reformers such as *Martin Luther* and *John Calvin* claimed that faith alone was the pivotal axis on which turned the individual's justification in the sight of God and thus salvation.

This was possible because the Reformers redefined faith as the individual sinner's subjective conviction that on account of Christ's merits one's sins were forgiven and God accounted one righteous and worthy of salvation. Sinners were saved by God's grace through faith because the uniting of the individual with Christ and the imputation of Christ's righteousness to the individual were brought about when the promise of salvation through Christ articulated in *Scripture* was accepted through faith. Far from such teachings inviting profligacy by removing *good works* from the process of salvation, Protestants argued that only those assured of salvation through faith could perform truly good works. Reliance on one's own efforts to merit salvation reflected an idolatrous self-interest and trusting in one's own powers that rendered sinful even apparently good works. Faith properly honored Christ by recognizing his sole sufficiency for salvation while avoiding blasphemously doubting the promises of God. Faith also provided assurance that eliminated selfish efforts to earn salvation, allowing grateful Christians empowered by the *Holy Spirit* to begin serving God and neighbor in love. Consequently a "faith" that did not issue in works of love was not authentic, saving faith.

The *Council of Trent* rejected what it saw as the belief that sins are forgiven merely on the basis of an arrogant overconfidence that they are forgiven. Understanding faith to be mere cognitive assent to Christian doctrines that could abide even in the absence of saving grace, the council affirmed that justification was "by faith" only in the sense that faith was the "foundation" of justification. In contrast to Protestants, the council asserted that faith alone, conceptually isolated from love, hope, and the good works that God empowered Christians to perform, neither justified sinners nor brought salvation.

Hamm (2004); Lane (2002).

DANIEL EPPLEY

Family   The reformation of the family (understood to be all those living in a household, including employees and servants) was a key concept of Protestant theology, which placed *marriage* and the family at the center of civil society. The most important difference from Catholicism was the demotion of *celibacy* as a sign of the spiritual elite and the promotion of marriage. There was an emphasis in all confessions on patriarchy and the importance of the father within the household, which has led to debate over the relative harsh treatment of both children and women in early modern families. Protestants abolished many of the Catholic impediments to marriage and relaxed some of the rules for *divorce*; however, evidence shows that the incidence of divorce did not differ significantly between Protestants and Catholics. The biggest difference in marriage patterns occurs geographically, where the average age of marriage in northwestern Europe was much later (mid-20s) than in the south and east (teens).

Flandrin (1979); Lynch (2003); Ozment (1983); Safley (1984); Wiesner (2008); Witte and Kingdon (2005).

AMY E. LEONARD

Farel, Guillaume (1489–1565)
Farel was a French Reformed pastor and theologian. After studying under *Faber Stapulensis* (Jacques Lefèvre d'Étaples), Farel served as a lay evangelist in the diocese of Meaux under the reformist bishop *Guillaume Briçonnet*. Dissatisfied with Briçonnet's moderate Catholic reform movement, Farel left Meaux in 1524 and spent the next decade preaching throughout the Rhine valley, Franche-Comte, and French-speaking Switzerland. In 1535–36 Farel led the city of *Geneva* to adopt the *Reformation*, and persuaded *John Calvin* to stay in Geneva as his colleague. In 1538 Farel and Calvin were driven out of Geneva, and Farel accepted the post of pastor in Neuchâtel, where he remained for the rest of his life. Farel wrote exclusively in French, and his work is pastoral and occasional. He was famous as a preacher, but his sermons have not survived. Besides his role in the French and Genevan Reformations, he was largely responsible for persuading the Waldensian leaders to join the Reformation.

Heyer (1990); Oberman (1999); White (2007).

EDWIN WOODRUFF TAIT

Fasting   Fasting had become part of Christian practices in the early centuries of the *church*, but in the medieval Christian church it developed into a regular part of the ritual of the Catholic faith. Tied to seasonal practices such as the Lenten fast, and the ascetic practices such as those followed in the monasteries, fasting was connected to the *sacrament* of *penance* within the Roman Church. At the time of the *Reformation*, the emphasis on salvation by *grace* meant that penance lost its theological force as a sacrament. As a result, the Reformers slowed the practice of fasting within the Protestant faiths, although the Protestant reformers did not forbid the practice and fasts were called at times by different Protestant faiths. Since the sixteenth century, fasting within the Christian churches has waned.

Mason (1998).

KRISTEN POST WALTON

Fathers   The influence and witness of the patristic age, the age of the Fathers, became increasingly more important throughout the period of the Reformations. Protestant reformers of all confessional stripes claimed to be returning the *church* to a purer, earlier form, not to be creating innovations. However, the manner in which this was true was problematic. The commonsense view frequently saw the "new" religion as introducing things not seen before. Soon, the Roman polemicists hit upon the devastating critique, "Where was your church before Luther?" In part, the study of the Fathers was motivated by the aim to demonstrate how the various efforts at reform were recoveries rather than inventions. As well, the study of the patristic authors and their age accorded well with the Renaissance drive for recourse to the sources.

Examples of the use and impact of the Fathers abound. *Martin Luther's* *Wittenberg* critic, *Andreas Bodenstein von Karlstadt*, was persuaded to join Luther's reforms by study of his new copy of the works of *Augustine*. *John Calvin* gained some of his early reputation at the Lausanne Disputation, where he skillfully and extemporaneously marshaled patristic citations to demonstrate Reformed conformity with *orthodoxy* and Roman innovation. Calvin's critic, Albert Pighius of Kampen, wrote against him in part because of Calvin's claim that the Fathers and especially Augustine denied the freedom of the *will*. Thomas Stapleton, a Roman theologian teaching at Louvain, commented upon *Scripture* according to the senses of the Fathers, explicitly against specific Protestant thinkers.

The use of the Fathers was enormously important in biblical *exegesis*, polemical treatises of all types, systematic formulations, and finally for (especially) magisterial Protestants, the founding of orthodoxy. Biblical exegesis by interpreters of both Roman and Protestant confessions drew deeply upon patristic sources, frequently without citation. The polemic use has been most frequently noted, but was hardly the most common application. In constructing theological syntheses on important topics such as *sacraments*, *Christology*, and ecclesiology, the Fathers were a ready and important source, as inspiration, as historical sources, and as conversation partners. Finally, though Protestants regularly claimed the *Bible* as the true source of Christian belief and practice, most willingly and explicitly accepted ancient creedal formulations as binding and true.

While Roman theologians could turn to the hierarchy as a foundation that the *Holy Spirit* would not allow to err, this dialectical strategy carried arguments into the patristic age, where problems abounded. Protestants would quickly point out instances of the hierarchy denying prior teaching, or the teaching of a particularly revered father such as Augustine. The exercise was also fraught with peril for intrepid Protestant theorists who accepted a Eusebian paradigm of the church being truest at its earliest forms, since their historical work sometimes brought to light a modern deviation from early *faith* and practice. The reforms of the early modern period increased the understanding and importance of the early church, but the full realization of these insights would not occur until long after the Reformations.

Backus (1997, 2003); Dipple (2005); Grane, Schindler, and Wriedt (1993).

R. WARD HOLDER

Fisher, John (ca. 1469–1535)

Fisher was an English theologian, bishop of Rochester (1504–35), and cardinal (1535). He attended Cambridge, of which he was later chancellor (1504–35). Fisher used his authority at Cambridge to promote humanist studies and made the training of preachers one of his priorities. He was esteemed for his preaching and as bishop was conscientious regarding the competence of his *clergy*. In the 1520s Fisher preached and wrote against *Martin Luther* and other Protestants, both defending and subsequently appealing to the *authority* of the *church* and its traditions and also analyzing and seeking to refute Protestant teachings. His polemical works were highly influential and played an important role at the *Council of Trent*. From 1527

Fisher was occupied with defending *Henry VIII*'s marriage to Catherine of Aragon and opposing Henry's subjugation of the church. These commitments eventually led to Fisher's imprisonment and ultimately his decapitation on charges of treason, shortly after he was created cardinal.

Bradshaw and Duffy (1989); Dowling (1999); Rex (1991).

DANIEL EPPLEY

Fornication   The term used for premarital sex in the *Reformation* period was "fornication." The Protestant elevation of *marriage* brought an increased intolerance of sexual activity outside marriage. In Calvinist churches that emphasized Christian discipline, fornication was one of the offenses most frequently investigated by *consistories*. In both Protestant and Catholic areas, prosecution for fornication intensified during the sixteenth century. Punishments included jail time and public acts of repentance. Although Calvinist areas especially tried to apply equal punishment to men and women, even then it was almost always the woman's reputation that was most harmed, due partly to increasing concerns about the illegitimate children who could result from fornication. Protestants most often focused on ensuring that fornicating fathers took responsibility for their illegitimate children, while Roman Catholics tended to focus on protecting the honor of the mother by establishing foundling homes for bastard children. During the sixteenth and seventeenth centuries, legal discrimination against illegitimate children increased across Europe.

Watt (2001); Wiesner-Hanks (2000); Witte and Kingdon (2005).

KAREN E. SPIERLING

Francis de Sales (1567–1622)   Born in Savoy, de Sales attended the *Jesuit* College of Clermont in Paris and studied law at the University of Padua. De Sales received his ordination in 1592 in his native Savoy and became provost of the Cathedral canons for the exiled diocese of Geneva residing in Annecy. In 1594 he began a successful missionary program in the duchy of Chablais among Reformed populations and would serve as bishop of the diocese of Geneva for twenty years (1602–22). In his most famous writing, *Introduction to the Devout Life*, de Sales provided guidance for laypeople to commune with God in their daily lives. De Sales maintained a wide correspondence with those seeking spiritual advice. One of his mentees was a widow, Jean de Chantal, who, along with de Sales, founded the Order of the Visitation. He was one of the most popular figures of post-Tridentine Catholicism and was canonized in 1665.

Kleinman (1962); Ravier (1988); W. Wright (1985a).

JILL R. FEHLEISON

Franciscans   The Franciscans were one of two orders of preaching friars established in the thirteenth century. The order had a long history of internal, even violent conflict over the proper observance of the Rule left by its founder, Francis of Assisi (ca. 1181–1226). Members struggled with how to institutionalize the goals and practices of Francis, who attempted to imitate the life of Christ, with the majority believing that modifications to the absolute vow of poverty allowed the order to better function within the Catholic Church. The Capuchins emerged in central Italy during the early sixteenth century when a small group of Franciscans left their houses in order to observe the Rule as literally as possible. The Capuchins faced intense opposition from the more moderate Franciscans but received full independence as a third branch of the order in 1619. They established missions throughout the world and promoted the major tenets of the *Counter-Reformation*.

E. Gleason (1994); Nimmo (1987).
JILL R. FEHLEISON

Franck, Sebastian (1499–1542)

Franck was the most radical of the early *Reformation* spiritualists. After studying in Ingolstadt and Heidelberg, he was ordained (1524) and subsequently became a Lutheran pastor. He later resigned his clerical post, became a printer, and published a wealth of material, some of it original but much excerpted from other sources, in Nuremberg, *Strasbourg*, Ulm, and Basel. In a letter to the spiritualist Johannes Campanus (1531), Franck described his vision of an invisible, spiritual *church*, existing throughout the ages, and warned that all external elements of religious observance were at best superfluous and at worst destructive. He elaborated on the details of the destruction wrought by such externals in the "Chronicle of Heretics," one of three chronicles contained in his *Chronica, Zeitbuch und Geschichtsbibel* (*Chronicle and History*, 1531), whose sixteen German editions and seven Dutch made it one of the most influential histories of the sixteenth century.

Hayden-Roy (1994); E. McLaughlin (2007); G. H. Williams (1992).
GEOFFREY DIPPLE

Frederick the Wise (1463–1525)

Frederick III was prince and *elector* of Saxony from 1486, and is remembered chiefly as *Martin Luther*'s prince and protector. He preferred negotiation to armed conflict, and was known as the "peace lover" (Ger. *Friedensreiche*, a play on the name *Friedrich*). In 1502 he established the University of Wittenberg. In 1519 he was even briefly considered a candidate for emperor. In 1518, at the

height of the *indulgence* controversy, he prevented Luther's extradition to Rome, and in 1521, following the *Diet of Worms*, provided him refuge at the Wartburg Castle. Frederick seems to have been a devout Catholic (he owned a collection of some 19,013 relics!), but at the Diet of Nurmberg in 1522 his delegation appeared with an evangelical slogan emblazoned on their sleeves—"The Word of God abides forever" (1 Pet. 1:25)—and on his deathbed he received the *sacrament* in both kinds, suggesting a sincere conversion to the new faith.

Junghans (2003).
MICKEY L. MATTOX

Free Will

The doctrine of free will (Lat. *liberum arbitrium*) is the notion that human beings have the ability to make choices independent of external and/or antecedent influences. In terms of *Reformation* thought, formulations concerning free will were usually pitted against assertions that the human *will* was bound or captive. Early modern theologians who argued for or against free will drew their proofs from Holy *Scripture*, the writings of previous Christian thinkers such as *Augustine* and from classical thinkers such as *Aristotle*, as well as from reason and experience.

The central assumption behind the concept of the free will is that the content of one's own *will* can be chosen. That is, one is free, for example, to decide whether to *want* to do good or evil, or whether to *want* to love and trust God. Hence, *liberum arbitrium* has also been rendered as "free choice of will" in light of the notion that humans can freely determine what they want to want.

Perhaps the best-known Reformation-era argument regarding the free will was the published debate between *Desiderius Erasmus* of Rotterdam and *Martin Luther* during the mid-1520s. As early as the Heidelberg Disputation in 1518, Luther had outlined his objections to the concept of the free will:

"Free will, after the fall, exists in name only." Luther's objections were initially countered by theologians such as Jacob Latomus (1475–1544) and *Johann Eck*. Erasmus joined the argument with the 1524 publication of *De libero arbitrio diatribe (Discourse on Free Will)*, in which he argued that the human will had final say regarding whether it would "turn toward or away from that which leads to eternal salvation." Luther responded a year later with *De servo arbitrio (On the Bondage of the Will)*. Borrowing a metaphor from Augustine, Luther compared the human will to a horse with two riders: "If God rides, it wills and goes where God goes . . . if Satan rides, it wills and goes where Satan goes." The classical Lutheran position, however, leaves room for some free agency regarding matters "below," that is, regarding matters *not* involving salvation.

Overall, the magisterial reformers developed and maintained a confession of *faith* that denied the will's ability to effect salvation, with the writings of *John Calvin* leading the way for the Reformed churches, and the teachings of Luther, *Philip Melanchthon*, and second-generation evangelicals such as *Martin Chemnitz* holding sway in Lutheran churches. The *Council of Trent* responded to these developments with several condemnations, including: "If anyone says that free will was lost and destroyed after Adam's sin, or that free will is a thing in name only . . . let him be anathema."

Forde (2005); Kolb (2005); Sproul (1997).
HANS WIERSMA

Freedom In the *Reformation* the concept of freedom played an important role in two theological disputes. The first debate centered on the Christian's relationship to the *law*. In the famous 1520 treatise, *On the Freedom of a Christian*, *Martin Luther* argued that because of *justification* by *grace* through *faith*,

Christians lived in a new paradoxical relationship to the law: "A Christian is perfectly free lord of all, subject to none"; and "A Christian is a perfectly bound servant, subject to all." Justification means that one is free to obey God's law and free from the fear of it. The second debate also featured Luther and focused on the relative freedom or bondage of the human *will* to *sin*. In a famous debate with *Desiderius Erasmus*, Luther argued that while human beings have a freedom of choice, that freedom is always exercised within a human nature that is bound to sinfulness.

Kolb (2005).
DAVID M. WHITFORD

French Confession The French or Gallican Confession was approved by the first National Synod in France in 1559. It is also known as the Confession of La Rochelle, where it was approved by the seventh National Synod in 1571, and signed by representatives from France, Geneva, and Navarre. The Reformed churches had sought *John Calvin*'s aid in writing a confession, and a draft in thirty-five articles was provided prior to the synod, often thought to be written by Calvin, possibly with the aid of *Theodore de Beza* and *Pierre Viret*. The synod expanded the first article on revelation to six, including an emphasis on natural revelation, making the final form forty articles. Despite small divergences from Calvin in this emphasis on natural revelation, the inclusion of obedience to *Scripture* as a kind of mark of the *church*, a threefold ministry, and a final qualification on obedience to the state, echoes of Calvin's theology are found throughout.

Barth (2002); Sunshine (1994, 2003).
GARY NEAL HANSEN

Friars Products of early thirteenth-century reforming energies, friars were distinguished by their mendicancy and active apostolate. The friars were consolidated into four major orders at the Second Council of Lyon (1274): *Dominicans*, *Franciscans*, Augustinians, and Carmelites. Together they provided many of the spiritual and intellectual leaders of the thirteenth and fourteenth centuries. Thought to have gone into decline in the fifteenth century, the four mendicant orders in fact underwent vigorous reform movements, which sometimes provided the foundation for broader initiatives to reform the whole church. To some (e.g., Ulrich von Hutten), the earliest stages of the *Reformation* looked like a continuation of traditional rivalries among the friars, with the Augustinians lining up behind *Martin Luther* and the Dominicans behind Johann Tetzel. By 1523, however, the battle lines were clear, and thereafter those friars who remained true to the old church played a prominent role in combating the Reformation.

———

M. Armstrong (2004); Dipple (1996); Elm (1989).

GEOFFREY DIPPLE

Geneva   In 1536 the Genevan government adopted the *Reformation*, according to the Swiss Reformed teachings followed by Bern, Geneva's military protector. That same year, *Guillaume Farel* persuaded *John Calvin* to help him lead the new Reformed Church in Geneva. Geneva's Reformation was shaped by local circumstances, including the government's determination to protect the new republic's independence from the duchy of Savoy, and local conflicts over Calvin's leadership of the church. By 1555 Calvin's supporters had defeated his political opponents. Thanks largely to Calvin's commitment to spreading reform to his native France, Geneva became the center of an international Reformed movement. The city's population nearly doubled in the 1550s with an influx of religious refugees, especially from France and *England*, and the church and city established a system for training ministers to spread Calvin's teachings beyond Geneva. Consequently, the influence of Calvin and the Genevan church spread into France, parts of the *Holy Roman Empire*, the Netherlands, Scotland, and England.

———

Kingdon (2007); Monter (1967); Naphy (1994).

KAREN E. SPIERLING

Geneva Bible   First published in 1560, following the English translations of the *Bible* in the 1530s, the Geneva Bible became the standard English version on both sides of the Atlantic until replaced by the King James Version. Translated by William Whittingham and other Marian exiles, including, perhaps, *Miles Coverdale*, the Geneva Bible was the first English version translated from the *Hebrew* and *Greek* texts of the Bible and was the first Bible to use numbered verses. The Geneva Bible was particularly known for the extensive marginal comments and annotations within it that helped to lay out the theology of the Reformers during the Elizabethan period. The notes covered approximately one-third of the work itself. The Geneva Bible was particularly influential over the *Puritans* of the sixteenth and seventeenth centuries, who brought a copy on the Mayflower. The Geneva Bible was printed more than two hundred times before 1644.

———

Hall (1957).

KRISTEN POST WALTON

Good Works   Good works (Lat. *bona opera*) were the object of much controversy during the *Reformation* era. Leaders of theological reform worked to amend the inherited system that understood that God's infused *grace* moved souls to *faith* and to the performance of good works necessary for salvation. *Martin Luther* subverted the inherited system by insisting that good works done to merit *justification* were actually *sins*. *Desiderius Erasmus* thought Luther's position unnecessarily extreme. *John Calvin* understood that human nature "polluted and contaminated" any work otherwise deemed "good" and that, outside of Christ, God was right to condemn even the most virtuous human. On the other hand, most Protestant reformers asserted some form of the notion that justifying faith necessarily produced good works. Differences of opinion among Reformers usually concerned the function of good works in regard to *sanctification*, union with Christ, and/or the "third use" of the *law*. The Roman Church clarified its own teaching on the function of good works during the sixth session of the *Council of Trent* (1547).

Forde (1969); Hughes (1982); Opocenský and Réamonn (1999).

HANS WIERSMA

Gospel   From the Greek *euangelion*, "gospel" means "good news." The word could refer to the four books of Scripture called "Gospels," or more typically, as in *Martin Luther*, Protestants would use the term to encapsulate *justification* by *faith*, the Pauline message that sinful human beings can be made righteous before God by faith. Luther is frequently viewed as having rediscovered this sense of gospel, though *Huldrych Zwingli* claimed to be teaching it before Luther was widely known. Luther typically contrasted gospel, which gives life and forgiveness, with biblical law, by which people see their guilt, bringing *death*. This sharp contrast was carried into Lutheran confessional documents, dividing Scripture's contents into two parts. Such statements should be read within Luther's doctrine of justification, to which obedience to law contrib-

utes nothing. Luther found one gospel throughout the Bible, seeing salvation promised in the Old Testament, and often seeking to interpret the Old Testament as christological prophecy.

T. Peters (2005); Strehle (1995); Wengert (1997).

GARY NEAL HANSEN

Grace   Because the issue of soteriology was so central to the doctrinal, ecclesiastical, and civil concerns in the early modern period, the doctrine of grace was frequently also at issue. The term "grace" (Gr. *charis*; Lat. *gratia*) contains the connotation of being free of cost. Patristic and medieval theologians had long recognized this, but struggled with the way in which God's free gift of grace could be reconciled with human moral effort in the process of salvation. Those issues returned with even more urgency in the Reformations of the sixteenth century.

An important early precedent for the doctrine of grace in the Reformations was the Pelagian controversy of the fifth and sixth centuries. Pelagius, a presbyter in Rome, had criticized *Augustine*, the bishop of Hippo in North Africa, for a doctrine of grace that would tend toward fatalism. Augustine, in his turn, condemned Pelagius for doctrines that tended to exalt human unaided *will*. Through a long series of both treatises and ecclesiastical political actions, the church adopted Augustine's mature position, which was very close to a view that humans were dependent on divine preceding action (prevenient grace) for any morally good action. This was formally pronounced at the Second Council of Orange, meeting in 529, and Pope Boniface II approved this in 531.

By the sixteenth century, mainstream soteriological theology had adopted a semi-Pelagianism that the Second Council of Orange had meant to prevent. In part, *Martin Luther* and *John Calvin*'s high doctrines of grace were meant as correctives to this tendency. Calvin's doctrine, and his position affirming double *predestination*, went further than the second Council of Orange had ever intended; it had anathematized predestination to evil.

While all confessional strains in the *Reformation* era asserted the need for grace, the meaning to which that term was assigned differed. Roman theologians far preferred to theorize about cooperating grace, and see human willing and God's grace in a relationship of collaboration, with God's movement leading. Protestant theologians tended to engage in seeing human willing and grace in almost an adversarial role—humans were saved by the surrender of their own wills. To the present, the doctrine of grace and its implications is one of the greatest differences between Catholic and Protestant thought.

Beachy (1977); Donnelly (1976); McGrath (1999).

R. WARD HOLDER

Gratian (fl. twelfth century) Gratian was the compiler of the *Concordantia discordantium canonum*, which was a collection of patristic and medieval texts that included excerpts from biblical commentaries, papal decrees, and pronouncements of church law. It is often referred to simply as the *Decreta* or the *Decretum Gratiani*. Gratian sought to bring the disparate texts into a harmonious system of *canon* (or church) *law*. It first appeared in the mid-twelfth century and was quickly adopted as the standard text for university lectures on canon law. It forms the beginning section of the *Corpus iuris canonici* (Body of Church Law). Though a number of Reformers were trained in canon law, all ultimately rejected large portions of it as well as Gratian's commentary upon it. In 1520, to mark his independence from the Roman Catholic Church, *Martin*

Luther burned a copy of the *Decretum* when he burned the papal bull threatening to excommunicate him.

Witte (2002).

DAVID M. WHITFORD

Grebel, Conrad (ca. 1498–1526) Grebel was the cofounder of Zurich Anabaptism. Born into a prominent Zurich family, Grebel joined the humanist study group around the reformer *Huldrych Zwingli* in 1521 and seems to have undergone a religious conversion in 1522. He and more Radical Reformers broke with Zwingli at the Second *Zurich Disputation* in 1523 when Zwingli accepted the Zurich city council's refusal to abolish the Catholic *Mass* immediately. Grebel began meeting separately with other radicals until in 1525 they publicly challenged the council decision, supported by Zwingli, that required infant *baptism* on pain of exile. Since the radicals believed the New Testament prescribed adult believers baptism, they baptized one another. As a result the group that came to be called "*Anabaptists*" (rebaptizers) from Zurich spread throughout Switzerland. Since adult rebaptism was punishable by death, many Zurich Anabaptists were executed. Grebel, however, died of illness in 1526.

Bender (1950); G. H. Williams (1992).

R. EMMET MCLAUGHLIN

Greek Study of the Greek language in the West began in fourteenth-century Italy as part of the Renaissance drive to recover the sources of civilization. Knowledge of Greek spread to France, Spain, and *England* in the fifteenth century, and to Germany and the Netherlands in the sixteenth. In the North the desire increasingly was to recover the sources of Christian antiquity—patristic theology and above all the New

Testament. This was exemplified in *Desiderius Erasmus*, who published numerous editions of Greek *fathers* and most importantly in 1516 was first to publish the Greek text of the New Testament. Reform-minded *humanism* thus created the resources for budding Protestantism, as when humanist-educated **Huldrych Zwingli** and **John Calvin** reformed their cities by preaching and teaching from the Greek New Testament, buttressing theology with patristics. Study of Greek became prominent in university programs and standard in the preparation of both Lutheran and Reformed ministers.

Johnson (2006); Lane (1999); N. Wilson (1992).

GARY NEAL HANSEN

Gutenberg, Johann (ca. 1400–1468)   The father of the printing press, Gutenberg was one of the most influential people in the *Reformation*, despite dying before it formally commenced. From Mainz in Germany, Gutenberg developed the printing press and produced the first printed text, the Gutenberg Bible, circa 1455. Although legal difficulties forced him to hand over some of his printing business to his partner, Gutenberg's original accomplishment remains undiminished. As a result of his invention, the ideas of the sixteenth-century Reformers, such as **Martin Luther** and **John Calvin**, were able to spread quickly through Europe, allowing for the permanence of the Protestant Reformation. Earlier thinkers, such as **John Wyclif** and **Jan Hus**, were unable to spread their words widely enough to create a similar movement. Gutenberg's press remains one of the harbingers of the modern world. Its invention allowed not only for the spread of ideas but also for the increase of literacy and *education*.

Füssell (2005); Kapr (1996); Man (2002).

KRISTEN POST WALTON

Hebrew   During the *Reformation*, study of the Old Testament in Hebrew, the original language of the overwhelming majority of the Old Testament, was immensely important. The first widely available edition of the Old Testament in Hebrew was the 1488 Soncino edition. A much improved edition was Daniel Bomberg's second edition of the *Rabbinic Bible* (*Mikraot Gedolot*) in 1525. Among Christian publishers, **Robert Estienne** was the most prolific of Hebrew editions of the Old Testament. Sebastian Münster, the cosmographer and Hebraist, published a number of Hebrew dictionaries in the 1520s and 1530s and a critical edition of the Old Testament in Hebrew and Latin in 1534.

S. Burnett (1996).

DAVID M. WHITFORD

Heidelberg   Heidelberg was the residence of the Palatine *Elector* and home to Germany's oldest university. It was one of the first centers of German *humanism*, and almost all of the later Reformers of southern Germany studied there in the early sixteenth century. Although there were earlier *evangelical* influences, the Palatinate did not fully adopt the *Reformation* until 1556. In the wake of a controversy over the **Lord's Supper** in 1559, Elector Frederick III converted to the Reformed faith, which he imposed in 1563 by issuing a new church ordinance and the *Heidelberg Catechism*. Frederick's son Ludwig VI reintroduced Lutheranism in 1578, but after his death in 1584 the Reformed faith was restored. The University of Heidelberg became a major center of Reformed theology into the seventeenth century, and the Palatinate's influence was key to the adoption of the Reformed faith by other smaller territories in northwestern Germany.

Bierma (2005); H. Cohn (1985).

AMY NELSON BURNETT

Heidelberg Catechism This catechism was commissioned by Frederick III (1515–76), *elector* of the Palatinate, and written by Zacharias Ursinus and a committee including Caspar Olevianus. It was published in German in 1563. Frederick wanted to create a unified Reformed teaching for his subjects, some of whom leaned toward Lutheranism. The second and third editions in the same year expanded the text slightly to its traditional form. The catechism follows *Martin Luther*'s model in its question-and-answer format, and by including commentaries on the classical catechetical texts: the Ten *Commandments*, the *Apostles' Creed*, and the Lord's Prayer. It has had wide acceptance and use among Reformed Christians, especially in the Dutch tradition. Its distinctive features include its tone, both hopeful and irenic, and its structure.

The tone is set in the introductory questions, which describe belonging to Jesus as humanity's only comfort in life and *death*. Throughout the text, the focus returns repeatedly to the benefits believers receive from specific teachings, including comfort and assurance. The catechism then presents the faith in three parts: Human Misery, Deliverance, and Gratitude. The text is also divided into fifty-two sections for weekly preaching.

Human Misery (questions 3–11) is by far the briefest section. Human beings are presented as convicted of *sin* by the *law* of God, and so damaged by the fall into sin that they are unable to do any good, instead actually hating God and neighbor.

Deliverance (questions 12–85) presents Christ's person and work, the Apostles' Creed as the summary of the *gospel*, righteousness through *faith* alone, the *sacraments*, and the keys of the kingdom. Here a number of typically Reformed themes emerge: *Providence* guides all things; the *church* is God's chosen people in all ages, even before the coming of Jesus; Jesus is bodily in heaven, and therefore not in the elements of the *Lord's Supper*; the promises communicated by the sacraments are drawn by analogy from their elements and actions; the "keys" opening and shutting heaven are *preaching* and *discipline*. The Lord's Supper in Heidelberg is more Calvinist than Zwinglian, emphasizing assurance in knowing the promise is for us, and deemphasizing remembrance.

The concluding section (questions 86–129) embraces the whole of Christian life in the winsome word "gratitude" as our response to deliverance in Christ. This section includes the commentary on the Ten Commandments, thereby framing the law according to Calvin's "third use" as a guide to the faithful for living God's will. Reformed emphases are seen in the opposition to idolatry, which precludes art in worship, and the sense that prohibitions implicitly contain requirements and vice versa. Prayer as the chief expression of gratitude, and the Lord's Prayer as Jesus' guide, conclude the text.

Bierma (2005); Klooster (2001); Spijker (2009).

GARY NEAL HANSEN

Helvetic Confessions (1536 and 1566) The Helvetic Confessions are two crucial doctrinal formulations of the Swiss Reformed churches. The first Helvetic Confession was part of the effort to reconcile the Swiss and Lutherans theologically after *Huldrych Zwingli*'s death in 1531. Its twenty-seven articles were distinctly Lutheran in tone, which made it difficult for the Swiss to accept. When *Leo Jud* translated it into German he rendered it more sympathetic to Zwingli's theology. In the end, there was no agreement and the Lutherans adopted the Wittenberg Accord of 1536. The Second Helvetic Confession was written by *Heinrich Bullinger* as a private document and was originally an analysis of the 1536 confession. With its considerable length, it was more a theological treatise than a confession and came to prominence when taken up by the *Elector* Palatine to defend his church against Lutheran criticism. The confession was then adopted by the Swiss in 1566 and became the principal statement of the Reformed faith.

Gordon (2002).

BRUCE GORDON

Henri IV (1553–1610; r. 1589–1610)

Henri was born a Protestant prince of Navarre to Jeanne d'Albret and Antoine de Bourbon. In 1572 he became king of Navarre and married King Charles IX's sister, Marguerite of Valois. Although the marriage was intended to resolve France's religious wars, the wedding ended with the *St. Bartholomew's Day Massacre*. Henri survived the massacre by abjuring Protestantism and fled the court in 1576. After years of mending *Huguenot* alliances, by the time of Francis of Anjou's death in 1584, Henri became the first Huguenot heir to the throne. Despite hostile opposition by the Catholic League, in 1589 the outcome of "The War of the Three Henrys" led to Henri's inheritance of the crown, though he was not immediately recognized. In 1593 Henri converted to Catholicism to ensure his claim to the throne, but this did not prevent him from granting Huguenot freedoms by the *Edict of Nantes* in 1598.

Love (2001); Pitts (2009); Wolfe (1993).

JENNIFER POWELL MCNUTT

Henry VIII (1492–1547; r. 1509–47)

Henry VIII, or Henry Tudor, was king of *England* and lord of Ireland. He became heir apparent on the death of his elder brother in 1502. Ascending the throne aged 17, he created an image of himself as an athletic, learned, Renaissance warrior prince. Real control of his government fell to the omnicompetent *Thomas Wolsey*, soon made a cardinal. Henry's

piety was theatrically traditional, and his marriage to his brother's widow, the Spanish princess Catherine of Aragon, was sonless but content. He ostentatiously opposed the early Lutheran movement, writing (or ghostwriting) a book against Luther and holding public book burnings in London.

In 1527 Henry unexpectedly repudiated his marriage, and demanded a papal annulment so that he might marry the French-raised courtier Anne Boleyn. The unsuccessful annulment campaign consumed English politics for seven years, destroying Wolsey, convincing Henry that the *papacy*'s powers were illegitimate, and driving him into uneasy alliance with *evangelical* Reformers (of whom Boleyn was one). Aided by *Thomas Cromwell* and *Thomas Cranmer*, in 1533 Henry solved his problem by rejecting all papal jurisdiction over the English church, a position formalized in the 1534 *Act of Supremacy*.

This schism was not a Protestant *Reformation*, but Henry became profoundly convinced of his new title of Supreme Head of the English church, and imposed an idiosyncratic, inconsistent, and brutal set of religious reforms on England. Doctrinally, Henry's "settlement" was broadly Erasmian: while traditional on *justification* and the *sacraments*, he published an English *Bible* and outlawed pardons, pilgrimages, and certain images. All religious houses in England were suppressed, partly but not purely an act of plunder. Papal loyalists were executed as traitors, and Protestants as heretics, in roughly equal numbers. However, it was the Protestants who proved better able to exploit this lethal religious ambiguity, taking power in a palace coup after Henry's death in 1547.

Rex (2006); Scarisbrick (1968); Wooding (2008).

ALEC RYRIE

Heresy
Heresy means "choosing," that is, choosing to reject the domi-

nant belief. Heresy is not just error or wrong belief, but willful nonbelief and the promulgation of that to others, even after being corrected. Those who claimed to know the "truth" were more of a threat than those who were outside the faith altogether. As Christianity solidified and standardized, *orthodoxy* was defined in contradistinction to heresy; heresy functioned in the clarification of orthodoxy. In the Christian West before the *Reformation*, heresy was defined as any belief in opposition to the Catholic Church. Many believed that a Christian society must attack and root out heretics, seen as being sent by the devil, since they could taint and corrupt true believers. The crime was serious enough to warrant secular and spiritual forces joining together to stamp it out with the use of *inquisitions*, torture, and execution, usually by burning to purge the body.

Heresy included both intellectual (often developed within the universities) and popular forms, which spread to the masses, usually following charismatic preachers. Repression of heresy was common in the early church but waned in the early Middle Ages. The twelfth to fifteenth centuries, however, saw the rise of numerous heresies and popular reform movements both within and outside the *church*, which were either vigorously attacked and repressed (such as the Cathars) or subsumed into the church (such as the mendicant orders). There was a fine line between heresy and accepted reform, often depending on how much authority one gave the clerical hierarchy.

Until the Reformation it was possible for the Catholic Church to minimize the damage or wipe out heresies completely, although pieces remained (and earlier heresies such as the Waldensians, Lollards, and Hussites can be seen as precursors to the Protestants). The situation changed in the fifteenth and sixteenth centuries as the role of secular governments, nationalism, and the invention of movable type brought new challenges to church hegemony, and heresy (or reform) spread too quickly and proved impossible to quench. State authority could turn against the church (as it did in the Hussite rebellion), and by the sixteenth century secular princes and city councils were actively supporting "heretical" movements. The Reformation shattered the sense of a unified Christian orthodoxy in the West, and "heresy" thus lost some of its specific meaning. With the development of new confessions, with newly defined doctrine, both Catholics and Protestants (with state support) continued to prosecute both heresy and "incorrect" popular belief, leading to attacks on *Anabaptists* and the witch persecutions.

———

Henderson (1998); Hunter et al. (2005); Lambert (1992); R. Moore (2007).

AMY E. LEONARD

Hoffmann, Melchior (ca. 1495–1543)

Hoffmann was an apocalyptic preacher and the founder of Dutch Anabaptism. Born in Schwäbisch-Hall, he was a furrier and lay preacher without formal university training. As a convinced follower of *Martin Luther* he began preaching in 1523 at Wolmar, Reval, and Dorpat. However, his involvement in iconoclastic riots led to his expulsion. Moving to Stockholm in 1526, he was again forced to leave in 1527 for the unrest he occasioned. Finding refuge with the king of Denmark, he preached in Kiel until his increasingly radical views of the *Lord's Supper* alarmed Luther. Hoffmann agreed with *Huldrych Zwingli* that the Supper was a memorial, though Hoffmann also saw it as the occasion of a spiritual union with Christ. A colloquy with Lutheran preachers at Flensburg (1529) led to his expulsion.

Already concerned by the lack of moral improvement in the wake of the Lutheran preaching, Hoffmann's encounter with *Anabaptists* in *Strasbourg* led to his rebaptism (1530). In

East Frisia he got to know *Andreas Bodenstein von Karlstadt* and began baptizing adults there and in the city of Emden. In response to the execution of some of his followers in the Hague at the end of 1531, he decided to suspend baptism for two years. He returned to Strasbourg convinced that it was the new Jerusalem and that the apocalypse was ordained for 1533. His prediction that the ungodly would be purged in preparation for Christ's second coming led to his arrest. In the wake of his failed prediction, two of his followers—Jan van Mathiis (ca. 1500–1534) and Jan van Leyden (1509–36)—assumed leadership of the Hoffmannites, revising Hoffmann's prediction and naming *Münster* as the new Jerusalem. Since Hoffmann was blamed for the resulting Anabaptist kingdom of Münster, he was kept in prison in increasingly hard conditions until his death in 1543.

Though Hoffmann was a prolific writer, his two most influential works were his *Commentary on the Revelation of John* (*Auslegung der heimlichen Offenbarung Joannis des heyligen Apostels unnd Evangelisten,* 1530), which laid out his apocalyptic predictions, and the *Ordinance of God* (*Die Ordonnantie Godts,* 1530), which argued for adult baptism followed by a sanctified life. Hoffmann was also the source for the heavenly flesh *Christology* that *Menno Simons* made popular in Dutch Anabaptism. Hoffmann probably derived the teaching from *Caspar Schwenckfeld,* whom he met in Strasbourg. Heavenly flesh Christologies maintained that the Virgin *Mary* contributed only a womb to Christ's conception and that the substance of Christ's humanity came directly from God.

Deppermann (1987); G. H. Williams (1992).
R. EMMET MCLAUGHLIN

Holy Roman Emperor (800–814, 962–1806)   This was the title of German rulers who governed the *Holy Roman Empire* from the coronation of Charlemagne (800) and later Otto I of Saxony (962) to the abdication of Francis II (1806). Invoking the heritage of Roman glory and the prerogative of Christian kingship, Holy Roman Emperors in theory ruled Western Christendom with the *papacy.* The emperor reigned in the temporal sphere while the pope presided in the spiritual realm. In reality, popes vied for political power with emperors in the Middle Ages, and territorial states undermined Imperial authority in the early modern period. In the mid-1300s seven permanent *electors* emerged who chose new emperors, though by 1438 the Imperial office became associated with the Habsburg dynasty from Austria. *Charles V* (r. 1519–56) attempted to impose strong centralized authority over the empire, but failed due to the *Reformation* and the resistance of European states.

Ficthner (2003); Maltby (2002); McKitterick (2008).
CHARLES PARKER

Holy Roman Empire (800–814, 962–1806)   This was the political domain claimed by Charlemagne (747–814; r. 800–814) and later Otto I of Saxony (912–973; r. 962–973) at Imperial coronations in 800 and 962, respectively. The concept of a Holy Roman Empire became clearer later, merging Roman and Christian imperial ideologies and encompassing Western Christendom. The empire always proved more theoretical construction rather than political reality. By the end of the Middle Ages, the primary territories included German and central European territories. Within the empire, many areas enjoyed significant autonomy. The major developments of the early modern period, the *Reformation,* the destructive religious and territorial wars, and the rise of strong states increasingly diminished the geopolitical significance of the empire. Finally on August 6, 1806,

the last emperor, Francis II (1768–1835; r. 1792–1806), terminated the Imperial office in order to keep Napoleon Bonaparte (1769–1821) from making it his own.

Barraclough (1959); R. Evans (1984); Folz (1969).
                                    CHARLES PARKER

Holy Spirit   Sometimes referred to as the Holy Ghost, the Holy Spirit is the third person of the *Trinity* in Christian theology, and acts as the conduit for God's *grace*. The Nicene Creed (325 CE) confirmed the doctrine of the Trinity to defend against the Arian heresy. Medieval theories taught that the Holy Spirit is distinct from the Father and the Son, but is nevertheless consubstantial with them and that the Holy Spirit guided the *church*. *Martin Luther* and other mainstream Protestants supported the Nicene Creed and the Trinity, but rejected the church as the conduit of the Holy Spirit. Instead, Luther emphasized the role of the Holy Spirit in the illumination of the meaning of *Scripture*.

Cameron (1991); Lohse (1986).
                        GRETA GRACE KROEKER

Hooker,   Richard   (1554–1600)
Hooker was an English pastor, theologian, and controversialist. He attended Oxford and from 1584 held a series of minor clerical appointments. He has been highly influential in English religious and political thought, primarily on account of his magnum opus, *Of the Laws of Ecclesiastical Polity*, an effort to persuade dissenters to obey the ecclesiastical laws of the *Elizabethan Settlement*. Of the *Laws'* projected eight books, the first four were published along with a preface in 1593, and the fifth was published in 1597; drafts of the last three were published posthumously.

In the first four books, Hooker responded to Puritan dissenters' claims "that scripture is the only rule of all things which in this life may be done" with an intricate discussion of *authority* in religious matters. While recognizing the authority of the divine *law* revealed in *Scripture*, he emphasized the importance and complexity of correctly interpreting Scripture and also argued that God has established additional laws to guide conduct, including natural laws discovered by reason and human laws "whereby politique societies are governed." As a society, the English church required human laws to maintain order; illicit disobedience of such laws was offensive to God and harmful to the church. At the same time, the church was not merely a human society; it was also the mystical body of Christ. The fifth book elaborated on this theme as part of a detailed defense of the ministry and worship prescribed in the *Book of Common Prayer*. The prescribed prayers of the church fostered "intercourse and commerce between God and us"; the *sacraments* of the church (*baptism* and the *Eucharist*) were effective means through which God communicated *grace*, uniting believers to Christ.

In the final three books, Hooker defended the *polity* of the church. Episcopacy was of apostolic origin and, while not immutable, was not to be discarded lightly considering the many benefits bishops brought to the church. Royal supremacy over the church, including authority to formulate ecclesiastical laws, was vested in the Crown in Parliament and was based on appointment by the community of Christians in *England* (i.e., the English church). Disobedience of ecclesiastical laws by English Christians was perverse because English Christians themselves were collectively responsible for the formulation of those laws. Any reform of ecclesiastical laws had to be carried out circumspectly and by the duly constituted authorities.

In addition to the *Laws*, several sermons and other writings of Hooker addressing a variety of pastoral and theological issues are extant. An area of contention in Hooker studies is the relationship of Hooker's thought to the Reformed tradition. Some scholars maintain that Hooker articulated a "middle way" between Protestantism and Catholicism, while others argue that he remained within the Reformed tradition.

Kirby (2003, 2008); McGrade (1997).

DANIEL EPPLEY

Hubmaier, Balthasar (ca. 1480–1528)

Hubmaier was the most significant theologian among early *Anabaptists*. He was trained in scholastic theology and earned a doctorate at the University of Ingolstadt. In 1521 Hubmaier became a priest in Waldshut in southern Germany. There he began to read the Pauline Epistles and became attracted to the works of *Desiderius Erasmus, Martin Luther,* and *Huldrych Zwingli.* While under Catholic persecution, he wrote the treatise *Von Kertzern und ihren Verbrennern* (*Concerning Heretics and Those Who Burn Them*). By 1525 Hubmaier had converted to Anabaptism and ushered in Anabaptist reforms to Waldshut. In July of 1525 Hubmaier wrote *Von dem Christlichen Tauff der Gläubigen* (*On the Christian Baptism of Believers*) as an Anabaptist response to Zwingli's baptismal writings. Arrested in Zurich, Hubmaier was tortured and forced to recant his Anabaptist beliefs before Zwingli and the town council. Exiled to Moravia, Hubmaier promoted Anabaptist beliefs in Nikolsburg. He was burned at the stake in Austria in 1528.

Estep and Bergsten (1978); Mabry (1994); Vedder (1905).

BRIAN C. BREWER

Huguenots

Huguenots were French Calvinists. More specifically, the term "Huguenot" referred to the political party of the French Calvinists—"Huguenot" was at least as much

a term of politics as religion. The term may have come from the Swiss German *Eidgenossen,* referring to those admitted to the Swiss Confederation, but that is still debated. French Calvinist churches were organized by the Synod of Paris in 1539. Their growing presence in France brought about a situation of a state with two Christian confessions, a condition that proved to be psychologically impossible. Though the crown attempted to stamp out the Calvinists, it was unsuccessful, even after the Guise-led massacre of unarmed Calvinist worshipers at Vassy in 1562 provoked the first of a series of French Wars of Religion. Neither royal nor Huguenot forces could finally win, prompting the former Huguenot King, *Henri IV,* to promulgate the *Edict of Nantes* in 1598. While the edict ended the wars, it did not finally settle the religious question.

Diefendorf (1991); Prestwich (1985); Sutherland (1980).

R. WARD HOLDER

Humanism

As it emerged in the Renaissance, humanism is a complex and, indeed, contested phenomenon, but there is general agreement about several of its components. First, Renaissance humanists focused on studies pertaining to life in the world (the *studia humanitatis,* or studies of humans) such as politics, ethics, and management of a family, as opposed to speculative theology and metaphysics. More specifically, *rhetoric,* the art of persuasion, replaced the scholastic emphasis on *dialectic,* the domain of abstract reasoning, as the most important of the *liberal arts,* because rhetoric concerns human interactions in society.

Second, Renaissance humanism was grounded in the literature of the ancient world, initially the pagan classics of Rome. Cicero was especially admired for his ethical *philosophy* and rhetorical theory, while historians such as Livy, Suetonius, and Tacitus were valued for their political insights. All were studied as exemplars of Latin prose, which Renaissance scholars strove to emulate. A popular subject for debate was whether the "moderns" could ever hope to rise to the level of excellence demonstrated by the ancient writers: some individuals believed that scholars of their own time could even surpass them, whereas others thought that later generations could only hope to approximate their greatness. In the fifteenth century the literature of ancient Greece came to be cultivated as avidly as that of Rome.

Third, humanists believed in the power of *education* to mold individuals in ways that contributed to moral excellence. Reading the classics would not only inspire students with the values that could enable them to cultivate virtue, but the very beauty and grandeur of the language would have the effect of enlarging their souls. The humanist program differed markedly from the theological studies pursued in the universities, which were heavily invested in logical demonstration and in the philosophical system of *Aristotle*. Humanists did not limit themselves to the pagan classics, but included the writings of the patristic period and, of course, *Scripture* itself. While humanists were overwhelmingly concerned with the education of men, some also encouraged learning in women, but they limited the scope of female education to subject matter that did not endanger chastity, and especially ruled out participation in public life, which was regarded as the necessary expression of male virtue.

Finally, humanists devoted themselves to textual scholarship, out of concern that the literature of the ancient world had been overwhelmingly corrupted through the physical deterioration of manuscripts, scribal error, and, in the case of Greek works that had been translated into Latin, bad translations. Utilizing the tools of philology and etymology, many of which they themselves developed, humanists published critical editions of the works of ancient writers, both pagan and Christian, the most noteworthy example being *Desiderius Erasmus*'s New Testament.

Protestant reformers benefited from the textual scholarship of humanists such as Erasmus, and indeed many were Erasmus's admirers and even colleagues in their youth; however, *Martin Luther* early on came to realize that he and Erasmus were not destined to be allies. Over time, there was an explicit divergence between humanists who remained Catholic while advocating a reform from within, and Protestant reformers who broke with the church.

Kristeller (1974a); Rabil (1988); Rummel (2000); Trinkaus (1970).

J. LAUREL CARRINGTON

Hus, Jan (1369–1415)

Hus was a Bohemian (Czech) priest and reformer who spoke out against church corruption during the Great Schism (1378–1417) and who espoused beliefs similar to the Oxford theologian *John Wyclif*. Hus championed the religious authority of *Scripture*, denied papal infallibility, and criticized *indulgences*. A popular preacher, Hus became an important figure at the University of Prague. His heterodox views and conflicts in the schism led the archbishop of Prague to excommunicate him in 1411. The emperor Sigismund persuaded Hus to explain himself at the church *Council of Constance* and promised him safe passage. Once at Constance, however, Hus was condemned for *heresy* and burned at the stake in 1415. Hus's execution outraged supporters (Hussites) and ignited years of warfare in Bohemia. Protestants, especially *Martin Luther*, regarded Hus as a like-minded reformer, and historians typically depict Hus and Wyclif as forerunners of the *Reformation*.

Spinka (1966, 1968).

CHARLES PARKER

Hut, Hans (ca. 1490–1527) Hut was a traveling book peddler turned Anabaptist evangelist in south Germany and Austria. He was a follower of *Thomas Müntzer* and was baptized by *Hans Denck*. Viewing the *Anabaptists* as the elect and *baptism* as an eschatological sign, Hut saw himself as the man described in Daniel 12:5 and Ezekiel 9:2–5 who was to seal the 144,000 elect by marking the foreheads of those baptized in the sign of the cross. He called for the cessation of violence among the peasants until Pentecost 1528, at which time he had predicted the second advent. Meanwhile, Hut urged the peasants to endure suffering and persecution as a way to faith. A key participant in the Martyrs' Synod in Augsburg, Hut was among the Anabaptist leaders arrested by authorities. He died of asphyxiation from an accidental fire in the Augsburg prison. The following day, his dead body was sentenced to death and was burned.

Goertz and Klaassen (1982); H. Klassen (1958); Packull (1977); Stayer (1976).
BRIAN C. BREWER

Hutter, Jakob (ca. 1500–1536) Hutter was already the leading Anabaptist in the Tyrol when he made his first visit to Moravia in 1529. The refugees he began sending to this "promised land" of the *Anabaptists* eventually made up the bulk of the communitarian Anabaptist population there. In 1533 he assumed a leadership role in the Auspitz Anabaptist community, but his allegedly high-handed actions led to a break in relations with other communitarian Anabaptist groups: the Philipites, also in Auspitz, and the Gabrielites in nearby Rossitz. Hutter's leadership in Auspitz lasted only two years and, amid intensified persecution in 1535, he returned to the Tyrol, where he was arrested in December and then executed in Innsbruck in March 1536. His impact on the teachings and practices of the Hutterite

Brethren is not completely clear; likely, his charismatic leadership role was subsequently formalized by the elders Peter Riedemann (fl. 1542–56) and Peter Walpot (fl. 1565–78).

Gross (1982); Packull (1995).
GEOFFREY DIPPLE

Hymns Hymns are a form of musical praise that predates the Christian era and continued to develop during the early modern period. Beginning in the 1520s, Europe's hymnody reflected the new theological developments and understandings of the *Bible* advanced by the various Reformed movements. *Martin Luther*'s first hymn, fittingly titled "We Lift Up a New Song," was written in 1523 and published as part of his first hymnbook in 1524. Luther appreciated the "unshackled art of music" and understood that hymns should reflect the "joyful" New Testament rather than the "lazy and tedious" Old Testament. *John Calvin* also understood that the difference between old and new *covenants* should be reflected in worship: Christian hymns should be kept simple and without ostentation. This principle informed the practice of unaccompanied congregational singing, the use of tunes with uniform metrics, and an appreciation of the Bible—especially the Psalms—as the only legitimate source for hymn texts. The English reformers did not follow Calvin's recommendations.

Garside (1979); Le Huray (1967).
HANS WIERSMA

Iconoclasm During the *Reformation* iconoclasm was directed toward the removal or destruction of Catholic sacred objects and images. The iconoclasts considered these objects to be idols and direct violations of the Decalogue. In general, Lutherans and Anglicans rejected iconoclasm, although they taught against superstitious uses of sacred objects and images. In the Swiss Reformation, however, iconoclasm found considerable support. In 1524 the Zurich magistracy called for the orderly removal of all religious images. Other Swiss cities followed, sometimes as a result of popular rioting (Basel, 1529). Wherever Reformed Protestantism spread, in Switzerland, France, Germany, the Low Countries, and the British Isles, it was accompanied by iconoclasm. *Anabaptists* also opposed images, but their general commitment to nonviolence limited image destruction. Although iconoclasm was not a central Protestant teaching, it did serve as an important cultural marker that could demonstrate the local triumph of Reformed Protestantism or become a rallying point for Roman Catholics.

N. Davis (1973); Eire (1986); Wandel (1995).

GREGORY J. MILLER

Ignatius of Loyola (1491–1556)

Ignatius was the thirteenth child of Beltrán de Loyola, a rich Basque nobleman. His youth was spent as a page and later a courtier. He was never a soldier, but courtiers were expected to serve as gentleman volunteers in emergencies. This he did when a French army attacked Pamplona in 1521. Loyola encouraged its defenders, but a cannonball smashed his legs. The city surrendered. French soldiers carried him back to Castle Loyola, where he spent nine months in convalescence. Bored, he began reading spiritual books. They changed his life. Now he would serve God, not some duke.

He decided to go on a pilgrimage to Jerusalem, but stopped at Manresa, where he stayed for over ten months. He kept notes about his deep religious and mystical experiences there, which later developed into his *Spiritual Exercises*, the core of Jesuit spirituality. The book version has enjoyed more than five thousand editions in dozens of languages. Finally he went to Jerusalem, where he planned to spend his whole life helping souls. The *Franciscan* superior, knowing such activities would anger the *Turks*, forced him to return to Venice and then to Barcelona in 1524.

Gradually Loyola realized that he needed formal *education* if he were to serve God by helping souls. After studying Latin at Barcelona, he then went on to the universities of Alcala and Salamanca. There his studies lacked focus, so he transferred to the University of Paris, where he studied from 1528 to 1535. Loyola profited from the organized Paris curriculum. The Paris model was taken up by the Jesuit Ratio Studiorum, the plan of studies for Jesuit colleges, which remained in use for four centuries. At Paris Loyola gathered six disciples. In 1534 the seven companions took a vow to go to Jerusalem and work for souls. When war between Venice and the Turks prevented the Jerusalem project, they went to Rome in 1538. The pope sent them to preach in Italian cities. Gradually they decided to start a new religious order, the Society of Jesus, popularly known as the *Jesuits*. They worked out a short preliminary rule in 1539 and presented it to *Paul III*, who approved the new Jesuit order in 1540. His companions elected Loyola their superior general and appointed him to draw up the Constitutions of the Order.

His *Spiritual Exercises*, a guide for making a thirty-day retreat, was published at Rome in 1548. That same year the Jesuits opened their first school for lay students at Messina in Sicily. It became the model for later Jesuit colleges: 34 by 1556, 372 by 1615. Gradually education became the main Jesuit ministry.

The new order was growing rapidly, counting roughly a thousand Jesuits by Loyola's death. Most were in Spain, Italy, and Portugal, but they were spreading in France and Germany. There were Jesuit missionaries at work in Asia (especially India), Africa (Ethiopia and the Congo), and Latin America.

During his last nine years Loyola in collaboration with his secretary, Juan Polanco, wrote more than six thousand surviving letters, mostly giving encouragement and direction to Jesuits. He also set up confraternities of wealthy people at Rome to aid people in trouble: a house for ex-prostitutes trying to make better lives, another to keep young women from falling into prostitution. Another confraternity helped noblemen who had fallen on hard times. Loyola also founded an orphanage for boys.

His last years saw a return of mystical experiences; they centered on *Scripture*, Christ, the *Trinity*, the *sacraments*, above all his daily *Mass*. He kept diaries of these experiences but destroyed most of them. After periods of declining health he died quietly on July 31, 1556. He was canonized in 1622.

Caraman (1990); Donnelly (2004); Ravier (1987).

JOHN PATRICK DONNELLY, S.J.

Image of God (Lat. *Imago Dei*)

Protestant reformers modified prior Christian conceptions of the image of God in several significant ways. First, the prior tradition identified the image of God in humanity as a capacity or active human power, while the Protestant reformers defined it as right relationship with God. Moreover, the prior tradition made a distinction between *similitudo* ("likeness") and *imago* ("image") and argued that at the fall, the likeness to God was lost, while the image was maintained. *Martin Luther* and *John Calvin* rejected this distinction and maintained a more complete corruption of the image of God in humanity at the fall. The Reformers confirmed, in agreement with prior tradition, that Jesus Christ is the image of God (Col. 1:15–20) who restores this image (and God's original intention) to believers. Finally, the Protestant reformers asserted that the image of God is found in both man and woman (though not necessarily equally),

whereas the prior tradition regularly identified it only in man.

L. Anderson (1994); T. Bell (2005); Børrensen (1995); Zachman (2007).

G. SUJIN PAK

Images   Veneration of images of Christ and the saints was a standard component of Christian worship in the pre-*Reformation* era. In early Christianity, sacred images are found in the catacombs and churches. A major dispute over images in the Eastern church led to the iconoclastic controversy, resolved at the Second Council of Nicaea (787) when the veneration of images was restored. Several medieval commentators, including Thomas Aquinas, attempted to provide a clear theological distinction between the proper and improper use of images. In the early Reformation era, there was a very strong reaction against the Catholic veneration of images. Reformed Protestants in particular condemned the use of images as a violation of the second commandment and as a practice insupportable on the basis of *Scripture*. *Iconoclastic* riots were common in the years surrounding the *Peasants' War* of 1525 in Germany, and later in Calvinist France, the Netherlands, and *England*. The *Council of Trent* (session 25) required that due honor and reverence be given to sacred images, but condemned treating images as objects of worship.

Eire (1986); Moeller (1972); Scribner (1981).

WILLIAM BRADFORD SMITH

Imputation   *Martin Luther*'s developed doctrine of *justification*, articulated more systematically by *Philip Melanchthon*, argued that human beings are "forensically" declared righteous by God on the basis of Christ's "alien righteousness" imputed to the believer. (Finnish Lutheran scholars have argued that the "forensic" view of justification is a distortion of Luther's theology, but this view remains controversial.) The Augustinian Catholic tradition, which identified justification with the forgiveness of *sin* and the infusion of *grace*, remained influential among many early Reformers, and the Lutheran theologian Andreas Osiander developed a theory basing justification on Christ's indwelling presence. Eventually, however, both Lutheran and Reformed confessional traditions embraced the doctrine of forensic imputation. The theory of double justification proposed at the *Regensburg* Colloquy of 1541 posited the imputation of Christ's righteousness as the basis for final justification, covering the imperfections in the believer's inherent righteousness. This view was rejected at the *Council of Trent*, leaving imputation as a dividing point between Roman Catholicism and magisterial Protestantism.

Braaten and Jenson (1998); McGrath (2005); Steinmetz (2001b).
                 EDWIN WOODRUFF TAIT

Incarnation   Orthodox   Christian teaching on the incarnation, formally defined at the Council of Chalcedon (451), asserts that the eternal Son of God took human form and that the historical Christ was both fully God and fully man. Chalcedon remained the sounding board for orthodox teaching throughout the Middle Ages and into the *Reformation*, in spite of disagreements among theologians about specifics of that teaching. For example, *Martin Luther*'s disagreement with *Huldrych Zwingli* about the real presence in the Eucharist highlighted differences between Lutheran and Reformed understandings of the exact nature of the union between Christ's divine and human natures.

While many of the Reformation radicals, too, held to the dictates of Chalcedon, several—most notably *Caspar Schwenckfeld* and *Melchior Hoffmann*—

championed positions that emphasized the divine origin of even Christ's flesh. This teaching became the litmus test for Melchiorite *Anabaptists*, including Mennonites, and figured prominently in divisions within the Anabaptist camp in the second half of the sixteenth century.

Blough (2007); Maier (1959); Stephens (1986); Willis (1966).
                 GEOFFREY DIPPLE

Index   Librorum   Prohibitorum (*Index of Forbidden Books*)   The Index was a list of books Roman Catholics were prohibited to read, sell, or even possess without special permission, on pain of excommunication. In reaction to the growing literature of the *Reformation* and developing science that challenged its positions, the Roman Catholic Church censored works it deemed to be contrary to faith and morals. While by the 1540s universities had begun proscribing books, *Pope Paul IV* promulgated the Pauline Index by the Congregation of Roman *Inquisition* in 1557 that included over a thousand condemnations, banning some 600 authors and over 450 individual titles considered heretical. The *Council of Trent* revised the Index, which was subsequently published by Pius IV in 1564. The regulations of the Index applied for four centuries. In 1966 Pope Paul VI abolished the Index because it was regarded as inconsistent with the freedom of inquiry promoted by the Second Vatican Council (1962–65).

Delph et al. (2006); McCabe (1931); Sheridan (2006).
                 BRIAN C. BREWER

Indulgences   To this day, no single issue, no single word, more surely evokes the tensions of the *Reformation* than does "indulgences." The practice as known in the sixteenth century had developed in the eleventh century in connection with the penances imposed by confessors as a part of the *sacrament* of *penance*. Penance included heartfelt contrition (*contritio cordis*), oral confession to a priest (*confessio oris*), priestly forgiveness of the guilt of *sin* (*absolutio*), and the assignment of penances in satisfaction of punishments owed (*satisfactio operis*). Indulgences pertain to the last element, that is, they presume the properly confessed and absolved Christian in a state of *grace*. In that condition, penitents who contributed money to a church or monastery, or who made a pilgrimage to pray at a shrine like St. James of Compostella or St. Peter's in Rome, were granted a partial reduction in the penances prescribed for their sins, for example, the reduction of an imposed period of fasting. In 1095 Pope Urban II declared a full ("plenary") indulgence for those who out of sincere devotion joined the crusade to liberate the church in Jerusalem. In the thirteenth century, Hugh of St. Cher contributed the notion of a *treasury of merit*—earned by Christ, Mary, and the saints—from which the church, particularly the pope, could draw in announcing a reduction of penance. Theologians like Thomas Aquinas and Bonaventure supported the practice and appealed to a "union of charity" on the basis of which the merits of one Christian could be shared with another (including those suffering in *purgatory*), and used to pay the penalties of sin. However, the practice was prone to abuses, both theological and financial.

In the early sixteenth century abuses of both kinds were in evidence following *Pope Leo X*'s declaration of a plenary indulgence in support of the building of the new St. Peter's in Rome. The *Dominican* Johann Tetzel, who preached this indulgence near Wittenberg, insinuated that they could remove not only the punishments but also the guilt of sin. *Martin Luther* objected, largely on pastoral grounds. Soon after the Ninety-Five Theses, in which the legitimacy of the practice seems to be admitted even as its theological support and pastoral utility are called into question, Luther came to see indulgences as contradictory to the gospel of *faith* in Christ alone for salvation. How much better to trust in the sure mercy of Christ rather than in one's own *good works*, especially works that were supposed to satisfy not only the *canon law* of the church but also the demands of divine justice? Elsewhere, *Huldrych Zwingli* followed his teacher Thomas Wyttenbach in opposing indulgences, and *John Calvin* dismissed them as evidence of corruption in the papal church.

Bagchi (1991); Lohse (1999).
MICKEY L. MATTOX

Infusion   Infusion refers to the manner in which God imparts *grace* to the believer, so that the believer may be made righteous. Generally speaking, the infusion of grace into the soul of the sinner moves the sinner to *faith* and to works that are necessary for *justification* and, therefore, salvation. As developed in Thomas Aquinas's "Treatise on Grace" in *Summa Theologiae*, infused grace "moves the *free will*" to faith and to charity, making one righteous. Without the infusion of grace at every level, cooperation with God in the process of salvation would be impossible. Such grace is infused via reception of the church's *sacraments*. *Martin Luther* and *Philip Melanchthon* objected to the notion that grace was a substance or essence that could be attached to souls. Instead, these Reformers, and later *John Calvin*, advanced the argument that divine righteousness was *imputed* (i.e., assigned or declared) on account of faith in Christ alone, apart from any movement of the "free will."

See also **Imputation** and **Free Will**

Forde (1991); McGrath (2005).
HANS WIERSMA

Innovation   Theological and biblical innovation played important roles in the intellectual and religious life of early modern Europe. In the *Reformation* context, theologians disagreed about who should be allowed to write theology. In general, it was considered dangerous to introduce new and innovative ways of studying and interpreting *Scripture* because it could lead to unorthodox or even heretical opinions and beliefs. Scholastic theologians argued that only those trained in scholastic methods and those who had achieved a doctorate of theology should be permitted to write about theological matters. Biblical humanists like *Desiderius Erasmus* and *Faber Stapulensis* (Jacques Lefèvre d'Étaples), however, insisted that the ancient languages, Latin and *Greek*, in particular, helped purify Scripture from scribal and translation errors and aided the study and comprehension of Scripture. Their training was largely philological rather than theological. Scholastic theologians worried that biblical humanists, untrained and uncontrolled, would introduce heterodoxies through changes in the Vulgate and commentaries on the *Bible*.

Nauert (2006); Rummel (1998, 2008).
GRETA GRACE KROEKER

Inquisition   The Inquisition was an ecclesiastical tribunal that tried cases of *heresy*, blasphemy, *witchcraft*, bigamy, and other moral transgressions. Its goal was to reconcile sinners with the *church* and to prevent religious prevarication. The Inquisition was first established in the Middle Ages to suppress the Cathar and Waldensian heresies, and was later revived in the early modern period. The most notorious inquisitorial tribunal was the Spanish Inquisition. It was established in 1478 and finally abolished in 1834. Inquisitions were also established in Portugal (1536) and Rome (1542), and these tribunals also operated into the nineteenth century. Each Inquisition developed its own national traits, but the basic procedures of the tribunals were the same.

For the Inquisition to act, an accusation of wrongdoing had to be brought before the tribunal. The Inquisition therefore encouraged people to denounce their neighbors and relied on a network of agents to report suspicious behavior. If the inquisitors found an accusation believable, they would collect further evidence from additional witnesses. In most instances, the inquisitors deemed the evidence insufficient for trial and suspended the case.

When a case went to trial, the inquisitors arrested the accused and confiscated the property. The proceedings were secret, and the accused did not know the charges that had been filed. The Inquisition, however, provided the accused with a defense lawyer and, to prevent false accusations, allowed the accused to present a list of enemies or people with whom that person had quarreled whose testimony was therefore discounted. The inquisitorial process was a series of questions and answers under oath to elicit a truthful confession. If the accused refused to answer the questions or equivocated, nonlethal torture, usually something similar to water boarding, was used to extract a confession. Any confession made under torture was later read back to the accused to confirm or to refute. Notaries meticulously recorded the proceedings. At the end of the trial, the inquisitors determined the guilt or innocence of the accused. In Spain and Portugal verdicts were publicly read at *autos de fe* (acts of faith), while in Italy verdicts were normally issued in private. Most people were reconciled to the church, but many people were executed (around 3,000 in Spain, 1,000 in Portugal, and 150 in Italy).

The Inquisition was also responsible for censorship. The *Index Librorum Prohibitorum* (*Index of Prohibited Books*, 1559) banned the reading of heretical and other inappropriate books. The Inquisition updated the Index periodically.

The Inquisition has been caricatured as a fanatically cruel and inhumane institution. Yet its procedures were more humane than secular courts at the time, and when compared to the number of witches executed by secular courts in northern Europe (around 40,000 between 1580 and 1650), the Inquisition was far from bloodthirsty. This does not excuse the Inquisition's actions, but placing them within their historical context is crucial for an objective understanding of this frequently misunderstood institution.

Kamen (1999); E. Peters (1988); Rawlings (2006).

SEAN T. PERRONE

Intercession of Saints

In late medieval *piety*, intercession referred to the practice of invoking deceased saints, and increasingly the Virgin *Mary*, for aid or mediation. Rejecting practices thought to compensate for *sin* such as the use of *indulgences*, *Martin Luther* criticized this practice as perpetuating the medieval notion to see Christ as the dreaded judge to be placated by the intercession of the saints and Mary, rather than as the gracious mediator. Although Luther believed that deceased saints could be venerated as examples of faith in Christ, he asserted that Christ alone should be invoked as mediator. The Confutation (1530), a Catholic response to the *Augsburg Confession,* defended both the veneration and the invocation of the saints by arguing that while Christ is the sole mediator of redemption, Mary and the saints are mediators of intercession. In response, *Philip Melanchthon's* Apology of the Augsburg Confession (1531) affirmed the honoring of saints but resisted the transition from intercession to invocation.

G. Anderson (1992); Symington (2006).

ESTHER CHUNG-KIM

Interpretation

The early and medieval church worked to define Catholic *orthodoxy* through a series of councils and guidance from the writings of the church *fathers*. While challenges to those interpretations can be traced to the very earliest of church controversies (including the Arian, Pelagian, and Manichean heresies), the Protestant reformers presented the most thorough challenge to the Catholic Church's doctrine and dogma. *Martin Luther, Huldrych Zwingli, John Calvin,* and many of their followers offered interpretations of *Scripture* that sometimes directly contradicted the teachings of the Roman Catholic Church. Reformers interpreted the *Bible* differently than the Roman Catholic Church, particularly on the issues of the number and efficacy of the *sacraments*, clerical *celibacy*, the real presence in the Eucharist, *predestination*, the existence of *purgatory*, and the freedom of the *will*.

See also Exegesis

Cameron (1991); Ozment (1980).

GRETA GRACE KROEKER

Jerome of Prague (1379–1416)

Jerome was a fifteenth-century church reformer influenced by the work of *John Wyclif* and connected with the Lollards in England. Originally from Prague, Jerome was forced to abandon his studies at both Oxford and Paris when his heterodox views became known. Back in Prague, he joined his friend *Jan Hus* in advocating the kinds of ideas that would gain traction a century later: Holy Communion under both kinds, the *Bible* in the vernacular, the inefficacy of *indulgences*, limits on papal *authority*, and so on. The publication of a 1410 papal bull against Wyclif's teachings meant the beginning of the end for Jerome. Under increasing threats, he continued to support Hus's Wyclif-inspired reforms. In 1415 Jerome arrived at the *Council of Constance* in order to provide support for the doomed Hus. There Jerome was arrested, imprisoned, and, on May 30, 1416, burned at the stake.

Fudge (1998); Zeman (1977).
HANS WIERSMA

Jesuits (Society of Jesus) The Society of Jesus was established by a bull (proclamation) of *Pope Paul III* on September 27, 1540. Their original purposes included *preaching*, teaching the *catechism*, and spiritual guidance. *Ignatius of Loyola*, whose *Spiritual Exercises* (1522–24) were foundational for the society, served as its first superior general.

The earliest Jesuits were not particularly devoted to the study of theology, but their intense spiritual formation and, after 1548, their involvement in educational institutions fostered an institutional culture that produced many outstanding theologians, including *Roberto Bellarmino*, *Francisco Suárez*, Luis de Molina, and *Peter Canisius*. In 1550 they added the defense of the faith to their stated purposes. Thus, even though they were not founded to oppose the *Reformation*, the Jesuits did help reinvigorate Catholicism, and their learning and devotion quickly made them formidable opponents of the Protestant cause. The society also experienced phenomenal growth. From the original group of Ignatius and six companions, the Jesuits grew by 1580 to include some five thousand members.

Like other Catholic orders, the Jesuits adopted a provincial system of administration, including, by the time of Loyola's death in 1556, nine provinces in Europe and three international ones. As a religious order, however, they were anything but typical. Unlike the mendicants or Benedictines, for example, the Jesuits had no female "second order." Instead, they adopted a "graduated" internal order and so incorporated some priests and laymen, "coadjutors," who would never take final, solemn vows. Those who obtained final membership in the society were priests only, men in solemn vows equipped individually for service. Their Formula and Constitutions did not require them to live in community, wear a habit, or chant the monastic hours. Moreover, to the three traditional religious vows of poverty, chastity, and obedience, they added a fourth vow of "special obedience to the sovereign pontiff regarding missions." They wished, in other words, to put themselves utterly at papal disposal, to be willing to go wherever they were needed for the sake of the church and its mission. These differences made the Jesuits controversial, even among Catholics, but they contributed to the society's unique capacity for service. Thus the Jesuits quickly became leaders in Catholic missions. *Francis Xavier* initiated their work in India in 1542, and Manuel de Nóbrega in Brazil. In 1583 Matteo Ricci led the mission to China, where he inaugurated a successful, if controversial, program of accommodation to Chinese culture.

Theologically, the Jesuits, led by Molina, adopted a distinctive approach to the questions of *nature* and *grace* that had occasioned so much controversy, defending *free will* as the determining factor in the efficacy of divine grace. In this they were opposed not only by the Protestants, but also by more conservative Catholics, particularly the *Dominicans*.

Bangert (1986); O'Malley (1993).
MICKEY L. MATTOX

Jewel, John (1522–71) An English polemicist and bishop of Salisbury (1560–71), Jewel was educated at Oxford and later emerged as a leading defender of the *Elizabethan Settlement*. In his "Challenge Sermon" (first presented in late 1559) and the ensuing controversy, Jewel challenged the legitimacy of the Catholic Church by maintaining that none of twenty-seven purportedly Catholic teachings had any basis in the primitive church (prior to 600 CE). Jewel's highly influential *Apologia pro Ecclesia Anglicana* (*Apology of the Church of England*, 1562) and *Defense of the Apology* (1567) defended the English church against the charge of **heresy**. From **Scripture** and, subordinately, the primitive church Jewel derived a minimalist vision of the essentials of the faith according to which the English church was clearly orthodox. All other aspects of religion he categorized as *adiaphora* to be ordered by the godly prince, obedience to whom in nonessentials was mandated by Scripture and crucial for ecclesiastical order.

Booty (1963); Jenkins (2006); Southgate (1962).

DANIEL EPPLEY

Jews, Judaism The *Reformation* reshaped the Jewish-Christian relationship in important ways, reinforcing old stereotypes and changing some Christian perceptions concerning the Jews and Judaism. Catholics continued to believe that Jews at times committed ritual murder and host desecration, and both Catholics and Protestants agreed that Jews stubbornly rejected the *gospel*. Yet Christians also gained a new appreciation for *Hebrew* and Jewish scholarship and began a new discussion concerning how Jews fit into a Christian society.

Beginning with *Johann Reuchlin*, who published the first reference grammar of Hebrew in 1506, an increasing number of Christians were able to study the Hebrew *Bible* and other Jewish texts in the original language. Hebrew learning was a priority for Protestant theologians committed to the ideal of *sola scriptura*. Together with an increased awareness of contemporary Judaism derived from Antonius Margaritha (d. 1542) and other Jewish convert writers, Christians gained a much more accurate understanding of Judaism as a religion, although they usually saw it in an unflattering light.

Increased access to Jewish literature meant that Christians were able to use information from it in both theology and profane scholarship. More than any other Reformation thinker, *Martin Luther* used the image of the Jew as unbeliever as a central element in his theology. His "chain of iniquity" linked Jews, sectarian Protestants, Catholics, and *Turks* as allies who together sought to overthrow the true *church*. Luther and other Reformation-era polemicists drew upon both the new literature on Judaism and older medieval polemical works in their books. *John Calvin* and other Reformed thinkers stressed the covenantal nature of the church as ancient Israel's successor. The period also saw an increase in the number of Latin translations of Jewish books, including some kabbalistic books by individuals such as Guillaume Postel (1510–81).

In both Catholic and Protestant lands there were renewed discussions of how Jews fit into a Christian society. Among Protestants the most public example of this debate took place in 1538–39, when Landgrave *Philipp of Hesse* considered the terms of Jewish settlement in his lands. *Pope Paul IV* changed the terms of Jewish settlement in Catholic lands with his bull *Cum nimis absurdum* (1555), decreeing that henceforth Jews would be tolerated under much stricter conditions. By the 1580s a number of Italian towns and cities forced their Jewish residents to live in small, densely populated, walled ghettos, which gave them a visible yet isolated place within society. The church also included Jewish books within its regimen of press controls, most notably banning the Talmud in 1553. Catholic authorities used these new measures to pressure Jews to convert, and their measures were moderately successful.

D. Bell and Burnett (2006); Oberman (1984); Ruderman (1992); Stern (1965).

STEPHEN G. BURNETT

John a Lasco (a.k.a. Jan Łaski, John the Younger, Johannes à Lasko; 1499–1560)   Lasco was a Polish leader among the Reformed churches. Educated in Italy, he was ordained in Poland in 1521, serving as a pastor, archdeacon, and titular bishop. In Basel he came to know both humanists and Reformers, including *Desiderius Erasmus*, *Huldrych Zwingli*, and *Johannes Oecolampadius*. After marrying in the Netherlands, he renounced Catholicism in 1540. From 1550 he served as a pastor to exiles in *England*, but under *Mary I* he was himself exiled. Returning to Poland he worked to establish the church along Reformed lines there. His writings included a confession, a *catechism*, and especially the *Forma ac ratio* (Form and Order, 1555), which recorded the church order and liturgy of the London Stranger Church. By these and his personal leadership he had influence in the Low Countries, England, the Palatinate, and Poland.

———

Dalton (1886); Rodgers (1994); Springer (2007).

GARY NEAL HANSEN

John Frederick I, Elector of Saxony (1503–54; r. 1532)   John Frederick was a staunch Lutheran, ruler of Electoral (or Ernestine) Saxony, signatory to the *Augsburg Confession*, and leader of the Protestant military alliance the Schmalkaldic League. By the 1529 Diet of Speyer, John Frederick was playing an increasingly important role in the administration of Saxony. Following the diet, he was instrumental in the foundation of the Schmalkaldic League. Throughout the 1530s and into the 1540s, he worked tirelessly on behalf of the Protestant cause within the *Holy Roman Empire*. In 1547 war broke out between Schmalkaldic League and Emperor *Charles V*. At the Battle of Mühlberg, John Frederick's army suffered a crushing defeat and he was taken prisoner. Originally sentenced to death by Charles V, he was forced to abdicate his electoral office—which was transferred to his cousin Maurice—and his sentence was reduced to life imprisonment. He was freed by Charles in 1552. He died in Weimar.

———

Brecht (vol. 2, 1985–93).

DAVID M. WHITFORD

John of the Cross (1542–91)   A *Discalced Carmelite* and mystic, John was canonized in 1726 and proclaimed Doctor of the Church in 1926. His name at birth was Juan de Yepes y Álvarez. He was initially associated with the *Jesuits*, but was finally enchanted by the *piety* of the Carmelites, formally joining them in 1563. He attended the University of Salamanca from 1564 to 1568. At Salamanca he became thoroughly imbued in the Thomistic tradition of the university. He was ordained to the priesthood in 1567. From 1568 he collaborated with *Teresa of Avila* in the reformation of the Carmelites. In addition to his reform work, John of the Cross contributed to the formation of a distinctively Carmelite mystical tradition, hailed by many as the crowning achievement of early-modern Spanish mysticism. In his writings he used Thomistic categories to refine the spiritual insights of Teresa of Avila.

———

Dombrowski (1992); Swietlicki (1986).

RADY ROLDAN-FIGUEROA

Jud, Leo (1482–1542)   Reformer, translator, and biblical scholar, Jud was born in Alsace and studied at Basel University, where he met the young *Huldrych Zwingli*. Jud became a priest before coming to the Benedictine Abbey of Einsiedeln when Zwingli was called to Zurich. Jud was a talented humanist and profoundly influenced by *Desiderius Erasmus*, whose works, in particular the Pauline paraphrases, he translated into German. Jud joined Zwingli in Zurich as the preacher in

St. Peter's Church and worked closely with him in establishing the *Reformation* in the city, drawing up the first Reformed baptismal liturgy. After Zwingli's death Jud remained a minister in the city but devoted himself to translations of works such as *Augustine*'s *De spiritu et litera*, Thomas à Kempis's *Imitation of Christ*, and Erasmus's works. He was closely involved in the vernacular translations of the *Bible* that appeared in Zurich during the 1520s and 1530s, and he translated the Old Testament into Latin for the Zurich Bible of 1543.

Gordon (2002); Potter (1976).

BRUCE GORDON

Julius II, Pope (1443–1513; r. 1503–13)

Born Giuliano della Rovere, Julius became one of the greatest pontifical patrons of the arts and strongest defenders of Rome's temporal kingdom in the entire early modern period. His uncle, who reigned as Sixtus IV from 1471, greatly advanced the young man's career, raising him to be a cardinal and granting him many rich benefices. Julius himself took the throne in 1503, and immediately set about safeguarding the temporal power of the *papacy*. He conducted several wars, forcing various Italian states to submit to papal claims. Simultaneously, he set about increasing the majesty of the Vatican, with a program of art patronage that recognized the work of Raphael, Michelangelo, and Bramante. He began the work of rebuilding St. Peter's Basilica in 1506, and thus indirectly affected the course of the later Protestant movement. While Julius was successful in many of his endeavors, he was not universally admired. *Desiderius Erasmus* wrote a scathing indictment of his warrior style in his *Moriae Encomium* (*Praise of Folly*).

Chambers (2006); Felix (1980).

R. WARD HOLDER

Junius Brutus

Junius Brutus is the pseudepigraphical name of the author of the 1579 tract *Vindiciae contra tyrannos*. The name is an allusion to Marcus Junius Brutus, one of the Roman senators who took part in the assassination of Julius Caesar in an attempt to save the Roman Republic. The most likely author is Philippe du Plessis Mornay (1549–1623), a minor French aristocrat, survivor of the *St. Bartholomew's Day Massacre* in 1572, and Protestant polemicist. A less likely possibility is Hubert Lanuet (1518–81), a French diplomat. The *Vindiciae* is part of a group of treatises and tracts written by French Protestants following the St. Bartholomew's Day Massacre on the right to resist secular authorities such as the king. The *Vindiciae* is divided into four sections framed as questions. Section one considers when one may resist a ruler who commands something contrary to the *law* of God. Section two asks whether one may resist a leader who violates God's law. Question three (the longest section) considers for whom, how, and by what right resistance is possible. The final section considers whether foreign rulers might aid those who resist.

E. Barker (1930).

DAVID M. WHITFORD

Justification

The doctrine of justification was one of the central points on which the emerging Protestant movement challenged the standard theology of the late medieval church. Medieval Western theologians, following *Augustine*, had defined *justificatio* as the act by which God makes human beings righteous, although this act was understood differently by different traditions of medieval theology. In the second decade of the sixteenth century, the Augustinian friar *Martin Luther* developed a theology of justification by *faith* alone, which was further developed by *Philip Melanchthon* and became the cornerstone for other Protestant soteriologies. According to the Lutheran view, God imputes the righteousness of Christ to those who abandon the effort to make themselves acceptable to God and trust only in God's promise. This view rested on a sharp distinction between *Law* (God's commands) and *Gospel* (God's promises), according to which the Law's condemnation drives us to the Gospel. Furthermore, while the Lutheran position drew on Augustine's doctrine of human depravity and his emphasis on the sovereignty of God's *grace*, it broke with the Augustinian tradition by making a sharp distinction between justification (God's declaration that human beings are righteous) and *sanctification* (the processes of being transformed by God's *grace*).

Huldrych Zwingli claimed to have developed the doctrine of justification by faith independently of Luther. However, Zwingli's account differs from Luther's by subordinating faith to *predestination*. According to Zwingli, one can be saved without faith by virtue of God's electing grace, which brings forth fruit in the form of *good works* and (when the gospel is heard) faith. Later Reformed theologians moved closer to the Lutheran position, leading to *John Calvin*'s synthesis in the *Institutes*. Nonetheless, Reformed theology continued to teach that regeneration preceded justification, and to ground saving faith in a confidence in God's electing grace. This allowed the Reformed to link good works closely with justification, since the same God who had predestined believers would ensure that they persevered in good works.

The language of justification by faith, without the precise definitions Lutheran theology assigned to the concept, was common among reform-minded humanists in the early sixteenth century. Reformist Catholics such as *Gasparo Cardinal Contarini* supported the compromise proposal of "double justification," drawn up by Catholic and Protestant negotiators at the *Regensburg*

Colloquy of 1541. In this proposal, justification begins with God's gracious imputation of Christ's righteousness to believers, followed by a lifelong process of sanctification in which God's grace transforms believers into holy people, and completed by the final *imputation* of Christ's righteousness in order to cover the remaining defects in the believer's holiness. Double justification was regarded with suspicion by Luther and rejected by the *Council of Trent*. Instead, Trent affirmed that the work of the *Holy Spirit* in the lives of believers was a sufficient and meritorious ground for their final acceptance by God.

By the end of the sixteenth century, the differences between Lutherans and Reformed had been reduced to nuances (if they had ever been more), but the differences between Protestants and Catholics had become matters of hardened polemic. Within Protestantism, "justification by faith alone" had come to be accepted as the pillar of the *Reformation*, a confessional self-understanding that obscured the nuances and hesitations of the historical record, even as it opened the door to further debate over just what the slogan meant within Protestanism.

Althaus (1966); McGrath (2005); Oberman (1992).

EDWIN WOODRUFF TAIT

Karlstadt, Andreas Bodenstein von (1486–1541)

A theologian and reformer, Karlstadt was dean at Wittenberg when *Martin Luther* received his doctorate there (1512). Initially a scholastic, he came to appreciate *Augustine* at the urging of Luther. As a result, Karlstadt published 151 Theses on Law and Grace several months before Luther's Ninety-Five Theses. During the *Leipzig Disputation* (1519), Karlstadt debated with *Johann Eck* regarding the human *will*. In 1521 Karlstadt presided over the first *"evangelical" mass*. Karlstadt's break with Luther was heralded by the Wittenberg "iconoclasm controversy" of 1522. Here Karlstadt urged the removal of images from Wittenberg's churches, a move that Luther opposed and that had the ultimate effect of sidelining Karlstadt from his teaching post. Because of his disenchantment with infant *baptism*, Karlstadt has been considered an *Anabaptist*. However, he moved to Switzerland and ultimately associated himself with the Swiss Reformed rather than with more "radical" Reformers.

Barge (2005); Sider (1974, 2001); Zorzin (1990).

HANS WIERSMA

Keys, Power of   The power of the keys refers to the *authority* to forgive and retain sins that Christ bestowed on his disciples (Matt. 18:18; John 20:22–23), and specifically on Peter (Matt. 16:19), in the Gospels. Protestants objected to the late medieval understanding of this authority, believing it should not be confined to ordained priests in the *sacrament* of *penance*. Protestants also objected to the way this authority had been used in the Middle Ages to argue for the supremacy of the *papacy* over temporal rulers. However, Protestants did not achieve a unified *evangelical* theology of the keys. Most agreed that all Christians possessed this authority but they disagreed on how it was to be exercised. Lutherans retained a modified version of private *confession* in which their pastors exercised the keys, while Reformed Protestants identified this authority with the public *preaching* of the gospel. *Anabaptists* opted for a communal exercise of the keys.

Rittgers (2004); Tentler (1977); Thayer (2002).

RONALD K. RITTGERS

Kingdom of God   *Martin Luther* argued for the kingdom of God through the dual but competing kingdoms of Christ and the world (or the devil). Christians are citizens of both. While God will ultimately heal and redeem the world through the kingdom of Christ, God presently rules over the two spheres independently of one another. God's reign, then, is over both secular and spiritual realms. *Huldrych Zwingli* emphasized the kingdom of God through humanity. Thus the *Holy Spirit*'s work in humans benefits the state. Christians then advance the state through citizenship and service. *John Calvin* saw the kingdom of God progressively through creation, the *church*, and finally through God's eschatological kingdom. The Christian must sojourn in this broken world until its final consummation, and the state should never violate God's laws or restrict true religion. Finally, the *Anabaptists* viewed the divine kingdom ecclesiologically, thus requiring the Anabaptist faith community's separation from government-sponsored institutions and churches.

Friedmann (1998); Fuhrmann (1951); Van Wyk (2001).

BRIAN C. BREWER

Knox, John (ca. 1514–72)   Born near Edinburgh, Knox was a Scottish reformer, often known as the founder of Scottish Presbyterianism. He was ordained a priest in 1536, but by 1544 had embraced Protestantism. Soon after becoming a Protestant preacher, Knox was imprisoned as a French galley slave from 1547 to 1549. After his release, he spent the next four years in Edward VI's England and became known for his radical biblicism and anti-Catholic liturgical views. With the ascension of *Mary I* to the throne in 1553, Knox fled England and by 1555 took refuge in Geneva, where he served as a pastor of a congregation from 1556 to 1559. He returned to Scotland in 1559 and fought for the Protestant cause in Scotland for his remaining years, which often brought him into conflict with the Catholic Mary Stuart (**Mary Queen of Scots**), who had returned to rule Scotland from 1561 to 1567. Knox died in Edinburgh on November 24, 1572.

Knox's theological contributions include his pamphlet *The First Blast of the Trumpet Against the Monstrous Regiment of Women* (1558), which argued that the rule of women in general (and in **England** and Scotland in particular) was "unnatural" and an abomination in the eyes of God. He later wrote *The History of the Reformation of Religion in Scotland* (1586/87), which recounted the events of the Scottish **Reformation**, argued for Scotland's covenanted significance, and appealed against accepting Catholic rule. Furthermore, Knox helped shape key documents of the Scottish Reformation, including the **Scots Confession** of Faith (1560) and the *First Book of Discipline* (1561). Key theological concepts of Knox's work include an emphasis on divine sovereignty, the sole *authority* of *Scripture*, resistance against idolatry (particularly in its Catholic forms), and the responsibility of civil authorities to help establish pure religion.

Kyle (2002); R. Marshall (2000); Mason, ed. (1998).

G. SUJIN PAK

Las Casas, Bartolomé de (1484–1566)

Las Casas was a *Dominican* priest, a bishop of the diocese of Chiapas in New Spain (modern-day Mexico), and an eventual crusader for the rights of native peoples after watching their annihilation by Christian settlers. Born in Seville, Las Casas could have witnessed the return of Christopher Columbus from the Indies in 1493. His father, Pedro, accompanied Columbus on his second voyage, returning home in 1498. Las Casas himself accompanied the expedition of Nicolás de Ovando to the Indies in 1502. He was ordained in Hispaniola in 1510. Though he carries

the title of the "Apostle to the Indies," Las Casas himself took part in the Spanish plantation system, called the *encomienda* system. Under this system, colonists were awarded both colonies to cultivate as large plantations, and native slaves to work the land. In exchange, the colonists were supposed to pay the Indians a modest wage and give them Christian instruction. The treatment of the native peoples was particularly brutal, and Las Casas would later write that he had seen cruelty on a scale that no living person had ever seen.

Moved by the inhumanity of the *encomienda* system and knowledgeable because of his own firsthand experience with it, Las Casas sought to foster changes in the system, appealing to the crown and to local authorities. From 1515 to 1522 he worked for reform, envisioning a utopian experiment where colonists and Native Americans would live side by side in peaceful coexistence. He managed to establish a colony of Carib Indians at a colony near Cumaná on the Venezuelan coast, where he prohibited the slavery practices that were common to other colonies. This effort ended horribly: while Las Casas was away from the colony, a group of Spanish colonists went slave raiding. The Caribs attacked in response, and some of Las Casas's people were killed. Las Casas's opponents would later use this episode as proof of the necessity of quelling native peoples by military force.

Bitter, Las Casas withdrew from society and entered the Dominican order in 1523. He became an ardent supporter of the rights of native peoples. He began to write apologetic books that defended native peoples and demonstrated the failure of colonial policies. His most widely read was probably the pamphlet *A Brief Account of the Destruction of the Indies* (*Brevísima relación de la destruición de las Indias*), published in 1552. This attacked the viciousness of the Spanish colonial practices, and held up to ridicule the Spanish claims of christianizing influence. As an alternative to native slavery, Las Casas for a time supported the idea of importing African slaves, an idea he later repudiated.

Back in Spain in 1550, Las Casas became embroiled in a dispute with Juan Ginés de Sepúlveda. Sepúlveda argued that the native peoples were inherently inferior, and needed to be controlled by the superior European Christians, positions that Las Casas denied on both biblical and philosophical grounds. At his death in Spain in 1566, he had not accomplished his goals of Christian treatment of native peoples, but had sown the seeds of Christian protest against such exploitation.

Friede and Keen (1971); Hanke (1994); Parish and Sullivan (1992).

R. WARD HOLDER

Lateran   Councils Five church councils (known as Lateran I, II, etc.) met between 1139 and 1517 at the Lateran basilica (the historic cathedral church of the pope as bishop of Rome). They are recognized in the Catholic Church as having ecumenical status (i.e., as ecumenical councils 9–12 and 18). The most significant is surely Lateran IV (1215). Convened under Pope Innocent III, the council affirmed *transubstantiation* and required all Christians who had reached the age of reason to participate annually in the *sacraments* of *penance* and Eucharist. Lateran V was convened in 1512 by *Julius II* and closed by *Leo X* in 1517, just months before *Martin Luther's* protest over *indulgences*. The council has usually been considered a decisive defeat for the conciliarist movement. Although it dealt broadly with moral reform and *heresy*, it was ineffectual enough to leave the church vulnerable to humanist and Protestant criticisms.

Duggan and Minnich (2003); Headley (1973); Oakley (1972).

MICKEY L. MATTOX

Latimer, Hugh (ca. 1485–1555) Educated at Cambridge, from 1529 onward Latimer preached against the *papacy, purgatory,* and *superstition.* He won patronage from *Henry VIII,* engaged in his own antipapal campaign. By 1533 he had emerged as the greatest English preacher of his generation, stirring up fervor and opposition wherever he went. He was made bishop of Worcester in 1535, and pursued *evangelical* reforms against considerable opposition. His rejection of the 1539 Act of Six Articles cost him his bishopric, and he withdrew to semiretirement until Edward VI's accession. Then he reemerged as the regime's champion preacher (and sometimes, friendly critic), linking evangelical reform to social justice; he refused a second bishopric. Imprisoned on *Mary I's* accession, he was tried and burned for *heresy* in 1555. His attributed last words—"We shall this day light such a candle by God's grace in England, as (I trust) shall never be put out"—are probably apocryphal.

Loades (1970); O'Day (1992); Wabuda (1998).

ALEC RYRIE

Law The Protestant reformers utilized conventional definitions of law inherited from the classical and Christian traditions. However, they devoted considerable attention to the functions of the law in the life of the Christian and of the community. For *Martin Luther,* the law has a civil or political use that serves to restrain human sinfulness so that people may be able to live together peaceably in society. The best articulation of civil law can be found in the Old Testament, but Luther also praised aspects of other legal systems, such as that of the Ottoman *Turks.* The spiritual function of the law was to demonstrate absolutely the human inability to achieve salvific righteousness. In this sense Law directly contrasts with *Gos-*

pel and its message of forgiveness. *John Calvin* agreed, but included a third use of the law that shows believers the path to *sanctification* and helps to foster *good works*.

Althaus (1966); Ebeling (1970); Hesselink (1992); Lohse (1986); Wendel (1997).
GREGORY J. MILLER

Lefèvre d'Étaples, Jacques *See* **Stapulensis, Faber**

Leipzig Disputation A series of academic disputations were held at Leipzig between June 27 and July 16, 1519, hosted by Duke Georg of Albertine Saxony. The Catholic side was represented by *Johann Eck* of the University of Ingolstadt; his opponents were *Andreas Bodenstein von Karlstadt* and *Martin Luther*. The disputation began with a debate between Eck and Karlstadt on the question of *free will* and *grace*. Luther and Eck were involved in two debates, July 4–14 and 15–16. In the course of the debates, Luther expanded on three points. First, he stressed that papal *authority* derived not from God but from human consent. Consequently, papal authority was not infallible. Second, the Roman Church was not superior to any other church in Christendom. Third, *Scripture* must be considered the ultimate authority in matters of faith. For his part, Eck stressed the similarities between Luther's positions and those of the condemned heresiarchs *John Wyclif* and *Jan Hus*. Eck's arguments led to the condemnation and burning of Luther's works at the universities of Cologne, Louvain, and Paris.

Bagchi (1991); Ziegler (1969).
WILLIAM BRADFORD SMITH

Leo X, Pope (1475–1521; r. 1513–21) Named at birth Giovanni, Leo was born to the powerful and affluent family of de Medici. For long he was known as the epitome of the kind of moral corruption of the *papacy* that prompted *Martin Luther*'s protest against the abuse of *indulgences*. He became cardinal at the ripe young age of thirteen. His abuses and the construction of St. Peter's demanded increasing amounts of wealth, leading to the spread of the selling of indulgences. He initially tried to contain the Luther affair by handling it as a local development limited in its implications for the church. Leo, however, changed his approach as it became clear that Luther's criticism was far reaching. On June 15, 1520, he issued the bull *Exsurge Domine* condemning the teachings of Luther. Alternative assessments of his pontificate call attention to his role as patron of the arts.

Doak (2006); Duffy (2006); Vaughan (1971).
RADY ROLDAN-FIGUEROA

Liberal Arts The seven liberal arts consist of the trivium of language arts (grammar, rhetoric, and dialectic) and the quadrivium of mathematical arts (arithmetic, geometry, astronomy, and music). The term "art" indicates a systematic study, while "liberal" marks these particular studies (as opposed to the mechanical arts) as the province of free choice. The foundations of these studies were developed in antiquity, while their codification was brought about through the efforts of fifth- and sixth-century scholars Martianus Capella, Boethius, and Cassiodorus. Early Christian authors such as *Augustine* and Jerome were ambivalent about pagan learning, yet the arts curriculum came to be the basis for university *education* in the High Middle Ages. Scholars of the early medieval period focused primarily on grammar (the analysis of both language and literature), which yielded to *dialectic* (systematic logic) in the High Middle Ages, while

Renaissance humanists gave primacy to *rhetoric* (the art of persuasion).

Abelson (1906); Wagner (1983).

J. LAUREL CARRINGTON

Libertine   In the sixteenth century "Libertine" first refers to a Protestant sect that *John Calvin* deemed heretical because of its pantheistic determinism, immoral character, and spiritualized *eschatology* that denied Christ's resurrection. Calvin initially used this term to refer to the Quintinists, a French-speaking group led by Quintin of Hainut and his followers Bertrand of Moulins, Claude Perceval, and Anthony Pocquet. In 1545 Calvin wrote a treatise against them entitled *Contre la secte phantastique et furieuse des Libertins que se nomments Spirtuels (Against the Fantastic and Furious Sect of the Libertines Who Call Themselves Spiritualists)*. Calvin later (1546–55) used this term to refer to a Genevan group led by Ami Perrin and the Favre family, who objected to Calvin's conceptions of church discipline. Historians have generally emphasized a sharp distinction between the "Libertines" of Geneva and the Quintinists. In the Dutch *Reformation*, "Libertines" referred to those who rejected Calvinist ecclesiastical discipline.

Farley (1982); Kaplan (1995); G. H. Williams (1992).

G. SUJIN PAK

Limbo   Limbo refers to a "place" in the afterlife, distinct from heaven, hell, and *purgatory*, free from suffering, but apart from the presence of God. As a Vatican commission confirmed in 2007, limbo was never a formally defined part of Catholic teaching, but a tradition that took root over the course of the Middle Ages. Most understood there to be two limbos: a *limbus infantium* for the souls of children dying before *baptism*, and a *limbus patrum* for the prophets and virtuous pagans who had lived before the incarnation. Limbo was an attempt to square God's justice with his mercy. Only baptized Christians could be admitted to heaven, but it was inconceivable that God would torment in hell for eternity the souls of newborn babies. Protestant reformers scoffed at limbo as a piece of unscriptural fantasy, but they had their own problems explaining to bereaved parents the likely fate of their dead infants.

Le Goff (1984); P. Marshall (2002).

PETER MARSHALL

Loci Communes   The *Loci Communes (rerum theologicarum)* was the first systematic presentation of *Reformation* theology, published in 1521 by *Philip Melanchthon*, the brilliant young humanist and theologian who had been appointed professor of *Greek* at the University of Wittenberg in 1518. It was intended to replace *Peter Lombard's Sentences*, which had been the standard theology text for over three hundred years. The term *loci communes* is translated as "commonplaces," but its meaning is richer. *Desiderius Erasmus* used it to refer to the "basic concepts" by means of which one could understand a text. Melanchthon applied this method to the problem of identifying the scriptural order for presenting Christian theology, taking the basic concepts of Paul's Letter to the Romans as the outline for his *Loci*, though he later had to add the doctrine of God and *Christology*. Melanchthon's commentaries typically consist of the identification of a text's loci, suggesting a dynamic relationship between *exegesis*, theology, and *preaching*.

Wengert (1998); Wengert and Graham (1999).

MICKEY L. MATTOX

Lord's Supper (Eucharist, Communion)   The *sacrament* of the

Lord's Supper, intended to express Christian unity, became the most divisive issue of the *Reformation*, drawing sharp lines between Catholic and Protestant, between Lutheran and Reformed, and to some degree even within Lutheran and Reformed camps.

In Catholic theology Christ was understood to be bodily present. As expressed in the doctrine of *transubstantiation*, what was brought in as bread and wine was changed in its very substance, becoming the body and blood of Christ. Since Christ was fully present in either element, the laity could be given Communion "in one kind," receiving the consecrated bread, or host, without the consecrated wine. The priest was understood to be presenting the sacrifice of Christ anew at every *Mass*, an offering made to God with intercessory power. Christ was understood to remain present even after the Mass, and could be adored in an uneaten host.

Martin Luther objected to all of this, notably in his 1520 treatise *De Captivitate Babylonica Ecclesiae* (*The Babylonian Captivity of the Church*). He argued that transubstantiation was unsound theology, being based on *Aristotle* rather than the *Bible*. Jesus had said specifically that all the disciples should drink from the cup, and so Communion in one kind was not acceptable. Christ's sacrifice was once for all, and so sacrificial language was inappropriate for the Mass. Luther himself was adamant that Christ was indeed physically present in the Eucharist because Jesus had said in the words of institution, "This is my body." The importance of the sacrament was its communication of the *gospel* promise of forgiveness of sins. Though he did not use the term, his understanding of Christ's presence has been called "*consubstantiation*" because the substance of Christ is present with the substance of the bread and wine.

Huldrych Zwingli and others met with Luther at the *Marburg Colloquy* in 1529 to seek Protestant unity. They were able to agree on everything but the Eucharist. The Reformed argued that the words "This is my body" should be read metaphorically and that one should instead emphasize Jesus' command in the same words of institution, "Do this in remembrance of me." Christ could not be bodily present in the earthly celebrations of the Supper, because he had ascended into heaven and was bodily present there. The Supper was for spiritual meditation, remembering Christ's work on our behalf.

John Calvin put the emphasis on a third portion of the words of institution: the body and blood are given "for you." Here he found the very personal promise of the *grace* of Christ. Christ is present, but spiritually rather than physically, and one should emphasize the gifts of spiritual nourishment and union symbolized in the elements.

T. Davis (2008); Rempel (1993); Wandel (2006).

GARY NEAL HANSEN

Love   Love is one of the three theological virtues recognized by the Christian *church* (alongside faith and hope). Protestant reformers modified prior theologies of love by placing *faith* as the primary virtue (despite 1 Cor. 13:13). They accomplished this in at least three important ways. First, Protestant reformers challenged the scholastic theology of love, which viewed love as an infused, uncreated virtue synonymous with God's *grace*. Such scholastics argued that humans are able to love God above all else by their own natural capacity. In contrast, *Martin Luther* and *John Calvin* argued that the gift of faith must be given before a habit of love can be acquired. Second, Protestant theologians redefined the fall not in terms of *Augustine*'s disordered loves but in terms of faith and unbelief. Third, the Protestant reformers emphasized that faith belongs to a believer's relationship to God, while love belongs to the believer's relationship with the neighbor; hence love became a fruit of faith. *Anabaptists* differed from Lutheran and Reformed views by retaining the primacy of love above faith.

Estep (1996); Kärkkäinen (2004).

G. SUJIN PAK

Low Countries The Low Countries comprised present-day Belgium, the Netherlands, and Luxembourg. This low-lying region belonged to the *Holy Roman Empire* during the Middle Ages. Divided by the Rhine, Scheldt, and Maas rivers, the area remained politically fragmented and linguistically diverse. Anglo-Saxon missionaries introduced Christianity in the 600s. Through intermarriage, Burgundy came into possession of the area in the early 1400s, as did the Habsburg dynasty at the century's end. A motley band of nobles, regents, and Calvinist partisans revolted in 1568 against the absolutist and **Counter-Reformation** policies of the Habsburgs. This war ended formally in 1648, affirming the independence of the northern provinces, the Dutch Republic, and the loyalty of the southern Spanish Netherlands to the Habsburgs. The Republic adopted Calvinism while the south remained Catholic. After French occupation (1795–1814) in the French Revolution, a united Kingdom of the Netherlands emerged briefly until 1831, when the south (Belgium) gained independence.

Arblaster (2006); Blom (1998); Israel (1995).

CHARLES PARKER

Luther, Martin (1483–1546) Luther was born on November 10, 1483, in Eisleben, Germany. He enrolled at the University of Erfurt in 1501. In July 1505 he entered the Augustinian monastery at Erfurt. The decision to enter the monastery was a difficult one. He was caught between his desire to please his parents and continue his education in law and his own desire to find salvation. The young Luther was haunted by insecurity (*Anfechtung*) about his salvation.

In 1511 he transferred from the monastery in Erfurt to one in **Wittenberg**, where, after receiving his doctor of theology degree, he became a professor of biblical theology at the newly founded University of Wittenberg.

In 1517 he posted a sheet of theses for discussion on the university's chapel door. The Ninety-Five Theses were a critique of *indulgences*. In Rome the Theses were regarded as an attack on papal *authority*.

Over the next two years, Luther continued to develop his theological outlook on the doctrine of *justification* by *faith*. In 1520 he published three significant treatises explaining his theology: *To the Christian Nobility of the German Nation, On the Freedom of a Christian,* and *On the Babylonian Captivity of the Church*. Through these treatises, Luther's mature theological perspective on salvation, *grace*, and authority within the church become apparent—often called the "three *solas*," *sola gratia* (solely grace), *sola fidei* (solely faith), *sola scriptura* (solely according to Scripture). Also in 1520 *Pope Leo X* promulgated the bull *Exsurge Domini (Arise O Lord)*, which threatened Luther with excommunication. Luther received the bull in October and publically burned it in December.

In January 1521 the pope excommunicated Luther. In March he was summoned by Emperor **Charles V** to Worms to defend himself. During the **Diet of Worms**, Luther refused to recant his position. At the conclusion of the diet, Luther was placed under imperial **ban**. He spent the next year in hiding at the Wartburg Castle. While in the Wartburg, he translated the New Testament into German. In May 1522 he returned to Wittenberg and began teaching again. In 1524 Luther left the monastery.

The year 1525 was eventful: he married Katharina von Bora; he first attempted to mediate a solution to the *Peasants' War,* and when those attempts failed he issued a diatribe against the violent uprising—*Against the Murdering Hordes of the Other Peasants*; and he participated in a famous written debate with *Desiderius Erasmus* on the nature of human freedom and the power of *sin*. In the late 1520s he wrote his Large and Short Catechisms, and in preparation for an imperial diet in 1530 he helped provide the framework for what would become the *Augsburg Confession*. During the 1530s he provided leadership within the emerging *evangelical* churches in Germany and continued to teach within the university. He died in 1546.

Brecht (1985–93); Oberman (1989).

DAVID M. WHITFORD

Magdeburg Centuries The *Magdeburg Centuries*, or *Ecclesiastica Historia, integram Ecclesiae Christi idea . . . secundum singulas Centurias . . . per aliquot studiosos & pios viros in urbe Magdeburgica* (*An Ecclesiastical History . . .* ordered by centuries . . . according to devoted and pious men from the city of Magdeburg), is the first comprehensive attempt at writing the history of the church since Eusebius. In 1559, in Basel, the first volume of what would ultimately grow to thirteen volumes was published. It begins in the first century and ends in the thirteenth. Matthias Flacius Illyricus, a staunch Lutheran polemicist and scholar, organized a small group of scholars who have come to be called the Magdeburg Centuriators. The *Centuries* are history written from a Protestant perspective. They remain important not only for what they say about early Protestant understandings of the Christian *church* but also because of the large number of historical texts that are preserved within their volumes.

Diener (1979); Whitford (2001).

DAVID M. WHITFORD

Magic In early modern Europe the line between magic, religion, and daily ritual was indistinct. Building on ancient, pseudo-ancient, Arab, and Jewish sources, intellectuals such as Cornelius Agrippa and Marsilio Ficino distinguished between natural and unnatural magic: natural magic used natural objects in wondrous ways, creating marvels, while unnatural magic used spirits to create false and artificial phenomena. Both Catholic and Protestant intellectuals increasingly condemned practitioners of ritual magic in the sixteenth century as consorting with demons. Despite such attacks, magic continued to be practiced throughout early modern European society. Amulets were used to protect travelers, livestock, and entrances to homes; charms could enhance a crop's yield or cause a broken bone to mend more quickly; and magicians were regular members of court or characters in courtly literature. "Cunning folk" were widely consulted and combined magic, herbology, psychology, and Christianity to find lost objects, cure people from common illnesses, and advise individuals on personal relationships.

Kieckhefer (1990); Walker (2000); S. Wilson (2000).

KATHRYN A. EDWARDS

Magistrates Magistrates were government officials or civil rulers. Their support was considered integral to the extent and speed of religious reforms during the early modern period. In the process, the Christian understanding of how Christians ought to relate to the government came into question. Citing the biblical warrant of Romans 13, most Protestant confessions considered magistrates as legitimate instruments of an earthly kingdom and appointed to serve the good of the community, even if by force. Lutheran and Reformed thinkers upheld the rights of rulers, permitted Christians to serve as magistrates, and argued that magistrates not only care for the welfare of the civil state but also protect the sacred ministry of the *church*. Meanwhile *Anabaptists* denied that the magisterial authority extended to Christ's spiritual kingdom and to members of his church, because Christ was the only true Christian magistrate and temporal authorities could not act as Christians, especially when they were involved in violence.

Hsia (1988); McClendon (1999); Urry (2006).

ESTHER CHUNG-KIM

Marburg Colloquy   The Marbug Colloquy was a meeting of theologians from German-speaking lands on October 1–4, 1529, facilitated by Landgrave *Philipp of Hesse*. Since 1525, *Martin Luther* and *Huldrych Zwingli* had become increasingly acrimonious in print over the presence of Christ in the *Lord's Supper*. Luther argued that Christ's words of institution, "This is my body," should be understood literally, while Zwingli argued that this scripture should be interpreted to mean, "This signifies my body." For both sides the issue was of critical importance, as it was symptomatic of significant differences in hermeneutics and soteriology. By bringing together theologians from both sides, Philipp hoped to forge a united *evangelical* theological union that could serve as the basis for a political alliance among evangelical estates in the empire. From the beginning the meeting was marred by mutual dislike and suspicion between Luther and Zwingli. The colloquy concluded without theological consensus and illustrates the splintering of the early *Reformation*.

Bornkamm (1983); Brecht (vol. 2, 1985–93); Lindberg (1996); Stephens (1986).

GREGORY J. MILLER

Marguerite de Navarre (1492–1549)   Born Marguerite d'Angoulême,

she married Henry of Albret, king of Navarre, in 1527. She was sister to Francis I of France (1494–1547; r. 1515–47), mother of Jeanne d'Albret of Navarre (1528–72; r. 1555–72), and grandmother of *Henri IV* of France (1553–1610), who converted from his Reformed faith prior to taking the throne. She had enormous influence, negotiating for her brother's release from captivity in 1525 and providing protection for humanists and Reformers, including *Faber Stapulensis*.

Though influenced by Lutheranism and Calvinism, her mystical faith was also shaped by teachings the Protestants would condemn. One of her works, *Le miroir de l'âme pécheresse* (*The Mirror of the Sinful Soul*), was condemned by the Sorbonne, though she remained officially Catholic. She also wrote a cycle of fictional stories known as *The Heptameron*, and *Les Prisons* (*The Prisons of Marguerite de Navarre*), which poetically details her mysticism.

Cholakian and Cholakian (2006); Cottrell (1986); Thysell (2000).

GARY NEAL HANSEN

Marian Exiles (1553–58)   When *Mary I* Tudor ascended the English throne in 1553, she returned *England* to the Roman Catholic religion that the country had worshiped before the English *Reformation* of her father, King *Henry VIII*, in 1534. Although originally not overly antagonistic to those who embraced Protestantism, soon Mary began to persecute certain Protestants within her kingdom. As a result, many of those who believed in the new faith fled England for the Continent, where they resided in cities from Frankfurt to Geneva. While away from England, these exiles, including *John Knox*, *Miles Coverdale*, John Foxe, and others, increased their ties to the continental Reformers, including *John Calvin* and *Theodore de Beza*, and they brought many important ideas upon their return to England after Mary's death in 1558.

The theology of the Marian exiles helped to shape the doctrine of the Elizabethan church and influenced the development of the English radical religions and Scottish Presbyterianism.

Danner (1999); Garrett (1938); M. Simpson (1978).

KRISTEN POST WALTON

Marpeck, Pilgram (ca. 1495–1556)

A native of Tyrol and the son of a city councilman in Rattenberg, Austria, Marpeck was a mining magistrate who became a significant *Anabaptist* leader, social radical, and civil engineer in south Germany. As a mining magistrate, Marpeck was required by Archduke Ferdinand to report miners who were sympathetic to Anabaptism. Upon the execution of the Anabaptist preacher Leonhart Schiemer, however, Marpeck resigned his magistrate's office and forfeited his substantial estate, moving to Bohemia and Moravia to become an Anabaptist elder. By the late 1520s he served *Strasbourg* as a lumbering supervisor and led an Anabaptist group associated with the Swiss Brethren. He later moved to Switzerland and traveled through Tyrol, Moravia, and south Germany, establishing churches through the region while debating *Caspar Schwenckfeld* and *Martin Bucer*. After 1544 Marpeck served as city engineer in Augsburg, subsidized Anabaptist publications, and led an Anabaptist community that met in his home.

Boyd (1992); W. Klassen (1968); Klaassen and Klassen (2008).

BRIAN C. BREWER

Marriage

Protestant reformers rejected clerical *celibacy*, instead elevating the state of marriage as the best possible model for faithful Christians. In response, Roman Catholics attacked the Protestant practice of clerical marriage as a violation of scriptural teachings. While Protestants no longer recognized marriage as a *sacrament*, they rejected the practice of clandestine marriages, insisting that engagements had to be announced at church services, that children needed parental consent to marry, and that weddings had to be performed by ministers, in a church. Church and secular leaders attempted to restrict the size and cost of wedding celebrations, as well as the myriad related "superstitious" customs. Protestants taught that husbands and wives were spiritual equals but that in the earthly relationship of marriage the husband was the head of the household. At the same time, they emphasized husbands' obligation to treat their wives with love and respect, although this could be a difficult ideal to enforce.

Carlson (1994); Harrington (1995); Karant-Nunn (1997); Wiesner (2008); Witte (1997).

KAREN E. SPIERLING

Martyrdom

From the Greek for witnessing or a witness, the term "martyr" was first applied to the apostles as the witnesses of Christ's life and resurrection (Acts 1:8, 22). As persecution of the early Christian movement grew, martyrs were identified as those who suffered for the faith, and eventually the designation was reserved for those who gave their lives. The classic age of Christian martyrs came before Constantine's legalization of Christianity in the Roman Empire (313), especially during the reign of Diocletian. Increasingly in the early church martyrs were venerated as *saints* and intercessors with God: the anniversaries of their deaths were observed as feasts, their *relics* were sought, and stories of their lives were widely read and embellished with legends.

The legalization of Christianity and its subsequent role as the official religion of the empire limited opportunities for orthodox Christians to die heroically for the faith. By the late Middle Ages, martyrdom had become for Western Christendom a "frontier phenomenon," associated primarily with missionaries and pilgrims to hostile lands. Nonetheless, stories of the martyrs remained popular, and in late medieval *piety* most Christians identified martyrdom increasingly with patient suffering, dying well, and devotion to Christ's passion. In late medieval Europe, those dying heroically for the faith and being celebrated in that role were more often sectarian heretics persecuted by the church than its faithful members.

Matters changed dramatically with the coming of the *Reformation*, the division of Europe into contending confessions, and institution of official religious persecution on a large scale within Christendom. Although the numbers of those martyred for religious beliefs in early modern Europe may seem small by most standards—recent estimates suggest around five thousand martyrs—their impact on the age and its developments was significant. By the mid-sixteenth century elaborate martyrological traditions developed to interpret these deaths. Catholic martyrs were venerated in a vast array of visual images, liturgical martyrologies, hagiographical collections, and narrative pamphlets. Likely better known are the great Protestant martyrologies: Ludwig Rabus's *History of God's Chosen Witnesses, Confessors, and Martyrs* (8 vols., 1552–58), Jean Crespin's *History of the Martyrs* (1st ed. 1554), Adriaen Cornelis van Haemstede's *History and Deaths of the Devout Martyrs* (1st ed. 1559), and John Foxe's *Actes and Monuments* (1st ed. 1563). A distinct *Anabaptist* martyrological tradition culminated in the 1685 edition of Thieleman van Braght's *Martyrs Mirror*.

Within these distinct martyrological traditions, correct doctrine became the most important criterion for distinguishing between true and false martyrs. Consequently, martyrologies were crucial in the creation of antagonistic, contending religious communities in early modern Europe and in ensuring that religious toleration was not a policy option in the early years of *confessionalization*.

—————
Gregory (1999); Kolb (1987); Wood (1993).
GEOFFREY DIPPLE

Mary   The Reformers' emphasis on faith in Jesus Christ as sole mediator of salvation meant that *prayer* and adoration should not be directed to Mary. Thus in the *Reformation* churches the image of Jesus' mother tilted sharply away from the medieval one of powerful intercessor, toward Mary as obedient handmaid of the Lord, a model of faith in God's Word. Nevertheless, the Reformers broadly affirmed the *Christology* defined at Chalcedon (451) and Ephesus (431), and confessed Mary as "Mother of God." *Martin Luther, Huldrych Zwingli,* and *John Calvin* also defended Mary's perpetual virginity. Zwingli and Luther taught that Mary was sinless, but for different reasons. Luther also accepted her assumption. The Anabaptist *Menno Simons,* following *Scripture* alone, saw Mary, and thus also Christ, differently: Scripture says that Christ only was "without sin"; thus Mary was sinful; Christ, therefore, was born *out of,* not *from,* her, bringing with him his own sinless "celestial flesh."

—————
Heal (2007); Kreitzer (2004).
MICKEY L. MATTOX

Mary I (1516–58; r. 1553–58)   Mary Tudor, queen of *England* and Ireland, was the only surviving child of *Henry VIII* and Catherine of Aragon. The annulment of her parents' marriage bastardized her, and eventually she was strong-armed into swearing to her father's supremacy. However, her religious conservatism was unmistakable, and she rejected the *Reformation* of her brother Edward VI. Excluded from the succession at his death, she mounted a swift, successful rebellion to become England's first queen regnant. By 1554 she had returned England to papal obedience (helped by her cousin and close ally, **Reginald Pole**), and married Philip of Spain, the future *Philip II*. Mary and Pole set about rebuilding English Catholicism in the parishes, a controversial program whose successes are easily underestimated. She also vigorously persecuted *heresy*; almost three hundred people were burned in 1555–58. Despite two false pregnancies, Mary's marriage was childless. She died on November 17, 1558, ending the Catholic restoration.

Duffy (2009); Duffy and Loades (2006); Loades (1989).

ALEC RYRIE

Mary Queen of Scots (1542–87)

Mary Stuart became the queen of Scots at the age of eight days. She was brought up largely in France, where she married her first husband, Francis II. Her mother, Marie de Guise, ruled Scotland as regent from 1553 to 1560. At the end of her mother's regency, the Scottish Covenanters, led by **John Knox** and others, reformed the Catholic Church in August 1560. Mary returned to her kingdom in 1561 after the death of her first husband and ruled as a Catholic in a Reformed country until the Lords forced her deposition in 1567. Mary's dramatic marriages to Henry Lord Darnley and James Lord Bothwell, and her later imprisonment and eventual execution in the **England** of **Elizabeth I**, provide the dramatic details of her life, but during her rule of Scotland, she largely allowed the Reformed church to prosper and make the roots that would allow it to develop later into Presbyterianism.

Doran (2007); Guy (2006); Walton (2007); Warnicke (2006).

KRISTEN POST WALTON

Mass

The central part of the Roman Catholic liturgy, the Mass makes up the larger liturgical setting for the celebration of the Eucharist. While there were unquestionably eucharistic services in the early church, the term "Mass" (*Misse*) first came into widespread use in the Western church after around 600 CE. The three primary components of the mass are the offertory, the words of consecration, and the distribution of the sacrament. According to Catholic tradition, Christ himself presided over the first mass (Matt. 26; Luke 22). Over time, the liturgical setting of the mass was greatly elaborated. These ceremonies, the canon of the mass, were understood not to rest entirely on the authority of **Scripture**. By the fifteenth century it was held that some of these could be omitted only at the risk of *sin*.

The liturgy of the Mass is a dramatic reenactment of the passion of Jesus Christ, the culmination of the worship service. In medieval theology the Mass was considered to constitute an offering. Rather than being merely a remembrance or symbolic representation of the passion, the Mass was in itself the same as and had the same effects as the actual offering of Christ on the cross. According to Thomas Aquinas, Christ was present as sacrificed in the context of the ceremony. The priest, taking on the role of Christ as representative of the church, the body of Christ, offered up, consecrated, and sacrificed Christ, the physical body of Christ, contained in the offerings of bread and wine (*Summa theologiae*, 3a q. 83 a. 1).

The idea of the Mass as sacrifice was hotly contested in the **Reformation**. **Martin Luther** found the sacrificial conception of the Mass as one of the most pernicious aspects of Catholic teachings, and the source of most abuses. Catholic theologians viewed the Mass as a propitiatory sacrifice and a good work, offered on behalf of the priest, the communicants, but also those for whom prayers were offered, including the dead. For Luther, the Eucharist was the "New Testament," that is, the promise of God, in blood; the Eucharist was a confirmation through sign and memorial of the promise of redemption.

John Calvin and the Reformed theologians went even further in their rejection of this concept. In particular, they complained that the Catholic emphasis on location and manner limited the presence of Christ, who could not be contained in such finite elements as the bread and wine. This does not mean that they advocated a doctrine of "real absence" but rather stressed that Christ's physical body had to remain in heaven, while his spiritual body was omnipresent. One experienced the presence internally, through *faith*. Nevertheless, for Calvin the bread and wine truly represented the presence of the body and blood of Christ, but in a spiritual sense rather than in the physical sense as according to Luther. *Huldrych Zwingli*, by contrast, viewed the *Lord's Supper* as a purely symbolic act.

In defense of the traditional opinion, Catholic writers offered up the example of Melchizedek (Gen. 14:18), who had offered up gifts of bread and wine. Christ had put an end to the Levitical priesthood and had been made eternal high priest according to the order of Melchizedek. On the cross he had not offered bread and wine, but his body and blood. In the Last Supper, however, he had instituted a sacrifice under the forms of bread and wine. Christ had thus instituted the Mass according to the priesthood of Melchizedek as a sacramental and memorial offering of the sacrifice performed once and for all on the cross. This viewpoint was confirmed in the decrees of the *Council of Trent* (sessions 21 and 25).

Lindberg (2002); McBride (2006); N. Thompson (2005).

WILLIAM BRADFORD SMITH

Maximilian I (1459–1519; king of Germany, 1486–1519; Holy Roman Emperor, 1508–19) Maximilian was the son of Emperor Frederick III and Eleanor of Portugal. Maximil-

ian was a Habsburg ruler who greatly expanded the Habsburg dynasty's land holdings and influence in Europe. Largely through marriage alliances, he added to the traditional possessions in Austria much of the Netherlands, Spain and the Spanish Empire, and Hungary and Bohemia. However, he was forced to recognize the independence of the Swiss Confederation in 1499, an important precursor to the Swiss *Reformation*. He was involved in the political reform of the empire, which included the reestablishment of the *Reichskammergericht* (Imperial Chamber Court) in 1495, a standing court that would play an important legal role in the Reformation. Maximilian was also a great patron of the arts and learning, inviting German intellectuals like Conrad Celtis to his court. He was succeeded as emperor by his grandson, *Charles V*.

Benecke (1982); Bonney (1991); Brady (1985b).

RONALD K. RITTGERS

Melanchthon, Philip (a.k.a. Philipp Schwarzerd; 1497–1560)
Melanchthon was a professor, a theologian, and one of northern Europe's leading reformers. Never ordained, Melanchthon would come to be known as *Praeceptor Germaniae* (Teacher of Germany). Melanchthon was born in Bretten in the Black Forest. At age twelve he began studies at the University of Heidelberg. His great uncle, the humanist *Johann Reuchlin*, gave him the name "Melanchthon," the latinized form of the German word *Schwarzerde* ("black soil"). Melanchthon completed his studies at Tübingen, where he received his master of arts degree at age 17. With a humanist's appreciation for classical literature and languages, he was called to *Wittenberg* in 1518 to teach *Greek*. In 1520 he married Katherina Krapp, the daughter of Wittenberg's mayor.

As a colleague of *Martin Luther*, Melanchthon soon found himself doing more than teaching language arts. Clearly influenced by Luther's central insight regarding *justification* by *faith*, Melanchthon proved himself an able exegete and theologian in his own right. Unhindered by his youth and lack of experience, he engaged already established Reformers in correspondence and debate, including *Desiderius Erasmus*. Melanchthon's many and far-ranging epistolary connections would later come to include *John Calvin* in Geneva.

In 1521 he published a handbook titled *Loci communes rerum theologicarum* (*Common Topics of Theological Matters*). Subsequent and expanded editions would simply be called *Loci communes theologici* (*Theological Commonplaces or Common Theological Topics*). Luther praised Melanchthon's opus: "Apart from Scripture, there is no better book." The *Loci Communes* became a standard textbook for theological students well into the seventeenth century.

However, Melanchthon's most enduring contribution to *Reformation* theology, and to the development of Christianity overall, came in regard to his participation in the politics of church reform. For more than four decades Melanchthon labored to advance the *evangelical* faith in difficult and often dangerous political waters. In this regard, Melanchthon's most significant contribution to Christendom is his work on the *Confessio Augustana* (*Augsburg Confession*) presented at the Diet of Augsburg (1530). This became the central defining document for the Lutheran position in matters of concord and conflict.

After 1530 Melanchthon continued to represent the Wittenberg position in increasingly turbulent times. In particular, Melanchthon appreciated the political need for harmony among German and Swiss Protestants. This led him to allow certain accommodations (for instance, in the 1540 *Confessio Augustana Variata*, subscribed to by Calvin) that left Melanchthon vulnerable to the charge of betraying core Lutheran principles.

Such charges would mount throughout the next two decades.

In 1546 Melanchthon offered an enduring eulogy at Luther's funeral. That same year war broke out. The defeat of the Schmalkaldic League in 1547 led to Interim agreements in Leipzig and then in Augsburg (1548) that demanded certain concessions from the losing side. Under significant political pressure, Melanchthon's strategy was to agree to terms he considered to be *adiaphora* (nonessential) but to insist that core evangelical principles be maintained. Many evangelical pastors refused to accept Melanchthon's accommodations and the Interim proved unenforceable. While the *Religious Peace of Augsburg* (1555) provided political calm, internal theological conflict with other evangelicals continued to occupy Melanchthon. Indeed, intra-Lutheran harmony would elude Melanchthon to his dying day, only to be realized seventeen years later with the publication of the Formula of Concord (1577).

Maag (1999); Stupperich (2006); Wengert (1998).

HANS WIERSMA

Memmingen Articles

Also referred to as the Twelve Articles of the Upper Swabian Peasants, the Memmingen Articles were formulated during a meeting of the largest Swabian peasant bands in Memmingen in early March 1525. These articles have been described as the manifesto of the German *Peasants' War* of 1525. Sebastian Lotzer, a furrier and secretary of the Baltringen band, likely distilled the articles from roughly three hundred grievances from the area. The local reforming preacher, Christoph Schappeler, probably added biblical citations and justifications. Many of the articles demand redress for specific social, economic, and legal grievances, but their general appeal to the *gospel* as the model for social reform and demands for communal authority over the local pastor reflect the influence of the **Reformation**. The articles were reprinted twenty-eight times, and were endorsed by all peasant bands except those in northern Switzerland and in the alpine regions of the Tyrol and Salzburg.

Blickle (1977, 1998); Scribner and Benecke (1979).

GEOFFREY DIPPLE

Mercenaries   The employment of mercenary soldiers by the *papacy* and the French played a significant role in shaping the Swiss **Reformation**. In his *Enchiridion Desiderius Erasmus* denounced the immorality of mercenary soldiers and their use by the Christian prince. *Huldrych Zwingli* was influenced by both Erasmus and his own experiences as a preacher in the Swiss armies that had campaigned in northern Italy. He was present at the slaughter at Marignano (1515). For Zwingli the mercenary service and the pensions paid to the leading families destroyed the fabric of Swiss society by fostering widespread corruption. He wrote fiercely against the practice in his *Warning Against Foreign Lords* (1522). The creation of a Christian community demanded the purgation of this offensive practice for which God would judge most severely. The rejection of the mercenary alliance with France was a central plank of Zwingli's campaign for reform, and under his successor *Heinrich Bullinger* Zurich continued to refuse to send mercenaries to the French king.

Augustijn (1991); Gordon (2002); Potter (1976).

BRUCE GORDON

Mercy   Mercy denotes undeserved kindness, compassion, and forgiveness. It is closely related to the concept of *grace*. Divine mercy, especially God's patience with and readiness to forgive sinners, is a prominent theme in the Bible and is integrally related to traditional Christian understandings of the redemptive work of Christ. The soteriological centrality of divine mercy was widely affirmed in the sixteenth century; *Desiderius Erasmus, Martin Luther, John Calvin*, the *Council of Trent*, and *Richard Hooker* all taught that God's mercy played a decisive role in the salvation of every person who entered heaven. Far more contentious were related issues such as the relationship between individuals' efforts and God's mercy in salvation and the roles played by priests, *sacraments*, and other mediators in accessing divine mercy. Often understood as a counterpoint to divine justice, mercy was sometimes presented as an aspect of God's justice inasmuch as God had promised to be merciful and justice demanded faithfulness to that promise.

Bromiley (1986); Demson (2005); Mattox (2008); Stafford (1985).

DANIEL EPPLEY

Merit   The term "merit" is used in Catholicism to connote the value of human effort as deserving of divine reward. Dating in use back at least to Tertullian (d. ca. 225), the term was used prominently in centuries preceding the **Reformation**. Catholics typically differentiated between two types of merit: "condign" merit and "congruent" merit, the former marking God's goodness bestowed because of human action, the latter highlighting the goodness conferred on humanity because of someone else's goodness, particularly God's goodness. Both types of merit attempted to maintain the primacy of *grace* for reward. In condign merit, the *Holy Spirit* moves the human to service that would be worthy of God's recompense. Thus grace aids the person to carry out an action for which God determined and promised requital. The person's actions, then, are associated with reward only secondarily, as the result of the Spirit's leadership. In contrast, congruent merit underscores the idea that some reward is given for action that is truly not earned or deserved but God bestows upon the person nevertheless through God's own goodwill. Regardless, the principal reward for merit is eternal life. However, the retention of the tradition in scholastic theology that some human works might claim divine remuneration, even salvation, became increasingly controversial at the advent of the Reformation and was strongly opposed by Protestant theologians in the sixteenth century.

The Catholic argument for grace's association in each meritorious action was particularly obscured by the medieval introduction of supererogation, the notion that saints achieved works that exceeded human requirement and whose benefits are stored in a *treasury of merit*. Such merits were transferable to other needy Christians. As sinners repented, the overabundant merits of Christ and other *saints* were available to be applied to their shortcomings. This theology inevitably dissolved to manipulation and the selling of *indulgences*, whereby sinners might receive eternal reward for themselves or for another through pecuniary donations and without *confession*.

Martin Luther initially challenged the abuse of indulgences and eventually wholly rejected the foundational conception of merit, basing his soteriology instead solely on God's grace to effect human *justification*. Human works could not contribute whatsoever to salvation. Likewise, *John Calvin* eschewed the term, though he qualified that the regenerate person was capable of receiving God's reward for faithful actions. Reward differed from merit for Calvin, because the latter intimated a divine obligation, the former merely an act of God's good pleasure.

The *Council of Trent*, however, upheld the theological validity and scriptural soundness of the term "merit."

God promises to reward humans for their good works based upon God's justice. The Tridentine decree reemphasized that merit is received first by virtue of grace and second by virtue of divine reward granted for human action.

Fodor and Bauerschmidt (2004); Kolb (2005); Wawrykow (1992).
                            BRIAN C. BREWER

Miracles   For early modern Europeans a miracle was God's temporary interruption of the workings of natural law. Only God could work miracles (*miracula*); anything else that seemed unnatural was merely a marvel (*mirabilia*). Miracles, the wonder they invoked, and the power they revealed were fundamental to the medieval and Catholic cult of the *saints*, and miracles became central to *Reformation* debates over power and legitimacy. While *Martin Luther* allowed for the possibility of miracles during his lifetime, he was skeptical about many that were dubbed such, and Protestant reformers generally argued that the "age of miracles" was past, continuing a debate from the fourteenth and fifteenth centuries. Among Catholic reformers miracles became one of the proofs of Catholic righteousness; the ability of Catholic exorcists to expel demons, Catholic saints' bodies to remain incorrupted after death, and Catholic holy women to levitate all testified to God's willingness to support his true *church*.

Cooper and Gregory (2005); Daston and Park (1998); Harline (2003); T. Jones and Sprunger (2002).
                         KATHRYN A. EDWARDS

Monasticism   Monasticism is the renunciation of the lay world in order to enter a community devoted to God and the religious life. Protestants vigorously attacked this practice and called for complete monastic dissolution. Critics claimed the monastic life was not supported by *Scripture*; that perpetual vows went against God; that *celibacy* was impossible for most people to maintain, leading to rampant sexual debauchery; that many novices were forced to enter against their will; and that monasticism presumed the religious were better and closer to God than lay Christians. One of the most damaging charges was that the monasteries were no longer useful to society: Christians did not need mediation between themselves and God, thus there was no salvific *merit* to praying for someone else's soul. The Catholic Church denied this reevaluation, and while it acknowledged some abuses within the houses, it accused detractors of exaggeration and argued for reform rather than dissolution. The *Council of Trent* reaffirmed the monastic life but stipulated that there should be tighter control and supervision, especially over women.

Dykema and Oberman (1993); Knowles (1976); Little (2002).

AMY E. LEONARD

Moral Conjecture   The late medieval period witnessed important developments in moral theology. Among them was the emergence of moral probability. Jean Gerson (1363–1469) applied the idea of probability to the consideration of moral questions. He considered absolute moral certainty of a mathematical kind to be beyond human intellectual abilities. Thus one can only make a probable conjecture, but not an absolutely certain pronouncement, about one's own state of *grace*. From this perspective, the quest for moral certainty is futile and even contradicts the means of grace that are available through the *church*. The Reformers rejected the idea of moral conjecture. *John Calvin* criticized the notion in his Romans commentary and in the *Institutes of the Christian Religion*. He asserted that the elect can be certain of their salvation on account

of the scriptural witness. The *Council of Trent* anathematized the Protestant position in its decree on *justification* of January 13, 1547.

Hobbins (2009); M. Stone (2000); Zachman (1993).

RADY ROLDAN-FIGUEROA

More, Thomas (1478–1535)   Best known as the author of *Utopia*, More was a lawyer, humanist, friend of *Desiderius Erasmus*, and Lord Chancellor to *Henry VIII* during a tumultuous period in English history. His refusal to support Henry's divorce of Queen Catherine and marriage to Anne Boleyn cost him the king's favor, his chancellorship, and ultimately his life.

More was the son of John More, a prominent London barrister and judge. In his youth he went to live in the household of Cardinal Morton, who sent him to Oxford, where he obtained an education rich in humanistic learning prior to taking up the study of law in 1494. From 1499 until 1503 he resided in the London Charterhouse, a monastery of the Carthusian order. More was attracted to the monastic life, but chose instead to enter public life with his election to the House of Commons in 1504, and to marry Jane Colt in 1505. He and his first wife had three daughters and a son before her death in 1511; More married Alice Middleton a month later.

His career flourished, reaching its height with his appointment as Lord Chancellor in 1529. Over the years he wrote prolificly: a laudatory biography of Pico della Mirandola (*Life of John Picus*, 1504), the *History of King Richard III* (1515–18), and the celebrated *Utopia* ("no place"), which he published in 1516 following an embassy to Bruges. Book 1 incorporates an extensive critique of European society in all of its brutality, with its drastic economic inequality, extensive use of capital punishment, and warmongering kings surrounded by flattering courtiers. Book 2, narrated by world traveler Raphael Hythloday ("nonsense-speaker"), describes an ideal commonwealth; its most notable features are community of property and a highly regimented society, in which all residents are conditioned from birth to follow a life of virtue based on reason.

More's devotion to the Roman Church prompted him to write fierce polemics against the Protestant reform, and to prosecute its English proponents as heretics. At first, he and King Henry were allies; in 1521 More helped him compose the Defense of the Seven Sacraments against Luther. However, around 1527 the king decided to divorce his queen, who had been married to his older brother, and with whom he had no son. The royal pair had received a papal dispensation to marry, which Henry sought to reverse to marry Anne Boleyn. The pope's refusal caused Henry to sever the English church from its allegiance to Rome, a decision More, who resigned his chancellorship in 1532, could not support. When he refused to sign the Act of Succession recognizing Henry's daughter by Anne, More was convicted of treason. He was executed on July 6, 1535, and canonized in 1935.

Fox (1983); Guy (2000); Marius (1984); C. Murphy et al. (1989).
J. LAUREL CARRINGTON

Mortal Sin

According to the medieval church, a mortal sin (sometimes called grave sin) is a willful and deliberate transgression against natural and divine law and causes irreparable damage to the salvation by depriving the sinner's soul of divine *grace*. In contrast, a *venial sin* was considered less grave and therefore did not result in the loss of sanctifying grace. Because the Protestant reformers rejected *free will*, they disagreed with the Catholic tenet that *sin* can be a deliberate choice, since humans always sin. They also rejected the distinction between mortal and venial sins and argued that all sin requires God's pardon through *faith*.

Cameron (1991); McGrath (1999).
GRETA GRACE KROEKER

Münster

A city in Westphalia (northwest Germany), Münster became home to the short-lived kingdom of chiliastic *Anabaptism*. Originating from reforms propagated by Bernard Rothmann's preaching in the heretofore Catholic-ruled city, Münster turned Anabaptist as Rothmann gained power. From February 1534 to June 1535, Münster fell under Anabaptist rule, which progressively became more fanatical. Strongly influenced by the writings of *Melchior Hoffmann*, Rothmann promoted radical Anabaptist beliefs while Jan Matthijs, a charismatic Dutch lay preacher, was made king. Catholic and Lutheran forces laid siege to the city, whereupon Matthijs was killed. Subsequently, another Dutch layman, Jan van Leyden, replaced Matthijs and declared Münster the new Jerusalem. Rothmann served as theologian, scripturally justifying the reforms introduced, which included communism and polygamy. Ultimately, Münster fell to the besieging forces and returned to Catholic rule. Consequently, most Anabaptists throughout Europe were thereafter improperly associated with zealotry and were persecuted, despite their *pacifism* and separatism.

Arthur (2000); von der Lippe and Reck-Malleczewen (2008); von Kerssenbrock (2007).
BRIAN C. BREWER

Müntzer, Thomas (ca. 1489–1525)

Often portrayed as a revolutionary representative of the common person, Müntzer, like *Martin Luther*, probably came from a family that benefited from the economic changes of the early sixteenth century. He had extensive formal education, and was ordained into the priesthood. During the winter of 1517/18 he was in Wittenberg and studied the writings of medieval German mystics, likely under the influence of *Andreas Bodenstein von Karlstadt*. He developed an independent, spiritualist theology, championing the exegetical competence of the Spirit-filled layperson over that of the learned scholars (*Schriftgelehrten*), during his conflict with the humanist reformer Johannes Sylvius Egranus while in Zwickau in 1520 and 1521. From June to November 1521, he was in Prague attempting to recruit the Bohemians for his reforming vision.

In early 1522 Müntzer had the opportunity to realize his reforming vision in the Thuringian city of Allstedt. There he implemented a series of liturgical reforms, which included the first *Reformation* translation of the *Mass* into German. He identified the rites of the church as primarily external signs of an inner salvific event, and he considered postponing *baptism* until the baptizand had reached the age of discernment, although there is no evidence that he ever became an Anabaptist. His growing rift with the *Wittenberg* reformers is evident in his writings from this time, especially in *Von dem gedichteten Glauben* (*On Counterfeit Faith*) and *Protestation oder Erbietung* (*Protestation or Proposition*). He decried their reliance on the written word, accusing them of worshiping a "dumb God," and criticized their soteriology, contrasting the cheap or easy *faith* of the Wittenbergers to true, experienced faith. Müntzer believed that this living, experienced faith transformed not only the individual, but social relations as well.

In Allstedt he still thought such a transformation was possible through existing political structures and, in his *Fürstenpredigt* (*Sermon to the Princes*) of July 13, 1524, he called on the rulers of ducal Saxony to defend his Reformation and lead the elect during the coming judgment. The failure of this

appeal and subsequent investigations by the authorities into the activities of Müntzer and his followers led him to flee the city on the night of August 7/8, 1524. In Mühlhausen he joined a reformation led by Heinrich Pfeiffer, but was expelled from the city and traveled in the southwest during the early stages of the *Peasants' War*, where some speculate he wrote the anonymous *Verfassungsentwurf* (*Draft of a Constitution*). Back in Mühlhausen by February 1525, he became embroiled in the Peasants' War, ultimately serving as chaplain of the peasant band at the Battle of Frankenhausen. Captured after the battle, he was interrogated and executed on May 27, 1525. Through *Hans Hut* and *Hans Denck* he influenced the development of south German–Austrian *Anabaptism* and Reformation spiritualism.

Friesen (1990); Goertz (1993); Scott (1989).
GEOFFREY DIPPLE

Musculus, Wolfgang (1497–1563)

Musculus was born in Lorraine and entered the Benedictine monastery in Lixheim in 1512. His advocacy of *Martin Luther*'s ideas led to his being dubbed "the Lutheran monk," and he married and left the monastery in 1527. Musculus spent three years in *Strasbourg* assisting *Martin Bucer* and Matthew Zell, before being called to Augsburg as a pastor. During his Augsburg years Musculus participated in the *Wittenberg* Concord of 1536 and the *Regensburg* Colloquy of 1541. In 1548 Musculus left Augsburg in the wake of the Interim, and eventually settled in Bern, where he taught theology until his death. Musculus is known for his systematic theology, the *Loci Communes*, as well as for his extensive biblical commentaries. He defended the supremacy of the civil authorities in ecclesiastical matters and is therefore seen as an influence on Thomas Erastus and on the Anglican tradition, and is also a significant figure in the development of federal theology.

———

Farmer (1997); Ives (1965); Schwab (1933).
EDWIN WOODRUFF TAIT

Music   Very little is known about music in the ancient world, where it originally held a liturgical function. During the early medieval period music was included in the quadrivium of the seven *liberal arts*, as the theoretical study of harmony in sound. Music in the Roman Church for the monastic office and the *Mass* became standardized as Gregorian chant (named for the late-sixth-century Pope Gregory I) over a period of several centuries. In the High and late Middle Ages, sacred music became increasingly complex. *Martin Luther* did not reject all aspects of this tradition, but advocated congregational singing in the form of the chorale, which provided the foundation for a rich heritage encompassing the chorale preludes of J. S. Bach. In contrast, *Huldrych Zwingli*, himself a talented musician, banned music from worship altogether because he believed there was no scriptural basis for its inclusion. *Martin Bucer, Johannes Oecolampadius,* and *John Calvin* supported singing as a legitimate form of public *prayer*.

———

Burkholder et al. (2010); Fisher (2007); Garside (1966, 1979).
J. LAUREL CARRINGTON

Myconius, Oswald (a.k.a. Oswald Geisshäusler; 1488–1552)   Myconius was a Swiss reformer, humanist, and friend, correspondent, and biographer of *Huldrych Zwingli*. He played an important role in the Swiss *Reformation*. Born in Lucerne, Myconius lived in both Zurich and Basel. In Zurich he taught at the cathedral school and encouraged the election of Zwingli as the people's priest. After Zwingli's death in 1531, he left Zurich for Basel, where he had attended university. There he pursued his interest in *humanism* and a friendship with the Basel reformer *Johannes Oecolampadius*, whom he succeeded as university professor. Although fundamentally a Zwinglian, he urged compromise with the Lutherans on the issues of the Eucharist and *excommunication*. He authored the First Basel Confession (1534), contributed to the *Helvetic Confession* (1536), and published a biography of Zwingli (1536).

———

Cameron (1991); Gordon (2002); Ozment (1980).
GRETA GRACE KROEKER

Natural Law (Lat. *lex naturalis*)
Natural law is the philosophical notion that *nature* supplies humanity with a rational and moral orientation that is naturally knowable. For Christian thinkers, the natural law is created by God, providing a universal basis for human legal codes, ethical systems, and moral theologies. Thomas Aquinas's attempts to synthesize *law* and Christian divine revelation were developed by later scholastic thinkers. When Reformers spoke of the "orders of creation," or of the law's "first use" or "civil use," they mainly had the natural law in mind. It was beginning with the law's "second use"— by which sinful humans recognize their existential guilt and need of a divine savior—that an independently functioning natural law became problematic. *Martin Luther* represented a break with the scholastic system by asserting that God redeems sinners entirely outside any rational, legal—that is, natural— framework. Others, such as *Desiderius Erasmus, Philip Melanchthon,* and *John Calvin*, tended to synthesize humanist and/or *evangelical* theology with Aquinas's original synthesis.

———

Arnold (1937); Cromartie (1997); Peschke (1967); VanDrunen (2006).
HANS WIERSMA

Nature   The Protestant reformers in general valued material life and the natural order. Although Protestantism has been accused of an instrumental understanding of nature that later made possible environmental abuses in Western culture, the Reformers instead taught that humans are to appreciate and enjoy the good things of creation, not as ends in themselves, but as a *revelation* of the goodness of God. *John Calvin*, for example, referred to the created order as the "theater of God's glory." The Reformers' commentaries on the Psalms are filled with expressions of the beauty of nature as revealing something of the magnificence of God. The ungodly cannot see the glory of God in the natural order and, as a result, give him no thanks, but rather hoard and plunder creation in their sinful covetousness. Christians, however, have responsibility to imitate God's loving care of the world through a careful stewardship of its resources.

Althaus (1966); Schreiner (1991); Schwanke (2004).

GREGORY J. MILLER

Nicodemites   Based on John 3, where Nicodemus approached Jesus reverently, but secretly by night, for fear of what others would think, *John Calvin* gave the name Nicodemites to those who claimed the Protestant faith, but secretly for fear of persecution. Particular questions for those trying to remain faithful and safe ranged from whether they could attend *Mass* to whether they could continue receiving a benefice or holding Roman Catholic clerical *office*. Those in such office might see opportunities for influence for the Protestant cause, but to Calvin open profession of the faith and participation in worship was required, even when that meant flight into exile or *martyrdom*. Calvin wrote numerous tracts and treatises on the topic from 1536 to 1562, especially to those in his native France. *Peter Mar-*

tyr Vermigli and *Wolfgang Musculus* also wrote treatises against such compromise in periods when English Protestants and German Lutherans were restricted.

Eire (1986); Higman (1984); D. Wright (2006).

GARY NEAL HANSEN

Ochino, Bernardino (1487–1564)
Born in Siena, Ochino became vicar-general of the observant *Franciscans* and later of the Capuchins. He preached throughout the Italian peninsula, and his *orthodoxy* came into question when he published sermons that reflected Protestant ideas, including *justification* by *faith* alone. Fearing for his safety, he fled to Switzerland, where *John Calvin* eventually entrusted him with a *preaching* position. In *Geneva* he published works that combined Franciscan mysticism with a strong Calvinist theology. After marrying, he traveled to *Basel* and *Strasbourg* but found stability only after moving to *England* at the invitation of the archbishop of Canterbury. That position was cut short, however, when the Catholic *Mary I* (Tudor) became queen. He returned to Switzerland, where he settled in Zurich as pastor to the Italian community. However, his controversial publications eventually led to his banishment. He fled to Poland and then to Moravia, where he died.

Gordon (2002); Taplin (2003).

GRETA GRACE KROEKER

Oecolampadius, Johannes (1482–1531)
Known as the Reformer of Basel, Oecolampadius was among the most significant biblical interpreters in the early *Reformation*. He studied law in Bologna and theology in Heidelberg and Tübingen before serving as tutor to the sons of the *Elector* of the Palatinate. He came to know *Philip Melanchthon* and became part of the circle around the

distinguished Hebraist *Johann Reuchlin*. He then worked for the printer Johannes Froben in Basel, where he came in contact with *Desiderius Erasmus*. He served as preacher in Augsburg before returning to the university at *Basel*, where he lectured on the Bible, most notably Romans and Isaiah. He was a subtle and sophisticated exegete of *Scripture*, and although his theology converged with *Huldrych Zwingli's*, he was an independent thinker much admired by his contemporaries. During the 1520s he led the Swiss Reformed party in disputations with Catholics (Baden, 1526) and he was decisive in the introduction of the Reformation in Basel in 1529.

Gordon (2002); Guggisberg (1982); Rupp (1969).

BRUCE GORDON

Office   The term "office" could be used in three distinct ways in the *Reformation* period. First, it could refer to the threefold office of Christ during his earthly ministry: prophet, priest, and king. This distinction went back to Eusebius (fourth century) but it received systematic definition especially in the work of *John Calvin* and the theologians of Protestant *orthodoxy*. Second, the term could refer to positions or functions within the *church* (e.g., pastor and superintendent in Lutheranism; pastor, teacher, deacon, and elder in Reformed Protestantism; and the various orders of the sacramental church office in Roman Catholicism—porter, lector, exorcist, acolyte, subdeacon, deacon, monk, priest, bishop—along with a host of purely functional or jurisdictional offices). Finally, the term could refer to the daily public prayers of the Roman Catholic Church, which were referred to as the Divine Office.

T. Parker (1995); Spijker (1996); van Liere (2004).

RONALD K. RITTGERS

Original Sin   The doctrine of original sin refers to the corruption of humanity resulting from the fall of Adam and Eve. Protestant reformers tended to define original sin in two ways. One side described the human nature and essence (rational soul) as wholly corrupt so that the very nature itself is the source of all other sins. The other side asserted that original sin was not a person's nature or essence but something in human nature; therefore they distinguished between the nature of fallen humanity and original *sin*, which was the work of the devil to corrupt human nature. The *Augsburg Confession* clearly taught that God was not the creator or cause of sin; rather original sin was like a spiritual poison or leprosy. Adherents to this Confession believed that the chief articles of the Christian *faith* contained the distinction balancing the human nature in which sin dwells but created and preserved by God, and the original sin itself that dwells in the nature.

Placher (1988); Tentler (1977); Wiley (2002).

ESTHER CHUNG-KIM

Orthodoxy   In regard to the *Reformation*, "orthodoxy" refers to various attempts from the mid-sixteenth century to the late seventeenth century to systematize, expound, and expand the theological insights of the first generation of Protestant leaders. Often utilizing scholastic reasoning, subtle argumentation, and Aristotelian logic, Protestant orthodoxy has a reputation of aridity and overrationalization. Yet the work of these theologians was essential in preserving and organizing the various Protestant confessions. Orthodoxy primarily was expressed in creedal statements, multivolume systematic theologies, and polemical writings. Of central importance in this period for Lutherans was the Formula of Concord (adopted 1577), which settled internal disputes and defined Lutheran doctrine over against

Reformed theology and the systematic theology of Johann Gerhard (d. 1637). For Reformed theology, the canons of the *Synod of Dort* (1618–19) combated Arminianism and established the parameters for Calvinist orthodoxy. Pietism may be regarded at least in part as a response to the intellectualizing emphasis of Protestant orthodoxy.

Kolb (2005); Muller (2003a, 2003b); Preus (1972).

GREGORY J. MILLER

Pacifism   The starting point for many Renaissance and *Reformation* discussions of pacifism and nonresistance was the teachings of *Desiderius Erasmus*, especially in his essay on the adage *Dulce bellum inexpertis* (War is sweet to the inexperienced) of 1515 and in the *Querela pacis* (Complaint of Peace) of 1517. Erasmus argued that participation in warfare contradicts not only Jesus' teachings in the Sermon on the Mount, but also human nature and *natural law*. While a number of Renaissance humanists shared his views, the magisterial reformers usually rejected them—the classic statement is *Martin Luther*'s in *Ob Kriegsleute auch in seligem Stand sein konnen* (*On Whether Soldiers, Too, Can Be Saved*). A number of Reformation radicals, most notably some of the *Anabaptists*, were pacifists. The clearest and earliest statement of Anabaptist nonresistance appears in the *Schleitheim* Articles (1527), which provided the framework for other Anabaptist positions as the sixteenth century progressed.

Adams (1962); Brock (1991); Olin (1979); Stayer (1976).

GEOFFREY DIPPLE

Papacy   On the eve of the *Reformation*, the Renaissance popes were solidly established not only as spiritual sovereigns, but also as temporal rulers prepared to defend their far-flung interests

by all means at their disposal, including military force. They were also powerful patrons of the arts and of humanist scholarship. By century's end, the pope's dual role as temporal and spiritual sovereign was more firmly established and the papacy had begun to take on the absolutist look of the emerging early modern state. The *church* itself was much improved and reformed, thanks largely to the papacy's own efforts to implement the reforms of the *Council of Trent*. These efforts in turn underscored the *authority* of the papal office. The building of the new St. Peter's Basilica in Rome, begun under *Julius II* and completed in 1626, was the centerpiece in a construction program that made Rome visually the center of Christendom.

Duffy (2006); Jedin, Dolan, and Holland (1993).

MICKEY L. MATTOX

Paris, University of   Founded in the twelfth century and often referred to as the Sorbonne, the University of Paris was the most important center of medieval and early modern French intellectual life. Although the humanist *Desiderius Erasmus* found other humanists when he studied theology there between 1495 and 1499, he lamented what he found to be a stifling intellectual atmosphere and left after four years without a doctorate. The university's Faculty of Theology nevertheless played a central role in the religious debates of the *Reformation*. In the mid-1520s the executive officer of the theology faculty, Noël Beda, led an attack against Erasmus, other humanists, and Protestant reformers, whom he assumed to be working in concert to undermine Roman Catholicism.

Nauert (2006); Rummel (1998, 2008).

GRETA GRACE KROEKER

Pastors   With the implementation of the *Reformation* in German and

Swiss lands during the 1520s, a complex process began by which former priests became pastors in the new Protestant churches. This involved several key theological, pastoral, and practical issues. The priesthood was no longer a *sacrament*, and the priest's sacrificial role at the *Mass* was replaced by the requirement to preach the Word of God and administer the two sacraments (*Baptism* and *Lord's Supper*). On this point the Lutherans and Reformed were in agreement, despite their varying theologies of the sacraments. The Protestant Reformation affirmed the separation of *clergy* from laity, but defined the former in terms of a vocation for which there had to be a legitimate calling and adequate training. The clergy were to marry, raise families, and serve as models of Christian conduct in their communities. There was no shortage of tension between the clergy and the laity, particularly as one of the pastor's duties was to participate in the oversight of the moral lives of the people.

Dixon and Schorn-Schütte (2003); Janse and Pitkin (2005); Parker and Carlson (1998); Pettegree (1993).

BRUCE GORDON

Paul III, Pope (1468–1549; r. 1534–49)

Born Allesandro Farnese, Paul III stamped the ecclesiastical history of the sixteenth century with his calling of the *Council of Trent*, causing some historians to call him the first reform pope. Educated at Rome and Florence, where he became acquainted with the Medicis, he moved up in the ranks of the church very quickly. Alexander VI created him as a cardinal in 1493, and he was unanimously elected as pope in 1534. Paul was not overly concerned about living a moral lifestyle, fathering four illegitimate children. However, his Renaissance habits also factored in his patronage of the arts. He commissioned Michelangelo to paint the Last Judgment in the Sistine Chapel, and engaged

him as the architect for the dome of St. Peter's Basilica. That love of beauty did not stop him from several reform-minded acts. He approved the foundation of the *Jesuit* order in 1540, elevated several reform-minded cardinals, and restored the office of the *Inquisition* in 1542. In 1545 his most significant reforming act was the calling and opening of the Council of Trent.

Fragnito (2001); Grendler (1977).

R. WARD HOLDER

Paul IV, Pope (1476–1559; r. 1555–59)

Born Gian Pietro Carafa to a prominent Neapolitan family with ties to the papacy, Paul IV progressed quickly through the church hierarchy. Erudite, as papal nuncio to England he began corresponding with *Desiderius Erasmus* but ultimately renounced *humanism*. A great supporter of reform and personally devout, he joined the Roman Oratory of Divine Love and helped establish the Theatine order along with Gaetano Thiene. As pope, Paul pursued an ill-advised war with Spain that led to the invasion of the papal states and defeat of its forces. Though strongly anti-Protestant, he chose not to revive the *Council of Trent* because he believed reform would be more effective solely under papal control. A leader of the *Inquisition*, he became increasingly intolerant as pope, restricting Jews in Rome to ghettos and establishing the *Index Librorum Prohibitorum* (*Index of Forbidden Books*). Remembered more for his severity than his *piety*, Paul did establish foundations for later substantive papal reform.

Jorgensen (1994); Pastor (1969); A. Wright (2000).

JILL R. FEHLEISON

Peasants' War

Involving up to 300,000 participants and 100,000 casualties, the German Peasants' War of 1525 was the largest mass insurrection in European history before the French Revolution. Noting that it included much more than just peasants and that it was not really a war for much of its course, some scholars have challenged the traditional nomenclature, preferring instead to speak of it as the Revolution of 1525.

In late summer and fall of 1524 peasant revolts appeared in the Black Forest and along the Upper Rhine, but many scholars consider the Peasants' War proper to have begun when the insurrection spread to Upper Swabia in late January 1525. This first phase of the revolt, lasting until the end of March, had the character more of a general strike than a war. In early March, at a meeting of the three largest Upper Swabian peasant bands, Sebastian Lötzer and Christoph Schappeler produced the *Memmingen Articles*. This "manifesto of the Revolution of 1525" went beyond a list of grievances to envision a just society patterned on the reawakened *gospel* of the *Reformation*. Schappeler likely also wrote at Memmingen a *Bundesordnung* (*League Ordinance*), which outlined a "republican" program for common governance of the peasant bands based on the political model of neighboring Swiss territories.

The term "war" better applies to the phase of the revolt beginning in early April. At the end of March and into April, the insurrection spread into Franconia, Württemberg, Thuringia, Alsace, and the Palatinate. At the same time the authorities began its forceful suppression. In this context, the peasants largely abandoned hopes of negotiated settlements and undertook the demolition of monasteries and castles, including at Weinsberg in Franconia, where the noble garrison was massacred. The changing attitudes of the Upper Swabian peasants are evident in the anonymous pamphlet, likely also written by Christoph Schappeler, *An die Versammlung gemeiner Bauerschaft* (*To the Assembly of the Common Peasantry*), which called into question the legitimacy of the lords' authority and justified open resistance to them.

Later uprisings in Salzburg and the Tyrol produced not only the greatest insurgent victory at Schladming on June 3, 1525, but also the most comprehensive political program of the rebellion, Michael Gaismaier's *Tiroler Landesordnung* (*Tyrolean Constitution*). A peasant rebellion in East Prussia in early September should not distract from the primarily south German nature of the Peasants' War.

The defeat of the insurgency may not have entirely excluded the common person from the subsequent political life of Germany, as once thought, nor may it have marked the definitive end of the popular Reformation, but it did encourage the transition from the Communal to the Princes' Reformation in many parts of the empire.

Blickle (1977, 1998); Scribner and Benecke (1979).

GEOFFREY DIPPLE

Penance   The medieval *sacrament* of penance (broadly affirmed at Trent)—with its internal sequence of contrition, confession, and works of *satisfaction*—was too closely tied to Catholic conceptions of *merit*, and to *purgatory*, not to have become the object of Protestant efforts at reform. Many Reformers also shared Luther's concern that penance had been tied too closely to the church's revenue stream through *indulgences*, and they criticized its tyranny over Christian consciences. Nevertheless, Protestant theology and *piety* emphasized the penitential quality of the life of *faith*. In his Small Catechism, for example, **Martin Luther** taught that *baptism* takes on its full meaning only when through daily penance and contrition "the old Adam" in us is put to death so that the "new man" may arise. Many Protestants abolished private confession and instead inserted a "general" or corporate confession into their liturgy.

Luther, however, commended private confession, and Lutherans generally retained it.

Rittgers (2004); Steinmetz (2002c).

MICKEY L. MATTOX

Pérez de Pineda, Juan (ca. 1500–1567)   Pérez de Pineda was a Spanish Reformed minister. The scholarly consensus is that he was an ordained priest and that he had a career as a diplomat at the service of *Charles V*. He apparently embraced Protestantism while in Spain, serving as rector of an orphanage in Seville. He found refuge in Geneva and served as minister in that city from about 1558 to 1561. He also served as minister among the French *Huguenots* in the city of Blois (France) from about 1562 to 1563, and as chaplain to Renée of France from about 1564 to 1567. His most important contribution was his revision of *Francisco de Enzinas*'s Spanish New Testament (Geneva, 1556). He also wrote the *Epístola Consolatoria* (*An Epistle of Consolation*, 1560) for those who suffered persecution in Seville. He edited several works by *Juan de Valdés* and published other works of a propagandistic character.

Kinder (1976, 1987); Roldan-Figueroa (2006b).

RADY ROLDAN-FIGUEROA

Perfection   The ability of the finite human to be in the state of perfection, without blemish, free from *sin* or completely holy, has been rejected by most Christians. However, Christians have been reminded of the scriptural injunction to "be perfect, . . . as your heavenly Father is perfect" (Matt. 5:48), or to "come to fullness in him" (Col. 2:10). Not surprisingly, then, various theologians over the centuries have attempted a doctrine of perfection. One theologian whose doctrine affected Catholic thought during the *Reformation* was

Thomas Aquinas (d. 1274), who had argued that perfection might be attained through works of charity marked by one's *love* for God and neighbor. Additionally, members of a Catholic religious order were seen as in a state of perfection upon taking vows of poverty, chastity, and obedience. Nevertheless, *Martin Luther* argued against the attainability of perfection in this life, noting that even the *saints* were not without sin.

Kleinig (2008); Raitt (1987); Wainwright (1988).

BRIAN C. BREWER

Perseverance   The notion of whether one will continue in the *faith* until *death* became important during the *Reformation*. The late medieval Catholic position was that claiming to be sure that one would persevere to the end was presumptuous; it was always possible to fall from *grace*. *John Calvin* emphasized assurance of salvation, teaching that the perseverance of the elect is securely in Christ's care. This became a pointed question in Reformed theology after Calvin, particularly in the Netherlands. On one side were those influenced by *Jacobus Arminius*, whose stronger emphasis on human agency led to the position that one could forfeit salvation after *justification*. Their opponents at the *Synod of Dort* made perseverance their fifth main point of doctrine, and thus an emphatic teaching of later Calvinism. They held that God graciously preserves the elect throughout life. The elect do *sin*, even gravely, but they will be led back to repentance.

Berkouwer (1958); Peterson and Williams (2004); Pinson (2002).

GARY NEAL HANSEN

Peter (ca. 1–64 CE)   Peter (born Simon) was one of the original twelve apostles, saint and martyr, and commonly accepted as the first bishop of

Rome. He was reputedly crucified upside down by the emperor Nero and buried in Rome. The Latin church, citing Matthew 16:18–19 and Peter's leadership role among the apostles, claimed that Christ endowed Peter with the responsibility of building his *church*; thus all who succeeded him (later known as popes) inherited his authority as superior of the church and head over all other bishops. Although the exact meaning and implications of the text were vigorously debated, the *papacy*'s authority was codified over the centuries through this "Petrine Doctrine." The Eastern church acknowledged Peter as one bishop among many and did not recognize the pope's authority over all Christians. Protestants, who mostly rejected the role of bishops and the papacy in general, contended that the church's arguments were based on basic misinterpretations of the biblical texts.

R. Brown et al. (1973); Cullmann (1958); Perkins (1994); T. Smith (1985).

AMY E. LEONARD

Peter Lombard (ca. 1098–1160)

Lombard was a theologian, compiler of *Sententiarum libri quator* (*Four Books of Sentences/Opinions*), and, for one year, the bishop of Paris. Born in Italy, he began his academic career in Paris around 1135 upon the recommendation of Bernard of Clairvaux. In the *Sentences* (1150), Lombard arranged passages of *Scripture*, the writings of the church *fathers* and later authorities, as well as his own commentary, around various doctrinal subjects (e.g., Book 1: "On the Unity of God and the Trinity"). The result was a systematic framework that helped define the parameters for subsequent philosophical and theological argument. Known as the *Magister Sententiarum* (Master of the Sentences), Lombard's influence on Thomas Aquinas and the development of late medieval *scholasticism* cannot be denied. As for *Reformation*-era theo-

logians, *Martin Luther* commented and lectured upon the *Sentences* early in his career before rejecting the scholastic framework Lombard helped inspire. *John Calvin*, in his *Institutes*, approved of Lombard on some points but rejected him on others, including on the matter of *free will*.

Colish (1994); Rosemann (2004).

HANS WIERSMA

Philip II (1527–98; r. 1556–98)

Philip II was born on May 21, 1527, in Valladolid, Spain. His parents were *Charles V*, the *Holy Roman Emperor* and King of Spain, and Isabel of Portugal. Upon his father's abdication of his possessions over the space of three years between 1554 and 1556, Philip gradually became ruler of a global monarchy comprising Spain and its American colonies, the Netherlands, Milan, Naples, and Sicily. In 1580 he inherited the crown of Portugal. His reign marks the apogee of Spanish power in the sixteenth century.

Philip was a conscientious ruler, who worked tirelessly to safeguard his inheritance, to carry out justice, and to uphold the Catholic faith in his realms. He read and annotated every official document dealing with state affairs, and he reserved all crucial decisions for himself. These practices have left us the image of a solitary king who ruled the world from his desk. Philip, however, always relied on a large bureaucracy to administer his empire. The Spanish monarchy under Philip also was not an absolutist state. It remained a composite monarchy, and Philip had to respect the traditional rights and privileges of his kingdoms or face rebellion (e.g., the Netherlands in 1566 and the kingdom of Aragon in 1591).

Philip's reign was marked by constant warfare. He inherited war with France, which he successfully brought to an end with his victory at the Battle of San Quentin (1557) and the subsequent Peace of Cateau-Cambrésis (1559).

Philip then turned his attention to Mediterranean threats. His forces won a decisive naval victory over the Ottomans at the Battle of Lepanto (1571), and he suppressed the Morisco Rebellion (1568–71) in Granada.

Philip's efforts to increase taxes, reform the episcopacy, and suppress Calvinism in the Netherlands led to a revolt in 1566. His attempt to quash this revolt proved ineffective as the seven northern provinces (which later became the Dutch Republic) continued to defy him. Their alliance with *England* in 1585 led to Philip's most notable failure when he launched the Spanish Armada three years later in 1588. In 1590 Philip overextended himself even more by intervening in the French Wars of Religion, which undermined Spanish efforts against the Dutch and the English by diverting scarce resources to France.

Appraising Philip's reign is difficult. Was he bent on world domination or was he simply trying to conserve his inheritance? People have debated this question since the sixteenth century, and their answers have often been based on partisan assessments of the king. For Protestants, Philip was a rabidly Catholic tyrant; for Catholics, he was the standard-bearer for the *Counter-Reformation*. What we know for certain of his character is that Philip was reserved, patient, and prudent. He was a great connoisseur and patron of artists (most notably Titian), had a personal library of over fourteen thousand volumes, and had the Escorial Palace-Monastery built. He was married four times and was devoted to his family. Philip died on September 13, 1598, in the Escorial.

Kamen (1997); G. Parker (1998); Pierson (1975).

SEAN T. PERRONE

Philipp of Hesse (1504–67)
Philipp was landgrave (territorial ruler) of Hesse after he reached majority in 1518. After 1524 he became an enthusiastic supporter of the Protestant cause, including, in 1531, the formation of the *evangelical* princes into a defensive alliance, the Schmalkaldic League, against the Catholic emperor. He also sponsored a series of inner Protestant colloquies designed to achieve Protestant theological unity in support of a military alliance, most famously the *Marburg Colloquy* (1529), which, however, failed to reconcile the factions of *Martin Luther* and *Huldrych Zwingli*. Philipp's leadership position was weakened in 1540 when, after receiving confessional counsel from Wittenberg, he took a second wife. *Philip Melanchthon* and Luther had sanctioned a secret second marriage solely out of pastoral necessity, but found themselves discredited when the arrangement became public. Imprisoned (1547–52) after the Schmalkaldic War, he eventually escaped and was restored to his rule. He also adopted a relatively tolerant policy toward the *Anabaptists*.

Hillerbrand (1967); W. Wright (1985b).
MICKEY L. MATTOX

Philosophy
Philosophy, the search for transcendent truth, has its origins in antiquity. While *Plato* and *Aristotle* are the two thinkers who most influenced Western philosophy, Stoics, Epicureans, and Skeptics also left their mark. Early theologians sought to reconcile this pagan tradition with Christianity, a project that would occupy scholars for centuries, especially the scholastic theologians of the High Middle Ages, who became preoccupied with Aristotelian logic and metaphysics. Their approach was derided by humanists, yet philosophy retained a vital presence during the Renaissance and *Reformation*. Marsilio Ficino translated the dialogues of Plato and developed an extensive Neoplatonic theology, while Aristotelians revitalized their field through philology, providing both scholarly Greek editions and Latin translations. *Lorenzo Valla*

undermined scholastic logic by recasting the relationship between language and meaning.

University-trained reformers such as *Martin Luther* and *Philip Melanchthon* were well versed in the philosophical tradition, aspects of which they both utilized and rejected. While he acknowledged the value of Aristotle's logic in the realm of knowledge, Luther held it useless as a basis for *faith*. In particular, late medieval scholastic theologians had developed a soteriology that gave a significant role to human agency, a position Luther vigorously refuted in 1517. Nonetheless, both Protestant and Catholic universities retained the study of logic, natural philosophy, moral philosophy, and metaphysics for years to come.

Copenhaver and Schmitt (1992); Hankins (2007); Kristeller (1974a).

J. LAUREL CARRINGTON

Philosophy of Christ (*Philosophia Christi*)

In his early works, especially the *Handbook of the Christian Soldier* (*Enchiridion militis Christiani*, 1503), *In Praise of Folly* (*Moriae encomium*, 1511), and *A Guide to True Theology* (*Ratio verae theologiae*, 1518), *Desiderius Erasmus* promoted his vision of the philosophy of Christ. Erasmus's philosophy of Christ challenged the usefulness of the complex theology of the scholastics and the complicated rituals, *superstitions*, and corruption of the Catholic Church. Erasmus urged Christians to trust Christ and demonstrate their *faith* in their everyday lives instead of through what he considered useless ceremonies. At the center of Erasmus's philosophy of Christ stood the *Bible* and the conviction that listening to the pure Word of God would encourage Christians to live lives inspired by Christ's life and sacrifice. Erasmus believed that this individual spiritual renewal of Christians through the imitation of Christ would lead to the spiritual renewal

of the Catholic Church, and that as a result, the corruption, hypocrisy, and superstition that he found so objectionable in the church would be replaced by a spiritual and practical transformation of Christendom.

The *philosophia Christi* represented the application of Renaissance humanist ideals to Christianity, including the return to early church sources in their purest forms (*ad fontes*), the reform of *education* and the rejection of scholastic *dialectic*, and the return to classical models, in this case, the spirit of the early Christian church. Those who embraced Erasmus's vision of a renewed and regenerated church through this *philosophia Christi* focused on the wisdom of the church *fathers* and the recovery of the Bible free from the errors of medieval translation and interpretation. Furthermore, they embraced biblical *humanism*, or the application of humanistic philological skills in *Greek*, Latin, and *Hebrew*, to the study of the Bible and theology.

While Erasmus's philosophy of Christ advocated for the reform of the church and Christendom, it was not, by extension, in line with *Martin Luther's* Protestant *Reformation*. Erasmus abhorred Luther's vehemence and immoderate tone and eventually wrote against Luther in *On the Freedom of the Will* (*De libero arbitrio*, 1524). Furthermore, while Luther rejected the efficacy of church tradition, Erasmus relied on the church fathers and church tradition to support his program of renewal. In both, he found the models for his philosophy of Christ.

Conroy (1974); Nauert (2006); Tracy (1996).

GRETA GRACE KROEKER

Piety

The Protestant *Reformation* can be understood as a dispute over Roman Catholic definitions and practices of Christian piety. Piety for the Protestant reformers entailed proper humility that feared and revered God and responded with the recognition and praise of God's *grace* and benevolence. The Protestant reformers sought to resituate piety in relation to the primacy of *faith* and *Scripture*, as they believed that the Roman Catholic Church had made piety to be a matter of human efforts and works righteousness. Instead, piety for the Protestant reformers belonged to the believer's proper posture of humility, reverence, and faith toward God (all of which are gifts given by God), rather than being defined by *good works* performed by the believer; yet such good works do and must proceed from proper piety. Thus at the heart of the issue for the sixteenth-century Reformers was the true worship of God. Radical Reformers, however, tended to retain an understanding of piety more in relation to good works performed. "Piety" is a central theological theme particularly of *John Calvin*'s writings.

Lee (1997); Ngien (2007).

G. SUJIN PAK

Pirckheimer, Caritas (1467–1532)

Abbess of the Franciscan convent St. Clara in Nuremberg, Pirckheimer was famous for her education and intelligence, as well as her opposition to the Protestant *Reformation*. She corresponded with leading northern humanists, including *Johann Reuchlin*, *Desiderius Erasmus*, Conrad Celtis, and her own brother, *Willibald Pirckheimer*; *Philip Melanchthon* specifically complimented her Latin. Pirckheimer criticized the Reformation and defended her convent against forced dissolution. She used theological arguments, pleas for sympathy, family connections, and practical reasoning about the utility of the convent to battle against the city council and the newly converted families. The confrontation turned violent when mothers stormed the house and forcibly dragged their daughters out. The letters, petitions, and eyewitness accounts were preserved in a collective house memoir (the *Denkwürdigkeiten*). Despite concerted efforts from the city, Pirckheimer was able to keep the convent open, with the majority of the nuns remaining; but no new novices were allowed, and the convent eventually died out in 1591.

P. Barker (1995); Strasser (1995); Woodford (2002).

AMY E. LEONARD

Pirckheimer, Willibald (1470–1530)

Pirckheimer was a Nuremberg patrician, politician, and German humanist. A central participant in northern *humanism*, he maintained extensive correspondence with leading intellectuals and Reformers of the time, including *Desiderius Erasmus*, *Martin Luther*, *Philip Melanchthon*, and Albrecht Dürer, one of his closest friends. He studied law in Italy but quickly gravitated toward humanist subjects. He returned to Nuremberg in 1495 and became a city magistrate and councilor to the emperor, even leading a contingent from Nuremberg in the Swiss war of 1499, although he did not distinguish himself there. His family had deep connections to Catholicism (seven of his sisters and three of his daughters became nuns). He acted as mediator between Luther and his critics, causing him to be named in the bull of excommunication against Luther. Although sympathetic to the *Reformation*, the treatment of his sister Caritas (abbess at the Nuremberg Poor Clare house) helped convince him not to convert to Protestantism.

Spitz (1963, 1972); Strauss (1976).

AMY E. LEONARD

Plato (427–347 BCE)

Plato was a student of Socrates and along with *Aristotle* is the foundation for Western *philosophy*. While Aristotelian philosophy was central to medieval *scholasticism*,

Plato's work sparked a *Greek* revival in the Renaissance. The revival and reinterpretation of Plato was centered in Florence during the fifteenth century. Cosimo de Medici was the greatest patron of Platonic studies and supported its chief scholar, Marsilio Ficino, and his informal Platonic Academy. Plato's philosophy proved more compatible with Christianity than that of Aristotle concerning the immortality of the soul. A disciple of Ficino, Giovanni Pico della Mirandola, believed the work of Plato prepared the way for Christianity. Plato's influence was never as pervasive as Aristotle's, and Neoplatonists were more philosophers than humanists. While the first Platonic scholars resided in sixteenth-century Catholic Italy, in the seventeenth century proponents were found on both sides of the confessional divide, including a Protestant group centered at Cambridge.

Kristeller (1974b); Nauert (2006); Robb (1935).

JILL R. FEHLEISON

Pole, Reginald Cardinal (1500–1558)

A grand-nephew of Edward IV, Pole was perhaps the most significant early opponent of the *Reformation in England*, and a crucial figure in international Catholic reform. Although courted by *Henry VIII*, Pole blasted him from Italian exile in 1536 in his *De unitate ecclesiae* (*Of the Unity of the Church*). Created cardinal and legate by *Paul III*, Pole was tasked with encouraging an invasion by the Catholic powers; in response, Henry planned his assassination. Pole was a key protagonist at the early stages of the *Council of Trent*, where he (unsuccessfully) promoted an understanding of *justification* similar to *Martin Luther*'s. In 1550 he came within a whisker of being elected pope. Instead, as archbishop of Canterbury, he masterminded the restoration of Catholicism in England after the accession of *Mary I* (Tudor), proposing substantive reforms and overseeing the suppression of Protestant dissidents. He died within hours of the queen in November 1558.

Duffy (2009); Fenlon (1972); Mayer (2000).

PETER MARSHALL

Polity

Though defined generally as the forms of government of a social institution, with regard to the Age of Reformation "polity" refers to the structure or government of a *church*. From the Catholic Church in which the polity basically revolves around the position of the bishop, each reformed religion established its own polity and manner of governance for its church. Some churches, such as the Anglican, retained a basic episcopal structure, but instituted the idea of the monarch or a secular prince gaining the position of leader of the church. The Swiss Reformed churches (and their counterparts on both sides of the Atlantic), on the other hand, established a more Presbyterian polity, while some of the more radical religions such as the *Anabaptists* and the Society of Friends formed a polity more based on congregationalism. The polity of the church created the structure of that church and the laws that governed it.

Höpfl (1982); Pocock (2009); Thomson (1980).

KRISTEN POST WALTON

Practical Syllogism

In the history of Calvinism, "practical syllogism" refers to the significance of works for personal assurance of salvation. The idea asserts that works can be drawn upon for personal confirmation of *election*. In this way election can be inferred a posteriori by paying attention to its signs, such as *good works*. The practical syllogism can be summarized in the following terms: "Those who are justified will do good works: But I do good works: therefore, I am justified." The mere assertion that *justification* can be inferred from works is problematic from a Protestant perspective, as it may appear to indicate that justification is somehow dependent upon works. Yet this is not the function of the practical syllogism. The place of the practical syllogism in *John Calvin*'s theology has been debated, while some scholars credit *Theodore de Beza* with its systematic use.

Strehle (1995); Venema (2007); Zachman (1993).
                              RADY ROLDAN-FIGUEROA

Prayer   For the Catholic much private prayer took place in public *worship*. Attending the Latin *Mass*, the faithful spent their time in devotional exercises, often using books of prayers. Protestants put their liturgies into the vernacular so that attending the service could largely be public prayer, whether sung, spoken, or listened to. Sung prayer was particularly important. For Lutherans this took the form of hymns. The Reformed sang metrical paraphrases of the Psalms, the authorized and required biblical prayers. Biblical models also shaped the spoken prayers in Reformed worship. Regarding private prayer *Martin Luther* advised his followers to use the Lord's Prayer as an outline to their meditations and supplications, while *John Calvin* said the Psalms were the best teachers. Prayer was request, but included such topics as praise and confession. Anglican public and private prayer was shaped by the offices of Matins and Evensong adapted from the Roman divine *office*.

Hammerling (2008); McKee (1992); Russell (2002).
                              GARY NEAL HANSEN

Preaching   Though the late medieval Christian church demonstrated an increased focus on preaching, the Protestant reformers insisted upon preaching as the pastor's chief duty—thus replacing the centrality of the Catholic *Mass* with the Protestant sermon. Preaching for the Protestant reformers was the proclamation of God's Word and the *gospel* of Jesus Christ as revealed in *Scripture*. *Martin Luther* and *John Calvin* viewed preaching as the communication of *faith* (cf. Rom 10:17) so that it formed, edified, and defined the church, thus becoming a central mark of the true *church*. Protestant preaching differed from what came before through its predominantly expository and catechetical style, indicating that a sermon's main purposes were instruction of believers in the biblical text and its applications. While Luther held to a very intimate bond between Word and *Holy Spirit*, so that preaching is an encounter with the Word of God, *Huldrych Zwingli* distinguished between human preaching ("external word") and the inner work of the Spirit ("internal Word"). Calvin emphasized that the Word of God is preached through the human if God wills the presence of the Spirit in it.

O. Edwards (2004); Old (2002); T. Parker (1992).
                              G. SUJIN PAK

Predestination   In theology "predestination" refers to God's determination in advance of those elected to salvation. Concerning predestination, Protestants disputed about whether God foreknew *good works* and counted them in the decision of *election* to salvation or not, whether God only elects to salvation (single predestination) or elects both to salvation and reprobation (double predestination), whether the proper place of predestination in the larger theological system is as part of the doctrine of God or the doctrine of salvation, and whether election occurs pre-fall (supralapsarianism) or post-fall (infralapsarianism). Predestination was already a contentious issue in late medieval Catholic theology, but the prevailing view on the eve of the Protestant Reformation was a form of single predestination, where God elected individuals to salvation based upon foreknowledge of their good works.

Early Lutheran and Reformed theologians rejected the view that God elected to salvation based upon foreseen merit—a view that undermined the doctrine of *justification* by *faith* alone. *Martin Luther* held to a strong doctrine of predestination; however, he considered it part of the hidden mystery of God and not a subject for public teaching and *preaching*. After Luther's death, *Philip Melanchthon* espoused the views that the human *will* cooperates in some way in salvation and that reprobation is the just desert for human sins. This led to a split in the Lutheran confession between Gnesio-Lutherans and Philippists. The 1577 Formula of Concord settled the controversy by stating that God elects to salvation based only upon God's *grace*, while reprobation is a matter of justice for human *sin*.

Predestination was a prominent doctrine among Reformed confessions and also a source of controversy. *Huldrych Zwingli* tied predestination to his doctrines of God and *providence* and argued that God elects to salvation and reprobation based only upon God's goodness with no account of human *merit*. Though *John Calvin* also viewed predestination as a matter of God's sovereign will, he placed it within his discussion of justification. He argued that salvation and damnation are equally acts of God's will, thus advocating a robust double predestination. In 1551 *Jerome Bolsec* challenged Calvin's doctrine of predestination, arguing that it made God a tyrant, and was exiled from Geneva. *Heinrich Bullinger*, Zwingli's successor in Zurich, also rejected Calvin's double predestination, argued that it made God the author of sin, and promoted the view that election is by grace, while reprobation is a matter of justice.

Theodore de Beza, Calvin's successor in Geneva, adopted supralapsarianism, which taught that God wills salvation and damnation even before the fall occurred. The more common Reformed view, however, became infralapsarianism, where God's decree of election to salvation comes after the fall.

Predestination became a central issue in the Dutch Reformation when *Jacobus Arminius* argued that predestination is a matter of God's foreknowledge of those who will have persevering faith. In response, the *Synod of Dort* reaffirmed double predestination, which the 1646 Westminster Confession also sanctioned. *England's Thirty-Nine Articles* advocated single predestination, while the 1595 Lambeth Articles affirmed double predestination. Yet by the early seventeenth century Anglicans embraced Arminianism. The Radical Reformers rejected the doctrine of predestination and asserted that the human will played a decisive role in both salvation and reprobation.

Opponents of the doctrine argued that such a teaching denied the importance of good works for the believer, was a form of fatalism, and made God the author of evil. Proponents responded that the good works of believers are important but have no place in the economy of salvation, that to teach that God was the author of evil was monstrous, and that this doctrine was not a choice, but the clear teaching of Scripture. The *Council of Trent*, in its sixth session meeting in 1547, formally anathematized those who hold some of the beliefs taught by Calvin and other predestinarian theologians.

Kolb (2005); Muller (1988); Venema (2002).

G. SUJIN PAK

Priesthood   The priesthood was an integral part of the Catholic religion. By the sixteenth century, becoming a priest was a *sacrament* called Holy Orders.

A member of the Catholic priesthood was separate from the layperson in the Catholic Church and held an important role within the church. Under the Protestant Reformation, the *clergy* took over a different role. Under the Protestant religions, a sacrament was not included as part of the process to become a member of the clergy, as the clergy were no longer seen as God's representatives on earth, but were instead looked to as guides within the religion. Protestants believed in a priesthood of all believers, while for Catholics, priests were male, followed a path of *celibacy*, and led the laity in public *worship* as intermediaries between humans and God. Priests were part of the episcopal structure of the Catholic Church.

P. Marshall (1994).
KRISTEN POST WALTON

Priesthood of Believers   As found in some of *Martin Luther*'s early writings, the common *priesthood* is nothing less, or more, than every Christian's calling to a life of sacrificial service and intercession before God on behalf of all who are in need, including the ability to assure one another of God's forgiveness (*absolution*). *Baptism* gives every Christian these priestly rights and duties. Since this priesthood is common, Luther dismissed the traditional distinction between the spiritual and temporal estates, which had placed the pope and his bishops beyond the governing authority of the German princes. Luther thought that the princes, acting through the common priesthood in the role of "emergency bishops," could rightly intervene in the affairs of the *church*, though not in the ministry per se. The authority of the church's pastoral *office* derives not from the common priesthood, but from the Word of God by and for which God established it.

Nagel (1997); Wengert (2005).
MICKEY L. MATTOX

Printer-Scholars   In the late fifteenth and early sixteenth century printer-scholars played an essential role in the preparation and dissemination of humanistic and theological projects. Johannes Froben (1460–1527) of Basel, Johannes Amerbach (1443–1513) of Basel, Aldus Manutius (1449–1515) of Venice, and Dirk Martens (1446/47–1534) of Flanders not only printed books important to *humanism* and the *Reformation*, but also provided intellectual centers that attracted some of the leading figures of the early modern period and aided the spread of the Reformation. Amerbach and Froben, in particular, helped make *Basel* a vibrant intellectual city and gathered to their printing houses scholars like *Johann Reuchlin, Beatus Rhenanus*, and *Desiderius Erasmus*, and artists like the Holbeins. In Zurich Christoph Froschauer (ca. 1490–1564) printed religious tracts by *Martin Luther* and *Huldrych Zwingli* and played a crucial role in promoting the cause of the Zurich reformers.

Bentley (1983); M. Edwards (1994); Gordon (2002); Nauert (2006).
GRETA GRACE KROEKER

Printing   In the 1450s *Johann Gutenberg* established the first European printing press in Germany and published his Gutenberg Bible circa 1455. The printing press allowed for religious (and other) ideas to spread more quickly across Europe during the sixteenth century. As a result, *Martin Luther*'s Ninety-Five Theses were able to spread quickly and the ideas took root, allowing him to commence the *Reformation*, which earlier Reformers such as *John Wyclif* and *Jan Hus* had not been able to do. The printing press was utilized extensively by both the Catholic and Reforming factions during the age of reformation, at which time propaganda was first used extensively. The printing press also allowed for more individuals to buy and read copies of the *Bible* themselves, which helped the flourishing of the new religions. Furthermore, printing, combined with Reformed beliefs that all should be able to read the Bible, meant that literacy rates began to soar during the sixteenth century, particularly in Reformed areas.

M. Edwards (1994); Eisenstein (1993); Gilmont (1998); Kingdon (1985b).

KRISTEN POST WALTON

Private Mass   A private *mass* is performed by a lone priest without other communicants present, often for an absent donor's *penance* or for souls of the dead. A widespread practice by the ninth century, churches and monasteries accepted donations to perform these masses, leading to an increase in the number of ordained priests whose primary duty was to perform the ritual and a proliferation of private chapels. Leaders of the *Reformation* universally condemned the practice as part of the larger battle over the Eucharist. *Martin Luther* argued that in a private mass the sacrificial aspect of the ritual was dominant but the crucial communion of the faithful was absent. Both Luther and *John Calvin* wrote that the private mass went against the intentions of the *Lord's Supper*, which was meant to be Christians partaking in the *sacrament* together. The *Council of Trent* reaffirmed private masses, asserting that the lone priest also celebrated for all faithful of the *church*.

Croken (1990); Metzger (1997); Wandel (2006).

JILL R. FEHLEISON

Prophecy   In the sense of predictions of cataclysm and divine judgment, prophecies were common in the later Middle Ages. In Florence Girolamo Savonarola (1452–98) preached condemnation of the Medici and the *papacy*. The *Reformatio Sigismundi* and the "Prophet of the Upper Rhine" pre-dicted violent political, religious, and social transformation in Germany in the century before the *Reformation*. Protestant prophecy was more closely tied to the text of the *Bible*, in particular the books of Revelation and Daniel. *Martin Luther* and Lutherans were particularly marked by apocalyptic foreboding. In Zwinglian Zurich, systematic biblical *exegesis* was itself termed "prophecy." Among more radical Protestants, a freer form of prophecy made its appearance with the *Zwickau prophets* and in *Anabaptism* (*Melchior Hoffmann*; Leonard and Ursula Jost, d. 1530). Catholic prophecy continued with figures such as the Venetian Virgin Giovanna Veronese (ca. 1496–1549). But prophets and their predictions commonly flourished in times of trouble. *Henry VIII's* reign (1509–47) saw many.

Barnes (1988); Jansen (1991); G. H. Williams (1992).

R. EMMET MCLAUGHLIN

Providence   Protestants, particularly within the Reformed tradition, placed special emphasis on God's providential governance of creation. This expressed itself in a belief that God caused all events, from the most to the least significant, leaving no independent role for *natural laws* or chance. For *John Calvin* providence encompassed human choices, including *sins*, that were divinely ordained (not merely permitted) without compromising God's righteousness or exculpating sinners. Because from the human perspective future events were contingent, Christians were warned against neglecting to order their lives in accord with God's revealed *will* or despising the mundane means through which God typically provided for their needs. Once an event had occurred, however, one could rest assured that it had been divinely foreordained. For some a source of comfort and freedom from worry, for others the doctrine of providence led to an anxious fixation on interpreting events to discover one's standing before God, especially one's predestined eternal fate.

Helm (2004); Schreiner (1991); Walsham (1999).

DANIEL EPPLEY

Purgatory Controversy over the existence of purgatory was a major feature of the *Reformation*, particularly in its early stages, and went to the heart of competing doctrines of salvation. The doctrine of a "third place" in the next life alongside heaven and hell developed over the course of the early Middle Ages and was in finished form by at least the twelfth century, when the noun *purgatorium* began to be used widely by theologians. Belief in purgatory reflected the commonsense view that only a small minority (monks, saints, and martyrs) were holy enough to merit immediate entry to heaven, but God was too merciful to consign the rest of humanity to unceasing torment in hell. Instead, they would be given an opportunity for their souls to be purified in advance of the Beatific Vision. The theological rationale was that while the *sacrament* of *penance* guaranteed forgiveness of *sins*, there was still a "debt" for them due to God, and penances performed in this life would be unlikely to pay off more than a portion of this necessary tariff: a spell in purgatory would secure the rest.

The existence of purgatory was formally defined by the Second Council of Lyons in 1274, and the Council of Florence in 1439, but the formulations said little about what souls could expect to find there. Preachers and devotional writers made up the deficit, usually suggesting purgatory was a place of fire and pain, distinguishable from hell only by its limited duration. Although the nature of time in purgatory was a complex theological issue, popular teaching usually put across the idea that souls could expect hundreds, or even thousands, of "years" of fiery purgation.

Yet Christians were not helpless in the face of this sobering prospect. The living had the ability, and the duty, to ease and shorten the sufferings of the dead: by praying for them, by having masses said on their behalf, or by acquiring *indulgences* (which from 1476 were available to assist souls already in purgatory). For those facing the prospect of *death*, securing the intercession of the community could be a strong priority, and gifts to churches, or legacies to kin and neighbors, were often contingent upon being "remembered." *Martin Luther* did not at first directly attack purgatory, though by 1530 he, along with most Reformers, had come to see it as incompatible with *justification* by *faith*. Protestants pointed out the word was not to be found anywhere in *Scripture* (Catholics countered that neither was the word "*Trinity*"). In Protestant states, institutions devoted to praying for the souls of the dead—monasteries, chantries, and fraternities—were abolished, though in Catholic societies the cult of the "Holy Souls" intensified in the Baroque era.

Koslofsky (2000); Le Goff (1984); P. Marshall (2002).

PETER MARSHALL

Puritans The term "Puritan" emerged as a term of abuse in *England* early in the reign of *Elizabeth I* (1558–1603). At that period, "Puritan" or (a near-synonym) "Precisian" were labels for those who wished both to purify the English church of perceived popish remnants, and to purify believers' lives of the dregs of idolatry. Early Puritanism's main ambitions were outward and structural. The most outspoken Puritans wished to replace the *Book of Common Prayer* with a purified liturgy such as that of Geneva, and to introduce presbyterian structures that would secure the English church's political independence. Many looked to the reformed Scottish church as a model. Naturally, the queen and her allies opposed this and successfully blocked Puritan agitation at every turn.

Other, more moderate Puritans aimed to reform the *church* from within; one such, Edmund Grindal, became archbishop of Canterbury in 1575. Grindal successfully promoted the *Geneva Bible* in England, but his refusal to suppress the "prophesyings" (public masterclasses in scriptural *exegesis* that the queen feared were disorderly and seditious) led to his house arrest and effective suspension. Puritan frustration with the queen boiled over in 1588 with the publication of a scurrilous set of anti-episcopal tracts under the pseudonym Martin Marprelate, giving the regime a pretext for a crackdown against Puritan activism.

Thereafter another face of Puritanism emerged, more pastoral than political. Puritan-leaning ministers such as Richard Greenham, Richard Rogers, and William Perkins developed a spirituality of inner renewal and rigorous personal discipline. Seeing itself as an elect remnant among a reprobate people, Puritanism became a self-conscious subculture in early-seventeenth-century England: striving for visible signs of *election* and holiness, Puritans were mocked, admired, and feared by the wider culture. Lacking *consistories* or external disciplinary structures, they embraced a formidable inner discipline. Their strong commitment to double *predestination* fostered rigorous self-observation. Yet almost all Puritans remained committed to the visible unity of the English church and condemned separatism.

Puritan emigrants to Ireland and (especially) New England were able to realize these ambitions to some extent, creating comprehensive godly structures and pursuing collective holiness: later seventeenth-century Massachusetts was in effect a Puritan society.

In England, however, the ceremonial revival under King Charles I (r. 1625–49) provoked an angry response from Puri-

tans, and helped to drive many previously conformist Protestants into their camp. The winning side in the English Civil War (1642–46) was defined in part by its Puritanism, indeed its presbyterianism; and following the execution of Charles I, the period of republican government (1649–60) has been described as one of Puritan rule. Yet Puritanism also splintered into competing sects during this period, and the restoration of the monarchy led to the final defeat of Puritan political ambitions.

J. Coffey and Lim (2008); Collinson (1967); Durston and Eales (1996).

ALEC RYRIE

Reason   Protestant reformers emphasized that after the fall human reason was corrupted and bred idolatry. *Martin Luther*, in particular, rejected any supremacy given to reason or *philosophy* in favor of the primacy of *faith* and *Scripture*. Though Luther expressed views that reason can become a useful tool after it has been redeemed and enlightened by faith, the weight of his statements were negative because he believed that reason led a person toward works righteousness rather than sole reliance on *faith* and God's *grace*. While *John Calvin* and *Philip Melanchthon* agreed with the primacy of faith and the view of Scripture as the foremost *authority*, they later sought to return to a more robust use of reason and philosophy as a handmaiden to faith and theology. Hence, Protestant *scholasticism* reaffirmed both the preeminence of faith and the use of reason and philosophy in service to faith. *Huldrych Zwingli*, as well as the *Anabaptists*, tended to set up a more radical antithesis between reason and faith, expressing greater skepticism concerning the reliability of reason.

Chia (2007); Gerrish (1962); Asselt and Dekker (2001).

G. SUJIN PAK

Reformation   In general, "reformation" connotes the restoration of something to its original state or condition. In the later Middle Ages there were increasing calls for a reformation of *church* and society in the wake of the papal schism and the development of the Hussite heresy in Bohemia. The conciliar movement called for a reform of the church "in head and members," while monastic reforms attempted to bring religious orders back to the principles associated with their founders. By the early sixteenth century, humanist concern with classical antiquity found its religious counterpart in editions of the New Testament and the church *fathers. Desiderius Erasmus* and his followers used these to promote reform following the model of the early church.

Martin Luther's theses criticizing the sale of *indulgences* were part of this effort to eliminate abuses and return the church to a more pristine form. Luther did not intend to divide Western Christendom, but his emphasis on the sole authority of the *Bible* led to a radical understanding of reformation, since it meant the rejection of beliefs and practices that were based on tradition. In his 1520 *Address to the German Nobility* he condemned the papacy for blocking reform by claiming the sole *authority* to interpret *Scripture* and institute reforms. *John Calvin* would argue in the prefatory letter to his *Institutes of the Christian Religion* that the Reformers were more faithful to the teachings and practices of the early church than were the supporters of the pope. For the Reformers, the church needed to be cleansed of medieval accretions and brought back into accord with Scripture.

The Reformers did not agree among themselves, however, in their interpretation of Scripture and about the extent and manner of reformation. The south Germans and Swiss urged a more radical reform of *worship*; more significantly, they disagreed with Luther's understanding of the *Lord's Supper*, which eventually led to the division between the Lutheran and Reformed churches. *Anabaptists* argued that infant *baptism* was not mentioned in the Bible and so rejected it, and a few radicals argued against the Nicene formulation of the *Trinity* for the same reason. In *England* the contrasting religious policies of King *Henry VIII* and each of his children made the Anglican Reformation quite different from developments on the Continent. By the mid-sixteenth century reform efforts within the Catholic Church combined with measures to stop the spread of Protestantism to produce a *Catholic Reformation*.

The splintering of the evangelical movement, the varying types of doctrinal and institutional reform, and the movement for Catholic renewal have led some historians to posit many "Reformations" during the sixteenth century rather than one unitary Reformation associated with Protestantism. Despite the diversity of goals and reform measures, though, all of these groups agreed in desiring to restore the church to its earlier, more pure state.

Cameron (1991); Hendrix (2004); Hillerbrand (2007); MacCulloch (2004).

AMY NELSON BURNETT

Regeneration   "Regeneration" refers to new birth of the Christian to life in Christ. Traditions differ as to when and how this happens, and it is often termed "*sanctification*." For the Catholic, regeneration is understood to happen in *baptism* wherein *original sin* is washed away and *grace* is infused, enabling life in *faith*, hope, and *love*. In Lutheran teaching baptism is also when regeneration happens, though the focus is on the proclamation on the *gospel* promise rather than on washing, and confessional documents also speak of faith bringing regeneration. *John Calvin* interpreted repentance as regeneration, a turning to God inseparable from faith but not to be confused with it. Sin no longer has dominion because of this new life, but for Calvin regeneration does not lead to sinless life. Only the *Anabaptist* communities, for whom baptism came as proclamation of a decided adult discipleship, expected a pure life of obedience to follow.

———
McGrath (1982); Trigg (1994); Wilcox (1997).

GARY NEAL HANSEN

Regensburg, Diet of   The Diet of Regensburg (Fr. Ratisbon) began in April 1541 under the authority of Emperor *Charles V.* The theological debates focused on the so-called Book of Regensburg drafted by *Martin Bucer* and Johannes Gropper, though neither *Martin Luther* nor *Philip Melanchthon* thought much of the work. When the Colloquy of Regensburg began on April 27 the book had been revised by *Gasparo Contarini* and formed the basis of the discussion. Numerous drafts were provided by both sides, including from Melanchthon and *Johann Eck.* The most significant issues were *justification,* the *sacraments,* and the *church* and its *authority.* By the end of May the Book of Regensburg contained 23 articles and was submitted, along with Protestant amendments, to the emperor. There was general belief that agreement had been reached on the vexed issue of justification. However, both Rome and the Catholic princes of the empire rejected the book. Many of the articles concerning Communion in both kinds, married clergy, and the Eucharist were deemed unacceptable compromises.

———
Brady (1995); Greschat (2004); Matheson (1972).

BRUCE GORDON

Reina, Casiodoro de (ca. 1520–94)
Reina was a Spanish Protestant translator of the Bible. He was a member of the Spanish observant branch of the

Order of Saint Jerome at the time of his conversion. He left Seville in 1557 and found refuge in Geneva. His irenic spirit made him sympathize with the fallen *Michael Servetus,* but he himself never articulated the theological ideas of the Aragonese thinker. He left Geneva and moved to *England.* In London he managed to organize a small Reformed Spanish congregation under the auspices of the Dutch and French Stranger churches. He wrote the *Confession de Fe Christiana* (Spanish Confession of Faith) in 1560. False charges of sodomy and *heresy* forced him to leave England. Thereafter he resided in Antwerp, Frankfurt, and Basel. In 1569 he published the first ever complete Spanish Bible to appear in print. By 1579 he had made a complete transition to Lutheranism.

———
Kinder (1975); Roldan-Figueroa (2005, 2006a and b).

RADY ROLDAN-FIGUEROA

Relics   *Saints'* relics—pieces of saints' bodies, clothing, or other connected items—were an important and popular part of late medieval Roman Catholic practice, as well as one of the first things attacked by critics like *Desiderius Erasmus.* Relics and the reliquaries that held them were at the center of many rituals connected to the cult of saints, both before and throughout the *Reformation* period. Roman Catholics believed that the physical connection to the saint gave a relic its power, and, according to orthodox Roman teachings, they venerated relics as representative of their respective saints. Collecting relics was seen as a *good work* to reduce one's time in *purgatory; Frederick the Wise, Martin Luther's* supporter, famously owned a collection of over nineteen thousand relics. Protestants viewed the use of relics as a superstitious practice that hindered true Christian faith. Relics were subject to iconoclastic attacks in some Protestant areas, particularly where the Swiss Reformed tradition was influential.

Dillenberger (1999); Duffy (2005); Eire (1986); Parish (2005).
KAREN E. SPIERLING

Religion   From the Middle Ages through the Age of the *Reformation*, religion was a regular part of life for almost every person living in Europe. Through 1517 the primary religion was Roman Christianity, which is now known as Catholicism. Religion was not simply a matter of attending *church* on Sundays, but instead, religion shaped every aspect of people's lives during this period. Holy days were days off work for the average person, the church was involved in every major life moment, and religion was something that one would fight and die for without much encouragement. In this period, religion was seen as a science, which laid out the absolute truths of how the world operated. With the Reformation, religion became an even more intense part of people's lives as both the Protestant and Catholic reforms further defined the church and religion. Only at the end of the seventeenth and beginning of the eighteenth century did people begin to respect the idea of an individual's right to follow his or her own *faith*.

Cameron (1991); Hsia (2005); G. H. Williams (1992).
KRISTEN POST WALTON

Resurrection   Though the Protestant reformers rejected *purgatory* as an unbiblical fiction, they strongly held to the physical resurrection of the dead to judgment or to eternal life. They taught that the Christian should face *death* not with fear but with confidence because Christ's righteousness has been applied to them. The Christian's faith in the resurrection is founded on Jesus' resurrection. At the resurrection, body and soul, separated at death, come together. The body that is resurrected is the same body that died, albeit transformed. The exact nature of this resurrected body and of the state of the person between death and the resurrection were not systematically expounded by the major Reformers. *Martin Luther* intimated that the soul of the dead enjoys a "sweet sleep" after death, but his thought is not entirely consistent. *John Calvin*'s summary of the resurrection is that the righteous are consoled forever while the reprobate suffer eternal destruction.

Althaus (1966); Partee (2008); Sauter (2004).
GREGORY J. MILLER

Reuchlin, Johann (1455–1522) Reuchlin was a German humanist and legal scholar who studied in Freiburg, Paris, and Basel. He published a *Hebrew* grammar and investigated the Jewish Kabbalah at a time when Hebrew studies were virtually unknown north of Italy. Beginning in 1511, he became the center of a controversy pitting scholastic theologians against humanist scholars, concerning the claim by Johannes Pfefferkorn, a converted Jew, that Hebrew books were insulting to Christianity and should be burned. Emperor *Maximilian I* requested the opinions of numerous scholars, of whom Reuchlin alone counseled against the recommendation. He and Pfefforkorn engaged in polemics that drew in supporters on both sides. In 1514 Reuchlin published *Letters of Famous Men*, a show of support by his humanist champions; the following year *Letters of Obscure Men* appeared, an anonymous satire on the scholastic theologians. *Martin Luther* sided publicly with Reuchlin, and in 1520 claimed that the same people who had attacked Reuchlin were now attacking him.

Levi (2002); Rummel (2002); Spitz (1963).
J. LAUREL CARRINGTON

Revelation   In theological terms "revelation" is divinely revealed knowledge that transcends human *reason* and empiricism. Catholic teaching denied that reason and revelation could clash since God, Reason itself, was the source of both. Any apparent disagreement was the result of human miscalculation. For the Catholic Church *Scripture* never stood alone but was only received embedded in the church's tradition of *interpretation* guided by the *Holy Spirit*. It was paralleled by an apostolic tradition of belief and practice that was not always reflected in written Scripture, as in the case of infant *baptism*. Magisterial Protestant reformers allowed for conflicts between reason and revelation, limited revelation to Scripture, and gave priority to individual interpretation, though crediting legally binding confessions issued by state churches. While radical spiritualists agreed in emphasizing the clash of reason and revelation, they argued for direct individual inspiration that preceded any understanding of the text and might extend beyond what was contained in Scripture.

Brunner (1946); Gilson (1938); G. H. Williams (1992).
                    R. EMMET MCLAUGHLIN

Rhenanus, Beatus (1485–1547) Philologist, textual scholar, historian, and editor, Rhenanus was born in Sélestat, the son of a prosperous butcher. He studied initially at Sélestat's famous Latin school and then in Paris, where he befriended *Faber Stapulensis* (Jacques Lefèvre d'Étaples). In 1511 he moved to Basel to work for the Froben press, becoming part of the circle that included *Desiderius Erasmus*. He favored the latter's humanistic reform, and like many humanists, he initially supported *Martin Luther*, but later turned against his approach when he realized its radical nature. By 1528 Rhenanus had moved back to Sélestat to pursue his scholarship in relative seclusion. Less celebrated than Erasmus, he nonetheless is significant for his method of textual criticism based on a careful examination of manuscripts, employing his deep knowledge of history and paleography, as opposed to conjecture. His works include a biography of Erasmus, a history of Germany, and annotated editions of Tacitus, Tertullian, and Pliny.

D'Amico (1988); Hirstein (1995).
                    J. LAUREL CARRINGTON

Rhetoric   Also called the art of persuasion, rhetoric has its Western roots in ancient Greece. According to *Aristotle's Rhetoric*, there are three components to a speech, each of which is a basis for persuasion: the speaker, by establishing oneself as a person of integrity; the audience, by appealing to the emotions of the listeners; and the subject matter, by presenting the pertinent facts and arguments. A second classification divides types of oratory according to function. Deliberative oratory, concerning future actions, refers to policy debates within an assembly; judicial or forensic oratory, having to do with past events, encompasses speech in a court of law; and epideictic oratory, rooted in present circumstances, covers speeches of praise or blame.

Aristotle regarded rhetoric as being closely related to *dialectic*, or logic (the construction of arguments), but the exact relationship between rhetoric and dialectic was either ill-defined or contentious from antiquity onward, as theorists considered rhetoric to embrace subject matter as well as style. In *Plato's Gorgias* Socrates criticizes rhetoric as a form of flattery, seeking to present opinion as attractive rather than to pursue truth with single-minded rigor; Cicero in *De oratore (On the Orator)*, on the other hand, deplores the disciplinary division between thinking and speaking well. In the Renaissance, humanists were sharply critical of the theologians and philosophers in the universities, who they believed dealt in abstractions that were both inaccessible to most people and irrelevant to the conduct of a good life. Humanists replaced the focus on dialectic that was characteristic of the universities with a focus on rhetoric, which is concerned with specific persons, of a particular time and place, involved in specific situations.

From its beginnings rhetorical theory pertained to speech rather than to the written word, but over time it came to be applied to literature, especially in circumstances where opportunities for public life were limited. The Renaissance humanist revival of rhetoric began in the context of the rich political culture of the Italian city-states; early humanists drew upon the medieval handbooks that instructed students in dictamen, the art of letter writing for diplomatic and legal purposes. Officials called notaries, who filled a growing need for such correspondence as well as for legal documents, were trained in Roman law. As interest in ancient literature developed, humanists came to focus on classical sources, particularly the rhetorical works of Cicero and Quintilian.

Rhetoric played a significant role in the *Reformation*, with the centrality the Reformers accorded to *Scripture* and with their emphasis on preaching. Many Reformers drew upon *Desiderius Erasmus*'s New Testament scholarship, which emphasized Scripture's rhetorical features. *Philip Melanchthon* authored two rhetorical treatises, *Institutiones rhetoricae* (*Instruction in the Art of Rhetoric*) and *Elementorum rhetorices libri II* (*The Elements of Rhetoric in Two Volumes*).

Kennedy (1980); J. Murphy (1983); Schneider (1990).

J. LAUREL CARRINGTON

Riemenschneider, Tilman (ca. 1460–1531)

One of sixteenth-century Germany's leading sculptors, Riemenschneider made his career as an artist, a city councilman, and eventually mayor of Würzburg, where he moved in 1483. Married for the first of four times in 1485, his wife's inheritance allowed him to advance from journeyman to master. Sculpting in stone and linden, he was known for pioneering the monochrome style, instead of the highly painted and gilded decorative techniques more common to his era. Two of his major commissions survive: the Münnerstadt Altarpiece (made between 1490 and 1492) and the Holy Blood Altarpiece in Rothenburg-ob-der-Tauber (made between 1501 and 1505). As a member of Würzburg's municipal council during the German *Peasants' War*, he paid for the city's support of the peasants with arrest, imprisonment, and torture. After his release in late 1525, he concentrated for the rest of his life on restoring work damaged during that war.

Bier (1982); Chapuis (1999, 2004); Kalden-Rosenfeld (2004).

KATHRYN A. EDWARDS

Righteousness

In theology "righteousness" is the quality or attribute of being morally upright or justifiable before God. In the centuries before the Reformation, Christian theology was ambiguous as to whether *Scripture* referred to the "righteousness of God" as the *grace* God bestowed upon the sinner (imputed righteousness) or whether it was God's own righteousness in contradistinction to human corruption in which human virtue received reward and human vice met divine punishment (distributive justice). The scholastic tradition held these two *interpretations* together in tension, thus intimating that both human and divine actions were required to accomplish a person's righteousness before God. However, *Martin Luther* challenged the latter notion, solidifying the righteousness of God as a passive gift in which God justifies by *faith*. In God's Word, Luther posited, God pardons sinners by imputing

Christ's righteousness to them. Later, *John Calvin* understood the righteousness of faith forensically, separating God's declaration of righteousness and the actual human renewal.

Billings (2008); Iwand (2008); Kang (2006).
BRIAN C. BREWER

Rome, Church of　The site of a vigorous network of Christians during the first century CE, Rome and the *church* there developed into the center of Latin Christendom under the *papacy* in the late Antique period and early Middle Ages. Rome became identified early with *Peter*, who according to Petrine theory was appointed by Christ (in Matt. 16:16–18) as head of the apostles and chief pastor of his church. According to tradition, Peter resided in Rome, served as its first bishop, and died dramatically as a martyr there. Paul also interacted with the congregation and was executed in Rome. The church's identification with these two apostles, especially Peter, and the city's position as Imperial metropole provided Roman bishops with compelling arguments for primacy over the universal, or catholic, church. After Constantine (272–337) moved the Imperial capital to Constantinople (330), church patriarchs there also laid claim to primacy. Church councils at Constantinople (381) and Chalcedon recognized their preeminence, though Roman bishops rejected these judgments on the basis of apostolic succession from Peter.

Over the course of the Middle Ages, the Roman Catholic Church came to exert jurisdiction over all churches in Europe, and popes worked out more expanded visions of papal *authority*. With the collapse of the Western empire at the end of the 400s, Roman bishops became widely recognized as the ultimate spiritual authority across Europe. In the 800s the paternal title "Pope" became reserved exclusively for the Roman bishop. The High Middle Ages

(1000–1350) marked a high watermark for papal authority. Popes continually asserted the primacy of the Roman see over the patriarchate of Constantinople, leading to schism in 1054; they pressed their prerogatives with political authorities, generating numerous conflicts, such as the lay investiture controversy; and, they called for military action against enemies of Christianity, calling Crusades (1096–1272) against Muslims and against Cathar heretics. The codification of church canons and the rise of theological study in universities produced a fully developed theological system. Roman Catholic theology was centered on the Trinitarian conception of God, seven *sacraments*, and clerical authority, which was set forth by the Fourth *Lateran Council* (1215) and affirmed by the *Council of Trent* (1545–63).

The Roman Church lost its grip over Western Christendom in the Protestant *Reformation* (1517–1648). Theological disputes and geopolitical rivalries fractured Christian unity, as Great Britain, the Netherlands, Scandinavia, Hungary, and large portions of Germany, Switzerland, and eastern Europe broke away permanently from the Roman Church. The advent of the Enlightenment, liberal revolutions, skeptical thought, and widespread warfare further eroded the church's influence in the eighteenth and nineteenth centuries. It remains, however, the largest Christian denomination in the world today, claiming over a billion members.

P. Brown (2003); Pelikan (1975–91); Southern (1990).
CHARLES PARKER

Sabbath　Early Christians initially observed Saturday, the seventh day of the Jewish week, as a day of rest and *prayer*. Gradually that observance shifted to Sunday, but during the *Reformation* two groups of religious radicals returned to observance of the Jewish Sabbath. From 1527 to 1550 Sabbatarian *Anabaptists* under the influence of Oswald Glaidt and Andreas Fischer were active in Moravia and Silesia. Their practices and teachings elicited responses from a number of Reformers, most notably from *Martin Luther* in his 1538 *Wider die Sabbather* (*Against the Sabbatarians*). Luther's fear that the Sabbatarian Anabaptists were evidence of successful Jewish proselytizing among Christians may have stoked the fires of his anti-Semitism. Beginning in 1588, a Sabbatarian wing of the Unitarian Church appeared in Transylvania. Expelled from the Unitarian Church in 1623, a small remnant survived persecution, ultimately converting to Judaism after the emancipation of Hungarian Jews in 1867.

Hasel (1972); Liechty (1988, 1993).

GEOFFREY DIPPLE

Sacramentarians

In general "sacramentarians" refers to the denial of salvific significance to any of the *sacraments*, but was specifically used to describe those who denied the real presence of Christ in the Eucharist, such as *Johannes Oecolampadius, Andreas Bodenstein von Karlstadt*, and *Huldrych Zwingli*. Some later Radical Reformers, such as *Caspar Schwenckfeld*, rejected the sacraments entirely. Sacramentarianism had many sources, most notably *Desiderius Erasmus*, and was directed against perceived superstitious practices. Zwingli argued that the sacrament does not communicate *grace*, but commemorates it. For Zwingli, the sacramental signs serve to aid the believer in recalling God's grace and as opportunities for the community to confess its *faith*. *Martin Luther* was adamantly opposed to sacramentarianism as embodying grievous errors concerning salvation and the church. He wrote fiercely against it in tracts such as *Against the Heavenly Prophets in the Matter of Images and Sacraments* (1525). For Luther, sacramentarianism made salvation dependent upon an individual's mental formations.

Brecht (vol. 2, 1985–93); Lindberg (1996); Macy (1992); Stephens (1986); G. H. Williams (1992).

GREGORY J. MILLER

Sacrament(s)

A sacrament (from Lat. *sacramentum*, "oath" or "bond") is a special ritual action believed to communicate divine *grace*. The theology of the sacraments was central to all Protestant reform movements as well as to the Roman Catholic response to Protestantism. Controversies over the sacraments, often bitter and deep, were chief among the causes of divisions among various reform movements. Because Christians in the sixteenth century considered the correct understanding of the sacraments to be essential for ecclesial life and salvation, to be wrong about the sacraments was not merely to hold a mistaken idea, but not to be a Christian at all.

Until the twelfth century there was no precise list of sacraments. Thereafter the Western Church came to consider the correct number of sacraments to be seven: *baptism*, Eucharist (*Lord's Supper*), *penance*, ordination, *unction*, *marriage*, and *confirmation*, although church life focused on baptism, penance, and the Eucharist.

Through the medieval period the most controversial of the sacraments was the Eucharist. The doctrine of *transubstantiation*, that is, that the bread and wine are transformed into the true body and blood of Christ, came to be dominant. This led to an understanding that the Eucharist contains grace as a bottle contains medicine. Popular devotional practice subsequently encouraged the worship of God in the host and understood the *Mass* to be a repetition of the passion.

The *Reformation* began with *Martin Luther*'s criticism of *indulgences*, directly related to the sacrament of penance. Luther thereafter developed his reform of the sacraments by limiting them to those in *Scripture* specifically initiated by Christ, that is, Eucharist and baptism. For Luther, salvation by *faith* alone required the efficacy of the sacraments to be completely due to the activity of God and not reliant on the individual. The faith of the individual did not make the sacraments efficacious, rather faith received the sacraments.

Other Reformers similarly reduced the number of sacraments to baptism and Communion, denying the *authority* of the church to authorize sacraments and emphasizing the role of Scripture alone in faith and practice. However, both Protestant sacraments became the loci for bitter dispute and division.

The first sustained conflict developed between Luther and *Huldrych Zwingli* over the sacrament of Communion, with Zwingli emphasizing that the believer confessed her faith in the Eucharist rather than received grace. The first controversy concerning baptism occurred in Zurich when *Conrad Grebel* and *Georg Blaurock* (called *anabaptist*, "rebaptized," by their foes) argued that baptism according to Scripture was based upon a confession of faith and therefore impossible for infants. In general, *Anabaptists* tended to emphasize interior aspects of the sacraments as essential, reinterpreting the sacraments as ordinances of the church, that is, helpful ecclesial practices but not conveyors of grace, or sometimes rejecting the need for sacraments entirely (such as *Caspar Schwenckfeld*). At the *Council of Trent* these various Protestant teachings concerning the sacraments were explicitly rejected and traditional understandings were made official.

Lindberg (1996); McGrath (1999); Ozment (1980); Steinmetz (2002c); Stephens (1992); G. H. Williams (1992).
GREGORY J. MILLER

Sacrifice

In its technical use, "sacrifice" (Lat. *sacrificium*) refers to the understanding that in the eucharistic liturgy the body and blood of Christ are presented to God as an offering for *sin*. This understanding was rejected by most Reformers, resulting in various revisions and reorientations of Christian *worship*. In 1523 both *Martin Luther* and *Huldrych Zwingli* published on the reform of the *Mass*, with Luther removing all language "that smacks of sacrifice." On the other hand, *Martin Bucer* attempted rapprochement with Rome on the matter of sacrifice. In *England Thomas Cranmer* wrote against the sacrifice of the Mass and, to discourage the *sacrificium*, stone altars were replaced with wooden tables (1550). In 1562 the *Council of Trent* decreed, "If anyone says that in the mass a true and proper sacrifice is not offered to God or that it is nothing else than Christ that is offered up and given to us to eat, *anathema sit* [let him be excommunicated]."

Senn (1997); B. Thompson (1980); N. Thompson (2005).
HANS WIERSMA

Sadoleto, Jacopo Cardinal (1477–1547)

An Italian cardinal, humanist, and reformer, Sadoleto was born in Modena and educated at the University of Ferrara. In 1513 *Pope Leo X* appointed him as his secretary, and he became bishop of Carpentras in 1517. Of irenic character, Sadoleto was assigned the task of seeking reconciliation with the Protestants. In 1536 *Pope Paul III* summoned Sadoleto to join the special commission that drafted the *Consilium de emendanda ecclesia* (Council of church reform), calling for comprehensive Catholic reform. By December 1536 he was named a cardinal. On March 18, 1539, Sadoleto wrote a letter to the Protestant churches in Geneva urging them to reunite with the Catholics. At a time when Protestantism in Geneva was still fragile, the letter argued that the Catholic Church is the universal church, while the Protestants seek dissension and innovation. *John Calvin* was chosen to respond to the letter, resulting in his famous defense of Protestantism.

Douglas (1959); Olin (2000).

G. SUJIN PAK

St. Bartholomew's Day Massacre

The massacre began on August 23, 1572, and went on for several days in Paris, then continued in cities throughout France for a few months. The massacre was incited by the marriage of the Protestant prince *Henri* of Navarre to the Catholic princess Margaret of Valois. The marriage itself was a failed effort to quell the religious wars.

The event began days earlier with a botched assassination plot against the leader of the *Huguenots*, Admiral Gaspard de Coligny. Recovering from his wound in a Paris apartment, he was dragged from his bed and murdered by a band of men led by the Duke of Guise. From that point, mob violence took over, and the atrocities were extraordinary. The estimates range between 3,000 and 30,000 people eventually killed, while many more thousands abjured Protestantism.

The extreme violence affected both the history and historiography of the event. It has become fashionable to interpret the brutality as "rites of violence," but it is significant that within months of the events, no political figure would take credit or blame for commanding the beginning of the massacre, forcing modern historians to interpret issues from circumstantial evidence.

Diefendorf (1991); Holt (1995); Kingdon (1988); Sutherland (1980).

R. WARD HOLDER

Saints

In the early church, individuals regarded as particularly holy were venerated as saints, their lives held up as models for imitation. During the Middle Ages Christian saints were treated increasingly as intercessors with the Divine. Excesses associated with the cult of saints were criticized both by those outside the late medieval church and by reformers within it. Renaissance humanists and Protestant reformers extended this criticism. Reformers argued that veneration of the saints detracted from Christ's role as the sole mediator with the Father and identified the saints with the community of the faithful rather than any spiritual elites. Vestiges of the cult of saints remained stronger in Lutheran territories than in other Protestant areas, especially in the south German and Swiss Reformations, where their veneration was early on a more serious point of contention than in Wittenberg. The *Council of Trent* moved against specific abuses associated with the veneration of the saints, but denied charges of idolatry and reaffirmed their intercessory role.

P. Brown (1981); Heming (2003); Hsia (2005); Kolb (1987).

GEOFFREY DIPPLE

Sanctification

Derived from the Latin terms *sanctus* ("holy") and *facere* ("to make"), "sanctification" means "making holy." Holiness is a perfection that properly belongs to God alone, one distinctively associated with God the *Holy Spirit* (*Spiritus Sanctus*). Sanctification thus suggests not only the believer's moral improvement but also a real encounter with God.

Martin Luther famously insisted that one's *justification* "before God" (*coram deo*) is not conditioned by prior holiness. To the contrary, the *gospel* is "good news" precisely because God for Christ's sake alone forgives sinners. One is justified before God by the "alien righteousness" (*iustitia aliena*) of Christ, imputed by God's *grace* through *faith* alone. Justification itself, however, is situated within the broader reality of sanctification, as can be seen in both Luther's Small Catechism and Large Catechism (both 1529). Indeed, the Holy Spirit effects the Christian life when he sets believers "on the bosom of the church" where through Word and Sacrament he "calls, gathers, enlightens, sanctifies, and preserves" them to life eternal. As God the Father is Creator and the Son Redeemer, so the Holy Spirit is "Sanctifier," and the *church* is the concrete locus in which his work is done. As suggested by the succession "calls, gathers, enlightens, and sanctifies," there is a processual and even a progressive sense in which the Christian is being sanctified. However, the acquisition of holiness never becomes the basis on which one stands justified before God. The sanctified believer is a venerable beginner who discovers her justification ever anew as faith returns her to Christ; sanctification, then, means progress from righteousness to righteousness.

Within the broader stream of Protestant theology, somewhat different understandings of sanctification prevailed. Beginning with *Philip Melanchthon*, "forensic" doctrines of justification tended to prioritize justification over sanctification and thus to temporalize the conceptual distinction between the two: first justification, then sanctification. Controversy ensued whenever the latter threatened to condition the former. Theologians struggled with questions like: Are good works *necessary* for salvation? What place is there for God's *Law* after justification by faith? In the Lutheran tradition, *good works* inevitably follow faith and repentance as "fruits of the Spirit," and the Law is a necessary, if still accusatory, guide for the life of faith.

For his part, *John Calvin* posited a greater continuity between Law and Gospel than the Lutherans, and thus emphasized sanctification and church discipline somewhat. Justification and sanctification reflect the "twofold grace of God"; they are inseparable, and, as with Luther, find their common source in the believer's union with Christ through faith. God also justifies the works of the Christian such that there is a "second righteousness," which

is proper to the Christian even if it depends on God's grace.

The *Council of Trent* decreed that justification is both the beginning and the uncertain goal of the Christian life. Faith initiates the process, but the faithful must cooperate with the infused gift of sanctifying grace in order to be further justified and so, at last, to merit eternal life.

Opocenský and Réamonn (1999); Wendel (1997).

MICKEY L. MATTOX

Satan As understood by clergy and laity alike, Satan was alive and well in the sixteenth century. A cosmology that included the activity of a physical devil and his minions was assumed by virtually all who lived in the early modern period. The corporeality of Satan was reinforced via the media of the age: sermons, paintings, woodcuts, morality plays, and parades. As the "prince of the world" (John 12:31), Satan sent "hordes of demons across the land, all threatening to devour us," as *Martin Luther* put it in the third stanza of "A Mighty Fortress Is Our God" (ca. 1528). Luther's strategy for chasing the devil away with flatulence serves as a humorous gloss upon what was for Luther and other Reformers a serious enterprise: resisting Satan's efforts to tempt the faithful into believing that *good works*, rather than faith in Christ, were necessary for salvation. This was in contrast to the medieval understanding that unconfessed and unabsolved mortal *sins* gave Satan final possession of souls. In terms of the many factions produced during the *Reformation*, it was a common rhetorical strategy—sometimes accompanied by prosecution, punishment, and death—to assert that members of opposing factions were in league with or possessed by Satan.

Muchembled (2004); Oberman (1989); Waite (2007).

HANS WIERSMA

Satisfaction   Satisfaction is the work of reconciliation that satisfies or fulfills the penalty of *sin*, usually through suffering, *prayer*, or *good works*. The priest often assigns works of satisfaction to bring a person in sin back into a right relationship with God. The original work of satisfaction referred to the satisfaction of Christ, who was the propitiation for human sins as his *sacrifice* voided the power of sin. Christ broke the cycle of sin caused by the first Adam, making it possible for those united to him to perform satisfactory works. Therefore, the satisfaction of Christ enabled the works of satisfaction by human penitents within the medieval church's sacramental system of *baptism* and *penance*. Noting the gravity of sin and inability of human works to merit forgiveness of sins, Protestant reformers challenged the notion that humans could satisfy the penalty of their sins. Instead, they emphasized Christ's work of satisfaction and the believer's faithful response to this gift of salvation. Meanwhile, Roman Catholics maintained the role of human participation in the reconciling work of satisfaction through the *sacrament* of penance.

Cessario (1990); McNeill (1990); Shuger (2008).

ESTHER CHUNG-KIM

Sattler, Michael (ca. 1490–1527) Sattler was an early Anabaptist leader, martyr, and the primary author of the *Schleitheim Confession.* Initially a Benedictine monk of St. Peter's of the Black Forest, where he possibly served as prior, by the early 1520s Sattler moved first to Lutheran and then Zwinglian Protestantism and finally converted to Anabaptism, joining the members of the Swiss Brethren in Zurich in 1525, only months after Anabaptism's formation. An Anabaptist missionary, Sattler preached and debated in the dependent territories north of Zurich and near *Strasbourg.* Sattler chaired a conference of the Swiss Brethren at Schleitheim in February of 1527, which produced the Schleitheim Confession. Arrested by Roman Catholic authorities along with his wife and other *Anabaptists* in Horb in early 1527, Sattler was tried and burned at the stake as a heretic at Rottenburg. The Schleitheim Confession and vivid accounts of Sattler's torturous execution were widely circulated, promoting early Anabaptist beliefs.

Bossert (1951); Snyder (1981, 1984).

BRIAN C. BREWER

Schism   A schism is a sinful breaking of communion by the splitting off of a group from the *church*. Although a schismatic is not necessarily a heretic, *Augustine* was influential in arguing that some kind of error is always at the root of schism. A medieval example of the grievous nature of the *sin* of schism can be seen in Dante's placement of schismatics near the bottom of hell, well below murderers and thieves. As embodied in the canons and decrees of the *Council of Trent*, especially in those of Pope Pius IV, Protestantism was officially referred to as a schism. Protestants did not consider themselves to be schismatics, but stated it was the Roman Church that had departed from the teaching of Jesus and the apostles. They argued, for example in the *Augsburg Confession* (1530), that the schismatic was the one who caused the separation, not the one who departed.

R. Holder (2009); Jedin (1957–61); Jensen (1992).

GREGORY J. MILLER

Schleitheim Confession   The Schleitheim Confession was an early (February 24, 1527) Anabaptist agreement and confession of faith probably drafted in Schleitheim, Switzerland, by *Michael Sattler,* a former Benedictine monk who would be executed by the Catholics along with his wife three months later. Though it represented the position of a small group of early *Anabaptists*, it has come to occupy an important position in the entire Anabaptist tradition.

Composed of seven articles, it is marked by clarity and concreteness, but also reflects the intense alienation that early Anabaptists experienced. Its dualistic worldview, separatism, discipline, and *pacifism* explain why some Protestants accused Anabaptists of being "new monks."

After an introduction that warns against antinomian tendencies probably among more spiritualistically inclined radicals, the confession presents seven articles on which agreement had been reached. (1) *Baptism* is to be given to all who believe themselves forgiven by their *faith* in Christ, but who have also repented and amended their lives. While salvation is achieved by Christ and appropriated by faith, it entails a new life in Christ and can be lost if that newness of life is lacking. (2) The community of the baptized will employ the *ban* to discipline brothers and sisters who lapse. The emphasis on the ban reflects both the possibility and the requirement of stricter standards of behavior than some understandings of *sola fide justification* would allow. (3) Only those who are baptized into the community may participate in the *Lord's Supper*, which is the remembrance of Christ's broken body and shed blood. The ban was intended to maintain the purity and unity of the body of Christ, which is the *church*. (4) Since the world is divided between light and darkness, Christ and Belial, believers must separate themselves from those who remain in the abomination of wickedness. Acceptance of this dualistic vision could make normal social intercourse with nonbelievers fraught with difficulties. (5) Pastors must be of good repute with those outside the faith to silence the slanderers. (6) The *sword*

(secular government) was ordained by God outside the perfection of Christ to punish the wicked and to protect the good. But within the perfection of Christ, among believers, only the ban is employed. And following Christ's command and example, no believer may bear the sword, sit in judgment, or otherwise serve in worldly government. Anabaptist refusal to shoulder many civic burdens, for example payment of war taxes or doing guard duty in cities, was a sore point for the ruling authorities. (7) Following Christ's command, oaths are forbidden to believers. In a society in which oaths of office, testimony, and allegiance were the visible bonds uniting society, this last provision was viewed as threatening the structure of society itself.

Snyder (1984); G. H. Williams (1992).
R. EMMET MCLAUGHLIN

Schmalkaldic Articles

After *Pope Paul III* called for a church council to meet at Mantua, the Schmalkaldic League called a diet at Schmalkalden in February 1537 to plan a response. The princes and theologians rejected the idea of a Mantuan council, demanding that the council be held in Germany, be free from papal control, and base its decisions entirely on *Scripture*. The princes then called on *Martin Luther* to draft a revised statement of *faith*. Luther agreed, in part to remedy what he saw as concessions to the Catholics in the *Augsburg Confession*. The articles stressed four points: salvation by faith alone; abolition of the *Mass* as a *sacrifice*; rejection of the divine right of the pope to rule; the right of princes to turn Catholic monasteries and foundations over to the territorial churches to be used as parish churches and schools. As well as constituting a more concise and forceful articulation of Lutheran doctrine, the Schmalkaldic Articles may also be seen as a Lutheran "Declaration of Independence" from the Roman Church and the starting point for Lutheran *confessionalization*.

———
Schlütter-Schindler (1986).
WILLIAM BRADFORD SMITH

Scholasticism   Scholasticism is a theological method developed during the thirteenth century and dominant in university life through the end of the Middle Ages, with the *Summa theologiae* of Thomas Aquinas perhaps its greatest exemplar.

Scholasticism includes three fundamental commitments. First, scholasticism was committed to the essential rationality of theology while maintaining that some Christian doctrines transcended **reason**. Related to this, scholastic theologians made extensive use of Aristotelian logic because it represented a universally valid system to which all intellectual disciplines should conform. Second, scholasticism was founded on the **authority** of ancient authors (especially **Scripture** and the church **fathers**) whose works could be divided up and utilized as individual statements. Finally, scholasticism was committed to the systematization of Christian knowledge. Beginning from first principles, scholastic theologians attempted to construct a comprehensive, coherent treatment of all aspects of theology organized under the framework of a *quaestio* (inquiry) followed by the dialectical lining up authorities pro and con, and then a resolution. Since all truth was from God, seemingly contradictory passages from authoritative sources required reconciliation through logical analysis.

Of seminal influence in the development of scholasticism was the *Sententiarum libri quatuor* (*Four Books of Sentences*) of **Peter Lombard** (d. 1160), which organized statements from the church fathers in a systematic framework. There were several movements

(or schools) within scholasticism as it developed through the fourteenth and fifteenth centuries.

Chief among the divisions were between the *via antiqua* and the *via moderna*. The *via moderna* is a school of thought originating in the fourteenth century associated with **William of Ockham**, Gregory of Rimini, and **Gabriel Biel** (among others), and usually understood to be a contrasting response to the *via antiqua* associated with Thomas Aquinas and **John Duns Scotus**. Theologians of the *via antiqua* were in general committed to the metaphysical position of realism, which holds that universal qualities truly exist. Theologians of the *via moderna* espoused nominalism, which holds that such universals have no ontological existence. Renaissance thinkers ridiculed scholasticism as pedantic and useless.

Most of the early Reformers also strongly rejected scholasticism, although sometimes for different reasons. **Martin Luther**, for example, accused the scholastic method as having too high a regard both for human reason and **Aristotle** (*Disputatio contra scholasticam theologiam*, 1517). Most importantly, the Protestant emphasis on the centrality of Scripture as the foundation for all of faith and practice encouraged the construction of theology on an entirely different basis, even when it was organized systematically.

After 1570, however, the scholastic method gained new life, especially in Reformed circles, as Protestant theologians utilized it to consolidate, organize, and defend the insights of the first generation of Reformers. The widespread use of the scholastic method across confessional lines has led to the denomination of this period in church history as the age of Protestant scholasticism.

———
McGrath (1999, 2005); Oberman (1986); Ozment (1980); Pieper (1960); Steinmetz (1980).

GREGORY J. MILLER

Schools By the time of the *Reformation* the number of schools had already increased in Europe, along with the rate of literacy. Schools were found in most towns in the fourteenth and fifteenth centuries. Rather than the primary driver of literacy among the laity, the Bible-centered reforms of Protestantism seem to have benefited from literacy. Both Protestant and Catholic reform movements worked to increase *education*. Boys were taught more Latin, but girls did go to school in many locations. *Martin Luther* thought education would make better Christians and citizens, and in the 1520s and 1530s school became compulsory in much of Protestant Germany, with curricula standardized regionally. In Spain in 1600 it was estimated that there were four thousand grammar schools. Increases in Catholic countries were prompted by the *Council of Trent*'s call for schools in all cathedrals and towns, and by the *Jesuits*, whose schools were both excellent and free.

Grafton and Jardine (1986); Moran (1985); Strauss and Gawthorp (1984).
GARY NEAL HANSEN

Schwabach Articles (1529) The Schwabach Articles were an early confession of Protestant *faith* drawn up by *Wittenberg* theologians at the order of Elector *John Frederick I* of Saxony. They received the approval of other Protestant theologians and rulers in Hesse, Saxony, Brandenburg-Ansbach, and Nuremberg. (The Nurembergers agreed to the articles in the town of Schwabach, from which the articles derive their name.) The seventeen articles were intended to help Wittenberg *evangelicals* throughout Germany present a united Protestant front against the threat of Imperial aggression after the majority of the Imperial estates voted to enforce the Edict of Worms (1521) at the Diet of Speyer (1529). They served as a basis for the ensuing discussion of Protestant theology at the *Marburg Colloquy* (1529), directly influencing the content of the Marburg Articles (1529) and eventually the *Augsburg Confession* (1530). Anti-Zwinglian from the start, they were never accepted by Swiss Protestants.

Christensen (1984); Kolb and Nestingen (2001).
RONALD K. RITTGERS

Schwenckfeld, Caspar (1489–1561) Schwenckfeld was a radical spiritualist reformer who emphasized direct communication with Christ to the exclusion of all mediation by *clergy*, the *Bible*, or *sacraments*. A nobleman, Schwenckfeld helped lead the Lutheran *Reformation* in Silesia to its initial success. However, he rejected *Martin Luther*'s defense of the real presence and increasingly doubted the role of externals in salvation. Driven into exile, Schwenckfeld spent the rest of his life in the cities or on noble country estates in southern Germany. For Schwenckfeld *faith* was directly inspired and only those with faith could understand *Scripture*. Participation in the glorified Christ, the "inner Eucharist," remade the Christian into a "new man." Schwenckfeld also held a heavenly flesh *Christology* that denied the creatureliness of Christ's humanity. The Schwenckfelders survived in south Germany until the seventeenth century, in Silesia until the nineteenth century, and in Pennsylvania north of Philadelphia to this day.

R. McLaughlin (1986); G. H. Williams (1992).
R. EMMET MCLAUGHLIN

Scots Confession Following the 1558–60 Scottish Covenanters' struggle against Catholic and French rule in Scotland, in the person of Marie de Guise, the August 1560 Reformation Parliament requested several Protestant reformers, including *John Knox* and John Spottiswoode, to write the Scottish Confession of Faith. They completed their task of writing the book in four days. The Scots Confession was based broadly on the ideas of Calvin and other Continental Reformers. The Confession sparked the beginning of Scotland as a Protestant nation and established the basics of the Knoxian Presbyterianism that would later form into true Presbyterianism. The Scots Confession abolished the pope, laid out the doctrine of *election*, and described the nature of the *church* in Scotland. In chapter 19 of the Confession, the signs of the true Kirk were recognized as *Scripture*, the proper administration of the *sacraments*, and ecclesiastical *discipline*. Though the first two signs were similar to many Reformed churches, the Scots took the emphasis on discipline directly from *Martin Bucer*'s tradition.

K. Brown (2004); Ryrie (2006); Walton (2008).

KRISTEN POST WALTON

Scotus, John Duns (1265–1308)

Scotus was a medieval philosopher and theologian, also known as *doctor subtilis* for his subtlety. He became a Franciscan friar circa 1280, and received the ordination to the priesthood in 1291. It appears that he studied at the Franciscan house of studies in Oxford from 1288 to 1301. He lectured at the University of Paris from 1302 to 1303, and, after a brief exile, he returned to Paris in 1304. He lectured at Cologne in 1307, where he died. The centerpiece of his theology was the assertion of the priority of the divine will over the divine intellect. He was also a critic of the Augustinian theory of knowledge known as "illuminationism." He advanced the doctrine of the immaculate conception of *Mary*, arguing that by a special act of divine *grace* Mary was conceived without *original sin*. His theology influenced disparate figures of the Reforma-

tion era like *John Calvin* and *Francisco Suárez*.

Ingham (2004); T. Williams (2003); Wolter (1990).

RADY ROLDAN-FIGUEROA

Scripture

In the Reformation the content, *authority*, and *interpretation* of Scripture were all in transition. The emphasis of *humanism* on reading ancient texts in their original languages led the Reformers to reject the Latin Vulgate. They emphasized *preaching* and teaching from the original *Greek* and *Hebrew* texts, and provided translations from these into vernacular languages for those less learned. The books of the Apocrypha were not canonical, lacking Hebrew originals, though early on they were still respected as edifying. The *Council of Trent* in 1546 went the opposite way, reaffirming the Vulgate, including the Apocrypha, as the Catholic Bible. Soon after, Protestant confessions began to include lists of canonical books that excluded the Apocrypha.

In the Middle Ages the Scriptures were seen as harmonious with the church's tradition, making for a seamless body of authoritative teaching. If Scripture was silent or difficult to understand, the *church* provided clarity. The Council of Trent in 1546 explicitly made the church's unwritten traditions, taken to be from Christ or the *Holy Spirit*, authoritative along with Scripture. Renaissance humanists, and Reformers after them, saw that there were places where the church's consensus strayed far from Scripture's explicit teaching. Protestants became convinced that Scripture held authority above any postbiblical tradition or teaching. Thus "Scripture alone" became the standard for Protestant teaching, the sufficient and authoritative rule for doctrine and practice. Scripture's authority would be made convincing to the reader by the work of the Holy Spirit, not by the testimony of the church.

Prominent theologians, including Thomas Aquinas (ca. 1225–1274), had long argued that the historical or literal sense of Scripture should be used for doctrine. However, much medieval interpretation gave great emphasis to three other levels of biblical meaning: the allegorical, in which a text was related to the spiritual life or, by metaphorical connections, to doctrine; the tropological, in which a text was related to morals and behavior; and the anagogical, in which a text was related to eschatological matters.

To the Reformers, these practices allowed one to make Scripture mean anything one wanted. The Protestant priority was instead to delve fully into the plain sense of Scripture, seeking the meaning intended by the human authors and the divine Author who spoke through them. To find this they used the humanist tools of linguistic and textual analysis, as well as theological rules such as interpreting unclear passages through clearer passages, and the rules of faith and love. The process would lead to knowledge of Christ who is the *scopus* or subject matter of the whole, and the materials of doctrine. Protestants, for example *Martin Luther* and *John Calvin*, tended to interpret the whole using the apostle Paul and his teaching on *justification* as a lens.

Muller (vol. 2, 2003b); Pelikan (1996); Steinmetz (1996).
GARY NEAL HANSEN

Seripando, Girolamo (1492?–1563)

Seripando was an Augustinian friar and reformer. He was born in Naples, and entered the order of Augustinian Hermits in 1507, receiving ordination to the priesthood in 1513. In 1538 he was appointed vicar-general of his order, and was elected general of the order in the following year. As general of the order that had nurtured *Martin Luther*, Seripando was concerned about the health of his order, and he executed a general visitation of the order to reform it and combat Lutheranism.

Seripando was one of the most influential figures at the **Council of Trent**. He displayed an Augustinian cast to his thought, and a conservatism in doctrinal matters that did not always please other members of the council. He worked unsuccessfully against the council's evaluation of tradition as an equal source of *authority* with *Scripture*. Like *Gasparo Cardinal Contarini*, he worked for the acceptance of the "double *justification*" stance by the council, but was ultimately unsuccessful. Though he retired from the generalship of the order in 1551 after a stroke, he eventually recovered and was appointed archbishop of Salerno in 1554 and was made a cardinal in 1561.

Cesareo (1999); Jedin (1947).
R. WARD HOLDER

Servetus, Michael (1511–53)
Servetus was a Spanish theologian and physician who was executed for his *anti-Trinitarian* beliefs by the Geneva town council with *John Calvin*'s consent. Servetus, intrigued by Christian theology early in life, saw the *Trinity* as a problem in converting Jews and Muslims and ultimately posited that doctrine as unbiblical by authoring *De Trinitatis erroribus* (*Concerning the Errors of the Trinity*). Consequently, he fled both Protestant and Catholic authorities and studied medicine in Paris, where he reportedly discovered the circulation of blood a century before William Harvey publicized it. He later served as the personal physician to the archbishop of Vienna. However, the authorship of his manuscript, *Restitutio Christianismi* (*The Restitution of Christianity*), sent to John Calvin, was discovered by Catholic authorities. Escaping arrest by the *Inquisition*, Servetus fled to Geneva, where he was recognized, arrested, and

tried for *heresy*. He was condemned and burned at the stake in 1553.

———

Bainton (2005); Fulton (1989); Hillar (2002).

BRIAN C. BREWER

Simons, Menno (ca. 1496–1561)

A farmer's son from Witmarsum in Frisia, Simons entered the clergy, becoming a vicar in neighboring Pingjum in 1524 and then pastor in Witmarsum in 1532. Like many sacramentarian priests in the Netherlands at the time, he questioned the doctrine of *transubstantiation*. After the execution in 1531 of Sicke Freerks, a prominent follower of *Melchior Hoffmann*, he began to doubt the legitimacy of infant *baptism* as well. In 1535 the armed seizure by *Anabaptists* of Oldeklooster, a nearby Cistercian monastery, occasioned a spiritual crisis, and the following year he left the Catholic Church and fled to East Frisia. In 1537 he was commissioned an Anabaptist elder by Obbe Philips, but did not assume an active leadership role until 1540. In 1539 or 1540 he completed *Dat Fundament des christelyken leers* (*The Foundation of Christian Doctrine*).

Debate continues about Menno's relationship to Melchiorite Anabaptism, and with it, his possible connections to the apocalyptic Anabaptist reformation in *Münster* (1534–35). Some scholars distance Menno from both of these phenomena, arguing that he came to his understanding of baptism through his reading of *Desiderius Erasmus*'s statements on the Great Commission (Matt. 28:19–20). Others note Menno's commitment to a distinctive Melchiorite *Christology*, which insisted that Christ's flesh came down from heaven, and they argue that this teaching and his soteriology, with its stress on rebirth and *sanctification*, were largely drawn from Hoffmann and the Münster theologian Bernhard Rothmann. This has informed an alternate understanding of Menno's early reforming activity, one that argues that Menno was baptized already in 1534, and that initially his opposition to the Münster reformation centered on its attempt to realize physically the spiritual kingdom of God. After the fall of Münster he was part of the spiritualizing current that swept Melchiorite Anabaptism, although his spiritualism was never as extreme as that of David Joris, his most serious rival for leadership of the Melchiorite movement. Into the 1540s Menno continued to campaign for acceptance of his reformation by church and government officials. Only in the 1550s did he somewhat reluctantly accept his role as leader of a minority separatist church, living under the cross without spot or wrinkle.

After the Habsburg government of the Netherlands put a price on his head in 1542, Menno left the Netherlands, eventually settling on a noble estate between Hamburg and Lübeck. During the 1540s and 1550s he became embroiled in a series of conflicts, both with dissenters within his movement and with Calvinist theologians without. The most serious of these came in the late 1550s over issues of banning and marital shunning and led to significant splits in the movement. In 1554/55 he published a second, significantly revised edition of *Dat Fundament*. He died January 31, 1561.

———

Friesen (1998); Isaak (2006); Voolstra (1997).

GEOFFREY DIPPLE

Sin

Sin is any thought, word, or deed that separates a person or community from God by its opposition to God's commands and purposes. *Martin Luther* reconceptualized *Augustine*'s view of disordered *love* as the sin originating the fall to define it as unbelief. *John Calvin* retained the view of *original sin* as unbelief, but kept more of the Augustinian emphasis on pride. Generally, the Protestant reformers sought to reinstate a more robust Augustinian conception of sin against what they saw as a rising Roman Catholic Pelagianism. Thus Luther (e.g., *De servo arbitrio* [*On the Bondage of the Will*], 1525) and Calvin emphasized the bondage of the human *will* to sin so that the will played no role in salvation and thereby underscored humanity's total depravity. Views concerning the relation between the human will and sin became a central dividing point between Catholics and Protestants and among Protestants themselves, as it directly related to their theories of salvation. *Anabaptists* (and later Arminians, Anglicans, and Methodists), not unlike sixteenth-century Roman Catholics, believed that the human will played some cooperating role in salvation.

Lane (1996); Winter (2002).

G. SUJIN PAK

Sleep of the Soul   The question of soul sleep emerged in the Reformation with the rejection of *purgatory*, though it was not a new topic. At the moment of *death*, according to the Reformers, souls went either to heaven or hell. The question remained, what was to be made of the Last Judgment? *Martin Luther* argued that until the resurrection the souls of the just sleep, but he never made this a doctrine. This ambiguity arose from his unwillingness to relinquish fully the possibility of postmortem purgation. *John Calvin*, following *Huldrych Zwingli* and *Heinrich Bullinger*, was adamant that the souls of the dead do not enter a third place. In one of his earliest works, the *Psychopannychia*, Calvin suggested that the dead might have some knowledge of the living, but no contact. Bullinger was more emphatic in separating the two. The issue was of great significance because it forced the Protestant reformers, theologically and pastorally, to address the question of the afterlife.

Karant-Nunn (1997); Koslofsky (2000); Quistorp (1955).

BRUCE GORDON

Stapulensis, Faber (a.k.a. Jacques Lefèvre d'Étaples, Jacobus Faber; ca. 1460–1536)   Born in Étaples in northern France, Stapulensis was an ordained priest and influential French biblical humanist. Although interested in the texts of the ancient world, particularly *Aristotle*, his most significant and controversial work was as a translator and exegete of the *Bible*. His commentary on the Pauline Epistles and the Gospels provoked a harsh response from the theologians of the University of Paris Faculty of Theology who found his emphasis on *faith* and *grace* threatening and heterodox and used his lack of a doctorate in theology to undermine his efforts at biblical *interpretation*. He fled Paris and spent the remainder of his life under the protection of King Francis I's sister, *Marguerite de Navarre*. Although he is known to have admired some Protestant reformers, he never formally broke with the Catholic Church.

Nauert (2006); Rummel (2008).

GRETA GRACE KROEKER

Staupitz, Johannes von (ca. 1460/69–1524)   Vicar-general of the observant Augustinians, Staupitz was *Martin Luther*'s religious superior and close spiritual adviser. Much of Luther's early theological development took place in the context of his close relationship with Staupitz, which has led scholars to investigate carefully the latter's own theology for signs of inspiration and/or dependence. Based primarily on his sermons on Job and some later works, researchers have found at the heart of his theology a robust doctrine of *election*. God's initiative in salvation is based on his own uncreated *love*. Election makes human beings pleasing to God, while the *grace* that flows from election makes God pleasing to the human being. In 1521 Staupitz resigned, with permission from Rome, from the Augustinian order and became abbot of the Benedictine monastery at Salzburg. Though he was initially sympathetic with Luther's protest, an exchange of letters just before Staupitz's death shows that the *Reformation* ruptured their friendship.

—————

Posset (2003); Saak (2002); Steinmetz (1980).
MICKEY L. MATTOX

Stoicism Along with Epicureanism, Stoicism is a product of the Hellenistic period, although none of the works of its founder, Zeno, survive. Stoics believed in a divine natural order, which unfolds by necessity according to its own logic. The basis for happiness lies in submitting to that order rather than becoming emotionally invested in particular outcomes, and in practicing virtue even under adverse circumstances. Stoics of the Roman imperial period include Seneca, Epictetus, and the emperor Marcus Aurelius. While Christianity bears a superficial resemblance to the self-restraint of Stoicism, there is in the latter no sense of devotion to a personal God; nonetheless, some Renaissance humanists were attracted to Stoicism because of their interest in ancient literature and *philosophy*. Before his conversion, *John Calvin* composed a humanist commentary on Seneca's *De clementia* (*On Clemency*). The most important figure in the sixteenth-century Stoic revival was Justus Lipsius (1547–1606), writing in response to the horrors of religious *war*.

—————

Colish (1990); Copenhaver and Schmitt (1992); Inwood (1999); Moreau (1999).
J. LAUREL CARRINGTON

Strasbourg An imperial city with around twenty thousand inhabitants, Strasbourg was one of the largest cities in Germany at the beginning of the sixteenth century. It was a major commercial and *printing* center located at the intersection of trade routes running both north-south and east-west. Matthew Zell began evangelical preaching in the city in 1521; he was soon joined by three others who would become prominent Reformers: *Martin Bucer, Wolfgang Capito*, and Caspar Hedio. By 1525 the city had essentially become *evangelical*, although masses continued to be said in the cathedral until officially abolished in 1529. With the outbreak of the eucharistic controversy, Strasbourg's pastors became Zwinglians, but the city's exposed political situation caused it to seek closer ties with the Lutherans, and Bucer was the driving force behind the Wittenberg Concord of 1536. With the hiring of pastors trained in *Wittenberg*, Strasbourg's church became more fully Lutheran, and in 1598 it accepted the Formula of Concord.

—————

Abray (1985); Brady (1978); Chrisman (1967); Kittelson (2000).
AMY NELSON BURNETT

Sturm, Johannes (Jean; 1507–89) From Schleiden in northwestern Germany, Sturm was introduced to *humanism* by the Brethren of the Common Life in Liège. He studied in Louvain and Paris, where he became involved with a circle of French humanists interested in religious reform. As a lecturer at the Collège de France he promoted a rhetorical approach to logic that would strongly influence his student Peter Ramus. In 1537 he moved to *Strasbourg* to teach *rhetoric* and *dialectic*. With *Martin Bucer* he reorganized the city's Latin schools to create a graded gymnasium and academy that combined the goals of *evangelical* piety with a humanist curriculum and pedagogy. Under Sturm's rectorship from 1538, the Strasbourg Academy became one of the leading schools in Germany; it was granted university status in 1631. By the 1560s Sturm's Reformed sympathies led to conflicts with the city's Lutheran pastors, and in 1581 he was removed from his post. He died eight years later.

—————

Ong (1958); Spitz and Tinsley (1995).
AMY NELSON BURNETT

Suárez, Francisco (1548–1617)

Suárez was a prominent *Jesuit* theologian. He studied at the University of Salamanca, joining the Society of Jesus in 1564. He taught at the Roman College from 1580 to 1585, the University of Alcala from 1585 to 1593, Salamanca from 1593 to 1597, and at Coimbra from 1597 to the end of his life. He wrote extensively in a wide range of topics. His most influential works were *Disputationes metaphysicae* (*Metaphysical Disputations*, 1597) and *De legibus, ac Deo legislatore* (*Laws and God the Legislator*, 1612); the latter became a seminal work in international law. Already in *De Verbo Incarnato* (*The Incarnate Word*, 1590) he endeavored to reconcile Thomas Aquinas and *John Duns Scotus* on the subject of the *incarnation*. He also made an important contribution to Roman Catholic congruism (i.e., the doctrine that God's *grace* is congruent with human freedom) in *Varia opuscula theologica* (*Shorter Theological Works*, 1599).

Fichter (1940); Pereira (2007).
RADY ROLDAN-FIGUEROA

Supererogatory Works

These works are a class of actions that go beyond duty and produce an excess of *merit*. The most extensive Christian exposition of supererogation was by Thomas Aquinas, who distinguished between precepts, which are duties of all, and *counsels of perfection*, which are a more expedient or guaranteed way of gaining eternal life. The key scriptural locus for the doctrine is in the story of the rich young ruler (Matt. 19:16–22), which was interpreted to mean there is a level of potential perfection above what is necessary to obtain salvation. From the Crusades onward, the merit produced through the supererogatory works of the *saints* was described as flowing into a treasury that could be applied to the lives of ordinary Christians by means of *indulgences*. The Reformers all strenuously rejected

this doctrine. The Protestant doctrine of *justification* by *faith* alone included the idea that no *good work* whatsoever earned merit before God.

Oberman (1986); Ozment (1980); Tentler (1977); Thayer (2002).
GREGORY J. MILLER

Superstition

Drawing on *Augustine*'s condemnations of *magic* and superstition, early modern theologians from diverse confessions argued that superstition (Lat. *superstitio*) was erroneous religious belief or ritual or one without God as its object. Well into the sixteenth century, the performance of legitimate rituals such as *baptism* by people who were not authorized to perform them would not be seen as superstitious, although authorities would almost certainly see them as illegitimate. Given that perceptions of superstition were frequently in the eye of the beholder, accusations of superstition grew frequent and vitriolic in the confessional debates of the sixteenth and seventeenth centuries. Protestant and separatist reformers, such as *Anabaptists*, condemned many Catholic rituals as superstitious because they saw them as violating biblical precedent. Despite extensive itemizations of superstitions and attempts to eradicate them, practices that theologians of all confessions saw as superstitious remained part of European life throughout the *Reformation*.

See also **Miracles; Witchcraft**

Bailey (2007); Klaniczay and Pócs (2006); Parish and Naphy (2002).
KATHRYN A. EDWARDS

Sword

Reformation era teachings on the "sword," a metaphor for the role of coercive force in Christian society, derived from medieval reflection on the relationship between civil and ecclesiastical *authority*. Appealing to the reference to two swords in Luke 22:38, Catholic thinkers argued for the superiority of ecclesiastical authority. Reformers who left the church argued instead on the basis of Romans 13:4 that temporal authorities held the only legitimate sword.

The teachings of magisterial reformers on legitimate use of the sword among Christians ran the gamut from *Martin Luther*'s sharp distinction between the spiritual and temporal realms, with relegation of all social concerns to the latter, to *Huldrych Zwingli*'s calls for the establishment of a just society by Christian rulers. Similarly, the Reformation Radicals adopted a range of positions on the sword from the revolutionary crusading endorsement of violence by *Thomas Müntzer* to the radical separatist nonresistance of some *Anabaptists*.

Biesecker-Mast (2006); Snyder (2006); Stayer (1976).

GEOFFREY DIPPLE

Synods   Synods, or meetings of clergy at a diocesan, provincial, or national level, played an important role in the early *church*. They continued to be held on an irregular basis throughout the Middle Ages, but they were revived especially by churches within the Reformed tradition in the sixteenth century. *Huldrych Zwingli* introduced a semi-annual meeting of all pastors in Zurich's territory in 1528, and the Zurich model was adopted by other Swiss Reformed churches, although they were not held with the same regularity. Synods were especially important in France and the Netherlands, where the Reformed churches operated independently of government supervision. In churches influenced by *John Calvin*'s understanding of church *office*, delegates to provincial and national synods included both pastors and elders or lay members of the consistories that oversaw each congregation. Synods defined doctrine, established uniform liturgical

and administrative policies, regulated financial questions, and settled disputes that could arise between churches, and so they were an important component of Reformed church governance.

Gordon (1992); Mentzer (2005); Sunshine (2003).

AMY NELSON BURNETT

Tabernacle   The tabernacle was the mobile form and place of God's dwelling among the Israelite people during their journey to the promised land and was often contrasted with the temple. The tabernacle was meant to be a symbol of heavenly realities and a place to behold God's glory. Based on the Epistle to the Hebrews, early Christians saw the tabernacle of Moses as a copy or shadow of a heavenly sanctuary that pointed to the image of the *church*, the body of Christ that prefigured the reality of heaven. Early exegetes developed the notion of the tabernacle of God in a christological sense by finding connections in the tabernacle of the union of human and divine natures in Christ.

Building on these christological themes, later exegetes interpreted the tabernacle as depicting the process of redemption through the shedding of blood, washing of water, and fragrant offering of intercession whereby sinners were brought from the profane earthly kingdom to the heavenly kingdom. For liturgical purposes, the tabernacle was a case or receptacle for liturgical vessels and the Eucharist. In response to Protestant views denying the permanence of the real presence of Christ in the elements, Catholics began to place the tabernacle at the center of the high altar for greatest visibility, so that by the end of the seventeenth century the placing of the tabernacle on the altar became the common practice in Roman Catholic churches.

A. Holder (1993); Kunzler (2001).

ESTHER CHUNG-KIM

Temporal Authority In the six-teenth century, as it had been in the medieval era, the relationship between the church leaders and the temporal authorities (emperors, kings, nobles, city magistrates) was complex and often con-tested. The area of deepest controversy concerned the degree to which temporal authorities (sometimes also translated in English as either "worldly" or "secular") had a responsibility to preserve and pro-tect true *religion* within their jurisdiction (often called the *cura religionis*).

See also **Authority**

Estes (2006); Whitford (2004).
DAVID M. WHITFORD

Teresa of Avila (1515–82)   Teresa was one of the most important female mystics and *Counter-Reformation saints*. She was born in Avila to a large Span-ish merchant family and educated at an Augustinian convent school. She became a Carmelite nun in 1535 and struggled with a lengthy illness. Twenty years later she had a vision of the wounded Christ that led her to a deeper personal faith. During her prayers and meditations, she increasingly had mystical experiences on the suffering of Christ. Her devotion led her to establish a stricter order known as the *Discalced Carmelites*, and she spread her reform and adherence to the primi-tive rule to both male and female houses. She was a close friend of another Span-ish mystic, *John of the Cross*, who aided Teresa in her reform efforts. Her ground-breaking autobiography, the *Life of Teresa of Avila*, and two other works, *The Way of Perfection* and *Interior Castle*, are impor-tant to Christian mysticism.

Bilinkoff (1989); Kavanaugh and Rodri-guez (2008); Slade (1995).
JILL R. FEHLEISON

Tetrapolitan Confession (1530) Also known as the Swabian Confes-sion, this was drawn up for the Diet of Augsburg in 1530 by *Martin Bucer* and *Wolfgang Capito*. Its title comes from the fact that it was signed by four cities: Memmingen, Constance, **Strasbourg**, and Lindau. Bucer had hoped to use the confession to unite the Zwinglians and Lutherans, and he worked hard, in par-ticular, to win over *Philip Melanchthon*. On the disputed article of the Eucha-rist, Bucer drew up a long explanation that he hoped would accommodate both sides. The language on the *Lord's Supper*, however, remained too close to *Huldrych Zwingli* for either *Martin Luther* or Melanchthon. In the end, the confession was not read before the diet and the Catholic reply was not made public. It was not until a year later in 1531 that the confession was printed, first in Strasbourg, where it retained influence for another thirty years.

Greschat (2004); Kittelson (1975).
BRUCE GORDON

Thirty Years' War (1618–48) The Thirty Years' War, one of the major con-flicts over *religion* in the Reformation era, centered in Germany during the first half of the seventeenth century. It began with a rebellion of the Protestant nobility in the kingdom of Bohemia and ultimately engulfed all of Europe. The conflict was closely connected with the spread of Calvinism and resistance to attempts by the Habsburg dynasty to subdue their Protestant subjects and extend the work of the *Counter-Reformation* in their own lands and beyond. The war had its ori-gins in the growing tensions between militant Catholic states, including Spain, Austria, and Bavaria, and Protestant, in particular Calvinist princes in Germany and the Netherlands. During the first decades of the seventeenth century, in the aftermath of confrontations in Ger-many and Austria, two military alliances formed: the Protestant Union, led by the Electors of the Palatinate, and the Catho-lic League, led by Bavaria in alliance with the Habsburgs. Both confederations played leading roles in the events leading up to and the first phases of the war.

The immediate cause of the war was the election of Frederick V, the Palatine Elector, as king of Bohemia in 1618. Protestant nobles in Bohemia, fearful of the Habsburg claimant to the throne, Ferdinand of Styria, rebelled. The rebels claimed that Ferdinand, by demanding the closure of Protestant churches, had violated the Letter of Majesty, a privilege granting limited toleration issued in 1609. The revolt culminated on May 21, 1618, when three Catholic counselors were thrown out of the window of the Hradschin palace, the famous Defenestration of Prague. Thereafter, the nobles deposed Ferdinand and elected Frederick of the Palatinate as king. This election not only deprived the Habsburg of one of the richest provinces in Europe, it altered the balance of power in the empire, giving the Protestants a majority in the electoral college. An army of the Catholic League, primarily made up of Bavarian troops under the command of John Tserclas, Count Tilly, invaded Bohemia. At the battle of White Mountain (November 8, 1620) the Protestants were defeated and Frederick was forced to take flight.

Over the next four years, Catholic armies under Tilly pursued and defeated the various remaining Protestant armies. In 1623 Tilly occupied the Palatinate, the last major Protestant stronghold. Attempts by the union to bring Sweden and Britain into the war failed. In 1625 the Danes were convinced to enter the conflict on the Protestant side, but were quickly defeated by the new imperial general, Albrecht von Wallenstein. Between 1626 and 1627 Wallenstein occupied most of Denmark and secured northern Germany for the Imperialists. In the aftermath of these campaigns, Ferdinand, now emperor, took two radical steps. Contrary to the Imperial constitution, he transferred the electoral dignity from the Counts Palatine to the Duke of Bavaria. He also issued the Edict of Restitution that called upon Protestants to return all ecclesiastical lands secularized since 1553. Both actions embittered those Protestant rulers, in particular the Lutherans, who had remained loyal to the emperor in the first phases of the war.

In 1630 Sweden entered the war. King Gustavus Adolphus of Sweden was concerned about the growing power of the Habsburgs in the Baltic. He also entered into an anti-Habsburg alliance with France in return for subsidies. As Gustavus Adolphus consolidated his position in northern Germany, the Imperial armies subdued the last remaining Protestant stronghold, the city of Magdeburg. The city was destroyed, and the "rape of Magdeburg" provided a rallying point for Protestant opposition. Gustavus Adolphus quickly overran much of Germany, defeating the Imperial forces at Breitenfeld, the Lech River, and Lützen in 1631 and 1632. At Lützen Gustavus Adolphus, the "Lion of the North," was killed. Although Sweden remained in the conflict, the defeat of the Swedes at Nördlingen in 1634 caused them to withdraw back to the north, leading to a stalemate. With the Swedish threat minimized, Ferdinand II had Wallenstein assassinated over fears of his ambition and growing power.

In 1629 France entered the war, initially by attacking Spanish positions in Italy, then through direct intervention in Germany and the Netherlands. By 1643 all sides had grown weary of the conflict. A preliminary peace treaty between Ferdinand II and the Protestant estates in 1635 laid the ground work for a final settlement. Between 1643 and 1648, representatives of the various sides met at Osnabrück and Münster to conclude a peace treaty, the *Peace of Westphalia*. The peace granted Calvinists official recognition alongside Lutherans and Catholics.

The war was immensely destructive of life and property. On account of warfare, plunder, and disease, approximately one-third of the German population was killed. In some regions, notably Brandenburg and Bavaria, depopulation was as high as 50 percent. Tax receipts from Bavaria suggest that it was not until the end of the century that the region had recovered.

Langer (1978); G. Parker (1997); Polišensky (1978); Wedgewood (1938).
WILLIAM BRADFORD SMITH

Thirty-Nine Articles   During the reign of King Edward VI of England (1547–53), the English church under *Thomas Cranmer*'s leadership prepared a formal statement of the reformed English church's beliefs, the Forty-Two Articles, eventually promulgated on June 19, 1553, with the requirement that all English clergy subscribe to them. However, Edward VI died on July 6, and Queen *Mary I* suppressed the articles. With the accession of *Elizabeth I* in 1558, the need for a statement of the English church's beliefs returned. In 1563 the Convocation of Canterbury drew up a lightly revised version of the Forty-Two Articles; several articles against *Anabaptist* doctrines were omitted as unnecessary, and the blunt anti-Lutheranism of the article on the Eucharist was softened. That article was dropped entirely at the last minute, so in 1563 Convocation approved Thirty-Eight Articles. In 1571 an English Parliament approved them, plus the omitted eucharistic article, giving the Thirty-Nine Articles of Religion the force of law.

Doctrinally, the articles belong to the broad Reformed Protestant family: they affirm standard Reformed tenets such as the sufficiency of *Scripture, justification* by *faith* and through *grace* alone, and infant *baptism*. However, they also assert the Royal Supremacy over the church (article 37), the validity of the *episcopate* (article 36), and the authority of each national church to approve traditions and to ordain or alter ceremonies. The article on *predestination* (article 17) is, at least by later Calvinist standards,

decidedly ambiguous, asserting the doctrine but without mentioning double predestination, irresistible grace, or limited *atonement*; instead, the doctrine's mystery and inscrutability are emphasized. Likewise, the treatment of the Eucharist as revised in 1563 (article 28) goes no further than to denounce *transubstantiation* and reservation, while declaring that Christ's body is received through faith, "after an heavenly and spiritual manner."

The articles' status has often been as ambiguous as their text. Initially, clergy were not required to subscribe to them (unlike the Forty-Two Articles); from 1571, only those ordained before 1558 were so required. Archbishop John Whitgift of Canterbury required more general subscription in the 1580s. It was after the Anglican Restoration of 1662 that the articles became most divisive, as large numbers of Puritan ministers were now unwilling to subscribe to them and were consequently ejected. Between 1672 and 1828, the Test Act required all civil officeholders in England to subscribe to the articles, as a means of excluding Protestant dissenters. In 1841, notoriously, John Henry Newman argued that the articles might be interpreted along more Catholic lines, a creative reinterpretation that won few converts but helped to consign the articles themselves to irrelevance. Although formally still in force in the Church of England, in modern times they have largely fallen out of use.

Chadwick (1988); Collinson (1967); MacCulloch (1996).
ALEC RYRIE

Torquemada, Tomas de (1420–98)
Torquemada was a *Dominican* friar and nephew of the theologian Juan Cardinal de Torquemada. Tomas became prior of the Santa Cruz convent in Segovia in 1452, and confessor to Ferdinand and Isabella in 1474. He helped draft the initial request for an *inquisition* in 1478,

and became head of the entire Spanish Inquisition in 1483. Pope Alexander VI considered his activities excessive and attempted to restrain him. Torquemada's Inquisition concerned itself primarily with Jews who allegedly continued to maintain their religion in secret. Torquemada also pressed for the expulsion of Jews in 1492, and excluded Christians of Jewish descent from membership in the convent he founded in Avila in 1482. This is ironic in light of the possibility that Torquemada himself was of Jewish descent, although this claim remains unproven.

J. Edwards (2005); Kamen (1998); Perez (2005).

EDWIN WOODRUFF TAIT

Tradition   The role of tradition (literally "to hand over") was one of the most contested areas during the Reformation. The Catholic Church stated that God's word was revealed and learned through both *Scripture* and tradition equally, while Protestants argued that all doctrine and *authority* was found in the *Bible* alone (*sola scriptura*). The *church* distinguished among different traditions, such as apostolic (coming from those who lived and worked with Christ), ecclesiastic (developed in the church later on), dogmatic (defining belief), and ceremonial (which regulated matters of a liturgical nature); but the *Council of Trent* was deliberately ambiguous on the role and relation of these. Protestants viewed tradition in a mostly negative light, arguing that the church had come to rely too much on human teaching and creations. They claimed to accept only those traditions that could be verified through the Bible, although later confessional texts (such as the *Augsburg Confession*) took on aspects of authoritative tradition.

Congar (1967); G. Evans (1992); Jedin (1957–61).

AMY E. LEONARD

Translation   Although some works of the Greek *fathers* were translated into Latin in the sixteenth century, and works by *Reformation* theologians were translated into various languages, most discussion of translation in the Reformation focuses on the *Bible*. Humanists had discerned significant translation problems with the Vulgate. Numerous scholars, Protestant and Catholic, worked either to revise the Vulgate or to provide entirely new Latin translations of the Bible. In these and in vernacular translation there was debate about whether to follow the wording of the original or to attempt to grasp the sense. Translation into vernacular languages was not new, but was spurred to prominence by Protestantism. While *Faber Stapulensis* (Jacques Lefèvre d'Étaples) based his French Bible (New Testament, 1523; complete, 1530) on the Vulgate, *Martin Luther* based his German Bible (New Testament, 1522; Old Testament, 1534) on the *Greek* and *Hebrew* originals. By the end of the sixteenth century the Bible was available in most European languages.

Greenslade (1963); Hobbs (1985); Norton (1984).

GARY NEAL HANSEN

Transubstantiation   Transubstantiation is a term commonly used to indicate the Roman Catholic doctrine concerning the mode of Christ's presence in the elements of the *Lord's Supper*. The Fourth *Lateran Council* (1215) enshrined *transubstantiatio* as a matter of catholic faith. The doctrine relies on the Aristotelian distinction of *substans* and *accidens* in its assertion that the eucharistic elements become the body and blood of Christ substantively, while retaining the accidental characteristics (i.e., material appearance) of bread and wine. Many sixteenth-century Reformers agreed, at the very least, that the reliance on *Aristotle* was unbiblical and, therefore, unnecessary. However, they rather famously disagreed in asserting their own formulations regarding whether and how Christ was present in Holy Communion. In response to the Reformers, the *Council of Trent* decreed anew (in 1551) that the conversion of bread and wine to Christ's flesh and blood is "fittingly and properly called 'transubstantiation.'"

P. Jones (1994); Wandel (2006).

HANS WIERSMA

Treasury of Merit   The theory of *indulgences*, to which *Martin Luther* took exception in 1517, was underpinned by the notion of a treasury of merit. Indulgences being certificates of remission of *satisfaction* due to God for *sins* already forgiven, they raised the question of where that satisfaction, necessary to meet the demands of God's justice, might come from. The answer, officially formulated by Clement VI in 1343, was that they drew on the superabundance of merit generated by the passion of Christ, and innumerable good deeds of *saints* down the ages. The church authorities controlled this deposit of surplus merit, and transferred it to needy sinners through indulgences. Though clearly open to abuse, and castigated by Protestant reformers, the idea was not self-evidently absurd— it expressed the interdependence of the communion of saints, and claimed scriptural grounding in Christ's pledge of the power of the keys (Matt. 16:19) to Peter and his successors.

Mullett (2004); Swanson (2007).

PETER MARSHALL

Trinity   Among major branches of *Reformation* Protestantism the doctrine of the Trinity was not in question: As taught since the ecumenical councils, there was understood to be one God who exists eternally as three distinct and coequal persons. These persons were understood by the terms in the baptismal formula of Matthew 28: Father, Son, and *Holy Spirit*. Nevertheless, *John Calvin* had to defend himself against charges of unorthodox Trinitarian views at Lausanne (1537) and by letter in Neuchâtel (1543).

Among the Radicals, however, the Trinity was directly questioned. *Michael Servetus* argued in *De Trinitatis erroribus* (*On the Errors of the Trinity*, 1531) that the doctrine was neither biblical nor reasonable, leading in part to his condemnation. Several early anti-Trinitarian leaders were Italians active in Switzerland, but their lasting influence centered in Poland. Such thinkers tended toward speculative christological views, and garnered accusations of ancient heresies including Arianism and Sabellianism.

See also **Anti-Trinitarianism; Christology**

Butin (1995); Helmer (1999); G. H. Williams (1992).

GARY NEAL HANSEN

Turk   In the sixteenth century "Turk" was used to designate both the inhabitants, leaders, and armies of the Ottoman Empire and more broadly as a shorthand designation for anyone of the Muslim faith. In 1453 Sultan Mehmed II conquered the city of Constantinople and brought the Byzantine Empire to an end. By the beginning of the sixteenth century, the Ottoman Empire was fully engaged in the Balkans. At the Battle of Mohács in 1526, Sultan Suleiman I defeated the forces of the Hungarian Kingdom, allowing Suleiman to occupy central Hungary and encroach upon central Europe. The "Turkish Threat" was a constant backdrop to nearly all of the imperial diets of the first half of the sixteenth century.

The Diet of Speyer in 1529 and of Augsburg in 1530 were called to specifically address Ottoman expansion into what is now Austria and the so-called Siege of Vienna in 1529. The Recess of the 1526 Diet of Speyer that provided the followers of *Martin Luther* with significant freedoms within the *Holy Roman Empire* were a response to *Charles V*'s need for support among the princes of evangelically leaning dominions in his fight against the Ottoman Empire. Both Roman Catholics and Protestants tended to view the expansion of the "Turkish Threat" as divine punishment for the *sins* and *heresy* of the other. Both sides used the Turks in propaganda against the other side. The Anabaptist *Michael Sattler*'s statement that he would not fight against the Turks should they invade helped cement an image in the minds of many sixteenth-century people that *Anabaptists* could not be trusted upon to defend their communities from outside aggression.

Fischer-Galati (1972); Miller (2002).

DAVID M. WHITFORD

Two Kingdoms *Martin Luther* advocated a theological outlook of two kingdoms, and used two sets of terms when speaking of them. The first, the "two realms" (*Zwei Reiche Lehre*), refers to the two spheres of one's existence: before God and before humanity. The *geistliche Reich* (the spiritual realm) is one's existence *coram deo* (before God). The *weltliche Reich* (the worldly realm) refers to one's existence *coram hominibus* (before humanity). Contained within these two realms is Luther's idea of "two governments" (*Zwei Regimente Lehre*). The first (*das geistliche Regiment*) is the spiritual government of the church exercised through the proclamation of the Word of God and proper administration of the *sacraments*. The second (*das weltliche Regiment*) is the worldly government of emperors, rulers, and ruled, which is governed by law and enforced by coercion.

Bornkamm (1966); Brady (1985a); W. Wright (2010).

DAVID M. WHITFORD

Tyndale, William (ca. 1494–1536)
Tyndale was an English translator and theologian. He was born in Gloucestershire and educated in Oxford. In the early 1520s, inspired by *Desiderius Erasmus*'s biblical scholarship, he conceived a desire to translate the New Testament into English. When the humanist bishop of London refused to support the project, Tyndale left for Germany in 1524. By 1525 he had a complete text, translated from the *Greek*. An effort to print it in Cologne was interrupted; the first finished edition appeared in Worms in 1526. It is an exceptionally good translation, scholarly and vivid. It was also, by now, unmistakably Protestant, drawing significantly on *Martin Luther*, although Tyndale was never a Lutheran in the precise sense.

His own theology, as laid out in a series of English treatises during the later 1520s, emphasized *justification* by *faith* but within a covenantal and communitarian framework, and avoided eucharistic controversies. His most influential book, *The Obedience of a Christian*, defended royal authority against papal claims and taught a high doctrine of obedience, a vision from which *Henry VIII* is said to have learned. However, Tyndale's blunt opposition to Henry's divorce won him his king's hatred, and he and his works remained proscribed. Now based in the Netherlands, and the leader of a group of English *evangelical* exiles, Tyndale produced a revised New Testament (1534); he also taught himself *Hebrew* and embarked on translating the Old Testament. *Thomas More*, England's stoutest defender of Catholicism, singled him out, and the two men carried out an ill-tempered and long-winded polemical exchange. With a price on his head, he was betrayed to the *Inquisition* in the Netherlands in 1535 and burned in 1536. His translation was incomplete, but a Bible based on his work was published in 1535 and a version legalized in 1537. His texts have formed the basis for subsequent English Bibles.

Daniell (2001); Day, Lund, and O'Donnell (1998); Werrell (2006).

ALEC RYRIE

Unction   Christians have used the practice of anointing with oil as a symbol of consecration and for the care of the sick or dying. As a symbol of consecration, unction was employed during *baptism, confirmation,* and ordination. Anointing the sick, based upon James 5:14–15 and Mark 6:13, developed into the *sacrament* of extreme unction by the end of the twelfth century and entailed the anointing of a person on their deathbed. The Protestant reformers rejected extreme unction as a valid sacrament, and many also discarded the use of oil as a consecratory symbol. In *De captivitate Babylonica ecclesiae* (*On the Babylonian Captivity of the Church*, 1520), **Martin Luther** argued that the practice of extreme unction is not a true sacrament but a human invention. **John Calvin** agreed and went further by rejecting the use of oil for consecratory purposes. In England **Thomas Cranmer**'s second prayer book (1552) omitted the use of unction. The Catholic Church reasserted the sacrament of extreme unction in session 14 (1551) of the *Council of Trent*.

Rowell (1993).

G. SUJIN PAK

Uses of Law   Prior to the Reformation, the Church generally assumed that the human will was free, able to obey God's law. Protestants strongly disagreed, arguing that the will was fallen and bound to sin. A point of disagreement between **Martin Luther** and **John Calvin** was the number of uses to which the biblical *law* is to be put. They agreed on two. First, as described by the apostle Paul, sinners see their own failings in contrast to the law's requirements. This brings conviction and repentance so that the guilty may be justified by God's *grace* through *faith*. Second, the law is useful in society, where it keeps even the ungodly under control: the threat of legal consequences keeps people from committing murder, theft, or adultery. Here, according to traditional wisdom, Luther stopped. Calvin went on to a third use

of the law, wherein the Christian person, after faith and repentance, begins to want to please God and looks around for guidance. What better guide than the Ten *Commandments*, or Jesus' summary of the law as *love* of God and neighbor? These are portrayed in the *Bible* not only as mirrors of human inadequacy and guilt, but as the positive description of the will of God for human life.

This reflects a difference in theological purpose between Luther and Calvin more than a difference in fact or substance: Luther tended to write topically, in response to issues and controversies of the moment. Also he was overwhelmingly concerned with the radical difference between his understanding of Paul's teachings on *justification* and teachings of the Roman Church, which he found frankly Pelagian: he was reacting to a late-medieval sense that obedience to the law, so far as one was able, was required as part of the process of justification, and was necessary before one could hope for grace. Luther's desire to emphasize the absolute inadequacy of any human efforts in bringing about justification led to rather polemically driven statements on the utter uselessness of *good works*, and a seeming unconcern for *sanctification*.

Calvin, on the other hand, was an organizer of the Reformation theological teachings, seeking to make sense of the Bible's teachings and the Protestant faith as a whole. He too reacted against any sense that obedience to the law helped in justification. However, he had to give guidance to people who had come to a justifying faith in Christ and needed help in living as Christians. Calvin embraced both a faith and a life guided by *Scripture*, and therefore embraced a doctrine of sanctification shaped by obedience to Scripture's commands—but out of love for God, not fear. In truth Luther too taught such a doctrine implicitly, as seen, for instance, in his catechisms.

Ebeling (1963); Hesselink (1992); Witte (2002).

GARY NEAL HANSEN

Usury   In the early sixteenth century, usury had multiple definitions. While some theologians followed Saint Anselm of Canterbury and argued that charging any interest was theft, most took Thomas Aquinas's position. He argued that usury existed when a moneylender charged interest and did not share the risk. Other theologians allowed some interest to be charged because, by loaning his money, a lender gave up the profits he could have earned from the money himself. With these debates and the rise of increasingly complex trade and financial systems, it is no surprise many Reformers entered the debate. In 1524 *Martin Luther* published a sermon "On Trade and Usury" (LW, vol. 45), where he condemned lenders who took interest without suffering substantial risk; *John Calvin* never directly addressed the question, although he did not consider lending money at interest as unlawful in all situations. The most explicit statements against taking interest came from the *Anabaptists* and other Radical Reformers.

Houkes (2004); D. Jones (2004); N. Jones (1989); Kerridge (2002).
KATHRYN A. EDWARDS

Vadian, Joachim (a.k.a. Vadianus or Joachim von Watt; 1484–1551)
A Swiss humanist, physician, and reformer, Vadian was born in St. Gallen. He received a master of arts and a doctorate of medicine at the University of Vienna, where he also became professor of *rhetoric* and was crowned poet laureate of the *Holy Roman Empire* by *Maximilian I.* He resigned these positions after befriending the future Anabaptist *Conrad Grebel*, who later became his brother-in-law. He returned to St. Gallen, where he became the city physician and also served as mayor. He studied the works of *Desiderius Erasmus, Martin Luther*, and *Philip Melanchthon* and corresponded with *Huldrych Zwingli.* Grebel attempted to establish St. Gallen as an Anabaptist

community, but as mayor Vadian suppressed the *Anabaptists* and instituted the *Reformation* in accordance with Zwinglian teaching.

Gordon (2002); Taplin (2003).
GRETA GRACE KROEKER

Valdés, Juan de (ca. 1490–1541)
Valdés was a Spanish humanist and theologian. He was deeply influenced by the *alumbrados* of Toledo. Like them he continued emphasizing throughout his career an inner spirituality rooted in the reading of the *Bible*, the practice of silent *prayer*, and a disdain for "outer" ceremonials. His intellectual formation at the University of Alcala exposed him to the writings of *Desiderius Erasmus*. He and his brother Alfonso de Valdés formed part of a vibrant movement of Spanish humanists. He published in 1529 his *Diálogo de doctrina Cristiana* (*Dialogue on Christian Doctrine*), a composition that incorporated large amounts of material inspired by works of *Martin Luther*. Soon after he left Spain and in 1534 settled in Naples. He became the central figure of a network of Italian humanists, among them the noble Giulia Gonzaga. He wrote commentaries on Romans and 1 Corinthians that were posthumously published in Geneva.

Crews (2008); Nieto (1970).
RADY ROLDAN-FIGUEROA

Valla, Lorenzo (1406–57)   Valla was born in Rome, where he was largely self-educated and eventually was employed by the papal court after teaching at Pavia and serving King Alfonso of Naples. Philologist, philosopher, rhetorician, and biblical scholar, Valla forged a powerful critique of scholastic logic, claiming that usage and context, not abstract formulae, are the basis for truth in language. He used his linguistic expertise to debunk the Donation of Constantine, an eighth-century forgery documenting that the fourth-century emperor Constantine gave the Roman Empire to Pope Sylvester I. Important works include the *Elegantiae linguae Latinae (Refinements of the Latin Language)*, a handbook on style; *De Vero Bono (On the True Good)*, endorsing a refined concept of pleasure as the highest good; the dialogue *De libero arbitrio (On Free Will)*, simultaneously supporting determinism and voluntarism; and the *Adnotationes (Annotations)* on the New Testament, a set of notes comparing the Vulgate with the original **Greek**.

Bentley (1983); Camporeale (1996); Nauta (2009).

J. LAUREL CARRINGTON

Venial Sin Roman Catholic theologians distinguish between sins that deprive the soul of sanctifying **grace** (called cardinal or mortal), and sins that hinder but do not destroy union with God (venial, from Lat. *venia*, "pardon"). The scriptural locus for this doctrine is found in 1 Corinthians 3:8–15, where the "wood, hay, stubble" are identified as venial sins. The doctrine is found in **Augustine**, expounded in Thomas Aquinas, and codified in the canons of the **Council of Trent** (sixth session, chap. 11). Venial sins do not need the grace of absolution, but can be remitted by contrition and pious works. Protestant reformers rejected the Roman Catholic distinction between venial and mortal sins. Both **Martin Luther** and **John Calvin** taught that all sins are mortal for the unredeemed, whereas for the Christian all sins are venial, not because they do not deserve death, but because of the forgiveness offered in Christ.

Oberman (1986); Ozment (1980); Tentler (1977); Thayer (2002).

GREGORY J. MILLER

Vermigli, Peter Martyr (1499–1562) An Italian theologian, Vermigli was born in Florence and became an Augustinian canon. He attended the University of Padua from 1518 and was ordained in 1525. He had a successful career as preacher, and was a friend of Italian evangelicals such as **Reginald Cardinal Pole, Gasparo Cardinal Contarini, Bernardino Ochino**, and **Juan de Valdés**. His Italian career came to an end in 1542 when he fled Italy in fear of the newly established **Inquisition**. Vermigli taught in **Strasbourg** for five years before moving to **England**, where he served as regius professor at Christ Church, Oxford. He returned to Strasbourg on the death of Edward VI, only to be forced to leave due to conflict with Johannes Marbach, the Lutheran head of the company of pastors. He lived in Zurich for the rest of his life, with frequent travels throughout Europe, including attendance at the Colloquy of Poissy together with **Theodore de Beza**. Scholarship on Vermigli has focused on his doctrine of **predestination**, his relationship to scholastic theology, and his eucharistic theology.

James (1998); McNair (1967); Steinmetz (2001b).

EDWIN WOODRUFF TAIT

Vernacular As a term meaning standard, common, or everyday, "vernacular" has been applied to subjects as diverse as architecture and disease. In the Reformation era, however, it was most commonly used when discussing the *translation* of religious works, especially the **Bible**. The fifteenth century saw the continued development of vernacular literatures throughout Europe and growing demands for vernacular Bibles by famous Reformers such as **Jan Hus** and **John Wyclif**. Pieces of biblical books and even entire Gospels were translated into vernaculars, but such practices were closely regulated. A fundamental tenet of the Lutheran, Reformed, and "radical" movements was the translation of the Bible into the vernacular, and by the mid-sixteenth century vernacular Bibles were available. Although the Catholic Church opposed the vernacularization of *Scripture*, fearing the escalation of *heresy* from inaccurate translation and individual *interpretation*, it produced and authorized many other vernacular religious texts during the late sixteenth and early seventeenth centuries.

Bentley (1983); Griffiths (2001); Muller (2003a).

KATHRYN A. EDWARDS

Vestments Clothing worn by the *clergy* are called "vestments." They emerged from the ancient world and were retained by the clergy of the medieval Roman Catholic Church. Vestments were worn during the *ceremonies* of the church and helped distinguish members of the clergy from the laity. Vestments include the surplice, the stole, the amice, the alb, the cincture, the chasuble, the dalmatic, the maniple, and the cope. Sometimes they were adorned with insignia. The status and role of the wearer determined the type and number of vestments worn. In addition, liturgical vestments differed from nonliturgical vestments. Vestments became an issue during the Protestant *Reformation*. *Martin Luther* saw vestments as optional, though he generally supported their use. *Huldrych Zwingli*, *John Calvin*, and the *Anabaptists* rejected vestments. The Anglican Church endured a great deal of controversy over the issue of clerical vestment, but finally settled on the inclusion of some vestments for clergy.

Brecht (1985–93); Cameron (1991).

GRETA GRACE KROEKER

Via antiqua, via moderna The *via antiqua* is a school of thought originating in the thirteenth century associated with Thomas Aquinas and *John Duns Scotus*. It is so-called in contrast to the later *via moderna* of **William of Ockham**, Gregory of Rimini, and **Gabriel Biel** (among others). The *via antiqua* is noted for its confident demonstration of the inherent rationality of Christian theology through the development of a series of harmonious interlocking arguments. The *via antiqua* included arguments about the existence and nature of God and about his work in the universe. In general, proponents of the *via moderna* ascribed to the philosophical system of nominalism, which denied the metaphysical existence of universal concepts. The *via moderna* made a distinction between the *potentia dei ordinata* (God's ordinary way of working in the world) and *potentia dei absoluta* (God's absolute freedom). The *via moderna* stressed God's freedom to have made the world in any way whatsoever, as well as God's freedom to work in the world outside of normal physical and spiritual means. While the *via moderna* has been accused of promoting the view that God acts in irrational and arbitrary ways, it is more correct to say that the *via moderna* stresses the incomprehensibility of God as he is in himself, and emphasizes his self-limiting, self-revealing, and covenantal way of working in the world through his *potentia ordinata*. The distinction between *via antiqua* and *via moderna* is particularly helpful in understanding the medieval background to the Reformation. In particular, Luther's *via moderna* schooling at the University of Erfurt greatly shaped his general distinction between *deus revelatus* (God revealed) and *deus absconditus* (God hidden) and specifically his sacramental theology. His dispute with *Huldrych Zwingli* over the *Lord's Supper* was in part a result of fundamental differences between these two schools of thought.

Oberman (1963, 1986); Ozment (1980).

GREGORY J. MILLER

Vincent de Paul (1581–1660) The son of a peasant, Vincent was born in the Dax region of France. He received his early ecclesiastical education from the *Franciscans* and studied theology at the University of Toulouse. Ordained as a priest in 1600, he moved around frequently in order to improve his social and economic status. He ended up as a tutor to the powerful Gondi family, who had close ties to the crown. During this time, he began to minister to the poor, which would become his life's work. He founded the Congregation of the Mission known as the Lazarists, and more importantly he established the Daughters of Charity with Louise de Marillac. This unique female order successfully fought *enclosure* by keeping its members, who offered aid to the poor and spread Tridentine Catholicism, as lay sisters. It offered women a clear alternative to the vocation of an enclosed nun.

Dinan (2006); Mezzadri (1992); Pujo (2003).

JILL R. FEHLEISON

Viret, Pierre (1511–71)   Viret was born in Switzerland. Though poor, he was able to attend the Collège Montaigu at the University of Paris, where he was converted to Protestantism. Under the influence of *Guillaume Farel* he became a minister around 1530, and joined Farel in Geneva in 1534. He was chief pastor in Lausanne from 1536 to 1559, when he was exiled to Geneva. In France from 1561 to his death, he preached to thousands in Nîmes, working to bring the *Reformation* in Lyons. He published some fifty works, the most important being *Instruction chrestienne* (*Christian Instruction*; 1564).

He was a close friend of *John Calvin*, and the two men's teachings were similar. However, Viret's eucharistic teaching leaned toward that of *Huldrych Zwingli* and, as well as advocating religious toleration, he was the first Calvin-

ist to articulate views that legitimized resistance to tyrannous governments.

Bruening (2008); Linder (1964, 1971).

GARY NEAL HANSEN

Visitation   The examination of churches, monasteries, and other ecclesiastical foundations by diocesan officials is called "visitation." Visitors generally considered three factors: the state of church finances, the moral qualities and professional conduct of the *clergy*, and the state of religious life in the parish or foundation generally. During the Reformation era, regular visitations were a major part of reform movements in both Catholic and Protestant states. Among Protestants, the parish visitations generally followed the model of the first Lutheran visitations: the Saxon visitation of 1527 and the Brandenburg-Nuremberg visitation of 1528. In the wake of the *Council of Trent*, visitations were conducted in Catholic territories. Regular visitations became one of the main mechanisms for enforcing religious norms during the confessional era.

Zeeden and Moliter (1977).

WILLIAM BRADFORD SMITH

Vives, Juan Luis (1492–1540)   Vives was a Spanish humanist. His parents were Jewish converts to Christianity, and members of his family were condemned by the *Inquisition* of Valencia. He studied at the University of Paris from 1509 to 1512. He soon became a disciple of *Desiderius Erasmus*. He revealed to the world the imprint of his master in his *Adversus pseudodialecticos* (1519), as he rehearsed Erasmus's criticism of the medieval church. He moved to *England* after the invitation of *Henry VIII*, who appointed him as tutor to Mary (*see Mary I*). However, he was imprisoned in 1527 as a result of his disapproval of the king's request for an annulment of his marriage with Catherine of Aragon. After his return to the Low Countries he continued writing, becoming a prolific author with very innovative ideas in the fields of *education* and care of the poor. He was an ardent advocate for the education of women.

Fantazzi (2008); Fernández-Santamaría (1998); Noreña (1970).

RADY ROLDAN-FIGUEROA

Vocation   In the Middle Ages "vocation" or "calling" (Lat. *vocare*, "to call") primarily referred to a divine calling to enter the priesthood or monastic life. Rejecting the medieval notion that entering a religious order or the ordained priesthood was spiritually superior to being a lay Christian, *Martin Luther* and other leading Protestants argued that vocation applied to all Christians. Every Christian was called by a "general" or "spiritual" vocation to join the priesthood of all believers through *faith* and *baptism*. By a "particular" or "external" vocation each Christian was also called to a station or role in society (governing, farming, preaching, etc.) as a sphere in which to practice Christian obedience. Thus they claimed equal dignity and sanctity before God for each particular vocation. Protestants also often used "calling" to refer to the procedure by which a pastor was installed by human authorities who mediated and confirmed an individual's vocation to ministry.

Douglas (1969); P. Marshall (1996); Placher (2005).

DANIEL EPPLEY

Vows   Vows became a regular part of church tradition by about the eighth century, and became attached to two of the *sacraments* formally recognized by the Roman Church following the Fourth *Lateran Council* in 1215: *marriage* and holy orders. When entering the church as a priest or as a monk or nun, a person had to make vows of chastity, poverty, and obedience. Marriage also required vows of commitment.

The Reformed religions did not recognize marriage and holy orders as sacraments, and *Martin Luther* argued that the religious vows were not necessarily permanent in his *Judgment of Monastic Vows* of 1521. Despite rejecting the two sacraments, the Protestant faiths did recognize the importance of vows, particularly with regard to marriage. The rejection of the monastic life and the promotion of marriage over chastity for the *clergy*, though, meant that the vows stressed by the Protestant religions differed from those of the Catholics.

Seymour (1885).

KRISTEN POST WALTON

War   Though Christ is often called the Prince of Peace, war has been intertwined with *religion* throughout the Christian era. With the onset of the *Reformation*, wars began to be fought across Europe between Christian faiths fighting for supremacy. Wars of religion erupted in most European countries affected by the Reformation, including France, the Netherlands, *England*, and the *Holy Roman Empire*. Many wars were fought during this time, from the *Peasants' War* of 1524–25 to the *Thirty Years' War* and the Treaty or *Peace of Westphalia* in 1648; Europe's rivers often ran red with blood of martyrs from many Christian faiths. War during this period produced many new ideas, from Montaigne's philosophy that embraced skepticism in religion, to the birth of deism and the decision following 1648 that the cost of religious war was too great. In addition, the geography of Europe transformed as a result of the wars fought for religion during the Age of Reformation.

Blickle, Brady, and Midelfort (1985); Holt (1995); G. Parker (1997).
KRISTEN POST WALTON

Westphal, Joachim (ca. 1510–71)

A preacher, theologian, and reformer at Hamburg, Westphal participated in several intra-Protestant disputes during the 1550s. He studied at Wittenberg through 1541. In the series of theological and political conflicts that arose after *Martin Luther*'s death in 1546, Westphal was numbered among the so-called Gnesio-Lutherans ("Genuine" Lutherans). Westphal did not share the irenic tendencies of his teacher, *Philip Melanchthon*, and opposed Melanchthon's efforts at compromise, beginning with the Augsburg Interim (1548). Along with other Gnesios, Westphal advanced the "ubiquity" doctrine in regard to the mode of the Christ's presence in Holy Communion. His writings against the *Zurich Consensus* (1549) and reformed teachings concerning the *Lord's Supper* elicited several published responses from *John Calvin*, including *A Final Warning to Joachim Westphal Who, Unless He Submits, Shall hereafter Be Treated as a Stubborn Heretic according to Paul's Command* (1557).

Pettegree (1987); Tylenda (1974, 1997).
HANS WIERSMA

Westphalia, Peace of (1648)   The

Peace of Westphalia was the set of treaties that brought an end to the *Thirty Years' War*. The peace comprised two separate agreements, the Peace of Osnabrück (*Instrumentum pacis Osnabrugense*) between Sweden and the *Holy Roman Empire*, and the Peace of Münster (*Instrumentum pacis Monasteriense*) between the empire and France. Both treaties were formally concluded on October 24, 1648.

Negotiations for a peace settlement began in 1640 when, after a series of military disasters and in light of the devastation of the empire, Emperor Ferdinand III called a meeting of the Imperial Diet at *Regensburg* (1640–41). Here Ferdinand agreed, against the demands of the *papacy*, to revoke the Edict of Restitution, a major point of Protestant disaffection. Meanwhile, various German states, including Brandenburg, Mecklenburg, Saxony, and Bavaria, sought to negotiate separate peace agreements with France and Sweden. After the French victory over Spain at Rocroy (May 18, 1643), Ferdinand gave his sanction for a general peace. After some delay, representatives from the empire, France, and Sweden assembled at Osnabrück and Münster, location agreed upon in a Franco-Swedish treaty of 1641, on December 4, 1644.

Negotiations continued steadily over the next four years even as the fighting showed little signs of letting up. Major points of controversy were territorial claims by the various belligerents, France and Sweden as well as the German states; the status of the Palatine Electorate, transferred to Bavaria twenty years earlier; the settlement of the war in the Netherlands; imperial justice; and official recognition of Calvinism. Most matters had been settled by the summer of 1646, but hostilities continued, primarily on account of Jules Cardinal Mazarin's decision to increase French demands. In the final settlement, France acquired control over much of Alsace and a toehold on the Rhine. Sweden received the former prince-bishoprics of Bremen and Verden as well as the western half of Pomerania. Eastern Pomerania and the former dioceses of Magdeburg and Halberstadt were ceded to Brandenburg. Saxony was confirmed in possession of Lusatia; likewise, Bavarian control over the Upper Palatinate was recognized. Switzerland was given its independence from the empire.

The Peace of Westphalia made the religious settlement agreed to at the Diet of Augsburg in 1555 permanent, granting official recognition in perpetuity to Protestantism, according to the formula *cuius regio, eius religio*. Article 5 followed the definition of Protestantism as the *religion* of the **Augsburg Confession**. Article 7, however, noted the presence of the "controversial religion . . . called by some Reformed" (i.e., Calvinism), and granted limited toleration to those princes who had adopted the new religion. Protestants, including Calvinists, were confirmed in their possession of all ecclesiastical rights and properties held prior to 1624.

The peace did not immediately end hostilities; fighting continued in some regions for another two years. Sweden did not finally withdraw from Saxony until 1650.

G. Parker (1997); Polišensky (1978); Wedgewood (1938); Zeumer (1904).
WILLIAM BRADFORD SMITH

Will   The role of the human will in salvation is a central issue in the **Reformation**. The issue was seen through Augustinian lenses, as the will was central in the Pelagian controversies in the early church. In the 1520s **Desiderius Erasmus** and **Martin Luther** debated "free choice." For Erasmus the scriptural injunctions to choose imply the sinner's ability to do so (e.g., Deut. 30:19); *merit*, too, seems to require *free will*. Luther argues that the scriptural imperatives are meant instead to reveal the folly of relying on our own will to effect salvation (cf. Rom. 7). The sinner's turn to God is an effect solely of God's *election* and *grace*. **John Calvin** takes a similar but somewhat more rigorous position. The **Council of Trent** said that salvation depends on grace at every point, but nevertheless insisted that in sinners the free will has not been extinguished. By grace one is "moved freely" toward salvation.

McSorley (1969); Saarinen (1994).
MICKEY L. MATTOX

William of Ockham (ca. 1285–1348)   William was a monk, philosopher/theologian, and founder of what came to be known as the *via moderna* (modern way). William was at the forefront of the conciliar reform movement that held that the church's highest earthly **authority** lay not with the **papacy** but with general councils. The idea behind "Ockham's razor"—that explanations of phenomena should be shaved of unnecessary assumptions—did not originate with William. Still, his form of philosophical nominalism sought to be realistic, thereby minimizing speculation about universals and absolutes. His theories regarding the way in which God exercises power among humans (*potentia ordinata*) would be developed by later nominalists (especially **Gabriel Biel**) into an intricate covenantal system known by the shorthand phrase *facere quod in se est* ("to do that which is within you to do"). It was **Martin Luther**'s alienation with this system that led to his famous theological "breakthrough" (ca. 1518).

See also **Via antiqua, via moderna**

Ozment (1980); Spade (1999); Tierney (1971); Vignaux (1971).
HANS WIERSMA

Witchcraft   As a crime tied to local conditions, personalities, and perspectives—and sometimes not even perceived as criminal—witchcraft in early modern Europe is notoriously difficult to synthesize. In the second half of the fifteenth century, however, writings about and trials for witchcraft escalated. Widely defined as *maleficia* (the practice of evil deeds), by the sixteenth century theologians and jurists also added the element of demonic conspiracy to their understanding of witchcraft. Between 1550 and 1720 approximately 110,000 individuals were accused of witchcraft and 60,000 executed throughout Europe, although certain regions and times had disproportionate activity. Men and women of all ages, classes, and educational levels were tried and condemned, with Protestants, Catholics, and *Anabaptists* all sharing convictions about the dangers of witches and their attendant demons. Although witchcraft trials declined substantially by the end of the seventeenth century, the last legal execution for witchcraft occurred in 1782 in the Swiss canton of Glarus.

Ankarloo and Clark (1999–2002); Behringer (2004); Clark (1997); Levack (2006).

KATHRYN A. EDWARDS

Wittenberg Though a relatively small Saxon town (about 2,000 inhabitants), Wittenberg housed one of Europe's most impressive collections of relics in the early sixteenth century. Nevertheless, owing to the presence of leading *evangelical* theologians like *Martin Luther, Philip Melanchthon*, and *Johannes Bugenhagen*, it became the center of the Lutheran *Reformation*. Wittenberg's humanist university, the so-called *Leucorea* (Greek for Wittenberg), where Luther and Melanchthon lectured, was the leading university of the evangelical movement; numerous Lutheran pastors received their training there. Wittenberg artists like *Lucas Cranach the Elder* helped to spread the evangelical message through paintings and woodcuts, and the town's printers turned it into one of the most important centers of book production in Germany. Luther, his family, and numerous guests lived in Wittenberg's Augustinian monastery, where Luther had once been a monk. Wittenberg also played an important role in the early history of the Radical Reformation owing especially to the conflict between Luther and *Andreas Bodenstein von Karlstadt*.

Brecht (vol. 1, 1985–93); Junghans (2003); Kirsch and Treu (1993).

RONALD K. RITTGERS

Wolsey, Thomas Cardinal (ca. 1472–1530) An Ipswich butcher's son, Wolsey rose to become *Henry VIII's* chief minister and one of the greatest European churchmen of his day. Having proven his abilities in administering the 1513 campaign against France, Wolsey was promoted to a succession of bishoprics, including the archdiocese of York. Henry persuaded the *papacy* to create him cardinal (1515) and to endow him with delegated papal powers as legate (1518). In this capacity, Wolsey dominated the church, while as Lord Chancellor (1515–29) he headed the civil administration. In his own day and since Wolsey attracted an unenviable reputation as a corrupt, power-hungry prelate. In fact (mistress and illegitimate son notwithstanding), he was a hard-working royal servant, a legal reformer, and a significant patron of the arts and *education*. But he failed in a key task Henry VIII set for him—to persuade Rome to grant the divorce from Catherine of Aragon—and died in disgrace.

Gunn and Lindley (1991); Gwyn (1990); Rex (1992).

PETER MARSHALL

Women No field of the *Reformation* has seen more of an explosion of research in the last forty years than that concentrating on women. Women were fundamental both as participants and as victims or beneficiaries of reform efforts. Both the Protestant and Catholic Reformations reaffirmed gender roles and generally desired to separate women and men into private (i.e., domestic) and public spheres, with varying degrees of success. Figures such as *Teresa of Avila, Caritas Pirckheimer, Katharina Schütz Zell*, Mary Ward, and Angela Merici wrote pamphlets, preached, started new orders, and converted believers. There was a backlash against these actions, and many women were forced to give up their public voice and activities.

Many scholars argue that the main effects of the Protestant Reformation for women were negative, with an increased focus on patriarchy and *marriage*, the closing of the convents and the brothels, and the expunging or demoting of female role models and symbols within the *church*, especially the Virgin *Mary*. Others counter that by valuing marriage more than celibacy the role of women in the family was enhanced and that the Protestant doctrine of the priesthood of all believers raised women to the spiritual equal of men. Further, the Protestant emphasis on *education* ultimately benefited women.

The dissolution of the convents was one of the most dramatic results of the Reformation. Reformers argued that *monasticism* hurt women, many of the nuns had been forced to enter, celibacy was unnatural, and that the Catholic hierarchy of merit placed women on a lower plane than men. On the other hand, the closing of the convents (and to a lesser degree, the brothels) took away one of the only public vocations for women and an arena of female community and empowerment. Women also had fewer options than men when their religious houses were closed, and many former nuns were left impoverished. The effects of dissolution were worse in *England* than in Germany, with as many as half the convents in some German areas successfully resisting closure. Religious women in Catholic areas were also affected by reform, as the church banned active female orders and sought closer control of nuns, demanding strict monastic *enclosure* for all religious women.

The Protestant emphasis on marriage as the center of civil society raised the value of the wife and mother, but also increased the father's control over the family. Divorce was theoretically easier for women to obtain, but evidence shows little difference between Protestant and Catholic divorce rates. Protestants advocated education for all,

girls and boys, but the establishment of girls' schools lagged far behind those for boys, and it is not clear how much better educated Protestant women were than Catholic.

Leonard (2005); S. Marshall (1989); Rapley (1990); Wiesner (2008).

AMY E. LEONARD

Worship   *Martin Luther*'s emphasis on *sola scriptura* led to new understandings of the purpose and experience of worship. Protestants insisted that worship should focus on the teaching of the Word of God (rather than experiencing divine mysteries), conducted all church services in the vernacular, and emphasized listening to sermons and praying aloud in unison. They restricted the use of images to different degrees, concerned that the laity would be misled into superstitious beliefs. Protestant liturgies varied considerably, from the frequency of the Eucharist to the order of weekly services. Zurich worship services had no music, whereas Luther put great emphasis on liturgical *music*, penning thirty hymns himself. *John Calvin* had the Psalms set to music, and the *Genevan Psalter* became a fundamental part of Reformed worship. Protestant liturgical changes sometimes led to alterations in church architecture, as well—for example, moving the pulpit to put *preaching* physically at the center of worship.

Eire (1986); Karant-Nunn (1997); Maag and Witvliet (2004); B. Thompson (1980); Yates (2008).

KAREN E. SPIERLING

Wyclif, John (ca. 1324–84)   Often termed the "Morningstar of the Reformation," Wyclif was an Oxford don who expressed his frustrations with a Roman Church existing in Avignon during the age of the Hundred Years War

(1337–1453) between France and *England*. Wyclif believed that men should be able to read the *Bible* for themselves and therefore translated it into English. He was one of the most important English thinkers of the Middle Ages both for his *philosophy* and his attempts to reform the *church*. Wyclif stressed the place of the state over the church on earth, believing that God, not the pope, was the true head of the church and that God had appointed the king. His ideas gained him the support of John of Gaunt (1340–99), a son of Edward III and the most powerful noble of the day. Wyclif also promoted other ideas of the Reformation, including emphasizing the importance of poverty within the church, and the importance of *Scripture*. His followers were known as Lollards.

Farr (1974); Hudson (1988); Lahey (2003).
KRISTEN POST WALTON

Xavier, Francis (1506–52)   Xavier
was born on April 7, 1506, at Xavier Castile near Pamplona (Spain) to a nobleman and noblewoman. In 1525 he matriculated at the University of Paris, where he met *Ignatius of Loyola* in 1528. On August 15, 1534, at the monastery of Montmartre in Paris, Loyola, Xavier, and other companions took a vow of poverty and chastity, and swore an oath to go to the Holy Land. In 1536, to fulfill their oath, the companions traveled to Venice but were unable to continue their journey to the Holy Land. So they began to do charitable work in the city's hospitals. At this time, Xavier was ordained to the priesthood. In 1540 *Pope Paul III* recognized the Society of Jesus (*Jesuits*) and charged the order with the propagation of the faith through word and deed.

That same year, King João III of Portugal asked the pope to send him members of the new order to evangelize in Asia. In response to the king's request, Loyola sent Xavier and Simon Rodriguez to Lisbon. Then, leaving Rodriguez

to train future Jesuit missionaries in Lisbon, Xavier set out for Asia in 1541.

Xavier successfully established missions in India, Malabar, Malacca, and Japan. He first preached among the pearl fishers near Cape Comorin, India, for two years. With the arrival of more Jesuit missionaries, he was appointed superior of the Jesuits' oriental mission in 1544. He then established a mission in the Spice Islands. While in Malacca, Xavier met Anjiro, a fugitive from Japan, whom he converted to Christianity. Anjiro made such a profound impression on Xavier that he resolved to go to Japan. In 1549 Xavier, two other Jesuits, and Anjiro (called Paul of the Holy Faith) went to Japan where they spent the next two years translating the catechism into Japanese, establishing churches, and baptizing people. Xavier's mission to Japan is probably his most famous, and it is the only case where Xavier's missionary activity did not follow in the wake of Portuguese expansion. While making preparations for a mission to China, Xavier died on December 3, 1552. For the last ten years of his life, Xavier had traveled throughout Asia, establishing missions and converting tens of thousands of people to Christianity.

Xavier was the first of many Jesuits to undertake missions abroad, and his apostolate in Asia became a model for future Jesuit missionaries to follow: he learned the local languages and adapted local customs to preach the gospel more effectively to the people. Xavier was canonized in 1622, declared patron saint of the Orient in 1748, and with Saint Teresa of the Child Jesus named protector of all missionary works in 1927.

Corrêa Monteiro (2006); Schurhammer (1973–82).
SEAN T. PERRONE

Zanchi, Girolamo (1516–90)   An
Italian Reformed theologian, Zanchi began his religious career with the

Augustinian Order of Regular Canons. By 1541 he was part of the priory of Lucca, at the time presided over by *Peter Martyr Vermigli*. He became acquainted with Protestant literature and engaged in *evangelical preaching*. In 1553 he moved to *Strasbourg* to take a position as professor of Old Testament. On account of his Reformed theology, however, he soon faced opposition by city and ecclesiastical authorities that were aligned, as the political situation of the city demanded, with Lutheranism. He left Strasbourg in 1563, and served as a preacher in Chiavenna until 1568. He taught at Heidelberg from 1567 to 1576, and then moved to another teaching position in Neustadt, where he remained until his death. He was the author of several theological works, including *De religione christiana fides* (*Confession of Christian Religion*, 1585).

Burchill (1984); Farthing (1999); Kittelson (2000).

RADY ROLDAN-FIGUEROA

Zell, Katharina Schütz (1498–1562)

Zell was an early Protestant reformer, writer, and teacher in *Strasbourg*. In 1523 she married the popular *evangelical* preacher Matthew Zell, which led to his excommunication and her pamphlet in defense of clerical *marriage*. One of the most public and vocal of the new pastors' wives, Schütz Zell devoted her life to teaching and helping the poor, sick, and religiously persecuted. She was notable for the amount and variety of her writings, her public persona (she gave the eulogy at her husband's funeral), and the longevity of her career, writing and publishing almost her entire adult life. Her vocal support of religious toleration, especially toward the *Anabaptists*, eventually earned her the condemnation of the city's Lutheran clergy, who accused her of being a "disturber of the peace of the church." Despite widespread suspicion of *heresy* (which she vigorously denied), there was never any proof, and when she died she received a Lutheran burial.

Bainton (1971); Chrisman (1972); McKee (1999, 2006).

AMY E. LEONARD

Zurich Consensus

The Zurich Consensus (Lat. *Consensus Tigurinus*) was an agreement on the *Lord's Supper*. In the years following 1544 the long-festering dispute between the Lutherans and Zwinglians reached a particular low. *John Calvin*, however, believed that unity was still possible. In his own writings he was largely in sympathy with the *Strasbourg* reformers (*Martin Bucer*) and critical of both the Lutheran doctrine of ubiquity and the Zwinglian emphasis on memorialism. The serious threat to the *Reformation* posed by the victory of *Charles V* in 1547 only heightened the necessity for union. To his horror Calvin had realized that *Martin Luther* counted him among the "sacramentarians," and his relations with the Lutherans deteriorated. This forced him to seek agreement with *Heinrich Bullinger*. Calvin traveled to Zurich and in 1549 an agreement (named for the city of Zurich) was reached that almost entirely reflected Bullinger's theological position. Calvin and Bullinger differed on the degree to which the bread and wine act as instruments of God's *grace*. Calvin later revised the document, but it did form the basis of a close relationship between the two men, who despite disagreements on questions of theology worked effectively to support and spread the Reformation.

Gordon (2002, 2009).

BRUCE GORDON

Zurich Disputations

As tensions concerning reform increased in Zurich, the town council took the unprecedented step of organizing and hosting a debate in January 1523 with the express purpose of establishing guidelines for faith and practice. *Huldrych Zwingli* should be considered the driving force behind these disputations, and his *67 Articles* (*Conclusions*) guided discussion. The ground-rule stipulation that *Scripture* alone would be accepted as authoritative in argumentation (visually expressed by the dominating presence of a large open *Bible*) made the result in favor of reform a foregone conclusion. The Zurich proceedings were soon imitated by other cities in the Swiss Confederacy and in the empire. A second disputation held in October 1523 focused on images and *sacraments*. The decision to end the *Mass* and remove images in an orderly manner did not satisfy the proponents of more extensive and rapid change, such as *Conrad Grebel*, who then turned away from Zwingli.

Lindberg (1996); Potter (1976); Stephens (1992); Wandel (1995).

GREGORY J. MILLER

Zwickau Prophets

Zwickau Prophets   Three men— Nicolas Storch, Marcus Stübner (or Thoma), and Thomas Drechsel—fled from Zwickau to Wittenberg in December 1521. Associated with *Thomas Müntzer* and led by Storch, a layman, the three "prophets" claimed to have new revelations of the *Holy Spirit*. They decried the poverty of the peasants, disavowed political and church authorities, and forecast the imminent return of Christ. With *Martin Luther* still in hiding in the Wartburg, the prophets established credibility with *Andreas Bodenstein von Karlstadt*, while an uncertain *Philip Melanchthon* wrote to Luther for advice. Reports of the prophets' radicalizing activities helped convince Luther to return to Wittenberg. Against the prophets' *schwärmerei* ("excited confusion" or "fanaticism") and the abuse of Christian liberty it seemed to inspire, Luther preached his Invocavit sermons (March 1522).

The prophets were eventually banished from Wittenberg. Although the Zwickau Prophets rejected infant *baptism*, the assertion that they initiated the *Anabaptist* movement is not correct.

Friesen (1990); Karant-Nunn (1987).

HANS WIERSMA

Zwingli, Huldrych (1484–1531)

Zwingli, Huldrych   (1484–1531) Zwingli was born in an alpine region of Switzerland to a prosperous peasant family with connections to local government and the church. Throughout his life Zwingli was a dedicated patriot who loved the Swiss land and people. He attended the University of Vienna, where he was significantly influenced by the *humanism* of Conrad Celtis and others. He received the bachelor (1504) and master (1506) of arts at the University of Basel, where he was instructed according to the *via antiqua* of Thomas Aquinas.

When he was 22 years old he was ordained priest and served the parish of Glarus. During two years of ministry as the people's priest at the important pilgrimage town of Einsiedeln (1516–18) he immersed himself in the Greek New Testament and began to preach in an Erasmian mold against religious abuses. In 1518 Zwingli accepted appointment as people's priest at the Great Minster in Zurich. He was already recognized as a great preacher and one of the best *Greek* scholars north of the Alps. Immediately upon beginning his responsibilities, he announced that he would preach "only the Scriptures."

By 1522 Zwingli's reform preaching had emboldened some of his listeners to violate the Lenten fast by eating sausages. Though Zwingli himself did not participate, he defended the fastbreakers and increased his calls for reform. In January 1523, at the First *Zurich Disputation*, the town council, under guidance by Zwingli, established control over religious life in the canton through the principle that *Scripture* alone rather than obedience to the ecclesiastical hierarchy was to determine faith and practice. Further action by the town council resulted in the permission of priests to marry (including Zwingli himself in April 1524), the removal of images (June 1524), and the abolition of the *Mass* (April 1525).

Zwingli was also intimately involved in efforts to spread the reform throughout Switzerland and beyond. To that end he eagerly sought the support of *Philipp of Hesse*. With *Martin Luther*, Zwingli was one of the key disputants in Philipp of Hesse's failed attempt to achieve a unified reformed position on the *Lord's Supper* at the *Marburg Colloquy* (October 1–4, 1529). In 1531, with the reluctant help of Bern, conflict was initiated with the Catholic cantons of Switzerland to force the issue of free *preaching* of Scripture.

The Second Kappel War that resulted was a disaster for Zurich, and Zwingli was among the battlefield casualties. However, Zwingli's death did not end the reform in Switzerland or efface his work. Under the leadership of his successor, *Heinrich Bullinger*, important aspects of the Zwinglian heritage were preserved and Zurich remained an important center for the European Reformation.

Though Zwingli published nearly ninety works and carried on a European-wide correspondence, he is perhaps best known for his symbolic interpretation of the Eucharist, his thoroughgoing rejection of religious images and holy objects, and his strong support of the *authority* of urban magistrates in religious matters. Most importantly, Zwingli's understanding of reform went far beyond liturgical or theological innovation to include an entire transformation of society based on Christian faith.

Eire (1986); Furcha and Pipkin (1984); Gäbler (1986); Potter (1976); Stephens (1992).

GREGORY J. MILLER

Primary Bibliography

BIBLES

Berry, L. E., ed. 1969. *Geneva Bible, a Facsimile of the 1560 edition*. Madison.

Bomberg, D., ed. 1525–26. *Mikraot Gedolot [Rabbinic Bible]*. 2nd ed. 4 vols. Venice.

Challoner, R., ed. 1989. *The Holy Bible, Translated from the Latin Vulgate. Diligently Compared with the Hebrew, Greek, and other Editions in Divers Languages. The Old Testament first published by the English college at Douay, A.D. 1609, and the New Testament first published by the English college at Rheims, A.D. 1582. With Annotations, References, and an Historical and Chronological index; the whole revised and diligently compared with the Latin Vulgate by Bishop Richard Challoner, A.D. 1749–1752*. Charlotte, NC.

Enzinas, F. de, ed. 1543. *El nuevo testamento de nuestro redemptor y salvador Jesu Christo, traduzido de Griego en lengua castellana por Françisco de Enzinas, dedicado a la Cesarea Magestad*. Antwerp.

The New Testament of Jesus Christ, 1582. Facsimile of the Rheims New Testament. 1975. Aldershot, UK.

Reina, C. de, trans. 1569. *La Biblia, que es los sacros libros del Viejo y Nuevo testamento*. Basel.

El Testamento nuevo de nuestro señor y salvator Jesu Christo. 1556. Geneva.

Tyndale, W. 1989. *Tyndale's New Testament*. Edited by D. Daniell. New Haven.

Wycliffe, J. 2002. *Wycliffe New Testament 1388: An edition in modern spelling, with an introduction, the original prologues and the Epistle to the Laodiceans*. Edited by W. Cooper. London.

Ximénes de Cisneros, F., and D. Lopez de Zuñiga. 1983–84. *Biblia complutensis*. Rome.

OTHER PRIMARY TEXTS

Agricola, J. 2008. *Introduction to the Art of Singing by Johann Friedrich Agricola*. Edited by J. Baird. Cambridge.

Anonymous. 1580. *Holie exercise of a true fast, described out of Gods word. Seene and allowed*. London.

Aquinas, Thomas. 1964. *Summa Theologica*. London.

Aristotle. 1991. *On Rhetoric: A Theory of Civic Discourse*. Translated by G. Kennedy. New York.

Arminius, J. *Writings*. 1956. 3 vols. Grand Rapids.

Augustine of Hippo. 1993. *On the Free Choice of the Will*. Edited and translated by T. Williams. Indianapolis.

Aurelius, M. 2006. *Meditations*. Edited and translated by M. Hammond. London.

Báñez, D. 1584. *Scholastica Commentaria in Primam Partem Angelici Doctoris S. Thomae*. Salamanca.

Báñez, D. 1587. *Scholastica commentaria in secundam secundae Angelici Doctoris D. Thomae*. Venice.

Báñez, D. 1594. *De iure & iustitia decisiones*. Salamanca.

Baylor, M., ed. 1991. *The Radical Reformation*. Cambridge Texts in the History of Political Thought. Cambridge.

Bellarmine, R. 1989. *Spiritual Writings*. Edited and translated by J. Donnelly and R. Teske. New York.

Beza, T. 1906. *A Tragedie of Abraham's Sacrifice Written in French (Abraham sacrifiant)*. Translated by A. Golding. Edited by M. Wallace. Toronto.

Beza, T. 1969. *Du droit des magistrates sur leur sujets (Right of magistrates)*. In *Constitutionalism and Resistance in the Sixteenth Century: Three Treatises*. Edited and translated by J. Franklin, 97–141. New York.

Beza, T. 1992. *Confession du foy du Chretien (The Christian Faith)*. Translated by J. Clark. East Essex, UK.

Biandrata, G. 1977. "To John Calvin, Esteemed Preceptor, from Giorgio Biandrata." Appendix 1 of "Warning That Went Unheeded: John Calvin on Giorgio Biandrata." Translated by J. Tylenda. *Calvin Theological Journal* 12, no. 1:52–54.

Biel, G. 1930. *Treatise on the Power and Utility of Moneys*. Translated by R. Burke. Philadelphia.

Biel, G. 1966. "The Circumcision of the Lord." Cited from H. Oberman, ed., *Forerunners of the Reformation*. New York.

Boethius. 1989. *Fundamentals of Music (De Institutione Musica)*. Translated by C. Bower. Edited by C. Palisca. New Haven.

Bolsec, J. 1875. *Histoire de la vie, mœrs, actes, doctrine, constance et mort de Jean Calvin, iadis ministre de Geneve*. Lyon.

Bond, R. ed. 1987. *Certain Sermons or Homilies (1547)*. Toronto.

Bracciolini, Poggio. 1900. "Description of the Death and Punishment of Jerome of Prague." Translated by M. Whitcomb. In *A Literary Source-book of the Italian Renaissance*, ed. M. Whitcomb, 40–47. Philadelphia.

Bray, G., ed. 1994. *Documents of the English Reformation*. London.

Braubach, M., and K. Repgen. 1962–. *Actis Pacis Westphalicae*. Münster.

Brenz, J. 1970–. *Johannes Brenz Werke. Eine Studienausgabe*. Edited by M. Brecht and G. Schäfer. Tübingen.

Bucer, M. 1972. *Common Places of Martin Bucer*. Translated and edited by D. Wright. Abingdon.

Bucer, M. 2009. *Concerning the True Care of Souls*. Carlisle, PA.

Buchanan, G. 1572. *Ane Detectioun of the Doingis of Marie Quene of Scotis*. St. Andrews.

Budé, G. 1967. *La Correspondance d'Érasme et de Guillaume Budé*. Paris.

Bullinger, H. 1849–52. *The Decades of Henry Bullinger*. Edited by T. Harding. 4 vols. Cambridge.

Bullinger, H. 1991. *Fountainhead of federalism: Heinrich Bullinger and the covenantal tradition with a translation of De testamento seu foedere Dei unico et aeterno (1534)*. Edited by C. McCoy and J. Baker. Louisville.

Burkholder, J., and C. Palisca, eds. 2010. *Norton Anthology of Western Music* (music score). New York.

Burkholder, J., and C. Palisca, eds. 2006. *Norton Recorded Anthology of Western Music* (sound recording). New York.

Burns, J., et al., eds. 1997. *Conciliarism and Papalism*. Cambridge.

Cajetan, T. 1978. *Cajetan Responds: A Reader in Reformation Controversy*. Washington, D.C.

Cajetan, T. 2005. *Opera omnia quotquot in Sacrae Scripturae expositionem reperiuntur*. Reprint, Hildesheim.

Calvin, J. 1561. *Institution of the Christian Religion*. London.

Calvin, J. 1954. *Calvin: Theological Treatises*. Edited by J. Reid. Louisville.

Calvin, J. 1958. *Psychopannychia*. Pages 413–90 in *Tracts and Treatises in Defense of the Reformed Faith*. Translated by H. Beveridge. Vol. 3 of *Calvin's Tracts and Treatises*. Grand Rapids.

Calvin, J. 1960a. *Calvin's New Testament Commentaries*. Edited by D. Torrance and T. Torrance, 12 vols. Grand Rapids.

Calvin, J. 1960b. *Institutes of the Christian Religion*. Edited by J. McNeill. Translated by F. Battles. Philadelphia.

Calvin, J. 1969. *Calvin's Commentary on Seneca's De Clementia*. Translated and edited by F. Battles and A. Hugo. Leiden.

Calvin, J. 1975. *John Calvin: Selections from His Writings*. Edited by J. Dillenberger. Missoula, MT.

Calvin, J. 1977. "John Calvin's Response to the Questions of Giorgio Biandrata." Appendix 2 of "Warning That Went Unheeded: John Calvin on Giorgio Biandrata." Translated by J. Tylenda. *Calvin Theological Journal* 12, no. 1:54–62.

Calvin, J. 1981. *Calvin's Commentaries*. Edited by the Calvin Translation Society. 22 vols. Reprint, Grand Rapids.

Calvin, J. 1982. *Treatises against the Anabaptists and against the Libertines*. Edited and translated by B. Farley. Grand Rapids.

Calvin, J. 1996. *Bondage and Liberation of the Will: A Defence of Orthodox Doctrine of Human Choice against Pighius*. Edited by A. Lane. Translated by G. Davies. Grand Rapids.

Calvin, J. 2001. *John Calvin: Writings on Pastoral Piety*. Edited and translated by E. McKee. New York.

Calvin, J. 2001. *John Calvin's Sermons on the Ten Commandments*. Edited by B. Farley. Grand Rapids.

Canons and Decrees of the Council of Trent. 1978. Translated by H. Schroeder. Reprint, Rockford, IL.

Cantorey, H., performer. 2007. *Music of the Reformation* (sound recording). Germany.

Capella, M. 1977. *The Marriage of Philology and Mercury (De Nuptiis Philologiae et Mercurii)*. Edited by W. Stahl, R. Johnson, and E. Burge. New York.

Capito, W. 2005–. *The Correspondence of Wolfgang Capito*. Edited by E. Rummel and M. Kooistra. Toronto.

Cassiodorus. 2004. *Institutions of Divine and Secular Learning and On the Soul (Institutiones)*. Translated by J. Halporn. Liverpool.

Cassirer, E., et al., eds. 1948. *The Renaissance Philosophy of Man*. Chicago.

Castellio, S. 1679. *A Conference of Faith*. London.

Castellio, S. 1747. *Divine dialogues: being sacred stories selected from the Holy Scriptures, with a short application to each story*. London.

Castellio, S. 1935. *Concerning Heretics: Whether They Are to Be Persecuted and How They Are to Be Treated: A Collection of the Opinions of Learned Men Both Ancient and Modern*. Translated by R. Bainton. New York.

Castellio, S. 1975. *Advice to a Desolate France: In the Course of which the Reason for the Present War Is Outlined, as Well as the Possible Remedy and, in the Main, Advice Is Given as to Whether Consciences Should be Forced, the Year 1562*. Translated by M. Valkhoff. Shepherdstown, WV.

The Catechism of the Council of Trent. 2008. Charlotte, NC.

Chemnitz, M. 1989. *Loci Theologici*. Edited and translated by J. Preus. St. Louis.

Cicero, M. T. 2001. *Cicero on the Ideal Orator*. Translated by J. May and J. Wisse. New York.

Clement VI. 1999. "Unigenitus." In *Documents of the Christian Church*, ed. H. Bettenson and C. Maunch, 182–83. New York.

Cochlaeus, J. 1529. *Septiceps Lutherus*. Leipzig. (Also published in German in the same year by the same publisher as *Sieben Köpfe Martini Lutheri Vom Hochwirdigen Sacrament des Altars*.)

Cochlaeus, J. 1549. *Historiae Hussitarum Libri Duodecim*. Mainz.

Cochlaeus, J. 1996. *Johannes Cochlaeus, Philippicae I-VII*. Edited by R. Keen. Bibliotheca Humanistica and Reformatorica. Houten, The Netherlands.

Cochlaeus, J., et al. 2001. "The Confutation of the Augsburg Confession."

In *Sources and Contexts of the Book of Concord*, ed. R. Kolb and J. Nestingen, trans. M. Tranvik, 105–39. Minneapolis.

Cochlaeus, J. 2002. "The Deeds and Writings of Martin Luther from the Year of the Lord 1517 to the Year 1546." Translated by E. Vandiver. In J. Cochlaeus et al., *Luther's Lives: Two Contemporary Accounts of Martin Luther*, translated and annotated by E. Vandiver, R. Keen, and T. Frazel, 53–351. Manchester, UK.

Cochrane, A., ed. 2003. *Reformed Confessions of the Sixteenth Century.* 2nd ed. Louisville.

Colet, J. 1985. *John Colet's Commentary on I Corinthians: A New Edition of the Latin Text, with Translation, Annotations, and Introduction.* Edited and translated by B. O'Kelly and C. Jarrott. Binghamton, NY.

Colet, J. 1989. *De Sacramentis (On the Sacraments).* In *John Colet*, ed. and trans. J. Gleason, 270–333. Berkeley.

Conroy, D. 1974. "The Ecumenical Theology of Erasmus of Rotterdam: A Study of the *Ratio Verae Theologiae*, Translated into English and Annotated." PhD. University of Pittsburgh.

Contarini, G. 1992. "The *Consilium de emendanda ecclesia*, 1537." In *The Catholic Reformation: Savonarola to Ignatius Loyola*, ed. J. Olin, 182–97. New ed. New York.

Coornhert, D. 2008. *Synod on the Freedom of Conscience.* Edited by G. Voogt. Amsterdam.

Cop, N. 1995. *Academic Discourse.* Appendix III in J. Calvin, *Institutes of the Christian Religion, 1536 Edition*, ed. and trans. by F. L. Battles, 363–72. Rev. ed. Grand Rapids.

Copernicus, N. *Complete Works.* 1978–85. Translated by Edward Rosen. 3 vols. Warsaw. Vol 1: *On the Revolutions* (facsimile); vol. 2: *On the Revolutions*; and vol. 3: *Minor Works.* Vols. 2 and 3 reprinted, Baltimore.

Corpus Iuris Canonici. 1879. Edited by A. Friedberg. Leipzig.

Corro, A. del. 1574. *Dialogus theologicus. Quo epistola Divi Pauli apostoli ad Romanos explanatur. Ex pr[a]electionibus Antonii Corrani Hispalensis.* London.

Corro, A. del. 1995. "Obras teológicas de Antonio del Corro: las dos redacciones de la 'Tabla de la obra de Dios' y la 'Monas theologica' (1569)." Edited by A. Kinder. *Diálogo Ecuménico* 30:311–39.

Corro, A. del. 2006. *Carta a los pastores luteranos de Amberes; Carta a Felipe II; Carta a Casiodoro de Reina; Exposición de la Obra de Dios, Obras de los Reformadores Españoles del Siglo XVI.* Sevilla.

Coverdale, M. 1975. *The Coverdale Bible, 1535.* Folkstone.

Coverdale, M. 2006. *Writings and Translations of Miles Coverdale, Bishop of Exeter: Containing the Old Faith, a spiritual and most precious pearl, fruitful lessons, a treatise on the Lord's Supper.* Edited by G. Pearson. Eugene, OR.

Cranach the Elder, L. 1963. *Cranach.* Edited by E. Ruhmer. Translated by J. Spencer. Greenwich, CT.

Cranach the Elder, L. 2007. *Cranach.* Edited by B. Brinkmann et al. London.

Cranmer, T. 1844. *Writings and Disputations of Thomas Cranmer Relative to the Sacrament of the Lord's Supper.* Edited by J. Cox. Cambridge.

Cranmer, T. 1846. *Miscellaneous Writings and Letters of Thomas Cranmer.* Edited by J. Cox. Cambridge.

Denck, H. 1975. *Selected Writings of Hans Denck.* Edited and translated by E. Furcha, with F. Battles. Pittsburgh.

Denck, H. 1991. *The Spiritual Legacy of Hans Denck: Interpretation and Translation of Key Texts.* Edited and translated by C. Bauman. Leiden.

Eck, J. 1979. *Enchiridion of Commonplaces of Johann Eck against Martin Luther and His Followers.* Translated by F. Battles. Grand Rapids.

Eck, J. 2001. "John Eck's Four Hundred and Four Articles for the Imperial Diet at Augsburg." Translated by

R. Rosin. In *Sources and Contexts of the Book of Concord*, ed. R. Kolb and J. Nestingen, 31–82. Minneapolis.

Elton, G., ed. 1982. *The Tudor Constitution*. 2nd ed. Cambridge.

Emser, J. 1921. *Hieronymus Emser: De disputatione Lipsicensi, quantum ad Boemos obiter deflexa est (1519). A venatione Luteriana aegocerotis assertio (1519)*. Edited by F. Thurnhofer. Munich.

English College (Douai, France). 1969. *The First and Second Diaries of the English College, Douay and an Appendix of Unpublished Documents*. Edited by the Fathers of the Congregation of the London Oratory. Farnborough, UK.

Enzinas, F. 1991. *Historia de Statu Belgico deque religione Hispanica*. Stuttgart.

Enzinas, F. 1995. *Epistolario*. Edited by I. J. García Pinilla. Geneva.

Erasmus, D. 1965. *Christian Humanism and the Reformation: Selected Writings of Erasmus*. Edited by J. Olin. New York.

Erasmus, D. 1965. *The Colloquies of Erasmus*. Translated by C. Thompson. Chicago.

Erasmus, D. 1969. "On the Freedom of the Will." In *Luther and Erasmus: Free Will and Salvation*. Edited by Gordon Rupp and Philip Watson, 35–100. Philadelphia.

Erasmus, D. 1974–. *Collected Works of Erasmus*. Toronto.

Erasmus, D. 1979. *The Praise of Folly*. Edited and translated by C. Miller. New Haven.

Erasmus, D. 1990. *The Erasmus Reader*. Edited and translated by E. Rummel. Toronto.

Fallico, A., and H. Shapiro, eds. and trans. 1967–69. *Renaissance Philosophy*. New York.

Ficino, M. 2001–6. *Theologica Platonica/Platonic Theology*. Edited by J. Hankins and W. Bowen. Translated by M. Allen and J. Warden. Cambridge.

Fisher, J. 1935. *Defence of the priesthood by John Fisher. . . . Translated from the original 'Sacri sacerdotii defensio contra Lutherum.'* Translated by P. Hallett. London.

Fisher, J. 2002. *English Works of John Fisher, Bishop of Rochester (1469–1535): Sermons and Other Writings, 1520–1535*. Edited by C. Hatt. Oxford.

Foxe, J. 2006. *Foxe's Book of Martyrs Variorum Edition Online*. http://www.hrionline.ac.uk/johnfoxe/ .

Francis de Sales. 1943. *St. Francis de Sales. Letters to Persons in Religion*. Edited and translated by H. Mackey. Westminster, MD.

Francis de Sales. 1988. *Francis de Sales, Jean de Chantal: Letters of Spiritual Direction*. Edited by W. Wright and J. Powers. New York.

Francis de Sales. 1995. *Thy Will Be Done: Letters to Persons in the World*. Manchester, NH.

"The French Confession of Faith, 1559." 1966. In *Reformed Confessions of the Sixteenth Century*, ed. A. Cochrane, 137–58. London.

Freudenberger, T., ed. 1959. *Hieronymus Emser: Schriften zur Verteidigung der Messe*. Munich.

Furcha, E., ed. and trans. 1986. *180 Paradoxes or Wondrous Sayings*. Lewiston, PA.

Giles, E. 1979. *Documents Illustrating Papal Authority, A.D. 96–454*. Westport, CT.

Harder, L., ed. 1985. *The Sources of Swiss Anabaptism: The Grebel Letters and Related Documents*. Scottdale, PA.

"The Heidelberg Catechism, 1563." 1966. In *Reformed Confessions of the Sixteenth Century*, ed. A. Cochrane, 305–31. London.

Henri IV. *The Edict of Nantes*. In *The Saint Bartholomew's Day Massacre: A Brief History with Documents*. Translated by B. Diefendorf, 144–47. Boston.

Hillerbrand, H., ed. 1964. *The Reformation: A Narrative History Related by Contemporary Observers and Participants*. New York.

Hoffman, M. 1957. "The Ordinance of God." In *Spiritual and Anabaptist Writers*. Edited and translated by

G. Williams and A. Mergal, 182–203. Philadelphia.

Hooker, R. 1593. *Of the Lawes of Ecclesiastical Politie Eyght Bookes.* London.

Hooker, R. 1977–82. *Of the Laws of Ecclesiastical Polity.* Edited by G. Edelen. Cambridge.

Hooker, R. 1977–98. *The Folger Library Edition of the Works of Richard Hooker.* Edited by W. Hill. Medieval and Renaissance Texts and Studies. Vols. 1–5. Cambridge. Vol. 6. Binghamton, NY. Vol. 7, Tempe, AZ.

Hubmaier, B. 1989. *Balthasar Hubmaier: Theologian of Anabaptism.* Edited by H. Pipkin and J. Yoder. Scottdale, PA.

Hughes, P., trans. 1966. *The Register of the Company of Pastors of Geneva in the Time of Calvin.* Grand Rapids.

Hus, J. 1972. *The Letters of John Hus.* Translated by M. Spinka. Manchester, UK.

Hus, J. 1974. *The Church.* Translated by D. Schaff. Westport, CT.

Hut, H. 1969. "Of the Mystery of Baptism." In *Patterns of Reformation.* Edited by G. Rupp, 379–87. London.

Hutten, U., et al. (attributed). 1964. *On the Eve of the Reformation: Letters of Obscure Men (Epistolae Obscurorum Virorum).* Translated by F. Stokes. New York.

Hutter, J. 1960. "Jakob Hutter's Last Epistle to the Church in Moravia, 1535." Edited by R. Friedmann. *Mennonite Quarterly Review* 34:37–47.

Hutter, J. 1964. "Jakob Hutter's Epistle Concerning the Schism in Moravia in 1533." Translated by the Society of Brothers. *Mennonite Quarterly Review* 38:329–43.

Hutter, J. 1979. *Brotherly Faithfulness: Epistles from a Time of Persecution.* Rifton, NY.

Ignatius of Loyola. 1985. *Letters of St. Ignatius Loyola.* Edited by W. Young. Chicago.

Ignatius of Loyola. 1991. *Ignatius of Loyola: The Spiritual Exercises and Selected Works.* Edited by G. Ganss. Mahwah, NJ.

Ignatius of Loyola. 1996. *Saint Ignatius of Loyola: Personal Writings.* Edited and translated by J. Munitiz and P. Endean. London.

Jayne, S. 1980. *John Colet and Marsilio Ficino.* Westport, CT.

Jewel, J. 1845–50. *The Works of John Jewel, Bishop of Salisbury.* Edited by J. Ayre. 4 vols. Cambridge.

John of the Cross. 1959. *Dark Night of the Soul.* Garden City, NY.

John of the Cross. 1979. *The Collected Works of St. John of the Cross.* 2nd ed. Washington, D.C.

John of the Cross. 1987. *Selected Writings.* Translated by K. Kavanaugh. New York.

Junius Brutus. 1924. *A Defence of Liberty against Tyrants.* Translated by H. Laski. London.

Karlstadt, A. 1995. *The Essential Carlstadt: Fifteen Tracts by Andreas Bodenstein von Karlstadt.* Edited by E. Furcha. Scottdale, PA.

Kingdon, R., and J.-F. Bergier, eds. 1964–95. *Registres de la Compagnie des Pasteurs de Genève.* Geneva.

Kingdon, R., et al., eds. 2000–. *The Registers of the Consistory of Geneva at the Time of Calvin.* Grand Rapids.

Kirby, T. 2009. "The *Zurich Agreement*: An English Translation of the *Consensus Tigurinus* of 1549." In *Consensus Tigurinus: Die Einigung zwischen Heinrich Bullinger und Johannes Calvin über das Abendmahl: Werden-Wertung-Bedeutung,* edited by E. Campi and R. Reich, 256–65. Zurich.

Klaassen, W., ed. 1981. *Anabaptism in Outline: Selected Primary Sources.* Kitchener, ON.

Knox, J. 1966. *The Works of John Knox.* Edited by D. Laing. 6 vols. Reprint, New York.

Knox, J. 1985. *The Political Writings of John Knox: The First Blast of the Trumpet against the Monstrous Regiment of Women and Other Selected Works.* Edited by M. Breslow. London.

Knox, J. 1994. *On Rebellion.* Edited by R. Mason. Cambridge.

Knox, J., et al. 1960. *The Scots Confession of 1560.* Edited by G. Henderson. Edinburgh.

Kolb, R., and J. Nestingen, eds. 2001. *Sources and Contexts of the Book of Concord.* Minneapolis.

Kolb, R., and T. Wengert, eds. 2000. *The Book of Concord: The Confessions of the Evangelical Lutheran Church.* Minneapolis.

Kohl, B., and R. Witt, eds. 1978. *The Earthly Republic: Italian Humanists on Government and Society.* Philadelphia.

Las Casas, Bartolomé de. 2003. *An Account, Much Abbreviated, of the Destruction of the Indies, and Related Texts.* Indianapolis.

Lasco, J. à. "Reformed Liturgies in Translation: Selections from à Lasco's Liturgy." Translated and edited by B. Thompson. *Theology and Life* 1:106–12.

Latimer, H. 1844. *Sermons by Hugh Latimer.* Edited by G. Corrie. Cambridge.

Latimer, H. 1845. *Sermons and Remains of Hugh Latimer.* Edited by G. Corrie. Cambridge.

Lipsius, J. 2006. *On Constancy.* Translated by J. Stradling. Edited by J. Sellars. Exeter, Devon, UK.

Lloyd, C., ed. 1825. *Formularies of Faith Put Forth by the Authority during the Reign of Henry VIII.* Oxford.

Lombard, P. 2007–9. *The Sentences.* Medieval Sources in Translation 42–45. 4 vols. Translated by G. Silano. Toronto.

Luther, M. 1883–. *D. Martin Luthers Werke: Kritische Gesamtausgabe.* 120 vols. Weimar.

Luther, M. 1955–86. *Luther's Works.* Edited by J. Pelikan and H. Lehmann. 55 vols. St. Louis and Philadelphia.

Luther, M. 1990. *The Bondage of the Will.* Translated by J. Packer and O. Johnston. Reprint, Grand Rapids.

Luther, M. 2002. *Discourse on Free Will: Erasmus and Luther.* Edited and translated by E. Winter. Reprint, New York.

Luther, M. 1967. *On the Councils and the Church.* In *Selected Writings of Martin Luther,* trans. and ed. T. Tappert, vol. 4:197–370. Philadelphia.

Luther, M. 2000. "The Small Catechism" and "The Large Catechism." In *The Book of Concord: The Confessions of the Evangelical Lutheran Church,* ed. R. Kolb and T. Wengert, 345–480. Minneapolis.

Luther, M., et al. 2001. "The Schwabach Articles," "The Marburg Articles," and "The Torgau Articles." In *Sources and Contexts of the Book of Concord,* ed. R. Kolb and J. Nestingen, trans. W. Russell, 83–104. Minneapolis.

Luther, M. 2005. *Martin Luther's Basic Theological Writings.* Edited by T. Lull and W. Russell. 2nd ed. Minneapolis.

Luther, M. 2007. *Luther's Spirituality.* Edited and translated by D. Krey and P. Krey. New York.

Marguerite de Navarre. 1984. *The Heptameron.* Translated by P. Chilton. New York.

Marguerite de Navarre. 1989. *The Prisons of Marguerite de Navarre.* Translated by H. Dale. Reading, UK.

Marguerite de Navarre. 2008. *Selected Writings: A Bilingual Edition.* Edited and translated by R. Cholakian and M. Skemp. Chicago.

Marpeck, P. 1978. *The Writings of Pilgram Marpeck.* Edited by W. Klassen and W. Klaassen. Scottdale, PA.

Marpeck, P. 1999. *The Later Writings of Pilgram Marpeck and his Circle.* Vol. 1: *The Exposé, A Dialogue and Marpeck's Response to Casper Schwenckfeld.* Edited by W. Klaassen, J. Rempel, and W. Packull. Kitchener, ON.

Melanchthon, P. 1969. "Loci Communes Theologici." In *Melanchthon and Bucer,* ed. W. Pauck, 18–154. Philadelphia.

Melanchthon, P. 1988. *A Melanchthon Reader.* Translated by R. Keen. New York.

Melanchthon, P. 2000. "The Augsburg Confession" and "The Apology of the Augsburg Confession." In *The Book of Concord: The Confessions of the Evangelical Lutheran Church.* Edited by R. Kolb and T. Wengert, 27–294. Minneapolis.

Mendham, J., ed. 2009. *An Index of Prohibited Books by Command of the Present Pope Gregory XVI in 1835.* Charleston, SC.

Montaigne, M. de. 1994. *The Complete Essays.* Edited by M. Screech. New York.

More, T. 1947. *The Correspondence of Sir Thomas More.* Edited by E. Rogers. Princeton.

More, T. 1963–. *The Yale Edition of the Complete Works of St. Thomas More.* New Haven.

More, T. 2002. *Utopia.* Edited by G. Logan and R. Adams. Cambridge.

Münster, S. 1523. *Dictionarium Hebraicum.* Basel.

Müntzer, T. 1988. *The Collected Works of Thomas Müntzer.* Edited and translated by P. Matheson. Edinburgh.

Müntzer, T. 1993. *Revelation and Revolution: Basic Writings of Thomas Müntzer.* Edited and translated by M. Baylor. Bethlehem, PA.

Musculus, W. 1555. *The Temporisour.* English translation by R. Pownall, based on the French translation by V. Wesel, Zurich. Available on microfilm and as downloadable computer file.

Musculus, W. 1556. *Of the Lawful and Unlawful Usurie amongst Christians.* English translation by J. Man. Wesel. Originally an appendix to Musculus's commentary on the Psalms. Available on microfilm.

Musculus, W. 1563. *Common Places of Christian Religion.* English translation by J. Man. London. Available on microfilm together with Musculus's treatises on oaths and on usury from his commentary on the Psalms.

Ochino, B. 2007. *Seven Dialogues.* Translated and edited by R. Belladonna. Toronto.

Olevianus, C. 1995. *A Firm Foundation: An Aid to Interpreting the Heidelberg Catechism.* Translated and edited by L. Bierma. Grand Rapids.

Olevianus, C., and Z. Ursinus. 2007. *The Heidelberg Catechism: A New Translation for the 21st Century.* Edited and translated by L. Barrett III. Cleveland.

Olin, J. 1990. *Catholic Reform from Cardinal Ximenes to the Council of Trent 1495–1563: An Essay with Illustrative Documents and a Brief Study of St. Ignatius Loyola.* New York.

Olin, J. 2000. *A Reformation Debate: Sadoleto's Letter to the Genevans and Calvin's Reply.* New ed. New York.

Pérez de Pineda, J. 1560a. *Breve tratado de la doctrina antigua de Dios, y de la nueva de los hombres, util y necessario para todo fiel Christiano.* Geneva.

Pérez de Pineda, J. 1560b. *Epistola para consolar a los fieles de jesu Christo, que padecen persecucion por la confession de su Nombre.* Geneva.

Pirckheimer, C. 2006. *Caritas Pirckheimer: A Journal of the Reformation Years, 1524–1528.* Translated by P. MacKenzie. Cambridge.

Plato. 1997. *Complete Works.* Edited by J. Cooper and D Hutchinson. Indianapolis.

Quintilian. 2001. *The Orator's Education.* Edited and translated by D. Russell. Cambridge.

Rebhorn, W., ed. and trans. 2000. *Renaissance Debates on Rhetoric.* Ithaca, NY.

Reina, C. de. 1573a. *Evangelium Ioannis: hoc est, iusta ac vetus apologia pro aeterna Christi divinitate.* Frankfurt.

Reina, C. de. 1573b. *Expositio primae partis quarti Matthaei, commonefactoria ad ecclesiam Christi.* Frankfurt.

Reuchlin, J. 1983. *On the Art of the Kabbalah (De arte cabalistica).* Translation by M. and S. Goodman. New York.

Reuchlin, J. 2000. *Recommendation Whether to Confiscate, Destroy, and Burn All Jewish Books: A Classic Treatise Against Anti-Semitism.* Translated and edited by P. Wortsman. New York.

Reuchlin, J. 2002. *The Case Against Johann Reuchlin: Religious and Social Contro-*

versy in Sixteenth-Century Germany. Edited by E. Rummel. Toronto.

Rhenanus, Beatus. 1966. *Briefwechsel des Beatus Rhenanus.* Edited by A. Horowitz and K. Hartfelder. Reprint, Hildesheim.

Rhenanus, Beatus. 1986. *Beatus Rhenanus, citoyen de Selestat, ami d'Erasme (1485–1547). Anthologie de sa Correspondance.* Edited and translated by R. Walter. Strasbourgh.

Rhenanus, Beatus. 1987. *Christian Humanism and the Reformation: Selected Writings of Erasmus, with the Life of Erasmus by Beatus Rhenanus.* Edited by J. Olin. 3rd ed. New York.

Ross, A., ed. and trans. 2009. *Introduction to the Devout Life.* New York.

Sadoleto, J. 1916. *Sadoleto on Education: A Translation of the De pueris recte instituendis.* Translated by E. Campagnac and K. Forbes. London.

Sattler, M. 1973. *The Legacy of Michael Sattler.* Edited by J. Yoder. Scottdale, PA.

Sattler, M. 1977. *The Schleitheim Confession.* Edited by J. Yoder. Scottdale, PA.

Schwenckfeld, C. 1907–61. *Corpus Schwenckfeldianorum.* Edited by C. Hartranft. Leipzig.

Schaff, P. 1900. *Nicene and Post-Nicene Fathers.* Vol. 14: *The Seven Ecumenical Councils.* New York.

Scott, T., and B. Scribner, eds. and trans. 1991. *The German Peasants' War: A History in Documents.* Atlantic Heights, NJ.

Scotus, John Duns. 1950–. *Opera Omnia.* Edited by C. Balic. Vatican.

Scotus, John Duns. 1975. *God and Creatures: The Quodlibetal Questions.* Translated by F. Alluntis and A. Wolter. Princeton.

Servetus, M. 2007. *Michael Servetus: A Translation of His Geographical, Medical and Astrological Writings with Introductions and Notes.* Translated by C. O'Malley. Whitefish, MT.

Servetus, M. 2008a. *Treatise Concerning the Supernatural Regeneration and the*

Kingdom of the Antichrist. Translated by C. Hoffman and M. Hillar. Lewiston, NY.

Servetus, M. 2008b. *Treatise on Faith and Justice of Christ's Kingdom.* Translated by C. Hoffman and M. Hillar. Lewiston, NY.

Sider, R., ed. 2001. *Karlstadt's Battle with Luther: Documents in a Liberal-Radical Debate.* Reprint, Eugene, OR. (Various writings of Karlstadt.)

Simons, M. 1956. *The Complete Writings of Menno Simons: c.1496–1561.* Translated by L. Verduin. Edited by J. Wenger. Scottdale, PA.

Simons, M. 1957. "On the Ban." In *Spiritual and Anabaptist Writers.* Edited and translated by G. Williams and A. Mergal, 261–71. Philadelphia.

Staupitz, J. 1981. "Eternal Predestination and Its Execution in Time." In *Forerunners of the Reformation.* Edited by H. Oberman, 175–203. Philadelphia.

Sturm, J. 1995. *Johann Sturm on Education.* Edited by L. Spitz and B. Tinsley. St. Louis.

Suárez, F. 1944. *Selections from Three Works of Francisco Suárez, S.J.: De legibus, ac Deo legislatore, 1612; Defensio fidei catholicae, et apostolicae adversus anglicanae sectae errores, 1613; De triplici virtute theologica, fide, spe, et charitate, 1621.* Oxford.

Tanner, N., ed. 1990. *Decrees of the Ecumenical Councils.* London.

Teresa of Avila. 2002. *The Complete Works of St Teresa of Avila.* Edited and translated by E. Peers. London.

Teresa of Avila. 2008. *Teresa of Avila: The Book of Her Life.* Translated by K. Kavanaugh, O.C.D., and O. Rodriguez, O.C.D. Indianapolis.

Tyndale, W. 1848–50. *Works.* Edited by H. Walter. 3 vols. Cambridge.

Ursinus, Z. 1985. *The Commentary of Dr. Zacharias Ursinus on the Heidelberg Catechism.* Translated by G. Williard. Reprint, Phillipsburg, NJ.

Valdés, J. de. 1981. *Valdés' Two Catechisms: The Dialogue on Christian Doctrine and the Christian Instruction for Children*. Translated by José C. Nieto et al. Lawrence, KS.

Valla, L. 1977. *On Pleasure = De voluptate*. Translated by A. Hieatt and M. Lorch. New York.

Valla, L. 2007. *On the Donation of Constantine*. Translated by G. Bowersock. Cambridge.

Vermigli, P. 1980. *The Political Thought of Peter Martyr Vermigli: Selected Texts and Commentary*. Edited and translated by R. Kingdon. Geneva.

Vermigli, P. 2000. *The Oxford Treatise and Disputation on the Eucharist*. Edited and translated by J. McLelland. Kirksville, MO.

Vermigli, P. 2003. *Predestination and Justification: Two Theological Loci*. Edited and translated by F. James. Kirksville, MO.

Vincent de Paul. 1993. *The Life of the Venerable Servant of God Vincent de Paul*. Edited by L. Abelly. Translated by W. Quinn. New Rochelle, NY.

Vincent de Paul. 1995. *Vincent de Paul and Louise de Marillac: Rules, Conferences, and Writings*. Edited by F. Ryan and J. Rybolt. New York.

Viret, P. 1573. *A Christian Instruction, Conteyning the Law and the Gospell*. London.

Vives, J. 1913. *Vives on Education: A Translation of the De tradendis disciplinis of Juan Luis Vives*. Cambridge.

Vives, J. 1968. *Introduction to Wisdom; A Renaissance Textbook*. New York.

Vives, J. L. 2000. *The Education of a Christian Woman: A Sixteenth-Century Manual*. Chicago.

Westphal, J. 1981. *Joachim Westphal und Peter Braubach: Briefwechsel zwischen dem Hamburger Hauptpastor, seinem Drucker-Verleger und ihrem Freund Hartmann Beyer in Frankfurt*. Edited by H. von Schade. Hamburg.

Wilbur, E., ed. 1932. *Two Treatises on the Trinity*. Cambridge.

William of Ockham. 1969. *Predestination, God's Foreknowledge, and Future Contingents*. Edited and translated by M. Adams and N. Kretzmann. New York.

William of Ockham, 1990. *Ockham: Philosophical Writings*. Translated by P. Boehner. Indianapolis.

William of Ockham, 1994. "William of Ockham: Five Questions on Universals from His Ordinatio." Translated by P. Spade. In *Five Texts on the Mediaeval Problem of Universals: Porphyry, Boethius, Abelard, Duns Scotus, Ockham*. Edited by P. Spade, 114–231. Indianapolis.

Williams, G., and A. Mergal, eds. 1957. *Spiritual and Anabaptist Writers*. Philadelphia.

Wilson, K. M., ed. 1987. *Women Writers of the Renaissance and Reformation*. Athens, GA.

Wycliffe, J. 2001. *The English Works of John Wyclif Hitherto Unprinted*. New York.

Wycliffe, J. 2002. *Wycliffe New Testament 1388: An Edition in Modern Spelling, with an Introduction, the Original Prologues and the Epistle to the Laodiceans*. Edited by W. Cooper. London.

Zanchi, G. 1605. *Operum theologicorum D. Hieronymi Zanchii*. 3 vols. Geneva.

Zanchi, G. 2007. *De religione Christiana fides—Confession of Christian Religion*. Edited by L. Baschera and C. Moser. 2 vols. Leiden.

Zell, K. 1999. *Katharina Schütz Zell*. Vol. 2: *The Writings, A Critical Edition*. Edited by E. McKee. Leiden.

Zell, K. 2006. *Church Mother: The Writings of a Protestant Reformer in Sixteenth-century Germany*. Translated by E. McKee. Chicago.

Zeumer, K. 1904. *Quellensammlung zur Geschichte der Deutschen Reichsverfassung*. Leipzig.

Ziegler, D., ed. 1969. *Great Debates of the Reformation*. New York.

Zuck, L.H., ed. 1975. *Christianity and Revolution: Radical Christian Testimonies*. Philadelphia.

Zwingli, U. 1905–. *Huldreich Zwinglis Sämtliche Werke*. 13 vols. Edited by E. Egli et al. Berlin.

Zwingli, U. 1912. *The Latin Works and the Correspondence of Huldreich Zwingli*. Edited by S. Jackson. New York.

Zwingli, U. 1953. *Zwingli and Bullinger*. Edited by G. Bromiley. Philadelphia.

Zwingli, U. 1977. *Huldrych Zwingli*. Edited by G. Potter. New York.

Zwingli, U. 1981. *Commentary on True and False Religion*. Edited by S. Jackson and C. Heller. Durham, NC.

Zwingli, U. 1984. *Huldrych Zwingli: Writings*. 2 vols. Edited and translated by E. Furcha and H. Pipkin. Allison Park, PA.

Zwingli, U. 1987. *Ulrich Zwingli. Early Writings*. Edited and translated by S. Jackson. Reprint, Durham, NC.

Secondary Bibliography

Abad, J. 1999. "The Printing Press in Alcalá de Henares: The Complutensian Polyglot Bible." In *The Bible as Book: The First Printed Editions*, ed. P. Saenger and K. van Kampen, 101–15. London.

Abelson, P. 1906. *The Seven Liberal Arts, a Study in Medieval Culture*. New York.

Abray, L. 1985. *The People's Reformation: Magistrates, Clergy, and Commons in Strasbourg, 1500–1598*. Ithaca.

Adams, R. 1962. *The Better Part of Valor: More, Erasmus, Colet, and Vives, on Humanism, War, and Peace, 1496–1535*. Seattle.

Ahlgren, G. 1996. *Teresa of Avila and the Politics of Sanctity*. Ithaca.

Althaus, P. 1966. *The Theology of Martin Luther*. Translated by R. Schultz. Minneapolis.

Althaus, P. 1972. *The Ethics of Martin Luther*. Philadelphia.

Anderson, G., ed. 1992. *The One Mediator, the Saints and Mary*. Minneapolis.

Anderson, L. 1994. "The Imago Dei Theme in John Calvin and Bernard of Clairvaux." In *Calvinus Sacrae Scripturae Professor: Calvin as Confessor of Holy Scripture*, ed. W. H. Neusner, 178–98. Grand Rapids.

Ankarloo, B., and S. Clark, eds. 1999–2002. *The Athlone History of Witchcraft and Magic in Europe*. 6 vols. Philadelphia.

Arblaster, P. 2006. *The History of the Low Countries*. New York.

Ariès, P. 1981. *The Hour of Our Death*. Translated by H. Weaver. London.

Armstrong, E. 1954. *Robert Estienne, Royal Printer*. Cambridge.

Armstrong, M. 2004. *The Politics of Piety: Franciscan Preachers during the Wars of Religion, 1560–1600*. Rochester, NY.

Arnold, F. 1937. *Zur frage des naturrechts bei Martin Luther, ein beitrag zum problem der natürlichen theologie auf reformatorischer grundlage*. Munich.

Arthur, A. 2000. *The Tailor-King: The Rise and Fall of the Anabaptist Kingdom of Münster*. New York.

Asselt, W. van, and E. Dekker, eds. 2001. *Reformation and Scholasticism: An Ecumenical Enterprise*. Grand Rapids.

Atwood, C. 2009. *The Theology of the Czech Brethren from Hus to Comenius*. University Park, PA.

Augustijn, C. 1991. *Erasmus: His Life, Works, and Influence*. Toronto.

Aulén, G. 1969. *Christus Victor: An Historical Study of the Three Main Types of the Idea of the Atonement*. New York.

Auth, C. 2000. *A Dominican Bibliography and Book of Reference, 1216–1992*. New York.

Avis, P. 2002. *The Church in the Theology of the Reformers*. Eugene, OR.

Avis, P. 2006. *Beyond the Reformation? Authority, Primacy, and Unity in the Conciliar Tradition*. London.

Backus, I. 1993. *The Disputations of Baden, 1526, and Berne, 1528: Neutralizing the Early Church*. Princeton.

Backus, I., ed. 1997. *The Reception of the Church Fathers in the West: From the Carolingians to the Maurists*. Leiden.

Backus, I. 2000. *Reformation Readings of the Apocalypse: Geneva, Zurich, and Wittenberg*. Oxford.

Backus, I. 2003. *Historical Method and Confessional Identity in the Era of the Reformation (1378–1615)*. Boston, Leiden.

Backus, I. 2004. "The Early Church as a Model of Religious Unity in the Sixteenth Century: Georg Cassander and Georg Witzel," *Conciliation and Confession*. Notre Dame.

Bagchi, D. 1991. *Luther's Earliest Opponents: Catholic Controversialists, 1518–1525*. Minneapolis.

Bailey, M. 2007. *Magic and Superstition in Europe: A Concise History from Antiquity to the Present*. Lanham.

Bainton, R. 1971. *Women of the Reformation in Germany and Italy*. Minneapolis.

Bainton, R. 2005. *Hunted Heretic: The Life and Death of Michael Servetus, 1511–1553*. Rev. ed. Providence.

Baker, J. 1980. *Heinrich Bullinger and the Covenant: The Other Reformed Tradition*. Athens, OH.

Bangert, W. 1986. *A History of the Society of Jesus*. 2nd ed. St. Louis.

Bangs, C. 1971. *Arminius: A Study in the Dutch Reformation*. Nashville.

Barge, H. 2005. *Andreas Bodenstein von Karlstadt*. 2 vols. Leipzig. Reprint, Boston.

Barker, E. 1930. "The Authorship of the *Vindiciae Contra Tyrannos*." *Cambridge Historical Journal* 3, no. 2:164–81.

Barker, P. 1995. "Caritas Pirckheimer: A Female Humanist Confronts the Reformation." *Sixteenth Century Journal* 26, no. 2:259–72.

Barnes, R. 1988. *Prophecy and Gnosis: Apocalypticism in the Wake of the Lutheran Reformation*. Stanford.

Barraclough, G. 1959. *The Medieval Empire: Idea and Reality*. London.

Barth, K. 2002. *The Theology of the Reformed Confessions*. Translated by D. Guder and J. Guder. Louisville.

Battles, F. 1977. "God Was Accommodating Himself to Human Capacity." *Interpretation* 31:19–38.

Bauman, C., ed. and trans. 1991. *The Spiritual Legacy of Hans Denck: Interpretation and Translation of Key Texts*. Leiden.

Bäumer, R. 1980. *Johannes Cochlaeus (1479–1552): Leben und Werk im Dienst der katholischen Reform*. Münster.

Baylor, M. 1991. *The Radical Reformation*. Cambridge.

Beachy, A. 1977. *The Concept of Grace in the Radical Reformation*. Nieuwkoop.

Becker, S. 1982. *The Foolishness of God: The Place of Reason in the Theology of Martin Luther*. Milwaukee.

Beeke, J. 1991. *Calvin, English Puritanism, and the Dutch Second Reformation*. New York.

Begheyn, P. 2006. "The Catechism (1555) of Peter Canisius, the Most Published Book by a Dutch Author in History." *Quaerendo* 36, nos. 1/2:51–85.

Behringer, W. 2004. *Witches and Witch-Hunts: A Global History*. Malden, MA.

Bell, D., and S. Burnett, eds. 2006. *Jews, Judaism and the Reformation in Sixteenth Century Germany*. Leiden.

Bell, T. 2005. "Man Is a Microcosmos: Adam and Eve in Luther's Lectures on Genesis (1535–1545)." *Concordia Theological Quarterly* 69:159–84.

Bender, H. 1950. *Conrad Grebel, c. 1498–1526, Founder of the Swiss Brethren, Sometimes Called Anabaptists*. Goshen, IN.

Benecke, G. 1982. *Maximilian I, 1459–1519: An Analytical Biography*. London.

Benedict, P. 2002. *Christ's Churches Purely Reformed: A Social History of Calvinism*. New Haven.

Benin, S. 1993. *The Footprints of God: Divine Accommodation in Jewish and Christian Thought*. Albany.

Benko, S. 1964. *The Meaning of Sanctorum Communio*. Translated by D. Scheidt. Naperville, IL.

Bentley, J. 1983. *Humanists and Holy Writ: New Testament Scholarship in the Renaissance*. Princeton.

Bergin, J. 1999. "The Counter-Reformation and Its Bishops." *Past and Present* 165 (November): 30–73.

Berkouwer, G. 1958. *Faith and Perseverance*. Grand Rapids.

Berkvens-Stevelinck, C., J. Israel, and G. Posthumus Meyers, eds. 1997. *The Emergence of Tolerance in the Dutch Republic*. Leiden.

Bernstein, E. 1983. *German Humanism*. Boston.

Biel, P. 1991. *Doorkeepers at the House of Righteousness: Heinrich Bullinger and the Zurich Clergy 1535–1575*. Bern.

Bier, J. 1982. *Tilmann Riemenschneider, His Life and Work*. Lexington.

Bierma, L. 1996. *German Calvinism in the Confessional Age*. Grand Rapids.

Bierma, L., ed. 2005. *An Introduction to the Heidelberg Catechism: Sources, History, and Theology*. Grand Rapids.

Biesecker-Mast, G. 2006. *Separation and the Sword in Anabaptist Persuasion: Radical Confessional Rhetoric from Schleitheim to Dordrecht*. Telford, PA.

Bilinkoff, J. 1989. *The Avila of Saint Teresa: Religious Reform in a Sixteenth Century City*. Ithaca, NY.

Billings, J. 2008. *Calvin, Participation, and the Gift: The Activity of Believers in Union with Christ*. New York.

Bireley, R. 1999. *The Refashioning of Catholicism, 1450–1700*. Washington, D.C.

Black, A. 1979. *Council and Commune: The Conciliar Movement and the Fifteenth Century Heritage*. London.

Black, C. 1989. *Italian Confraternities in the Sixteenth Century*. New York.

Blackwell, R. 1991. *Galileo, Bellarmine, and the Bible: Including a Translation of Foscarini's Letter on the Motion of the Earth*. Notre Dame, IN.

Blickle, P. 1977. *The Revolution of 1525*. Baltimore.

Blickle, P. 1998. *From the Communal Reformation to the Revolution of the Common Man*. Leiden.

Blickle, P., T. Brady Jr., and H. Midelfort, trans. 1985. *The Revolution of 1525: The German Peasants' War from a New Perspective*. Baltimore.

Blockmans, W. 2002. *Emperor Charles V, 1500–1558*. Translated by I. van den Hoven-Vardon. London.

Blom, J. 1998. *A History of the Low Countries*. New York.

Blough, N. 2007. *Christ in Our Midst: Incarnation, Church and Discipleship in the Theology of Pilgram Marpeck*. Kitchener, ON.

Bockmuehl, K. 1997. *The Christian Way of Living: An Ethics of the Ten Commandments*. Vancouver.

Bohlman, R. 1983. *Principles of Biblical Interpretation in the Lutheran Confessions*. St. Louis.

Bond, R. ed. 1987. *Certain Sermons or Homilies (1547)*. Toronto.

Bonger, H. 2004. *The Life and Work of Dirck Volkertszoon Coornhert*. Translated by G. Voogt. Amsterdam.

Bonney, R. 1991. *The European Dynastic States, 1494–1660*. Oxford.

Booty, J. 1963. *John Jewel as Apologist of the Church of England*. London.

Booty, J. 1976. "History of the 1559 Book of Common Prayer." In *The Book of Common Prayer 1559*, ed. Booty, 327–82. London.

Bornkamm, H. 1966. *Luther's Doctrine of the Two Kingdoms in the Context of His Theology*. Philadelphia.

Bornkamm, H. 1983. *Luther in Mid-Career, 1521–1530*. Philadelphia.

Børrensen, K., ed. 1995. *The Image of God: Gender Models in Judaeo-Christian Tradition*. Minneapolis.

Bossert, G., Jr. 1951. "Michael Sattler's Trial and Martyrdom in 1527." *Mennonite Quarterly Review* 25, no. 3:201–18.

Bostick, C. 1998. *The Antichrist and the Lollards: Apocalypticism in Late Medieval and Reformation England*. Leiden.

Boyd, S. 1992. *Pilgram Marpeck: His Life and Social Theology*. Durham.

Braaten, C., and R. Jenson, eds. 1998. *Union with Christ: The New Finnish Interpretation of Luther*. Grand Rapids.

Bradshaw, B., and E. Duffy, eds. 1989. *Humanism, Reform and the*

Reformation: The Career of Bishop John Fisher. Cambridge.

Brady, T. 1978. Ruling Class, Regime and Reformation at Strasbourg 1520–1555. Leiden.

Brady, T. 1985a. "Luther and Society: Two Kingdoms or Three Estates? Tradition and Experience in Luther's Social Teaching," Lutherjahrbuch 52:197–224.

Brady, T. 1985b. Turning Swiss: Cities and Empire, 1450–1550. Cambridge.

Brady, T. 1995. Protestant Politics: Jacob Sturm (1489–1553) and the German Reformation. Atlantic Highlands, NJ.

Braswell, M. 1983. The Medieval Sinner. London.

Bray, J. 1975. Theodore Beza's Doctrine of Predestination. Niewkoop.

Brecher, A. 1883. "Lang, Johannes." In Allgemeine Deutsche Bibliographie 17:635–37. Leipzig.

Brecht, M. 1985–93. Martin Luther. Translated by J. Schaaf. 3 vols. Philadelphia.

Brigden, S. 2000. New Worlds, Lost Worlds: The Rule of the Tudors, 1485–1603. New York.

Brock, P. 1991. Freedom from Violence: Sectarian Nonresistance from the Middle Ages to the Great War. Toronto.

Brodrick, J. 1961. Robert Bellarmine: Saint and Scholar. Westminster, MD.

Brodrick, J. 1998. Saint Peter Canisius. Chicago.

Bromiley, G. 1978. Historical Theology: An Introduction. Grand Rapids.

Bromiley, G. 1986. "Mercy in the Book of Common Prayer." In God Who Is Rich in Mercy: Essays Presented to Dr. D. B. Knox, ed. P. O'Brien and D. Peterson, 345–60. Grand Rapids.

Brown, C. 2005. Singing the Gospel: Lutheran Hymns and the Success of the Reformation. Cambridge.

Brown, G. 1933. Italy and the Reformation to 1550. Oxford.

Brown, K. 2004. "The Reformation Parliament." In Parliament and Politics in Scotland, 1235–1560, ed. K. Brown and R. Tanner, 203–32. Edinburgh.

Brown, P. 1981. The Cult of Saints: Its Rise and Function in Latin Christianity. Chicago.

Brown, P. 2000. Augustine of Hippo. Expanded edition. Berkeley.

Brown, P. 2003. The Rise of Western Christendom: Triumph and Diversity, AD 200–1000. 2nd ed. London.

Brown, R., K. Donfried, and J. Reumann. 1973. Peter in the New Testament: A Collaborative Assessment by Protestant and Roman Catholic Scholars. Minneapolis.

Bruening, M. 2008. "Pierre Viret and Geneva." Archiv für Reformationsgeschichte 99:175–97.

Brundage, J. 1995. Medieval Canon Law. New York.

Brunner, E. 1946. Revelation and Reason: The Christian Doctrine of Faith and Knowledge. Translated by O. Wyon. Philadelphia.

Bulman, R., and F. Parrella, eds. 2006. From Trent to Vatican II: Historical and Theological Investigations. Oxford.

Bunge, M., ed. 2001. The Child in Christian Thought. Grand Rapids.

Burchill, C. 1984. "Girolamo Zanchi: A Portrait of a Reformed Theologian and His Work." Sixteenth Century Journal 15:185–207.

Burgess, J., ed. 1980. The Role of the Augsburg Confession: Catholic and Lutheran Views. Philadelphia.

Burke, P. 2009. Popular Culture in Early Modern Europe. 3rd ed. Burlington, VT.

Burkholder, J., D. Grout, and C. Palisca, eds. 2010. A History of Western Music. 8th ed. New York.

Burnett, A. 1994. The Yoke of Christ: Martin Bucer and Christian Discipline. Kirksville, MO.

Burnett, A. 1995. "Confirmation and Christian Fellowship: Martin Bucer on Commitment to the Church." Church History 64:202–17.

Burnett, A. 2004. "The Educational Roots of Reformed Scholasticism: Dialectic and Scriptural Exegesis in the Sixteenth Century." Nederlands archief voor kerkgeschiedenis 84:299–317.

Burnett, S. 1996. From Christian Hebraism to Jewish Studies. Leiden.

Butin, P. 1995. Revelation, Redemption, and Response: Calvin's Trinitarian

Understanding of the Divine-Human Relationship. Oxford.

Cameron, E. 1991. *The European Reformation.* Oxford.

Campenhausen, H. 1969. *Ecclesiastical Authority and Spiritual Power in the Church of the First Three Centuries.* Stanford.

Campi, E., and P. Opitz, eds. 2007. *Heinrich Bullinger: Life, Thought, Influence: Zurich, Aug. 25–29, 2004, International Congress Heinrich Bullinger (1504–1575).* Zurich.

Camporeale, S. 1996. "Lorenzo Valla's 'Oratio' on the Pseudo-Donation of Constantine: Dissent and Innovation in Early Renaissance Humanism." *Journal of the History of Ideas* 17, no. 1:9–26.

Caraman, P. 1990. *Ignatius Loyola: A Biography of the Founder of the Jesuits.* San Francisco.

Carleton, J. 1902. *The Part of Rheims in the Making of the English Bible.* Oxford.

Carlson, E. 1994. *Marriage and the English Reformation.* Oxford.

Catholic Encyclopedia. 1907–12. 15 vols. New York.

Cesareo, F. 1999. *A Shepherd in Their Midst: The Episcopacy of Girolamo Seripando (1535–1563).* Villanova, PA.

Cessario, R. 1990. *The Godly Image.* Petersham, MA.

Cessario, R. 2005. *A Short History of Thomism.* Washington, D.C.

Chadwick, H. 1988. "Tradition, Fathers and Councils." In *The Study of Anglicanism,* ed. S. Sykes and J. Booty, 100–114. London.

Chambers, D. 2006. *Popes, Cardinals, and War: The Military Church in Renaissance and Early Modern Europe.* New York.

Chapuis, J. 1999. *Tilman Riemenschneider, Master Sculptor of the Late Middle Ages.* New Haven.

Chapuis, J. 2004 *Tilman Riemenschneider, c. 1460–1531.* New Haven.

Chatellier, L. 1989. *The Europe of the Devout: The Catholic Reformation and the Formation of a New Society.* Cambridge.

Chia, R. 2007. "Protestant Reflections on Pope Benedict XVI's Faith, Reason and the University." *Dialog: A Journal of Theology* 46:66–77.

Cholakian, P., and R. Cholakian. 2006. *Marguerite de Navarre: Mother of the Renaissance.* New York.

Chrisman, M. 1967. *Strasbourg and the Reform: A Study in the Process of Change.* New Haven.

Chrisman, M. 1972. "Women and the Reformation in Strasbourg, 1490–1530." *Archiv für Reformationsgeschichte* 63:143–67.

Christensen, C. 1984. "John of Saxony's Diplomacy, 1529–1530: Reformation or Realpolitik?" *Sixteenth Century Journal* 15, no. 4:419–30.

Church, F. 1932. *The Italian Reformers 1534–1564.* New York.

Clark, S. 1997. *Thinking with Demons: The Idea of Witchcraft in Early Modern Europe.* New York.

Cochrane, A. 2003. *Reformed Confessions of the Sixteenth Century.* Reprint, Louisville.

Coffey, D. 2001. *The Sacrament of Reconciliation.* Collegeville, MN.

Coffey, J., and P. Lim, eds. 2008. *The Cambridge Companion to Puritanism.* Cambridge.

Cohn, H. 1985. "The Territorial Princes in Germany's Second Reformation, 1559–1622." In *International Calvinism 1541–1715,* ed. Menna Prestwich, 139–65. Oxford.

Cohn, N. 1984. *The Pursuit of the Millennium: Revolutionary Millenarians and Mystical Anarchists in the Middle Ages.* London.

Colish, M. 1990. *The Stoic Tradition from Antiquity to the Early Middle Ages.* Leiden.

Colish, M. 1994. *Peter Lombard.* Leiden.

Collins, D. 2008. *Reforming Saints: Saints' Lives and Their Authors in Germany 1470–1530.* Oxford.

Collins, R. 1968. *Calvin and the Libertines of Geneva.* Toronto.

Collinson, P. 1967. *The Elizabethan Puritan Movement.* London.

Collinson, P. 2007. *Elizabeth I.* Oxford.

Compier, D. 2001. *John Calvin's Rhetorical Doctrine of Sin.* Lewiston, NY.

Congar, Y. 1967. *Tradition and Traditions: An Historical and a Theological Essay.* New York.

Conroy, D. 1974. "The Ecumenical Theology of Erasmus of Rotterdam: A Study of the Ratio Verae Theologiae, Translated into English and Annotated." PhD diss. University of Pittsburgh.

Cooper, K., and J. Gregory, eds. 2005. *Signs, Wonders, Miracles: Representations of Divine Power in the Life of the Church, Papers Read at the 2003 Summer Meeting and the 2004 Winter Meeting of the Ecclesiastical History Society.* Rochester, NY.

Copenhaver, B., and C. Schmitt. 1992. *Renaissance Philosophy.* Oxford.

Coriden, J. 2004. *An Introduction to Canon Law.* Mahwah, NJ.

Corrêa Monteiro, M. 2006. *Saint Francis Xavier: A Man for All Others.* Lisbon.

Corthell, R., ed. 2007. *Catholic Culture in Early Modern England.* Notre Dame, IN.

Cottrell, R. 1986. *The Grammar of Silence: A Reading of Marguerite de Navarre's Poetry.* Washington, D.C.

Cressy, D. 1997. *Birth, Marriage & Death: Ritual, Religion, and the Life-cycle in Tudor and Stuart England.* Oxford.

Crews, D. 2008. *Twilight of the Renaissance: The Life of Juan de Valdés.* Toronto.

Croken, R. 1990. *Luther's First Front: The Eucharist as Sacrifice.* Ottawa.

Cromartie, M., ed. 1997. *A Preserving Grace: Protestants, Catholics, and Natural Law.* Grand Rapids.

Cullmann, O. 1958. *Peter: Disciple, Apostle, Martyr: A Historical and Theological Essay.* New York.

Curry, P. 1989. *Prophecy and Power: Astrology in Early Modern England.* Princeton.

Cuthbert, Fr. 1929. *The Capuchins: A Contribution to the History of the Counter-Reformation.* New York.

Dallman, W. 1925. *Miles Coverdale, Bishop of Exeter.* St. Louis.

Dalton, H. 1886. *John a Lasco: His Earlier Life and Labours; A Contribution to the History of the Reformation in Poland, Germany, and England.* London.

D'Amico, J. 1988. *Theory and Practice in Renaissance Textual Criticism: Beatus Rhenanus between Conjecture and History.* Berkeley.

Dán, R., and A. Pirnát. 1982. *Antitrinitarianism in the Second Half of the Sixteenth Century.* Leiden.

Daniell, D. 2001. *William Tyndale: A Biography.* 2nd ed. New Haven.

Daniel-Rops, H. 1964. *The Catholic Reformation.* New York.

Danner, D. 1999. *Pilgrimmage to Puritanism: History and Theology of the Marian Exiles at Geneva, 1555–1560.* New York.

Daston, L., and K. Park. 1998. *Wonders and the Order of Nature, 1150–1750.* New York.

Davies, B., and B. Leftow. 2004. *The Cambridge Companion to Anselm.* Cambridge.

Davis, N. 1973. "The Rites of Violence: Religious Riots in Sixteenth-Century France." *Past and Present* 59:51–91.

Davis, T. 2008. *This Is My Body: The Presence of Christ in Reformation Thought.* Grand Rapids.

Day, J., E. Lund, and A. O'Donnell, eds. 1998. *Word, Church, and State: Tyndale Quincentenary Essays.* Washington, D.C.

De Boer, W. 2001. *The Conquest of the Soul: Confession, Discipline and Public Order in Counter-Reformation Milan.* Leiden.

De Lubac, H. 1998–2009. *Medieval Exegesis.* Translated by M. Sebanc. 3 vols. Grand Rapids.

De Lubac, H. 2007. *History and Spirit: The Understanding of Scripture According to Origen.* Translated by A. Nash. San Francisco.

Delph, R., M. Fontaine, and J. Martin, eds. 2006. *Heresy, Culture and Religion in Early Modern Italy.* Kirksville, MO.

Demson, D. 2005. "John Calvin." In *Reading Romans through the Centuries:*

From the Early Church to Karl Barth, ed. J. Greenman and T. Larsen, 137–48. Grand Rapids.

Denzinger, H. 2007. *The Sources of Catholic Dogma*. Translated by R. Deferrari. Fitzwilliam.

Deppermann, K. 1987. *Melchior Hoffman: Social Unrest and Apocalyptic Visions in the Age of Reformation*. Edinburgh.

DeWind, H. 1952. "Anabaptism and Italy." *Church History* 21:20–38.

Diefendorf, B. 1991. *Beneath the Cross: Catholics and Huguenots in Sixteenth-Century Paris*. Oxford.

Diefendorf, B. 2009. *The Saint Bartholomew's Day Massacre: A Brief History with Documents*. Boston.

Diener, R. 1979. "The *Magdeburg Centuries*: A Bibliothecal and Historiographical Analysis." Th.D. diss. Harvard University.

Dillenberger, J. 1999. *Images and Relics: Theological Perceptions and Visual Images in Sixteenth-Century Europe*. Oxford.

Dinan, S. 2006. *Women and Poor Relief in Seventeenth-century France: The Early History of the Daughters of Charity*. Burlington, VT.

Dipple, G. 1996. *Antifraternalism and Reformation Anticlericalism: Johann Eberlin von Günzburg and the Campaign against the Friars*. Aldershot, UK.

Dipple, G. 2005. *"Just as in the Time of the Apostles": Uses of History in the Radical Reformation*. Kitchener, ON.

Dixon, C., and L. Schorn-Schütte, eds. 2003. *The Protestant Clergy of Early Modern Europe*. London.

Doak, R. 2006. *Pope Leo X: Opponent of the Reformation*. Minneapolis.

Dombrowski, D. 1992. *St. John of the Cross: An Appreciation*. Albany.

Donnelly, J. 1976. *Calvinism and Scholasticism in Vermigli's Doctrine of Man and Grace*. Leiden.

Donnelly, J. 1981. "Peter Canisius." In *Shapers of Religious Traditions in Germany, Switzerland, and Poland, 1560–1600*, ed. J. Raitt, 141–56. New Haven.

Donnelly, J. 2004. *Ignatius of Loyola: Founder of the Jesuits*. New York.

Doran, S. 2000. "Elizabeth I's Religion: The Evidence of Her Letters." *Journal of Ecclesiastical History* 51:699–720.

Doran, S. 2007. *Mary, Queen of Scots: An Illustrated Life*. London.

Douglas, R. 1959. *Jacopo Sadoleto, 1477–1547: Humanist and Reformer*. Cambridge.

Douglas, R. 1969. "Talent and Vocation in Humanist and Protestant Thought." In *Action and Conviction in Early Modern Europe: Essays in Memory of E. H. Harbison*, ed. T. Rabb and J. Seigel. Princeton.

Dowling, M. 1999. *Fisher of Men: A Life of John Fisher, 1469–1535*. New York.

Dubay, T. 1989. *Fire Within: St. Teresa of Avila, St. John of the Cross, and the Gospel, on Prayer*. San Francisco.

Duffy, E. 2005. *The Stripping of the Altars: Traditional Religion in England, c. 1440–c. 1580*. 2nd ed. New Haven.

Duffy, E. 2006. *Saints and Sinners: A History of the Popes*. 3rd ed. New Haven.

Duffy, E. 2009. *Fires of Faith: Catholic England under Mary Tudor*. New Haven.

Duffy, E., and D. Loades, eds. 2006. *The Church of Mary Tudor*. Aldershot, UK.

Duggan, C., and N. Minnich. 2003. "Lateran Councils." In *New Catholic Encyclopedia*. 2nd ed. Vol. 8:350–55. Detroit.

Durnbaugh, D. 1985. *Believers' Church: The History and Character of Radical Protestantism*. Reprint, Scottdale, PA.

Durston, C., and J. Eales. 1996. *The Culture of English Puritanism*. Basingstoke.

Dvornik, F. 1958. *The Idea of Apostolicity in Byzantium and the Legend of the Apostle Andrew*. Cambridge.

Dyk, C., and K. Koop. 2006. *Confessions of Faith in the Anabaptist Tradition, 1527–1660*. Kitchener, ON.

Dykema, P., and H. Oberman, eds. 1993. *Anticlericalism in Late Medieval and Early Modern Europe*. Leiden.

Ebeling, G. 1963. "On the Doctrine of the *Triplex Usus Legis* in the Theology of the Reformation." In *Word and Faith*, 62–78. Translated by J. Leitch. Philadelphia.

Ebeling, G. 1970. *Luther: An Introduction to His Thought*. Philadelphia.

Edmondson, S. 2004. *Calvin's Christology*. Cambridge.

Edwards, J. 2000. *The Spain of the Catholic Monarchs, 1474–1520*. Malden.

Edwards, J. 2005. *Torquemada and the Inquisitors*. Stroud.

Edwards, M. 1994. *Printing, Propaganda, and Martin Luther*. Minneapolis.

Edwards, O. 2004. *A History of Preaching*. Abingdon.

Ehmer, H. 2002. "Johannes Brenz." In *The Reformation Theologians*, ed. C. Lindberg, 124–39. Oxford.

Eire, C. 1986. *War Against the Idols: The Reformation of Worship from Erasmus to Calvin*. Cambridge.

Eisenstein, E. 1993. *The Printing Revolution in Early Modern Europe*. Cambridge.

Elm, K., ed. 1989. *Reformbemühungen und Observanzbestrebungen im spätmittelalterlichen Ordenswesen*. Berlin. [Includes valuable chapters in English.]

Elton, G. 1972. *Policy and Police: The Enforcement of the Reformation in the Age of Thomas Cromwell*. Cambridge.

Elton, G. 1973. *Reform and Renewal: Thomas Cromwell and the Common Weal*. Cambridge.

Eppley, D. 2007. *Defending Royal Supremacy and Discerning God's Will in Tudor England*. Aldershot, UK.

Estep, W. 1996. *The Anabaptist Story: An Introduction to Sixteenth-Century Anabaptism*. 3rd ed. Grand Rapids.

Estep, W., and T. Bergsten. 1978. *Balthasar Hubmaier: Anabaptist Theologian and Martyr*. Valley Forge.

Estes, J. 2002. "Johannes Brenz and the German Reformation." *Lutheran Quarterly* 16:373–414.

Estes, J. 2006. *Peace, Order and the Glory of God: Secular Authority and the Church in the Thought of Luther and Melanchthon*. Leiden.

Estes, J. 2007. *Christian Magistrate and Territorial Church: Johannes Brenz and the German Reformation*. Toronto.

Evangelisti, S. 2003. "'We Do Not Have It, and We Do Not Want It': Women, Power, and Convent Reform in Florence." *Sixteenth Century Journal* 34, no. 3:677–700.

Evans, G. 1992. *Problems of Authority in the Reformation Debates*. Cambridge.

Evans, R. 1984. *The Making of the Hapsburg Monarchy, 1550–1700: An Interpretation*. Oxford.

Evennett, H. 1968. *The Spirit of the Counter-Reformation*. Edited by J. Bossy. Cambridge.

Fanning, W. 1908. "Confraternity (Sodality)." In *Catholic Encyclopedia*, ed. C. Herbermann et al. New York.

Fantazzi, C. 2008. *A Companion to Juan Luis Vives*. Leiden.

Farge, J. 1985. *Orthodoxy and Reform in Early Reformation France: The Faculty of Theology of Paris, 1500–1543*. Leiden.

Farley, B., ed. and trans. 1982. *Treatises against the Anabaptists and against the Libertines*. Grand Rapids.

Farley, B., ed. 2000. "Introduction." In *John Calvin's Sermons on the Ten Commandments*, 30–48. Reprint, Grand Rapids.

Farmer, C. 1997. *The Gospel of John in the Sixteenth Century*. Oxford.

Farr, W. 1974. *John Wyclif as Legal Reformer*. Leiden.

Farthing, J. 1999. "Patristics, Exegesis and the Eucharist in the Theology of Girolamo Zanchi." In *Protestant Scholasticism: Essays in Reassessment*, ed. C. Truman and R. Clark, 79–95. Carlisle, PA.

Felix, G. 1980. *The Pope, His Banker, and Venice*. Cambridge.

Fenlon, D. 1972. *Heresy and Obedience in Tridentine Italy: Cardinal Pole and the Counter Reformation*. Cambridge.

Fernández-Santamaría, F. 1998. *The Theater of Man: J. L. Vives on Society*. Philadelphia.

Fichter, J. 1940. *Man of Spain: Francis Suarez*. New York.

Fichtner, P. 2003. *The Habsburg Monarchy, 1490–1848: Attributes of Empire*. New York.

Fischer-Galati, S. 1972. *Ottoman Imperialism and German Protestantism*. Cambridge.

Fisher, A. J. 2007. "Music and Religious Change." In *Cambridge History of Christianity*, vol. 6: *Reform and Expansion 1500–1660*, ed. R. Hsia, 386–406. Cambridge.

Fisher, J. 1978. "Initiation, 5: Lutheran, Anglican, and Reformed Rites." In *The Study of Liturgy*, ed. Cheslyn Jones et al., 120–32. New York.

Flandrin, J. 1979. *Families in Former Times.* Cambridge.

Flynn, M. 1991. "Mimesis of the Last Judgment: The Spanish Auto de Fe." *Sixteenth Century Journal* 22:281–97.

Fodor, J., and F. Bauerschmidt, eds. 2004. *Aquinas in Dialogue: Thomas for the Twenty-first Century.* Malden, MA.

Folz, R. 1969. *The Concept of Empire in Western Europe from the Fifth to the Fourteenth Century.* New York.

Forde, G. 1969. *Law-Gospel Debate: An Interpretation of Its Historical Development.* Minneapolis.

Forde, G. 1991. *Justification by Faith: A Matter of Life and Death.* Mifflintown, PA.

Forde, G. 2005. *Captivation of the Will: Luther and Erasmus on Freedom and Bondage.* Grand Rapids.

Forde, G., M. Mattes, and S. Paulson, eds. 2007. *The Preached God: Proclamation in Word and Sacrament.* Grand Rapids.

Forster, M. 1992. *The Counter-Reformation in the Villages: Religion and Reform in the Bishopric of Speyer, 1560–1720.* Ithaca.

Fox, A. 1983. *Thomas More: History & Providence.* New Haven.

Foxgrover, D., ed. 2004. *Calvin and the Company of Pastors: Papers Presented at the 14th Colloquium of the Calvin Studies Society, May 22–24, 2003, The University of Notre Dame, Notre Dame, Indiana.* Grand Rapids.

Fragnito, G. 2001. *Church, Censorship and Culture in Early Modern Italy.* Cambridge.

Freitag, J. 2001. *Luther in Erfurt und die katholische Theologie.* Leipzig.

Frend, W. 1984. *The Rise of Christianity.* Philadelphia.

Friede, J., and B. Keen. 1971. *Bartolomé de las Casas in History: Toward an Understanding of the Man and His Work.* Dekalb, IL.

Friedmann, R. 1998. *The Theology of Anabaptism: An Interpretation.* Scottdale.

Friesen, A. 1990. *Thomas Muentzer, a Destroyer of the Godless: The Making of a Sixteenth-Century Religious Revolutionary.* Berkeley.

Friesen, A. 1998. *Erasmus, the Anabaptists, and the Great Commission.* Grand Rapids.

Froehlich, K. 2004. "Luther on Vocation." In *Harvesting Martin Luther's Reflections on Theology, Ethics, and the Church*, ed. Timothy Wengert, 121–33. Grand Rapids.

Fuchs, W. 1970. *Das Zeitalter der Reformation.* Stuttgart.

Fudge, T. 1998. *The Magnificent Ride: The First Reformation in Hussite Bohemia.* Brookfield, VT.

Fuhrmann, P. 1951. *Luther's Vision of the Kingdom of God.* Westminster, MD.

Fulton, J. 1989. *Michael Servetus: Humanist and Martyr.* Reprint, New Castle.

Furcha, E., and H. Pipkin. 1984. *Prophet, Pastor, Protestant: The Work of Huldrych Zwingli after Five Hundred Years.* Allison Park, PA.

Füssell, S. 2005. *Gutenberg and the Impact of Printing.* Translated by D. Martin. Aldershot, UK.

Gäbler, V. 1986. *Huldrych Zwingli: His Life and Work.* Philadelphia.

Gamble, R., ed. 1992. *Calvin's Ecclesiology: Sacraments and Deacons.* New York.

Ganoczy, A. 1987. *The Young Calvin.* Translated by D. Foxgrover and W. Provo. Philadelphia.

García Pinilla, I. J., and J. Nelson. 2001. "The Textual Tradition of the Historia de Statu Belgico et Religione Hispanica by Francisco de Enzinas (Dryander)." *Humanistica Lovaniensia: Journal of Neo-Latin Studies* 50:267–86.

Garrett, C. 1938. *Marian Exiles: A Study in the Origins of Elizabethan Puritanism.* Cambridge.

Garside, C. 1966. *Zwingli and the Arts.* New Haven.

Garside, C. 1979. *The Origins of Calvin's Theology of Music, 1536–1543.* Philadelphia.

Gassman, G., and S. Hendrix. 1999. *Fortress Introduction to the Lutheran Confessions.* Minneapolis.

Gerrish, B. 1962. *Grace and Reason: A Study in the Theology of Luther.* Oxford.

Gilmont, J. 1998. *Printing and the Book.* Edited and translated by K. Maag. Aldershot, UK.

Gilson, E. 1938. *Reason and Revelation in the Middle Ages.* New York.

Gingerich, O. 2004. *The Book Nobody Read: The Revolutions of Nicolaus Copernicus.* New York.

Gleason, E. 1993. *Gasparo Contarini: Venice, Rome and Reform.* Berkeley.

Gleason, E. 1994. "The Capuchin Order in the Sixteenth Century." In *Religious Orders of the Catholic Reformation: In Honor of John C. Olin on His Seventy-Fifth Birthday,* ed. R. DeMolen, 31–57. New York.

Gleason, J. 1989. *John Colet.* Berkeley.

Goertz, H.-J. 1993. *Thomas Müntzer: Apocalyptic, Mystic, and Revolutionary.* Edinburgh.

Goertz, H.-J. 1996. *The Anabaptists.* London.

Goertz, H.-J., and W. Klaassen, eds. 1982. *Profiles of Radical Reformers: Biographical Sketches from Thomas Müntzer to Paracelsus.* Scottdale, PA.

Goldberg, P. 1999. "Performing the Word of God: *Corpus Christi* Drama in the Northern Province." In Diana Wood, ed., *Life and Thought in the Northern Church c1100-c1700.* Woodbridge.

Gootjes, N. 2007. *The Belgic Confession: Its History and Sources.* Grand Rapids.

Gordon, B. 1992. *Clerical Discipline and the Rural Reformation. The Synod in Zürich, 1532–1580.* Bern.

Gordon, B. 2002. *The Swiss Reformation.* Manchester, UK.

Gordon, B. 2009. *Calvin.* New Haven.

Gordon, B., and E. Campi, eds. 2002. *Architect of Reformation: An Introduction to Heinrich Bullinger, 1504–1575.* Grand Rapids.

Gordon, B., and P. Marshall, eds. 2000. *The Place of the Dead: Death and Remembrance in Late Medieval and Early Modern Europe.* Cambridge.

Grafton, A., and L. Jardine. 1986. *From Humanism to the Humanities: Education and the Liberal Arts in Fifteenth- and Sixteenth-Century Europe.* Cambridge.

Graham, M. 1996. *The Uses of Reform: "Godly Discipline" and Popular Behavior in Scotland and Beyond, 1560–1610.* Leiden.

Grane, L. 1987. *The Augsburg Confession: A Commentary.* Translated by John Rasmussen. Minneapolis.

Grane, L., A. Schindler, and M. Wriedt, eds. 1993. *Auctoritas Patrum: Contributions on the Reception of the Church Fathers in the 15th and 16th Centuries.* Mainz.

Green, I. 1996. *The Christian's ABC: Catechisms and Catechizing in England, c. 1530–1740.* New York.

Greengrass, M. 1987. *The French Reformation.* Oxford.

Greenslade, S., ed. 1963. *The Cambridge History of the Bible. The West from the Reformation to the Present Day.* Cambridge.

Gregory, B. 1999. *Salvation at Stake: Christian Martyrdom in Early Modern Europe.* Cambridge.

Grendler, P. 1977. *The Roman Inquisition and the Venetian Press, 1540–1605.* Princeton.

Grendler, P. 2004. "The Universities of the Renaissance and Reformation." *Renaissance Quarterly* 57, no. 1:1–42.

Greschat, M. 2004. *Martin Bucer: A Reformer and His Times.* Translated by Stephen E. Buckwalter. Louisville.

Griffiths, R., ed. 2001. *The Bible in the Renaissance: Essays on Biblical Commentary and Translation in the Fifteenth and Sixteenth Centuries.* Burlington, VT.

Grimm, H. 1973. *The Reformation Era, 1500–1650.* New York.

Gritsch, E., and R. Jenson. 1976. *Lutheranism: The Theological Movement and Its Confessional Writings.* Philadelphia.

Gross, L. 1982. "Jakob Hutter: A Christian Communist." In *Profiles of Radical Reformers: Biographical Sketches from Thomas Müntzer to Paracelsus,* ed. H.-J. Goertz and W. Klaassen, 158–67. Scottdale, PA.

Guggisberg, H. 1982. *Basel in the Sixteenth Century: Aspects of the City Republic before, during, and after the Reformation.* St. Louis.

Guggisberg, H. 2003. *Sebastian Castellio, 1515–1563: Humanist and Defender of Religious Toleration in a Confessional Age.* Aldershot, UK.

Gunn, S., and P. Lindley, eds. 1991. *Cardinal Wolsey: Church, State and Art.* Cambridge.

Guppy, H. 1935. *Miles Coverdale and the English Bible, 1488–1568.* Manchester, UK.

Guy, J. 2000. *Thomas More.* New York.

Guy, J. 2006. *Queen of Scots: The True Life of Mary Stuart.* Boston.

Guzman, N. 2009. *Martin Luther's Ethics of Creation: A Morality of Nature.* Saarbrücken.

Gwyn, P. 1990. *The King's Cardinal: The Rise and Fall of Thomas Wolsey.* London.

Haigh, C., ed. 1987. *The English Reformation Revised.* Cambridge.

Haigh, C. 1993. *English Reformations: Religion, Politics, and Society under the Tudors.* Oxford.

Halkin, L.-E. 1993. *Erasmus: A Critical Biography.* Oxford.

Hall, B. 1957. *Genevan version of the English Bible.* London.

Hall, B. 1985. "*Hoc est corpus meum*: The Centrality of the Real Presence for Luther." In *Luther: Theologian for Catholics and Protestants,* ed. George Yule, 112–44. Edinburgh.

Hamilton, A. 1992. *Heresy and Mysticism in Sixteenth-Century Spain: The Alumbrados.* Toronto.

Hamm, B. 2004. *The Reformation of Faith in the Context of Late Medieval Theology and Piety: Essays by Berndt Hamm.* Edited by R. Bast. Leiden.

Hammann, K. 1989. *Ecclesia Spiritualis: Luthers Kirchenverständnis in den Kontroversen mit Augustin von Alveldt und Ambrosius Catharinus.* Göttingen.

Hammerling, R., ed. 2008. *A History of Prayer: The First to the Fifteenth Centuries.* Leiden.

Hanke, L. 1994. *All Mankind Is One: A Study of the Disputation between Bartolomé de Las Casas and Juan Ginés de Sepúlveda in 1550 on the Intellectual and Religious Capacity of the American Indians.* Dekalb, IL.

Hankins, J. 1990. *Plato in the Italian Renaissance.* Leiden.

Hankins, J., ed. 2007. *The Cambridge Companion to Renaissance Philosophy.* New York.

Harline, C. 1995. "Actives and Contemplatives: The Female Religious of the Low Countries Before and After Trent." *Catholic Historical Review* 89, no. 4:541–67.

Harline, C. 2003. *Miracles at the Jesus Oak: Histories of the Supernatural in Reformation Europe.* New York.

Harrington, J. 1995. *Reordering Marriage and Society in Reformation Germany.* Cambridge.

Hasel, G. 1972. "Capito, Schwenkfeld and Crautwald on Sabbatarian Anabaptist Theology." *Mennonite Quarterly Review* 46:41–57.

Hauben, P. 1967. *Three Spanish Heretics and the Reformation.* Geneva.

Hayden-Roy, P. 1994. *The Inner Word and the Outer World: A Biography of Sebastian Franck.* New York.

Headley, J. 1973. "Luther and the Fifth Lateran Council." *Archiv für Reformationsgeschichte* 64:55–78.

Heal, B. 2007. *The Cult of the Virgin Mary in Early Modern Germany: Protestant and Catholic Piety, 1500–1648.* Cambridge.

Heim, F., and J. Hirstein, eds. 2000. *Beatus Rhenanus (1485–1547), lecteur et éditeur des textes anciens.* Turnhout.

Heinze, R. 2005. *Reform and Conflict: From the Medieval World to the Wars of Religion, A.D. 1350–1648.* Grand Rapids.

Helm, P. 2004. *John Calvin's Ideas.* Oxford.

Helmer, C. 1999. *The Trinity and Martin Luther: A Study on the Relationship between Genre, Language and the Trinity in Luther's Works (1523–1546).* Mainz.

Helmholz, R. 1990. *Roman Canon Law in Reformation England.* Cambridge.

Heming, C. 2003. *Protestants and the Cult of Saints in German-Speaking Europe, 1517–1531.* Kirksville, MO.

Hendel, K. 2004. "Johannes Bugenhagen, Organizer of the Lutheran Reformation." *Lutheran Quarterly* 18, no. 1:43–75.

Henderson, J. 1998. *The Construction of Orthodoxy and Heresy: Neo-confucian, Islamic, Jewish, and Early Christian Patterns.* Albany, NY.

Hendrix, S. 2004. *Recultivating the Vineyard: The Reformation Agendas of Christianization.* Louisville.

Hesselink, I. 1992. *Calvin's Concept of the Law.* Allison Park, PA.

Heyer, H. 1990. *Guillaume Farel: An Introduction to His Theology.* Edited and translated by Blair Reynolds. New York.

Higman, Francis M. 1984. "The Question of Nicodemism." In *Calvinus ecclesiae Genevensis custos: Die Referate des Congrès International des Recherches Calviniennes vom 6.- 9. September 1982 in Genf,* ed. W. Neuser, 165–70. Frankfurt.

Hillar, M. 2002. *Michael Servetus: Intellectual Giant, Humanist, and Martyr.* Lanham, MD.

Hillerbrand, H. 1967. *Landgrave Philipp of Hesse, 1504–1567: Religion and Politics in the Reformation.* St. Louis.

Hillerbrand, H. 1984. *Men and Ideas in the Sixteenth Century.* Prospect Heights, IL.

Hillerbrand, H. 2007. *The Division of Christendom: Christianity in the Sixteenth Century.* Louisville.

Hinnebusch, W. 1966. *A History of the Dominican Order.* Staten Island, NY.

Hirsch, E. 1981. *Introduction to De arte dubitandi et confidendi, ignorandi et sciendi, by Sebastien Castellio.* Leiden.

Hirstein, J. 1995. *Tacitus' Germania and Beatus Rhenanus (1485–1587): A Study of Editorial and Exegetical Contribution of a Sixteenth Century Scholar.* Frankfurt am Main.

Hobbins, D. 2009. *Authorship and Publicity before Print: Jean Gerson and the Transformation of Late Medieval Learning.* Philadelphia.

Hobbs, R. 1985. "Zwingli and the Old Testament." In *Huldrych Zwingli, 1484–1531: A Legacy of Radical Reform,* ed. E. J. Furcha, 144–78. Montreal.

Holborn, H. 1959. *A History of Modern Germany: The Reformation.* Princeton.

Holder, A. 1993. "The Mosaic Tabernacle in Early Christian Exegesis." *Studia Patristica* 25:101–6. Leuven.

Holder, R. 2006. *John Calvin and the Grounding of Interpretation. Calvin's First Commentaries.* Leiden.

Holder, R. 2009. *Crisis and Renewal: The Era of the Reformations.* Louisville.

Holt, M. 1995. *The French Wars of Religion, 1562–1629.* Cambridge.

Holtrop, P. 1993. *The Bolsec Controversy on Predestination from 1551 to 1555: The Statements of Jerome Bolsec and the Responses of John Calvin, Theodore Beza and Other Reformed Theologians.* New York.

Homza, L. 2000. *Religious Authority in the Spanish Renaissance.* Baltimore.

Höpfl, H. 1982. *The Christian Polity of John Calvin.* Cambridge.

Houkes, J. 2004. *An Annotated Bibliography on the History of Usury and Interest from the Earliest Times through the Eighteenth Century.* Lewiston, NY.

Houlbrooke, R. 1998. *Death, Religion and the Family in England 1480–1750.* Oxford.

Hsia, R. 1988. *The German People and the Reformation.* Ithaca.

Hsia, R. 1989. *Social Discipline in the Reformation: Central Europe 1550–1750.* London.

Hsia, R. 2005. *The World of Catholic Renewal 1540–1770*. 2nd ed. Cambridge.

Hudson, A. 1988. *The Premature Reformation: Wycliffite Texts and Lollard History*. Oxford.

Hughes, P. 1982. *Faith and Works: Cranmer and Hooker on Justification*. Wilton, CT.

Hunter, I., J. Laursen, and C. Nederman, eds. 2005. *Heresy in Transition: Transforming Ideas of Heresy in Medieval and Early Modern Europe*. Aldershot, UK.

Ingham, M. 2004. *The Philosophical Vision of John Duns Scotus: An Introduction*. Washington, D.C.

Inwood, B., ed. 1999. *The Cambridge Companion to the Stoics*. Cambridge.

Isaak, H. 2006. *Menno Simons and the New Jerusalem*. Kitchener, ON.

Iserloh, E. 1981. *Johannes Eck: Scholastiker, Humanist, Kontroverstheologe*. Münster.

Israel, J. 1995. *The Dutch Republic: Its Rise, Greatness, and Fall, 1477–1806*. Oxford.

Ives, R. 1965. *The Theology of Wolfgang Musculus*. Manchester, UK.

Iwand, H. 2008. *Righteousness of Faith according to Luther*. Eugene, OR.

Izbicki, T., and J. Rollo-Koster, eds., 2009. *A Companion to the Great Western Schism*. Leiden.

James, F. 1998. *Peter Martyr Vermigli and Predestination: The Augustinian Inheritance of an Italian Reformer*. Oxford.

Janse, W., and B. Pitkin. eds. 2005. *The Formation of Clerical and Confessional Identities in Early Modern Europe*. Leiden.

Jansen, S. 1991. *Political Protest and Prophecy Under Henry VIII*. Woodbridge, UK.

Janz, D. 1983. *Luther and Late Medieval Thomism: A Study in Theological Anthropology*. Waterloo.

Jedin, H. 1947. *Papal Legate at the Council of Trent, Cardinal Seripando*. St. Louis.

Jedin, H. 1957–61. *A History of the Council of Trent*. Translated by E. Graf. 2 vols. St. Louis.

Jedin, H. 1967. *Crisis and Closure of the Council of Trent*. London.

Jedin, H., J. Dolan, and D. Holland. 1993. *History of the Church*. New York.

Jenkins, G. 2006. *John Jewel and the English National Church: The Dilemmas of an Erastian Reformer*. Aldershot, UK.

Jensen, D. 1973. *Confrontation at Worms: Martin Luther and the Diet of Worms*. Provo, UT.

Jensen, D. 1992. *Reformation Europe: Age of Reform and Revolution*. Lexington, MA.

Jenson, M. 2006. *Gravity of Sin: Augustine, Luther and Barth on homo incurvatus in se*. London.

Johnson, D. 2006. "Musa Posseliana: Johannes Posselius the Elder (1528–91) and the Lutheran Greek Program." *Reformation and Renaissance Review* 8:186–209.

Jones, D. 2004. *Reforming the Morality of Usury: A Study of the Differences that Separated Protestant Reformers*. Lanham, MD.

Jones, N. 1989. *God and the Moneylenders: Usury and the Law in Early Modern England*. New York.

Jones, P. 1994. *Christ's Eucharistic Presence: A History of the Doctrine*. New York.

Jones, R. 2005. *Coornhert and the Collegiants: A Movement for Spiritual Religion in Holland*. Whitefish, MT.

Jones, T., and D. Sprunger, eds. 2002. *Marvels, Monsters, and Miracles: Studies in the Medieval and Early Modern Imaginations*. Kalamazoo, MI.

Jorgensen, K. 1994. "The Theatines." In *Religious Orders of the Catholic Reformation*, ed. R. DeMolen, 1–30. New York.

Junghans, H. 2003. "Luther's Wittenberg." In *The Cambridge Companion to Martin Luther*, ed. D. McKim, 20–35. Cambridge.

Kalden-Rosenfeld, I. 2004. *Tilman Riemenschneider: The Sculptor and His Workshop, with a Catalog of Works Generally Accepted as by Riemenschneider and His Workshop*. Translated by H. Grieve. Königstein in Taunus.

Kamen, H. 1997. *Philip of Spain.* New Haven.

Kamen, H. 1998. *The Inquisition: A Historical Revision.* New Haven.

Kamen, H. 1999. *The Spanish Inquisition: A Revision.* New Haven.

Kang, P. 2006. *Justification: The Imputation of Christ's Righteousness from Reformation Theology to the American Great Awakening and the Korean Revivals.* New York.

Kaplan, B. 1995. *Calvinists and Libertines: Confession and Community in Utrecht, 1578–1620.* Oxford.

Kaplan, B. 2007. *Divided by Faith: Religious Conflict and the Practice of Toleration in Early Modern Europe.* Cambridge.

Kapr, A. 1996. *Johann Gutenberg: The Man and His Invention.* Translated by D. Martin. Aldershot, UK.

Karant-Nunn, S. 1987. *Zwickau in Transition, 1500–1547: The Reformation as an Agent of Change.* Columbus, OH.

Karant-Nunn, S. 1997. *The Reformation of Ritual: An Interpretation of Early Modern Germany.* London.

Kärkkäinen, V. 2004. "'The Christian as Christ to the Neighbor': On Luther's Theology of Love." *International Journal of Systematic Theology* 6:101–17.

Kaufman, P. 1982. *Augustinian Piety and Catholic Reform: Augustine, Colet and Erasmus.* Macon, GA.

Kavanaugh, K., O.C.D., and O. Rodriguez, O.C.D., trans. 2008. *Teresa of Avila: The Book of Her Life.* Indianapolis.

Kawerau, G. 1903. *Hieronymus Emser: Ein Lebensbild aus der Reformationszeit.* Halle.

Keen, R. 2002. "Johannes Cochlaeus: An Introduction to His Life and Work." In *Luther's Lives: Two Contemporary Accounts of Martin Luther,* trans. and annotated by E. Vandiver, R. Keen, and T. Frazel, 40–52. Manchester, UK.

Kendall, R. 1981. *Calvin and English Calvinism to 1649.* Oxford.

Kennedy, G. 1980. *Classical Rhetoric and Its Christian and Secular Tradition from Ancient to Modern Times.* Chapel Hill, NC.

Kerridge, E. 2002. *Usury, Interest, and the Reformation.* Burlington, VT.

Kerssenbrock, H. von. 2007. *Narrative of the Anabaptist Madness: The Overthrow of Münster, the Famous Metropolis of Westphalia.* Translated by C. Mackay. Leiden.

Kieckhefer, R. 1990. *Magic in the Middle Ages.* New York.

Kinder, A. 1975. *Casiodoro de Reina: Spanish Reformer of the Sixteenth Century.* London.

Kinder, A. 1976. "Juan Pérez de Pineda (Pierius): A Spanish Calvinist Minister of the Gospel in Sixteenth-Century Geneva," *Bulletin of Hispanic Studies* 43:283–300.

Kinder, A. 1986. "Antonio del Corro." In *Bibliotheca Dissidentium: Répertoire des non-conformistes religieux des seizième et dix-septième siècle,* ed. A. Séguenny, 121–76. Baden-Baden.

Kinder, A. 1987. "Two Previously Unknown Letters of Juan Pérez de Pineda, Protestant of Seville in the Sixteenth Century." *Bibliothèque d'Humanisme et Renaissance* 49:111–20.

Kinder, A. 1994. *Alumbrados of the Kingdom of Toledo; Jacobus Acontius.* Baden-Baden.

Kingdon, R. 1985a. "Calvin and 'Presbytery': The Geneva Company of Pastors." *Pacific Theological Review* 18:43–55.

Kingdon, R. 1985b. *Church and Society in Reformation Europe.* London.

Kingdon, R. 1987. "The Episcopal Function in Protestant Churches in the Sixteenth and Seventeenth Centuries." In *Miscellanea historiae ecclesiasticae VIII: L'institution et les pouvoirs dans les églises de l'antiquité à nos jours,* ed. B. Vogler, 207–20. Brussels.

Kingdon, R. 1988. *Myths about the St. Bartholomew's Day Massacres, 1572–1576.* Cambridge.

Kingdon, R. 1994. "The Geneva Consistory in the Time of Calvin." In *Calvinism in Europe, 1540–1620,* ed. Andrew Pettegree et al., 21–34. Cambridge.

Kingdon, R. 1995. *Adultery and Divorce in Calvin's Geneva.* Cambridge.

Kingdon, R. 2007. *Geneva and the Coming of the Wars of Religion.* New ed. Geneva.

Kirby, W., ed. 2003. *Richard Hooker and the English Reformation.* Dordrecht.

Kirby, W., ed. 2008. *A Companion to Richard Hooker.* Leiden.

Kirk, J. 1989. *Patterns of Reform.* Edinburgh.

Kirsch, W., and M. Treu. 1993. *Wittenberg: The Town of Martin Luther.* Berlin.

Kittelson, J. 1975. *Wolfgang Capito: From Humanist to Reformer.* Leiden.

Kittelson, J. 2000. *Toward an Established Church: Strasbourg from 1500 to the Dawn of the Seventeenth Century.* Mainz.

Klaassen, W., and W. Klassen. 2008. *Marpeck: A Life of Dissent and Conformity.* Waterloo, ON.

Klaniczay, G., and E. Pócs, eds. 2006. *Christian Demonology and Popular Mythology: Demons, Spirits, and Witches.* Bucharest.

Klassen, H. 1958. "The Life and Teachings of Hans Hut." *Mennonite Quarterly Review* 32:171–205, 267–304.

Klassen, W. 1968. *Covenant and Community: The Life, Writings, and Hermeneutics of Pilgram Marpeck.* Grand Rapids.

Klauser, T. 1979. *A Short History of the Western Liturgy: An Account and Some Reflections.* Translated by J. Halliburton. 2nd ed. Oxford.

Kleinig, J. 2008. "Luther on the Reception in God's Holiness." *Pro Ecclesia* 17:76–91.

Kleinman, R. 1962. *Saint François de Sales and the Protestants.* Geneva.

Klooster, F. 2001. *Our Only Comfort: A Comprehensive Commentary on the Heidelberg Catechism.* 2 vols. Grand Rapids.

Knowles, D. 1976. *Bare Ruined Choirs: The Dissolution of the English Monasteries.* Cambridge.

Kolb, R. 1987. *For All the Saints: Changing Perceptions of Martyrdom and Sainthood in the Lutheran Reformation.* Macon, GA.

Kolb, R. 1996. *Luther's Heirs Define His Legacy: Studies on Lutheran Confessionalization.* Brookfield, VT.

Kolb, R. 2002. "Martin Chemnitz." In *The European Theologians,* ed. C. Lindberg, 140–53. Oxford.

Kolb, R. 2005. *Bound Choice, Election, and Wittenberg Theological Method: From Martin Luther to the Formula of Concord.* Grand Rapids.

Kolb, R., and C. Arand. 2008. *The Genius of Luther's Theology: A Wittenberg Way of Thinking for the Contemporary Church.* Grand Rapids.

Kolb, R., and J. Nestingen. 2001. *Sources and Contexts of the Book of Concord.* Minneapolis.

Koslofsky, C. 2000. *The Reformation of the Dead. Death and Ritual in Early Modern Germany, 1450–1700.* New York.

Kreitzer, B. 2004. *Reforming Mary: Changing Images of the Virgin Mary in Lutheran Sermons of the Sixteenth Century.* Oxford.

Kriechbaum, F. 1967. *Grundzüge der Theologie Karlstadts: Eine systematische Studie zur Erhellung der Theologie Andreas von Karlstadts . . . aus seinen eigenen Schriften entwickelt.* Hamburg.

Krieger, C., and M. Lienhard, eds. 1993. *Martin Bucer and Sixteenth Century Europe. Actes du colloque de Strasbourg, 28–31 août 1991.* 2 vols. Leiden.

Kristeller, P. 1974a. *Medieval Aspects of Renaissance Learning; Three Essays.* Edited and translated by E. Mahoney. Durham, NC.

Kristeller, P. 1974b. "The Role of Religion in Renaissance Humanism and Platonism." In *The Pursuit of Holiness in Late Medieval and Renaissance Religion,* ed. C. Trinkaus and H. Oberman, 367–70. Leiden.

Kuhn, T. 1985. *Copernican Revolution: Planetary Astronomy in the Development of Western Thought.* Reprint, Cambridge.

Kunzler, M. 2001. *The Church's Liturgy.* Berlin.

Kyle, R. 2002. *The Ministry of John Knox: Pastor, Preacher and Prophet.* Lewiston, NY.

Lahey, S. 2003. *Philosophy and Politics in the Thought of John Wyclif*. Cambridge.

Lake, P., and M. Questier. 2002. *The Anti-Christ's Lewd Hat: Protestants, Papists and Players in Post-Reformation England*. New Haven.

Lambert, M. 1992. *Medieval Heresy: Popular Movements from the Gregorian Reform to the Reformation*. 2nd ed. Oxford.

Lane, A., ed. 1996. *Bondage and Liberation of the Will: A Defence of Orthodox Doctrine of Human Choice against Pighius*. Translated by G. Davies. Grand Rapids.

Lane, A. 1999. *John Calvin: Student of the Church Fathers*. Grand Rapids.

Lane, A. 2002. *Justification by Faith in Catholic-Protestant Dialogue: An Evangelical Assessment*. London.

Langer, H. 1978. *The Thirty Years' War*. Poole.

Le Goff, J. 1984. *The Birth of Purgatory*. Translated by A. Goldhammer. Aldershot, UK.

Le Huray, P. 1967. *Music and the Reformation in England, 1549–1660*. Cambridge.

Lea, H. 1932. *History of Sacerdotal Celibacy in the Christian Church*. 4th ed. London.

Lee, S. 1997. "Calvin's Understanding of Pietas." In *Calvinus Sincerioris Religionis Vindex: Calvin as Protector of the Purer Religion*, ed. W. Neusner and B. Armstrong, 225–39. Kirksville, MO.

Lehmberg, S. 1970. *The Reformation Parliament, 1529–36*. Cambridge.

Leith, J. 1982. *Creeds of the Churches: A Reader in Christian Doctrine from the Bible to the Present*. 3rd ed. New York.

Leonard, A. 2005. *Nails in the Walls: Catholic Nuns in Reformation Germany*. Chicago.

Leppin, V., et al., eds. 2006. *Johann Friedrich I: Der lutherische Kurfürst*. Gütersloh.

Levack, B. 2006. *The Witch-Hunt in Early Modern Europe*. 3rd ed. New York.

Levi, A. 2002. *Renaissance and Reformation: The Intellectual Genesis*. New Haven.

Liechty, D. 1988. *Andreas Fischer and the Sabbatarian Anabaptists: An Early Reformation Episode in East Central Europe*. Scottdale, PA.

Liechty, D. 1993. *Sabbatarianism in the Sixteenth Century: A Page in the History of the Radical Reformation*. Berrien Springs, MI.

Lillback, P. 2001. *The Binding of God: Calvin's Role in the Development of Covenant Theology*. Grand Rapids.

Lindberg, C. 1996. *The European Reformations*. Oxford.

Lindberg, C., ed. 2002. *The Reformation Theologians*. Oxford.

Linder, R. 1964. *The Political Ideas of Pierre Viret*. Geneva.

Linder, R. 1971. "The Bible and Biblical Authority in the Literary Works of Pierre Viret." *Sixteenth Century Journal* 2:55–71.

Little, L. 2002. "Monasticism and Western Society: From Marginality to the Establishment and Back." *Memoirs of the American Academy in Rome* 47: 83–94.

Loades, D. 1970. *The Oxford Martyrs*. New York.

Loades, D. 1989. *Mary Tudor: A Life*. Oxford.

Lohse, B. 1986. *Martin Luther: An Introduction to His Life and Work*. Philadelphia.

Lohse, B. 1999. *Martin Luther's Theology: Its Historical and Systematic Development*. Translated by R. Harrisville. Edinburgh.

Longenecker, S., ed. 1997. *The Dilemma of Anabaptist Piety: Strengthening or Straining the Bonds of Community?* Bridgewater, VA.

Love, R. 2001. *Blood and Religion: The Conscience of Henri IV 1553–1593*. Montreal.

Lualdi, K., and A. Thayer, eds. 2000. *Penitence in the Age of Reformations*. Aldershot, UK.

Lubieniecki, S., and G. H. Williams. 1995. *History of the Polish Reformation: And Nine Related Documents*. Minneapolis.

Luke, C. 1989. *Pedagogy, Printing, and Protestantism: The Discourse on Childhood*. Albany.

Lupton, J. 1909. *A Life of John Colet, D. D., Dean of St. Paul's and Founder of St. Paul's School*. London.

Luria, K. 2005. *Sacred Boundaries: Religious Coexistence and Conflict in Early-Modern France*. Washington, D.C.

Lynch, K. 2003. *Individuals, Families, and Communities in Europe, 1200–1800: The Urban Foundations of Western Society*. Cambridge.

Maag, K. 1995. *Seminary or University? The Genevan Academy and Reformed Higher Education, 1560–1620*. Aldershot, UK.

Maag, K., ed. 1999. *Melanchthon in Europe: His Work and Influence beyond Wittenberg*. Grand Rapids.

Maag, K., and J. Witvliet. 2004. *Worship in Medieval and Early Modern Europe: Change and Continuity in Religious Practice*. Notre Dame, IN.

Mabry, E. 1994. *Balthasar Hubmaier's Doctrine of the Church*. Lanham, MD.

MacCulloch, D. 1996. *Thomas Cranmer: A Life*. New Haven.

MacCulloch, D. 2001a. *The Boy King: Edward VI and the Protestant Reformation*. New York.

MacCulloch, D. 2001b. *The Later Reformation in England 1547–1603*. 2nd ed. Basingstoke.

MacCulloch, D. 2004. *The Reformation*. New York.

Macy, G. 1992. *The Banquet's Wisdom: A Short History of the Theologies of the Lord's Supper*. New York.

Maier, P. 1959. *Caspar Schwenkfeld on the Person and Work of Christ: A Study of Schwenkfeldian Theology at Its Core*. Assen.

Makowski, E. 1997. *Canon Law and Cloistered Women: Periculoso and Its Commentators, 1298–1545*. Washington, D.C.

Mallinson, J. 2003. *Faith, Reason, and Revelation in Theodore Beza, 1519–1605*. Oxford.

Maltby, W. 2002. *The Reign of Charles V*. New York.

Man, J. 2002. *John Gutenberg: How One Man Remade the World with Words*. New York.

Manetsch, S. 2000. *Theodore Beza and the Quest for Peace in France, 1572–1598*. Leiden.

Mann, J. 2000. "Melanchthon's Response to Antinomianism: How the Antinomian Questions Shaped the Development of his Theology." *Concordia Journal* 26:305–25.

Marius, R. 1984. *Thomas More: A Biography*. New York.

Marshall, Paul. 1996. *A Kind of Life Imposed on Man: Vocation and Social Order from Tyndale to Locke*. Toronto.

Marshall, Peter. 1994. *The Catholic Priesthood and the English Reformation*. Oxford.

Marshall, Peter. 2002. *Beliefs and the Dead in Reformation England*. Oxford.

Marshall, Peter. 2003. *Reformation England 1480–1642*. London.

Marshall, Peter. 2007. "Leaving the World," In *Reformation Christianity*, ed. P. Matheson, 168–88. Minneapolis.

Marshall, R. 2000. *John Knox*. Edinburgh.

Marshall, S. 1989. *Women in Reformation and Counter-Reformation Europe: Public and Private Worlds*. Bloomington, IN.

Mason, R. 1998. "Playing God's Card—Knox and Fasting, 1565–66." In *John Knox and the British Reformations*, ed. R. Mason, 176–98. Aldershot, UK.

Mason, R., ed. 1998. *John Knox and the British Reformations*. Aldershot, UK.

Matheson, P. 1972. *Cardinal Contarini at Regensburg*. Oxford.

Mattox, M. 2008. "Fortuita Misericordia: Martin Luther on the Salvation of Biblical Outsiders." *Pro Ecclesia* 17:423–41.

Mayer, T. 2000. *Reginald Pole: Prince and Prophet*. Cambridge.

McBride, A. 2006. *A Short History of the Mass*. Cincinnati.

McCabe, J. 1931. *The History and Meaning of the Catholic Index of Forbidden Books*. Girard, KS.

McClendon, M. 1999. *The Quiet Reformation*. Palo Alto.

McCormick, I., trans. 1983. *The Capuchin Reform: Essays in Commemoration of Its 450th Anniversary, 1528–1978*. Pittsburgh.

McGinn, B. 1994. *Antichrist: Two Thousand Years of Human Fascination with Evil*. San Francisco.

McGrade, A., ed. 1997. *Richard Hooker and the Construction of Christian Community*. Tempe.

McGrath, A. 1982. "Humanist Elements in the Early Reformed Doctrine of Justification." *Archiv für Reformationsgeschichte* 73:5–20.

McGrath, A. 1999. *Reformation Thought: An Introduction*. Malden, MA.

McGrath, A. 2005. *Iustitia Dei: A History of the Christian Doctrine of Justification*. 3rd rev. ed. Cambridge.

McKee, E. 1984. *John Calvin on the Diaconate and Liturgical Almsgiving*. Geneva.

McKee, E. 1988. *Elders and the Plural Ministry: The Role of Exegetical History in Illuminating John Calvin's Theology*. Geneva.

McKee, E. 1992. "John Calvin's Teaching on the Lord's Prayer." *Princeton Seminary Bulletin*, supplementary issue, n.s., 2:88–106.

McKee, E. 1998. "The Offices of Elders and Deacons in the Classical Reformed Tradition." *Major Themes in the Reformed Tradition*, ed. D. K. McKim, 344–53. Grand Rapids.

McKee, E. 1999. *Katharina Schütz Zell*. Vol. 1: *The Life and Thought of a Sixteenth-Century Reformer*. Leiden.

McKee, E. 2006. *Church Mother: The Writings of a Protestant Reformer in Sixteenth-Century Germany*. Chicago.

McKim, D., ed. 2006. *Calvin and the Bible*. Cambridge.

McKitterick, R. 2008. *Charlemagne: The Formation of a European Identity*. Cambridge.

McLaughlin, E. 2007. "Spiritualism: Schwenkfeld and Franck and Their Early Modern Resonances." In *A Companion to Anabaptism and Spiritualism, 1521–1700*, ed. J. Roth and J. Stayer, 119–61. Leiden.

McLaughlin, R. 1986. *Caspar Schwenckfeld, Reluctant Radical: His Life to 1540*. New Haven.

McNair, P. 1967. *Peter Martyr in Italy, an Anatomy of Apostasy*. Oxford.

McNeill, J. 1990. *Medieval Handbooks of Penance*. New York.

McSorley, H. 1969. *Luther: Right or Wrong? An Ecumenical-Theological Study of Luther's Major Work, The Bondage of the Will*. Minneapolis.

Mentzer, R., ed. 1994. *Sin and the Calvinists: Morals Control and the Consistory in the Reformed Tradition*. Kirksville, MO.

Mentzer, R. 2005. "The Synod in the Reformed Tradition." In *Synod and Synodality: Theology, History, Canon Law and Ecumenism in New Contact. International Colloquium Bruges 2003*, ed. A. Melloni and S. Scatena, 173–84. Münster.

Metzger, M. 1997. *History of the Liturgy: The Major Stages*. Translated by M. Beaumont. Collegeville, MN.

Mezzadri, L. 1992. *A Short Life of Saint Vincent de Paul*. Dublin.

Miller, G. 2002. "Fighting Like a Christian: The Ottoman Advance and the Development of Luther's Doctrine of Just War." In *Caritas et Reformatio*, ed. D. Whitford, 41–58. St. Louis.

Mladenovic, P. 1965. *Jan Hus at the Council of Constance*. Translated by M. Spinka. New York.

Moeller, Bernd. 1972. *Imperial Cities and the Reformation*. Philadelphia.

Monter, W. 1967. *Calvin's Geneva*. New York.

Moore, J. 1984. *Anabaptist Portraits*. Scottdale, PA.

Moore, R. 2007. *The Formation of a Persecuting Society: Authority and Deviance in Western Europe, 950–1250*. 2nd ed. Malden, MA.

Moran, J. 1985. *The Growth of English Schooling, 1340–1548: Learning, Liter-*

acy, and Laicization in Pre-Reformation York Diocese. Princeton.

Moreau, P.-F. 1999. *Le stoicisme au XVIe et au XVIIe siècle: Le retour des philosophies antiques à l'âge classique.* Paris.

Moser, P. 2005. *Lucas Cranach: His Life, His World, and His Art.* Translated by K. Wynne. Bamberg.

Mozley, J. 1953. *Coverdale and His Bibles.* London.

Muchembled, R. 2004. *A History of the Devil: From the Middle Ages to the Present.* Cambridge.

Muir, E. 2005. *Ritual in Early Modern Europe.* 2nd ed. Cambridge.

Muller, R. 1988. *Christ and the Decree: Christology and Predestination in Reformed Theology from Calvin to Perkins.* Grand Rapids.

Muller, R. 1991. *God, Creation, and Providence in the Thought of Jacob Arminius: Source and Directions of Scholastic Protestantism in the Era of Early Orthodoxy.* Grand Rapids.

Muller, R. 2000. *The Unaccommodated Calvin: Studies in the Foundation of a Theological Tradition.* Oxford.

Muller, R. 2003a. *After Calvin: Studies in the Development of a Theological Tradition.* Oxford.

Muller, R. 2003b. *Post-Reformation Reformed Dogmatics: The Rise and Development of Reformed Orthodoxy, ca. 1520 to ca. 1725.* 2nd ed. 4 vols. Grand Rapids.

Muller, R., and J. Thompson, eds. 1996. *Biblical Interpretation in the Era of the Reformation.* Grand Rapids.

Mullett, M. 1999. *The Catholic Reformation.* New York.

Mullett, M. 2004. *Martin Luther.* London.

Mulsow, M., and J. Rohls. 2005. *Antitrinitarians, Calvinists, and Cultural Exchange in Seventeenth-Century Europe.* Leiden.

Murphy, C., H. Gibaud, and M. Di Cesare, eds. 1989. *Miscellanea Moreana: Essays for Germain Marc'hadour.* Binghamton, NY.

Murphy, J., ed. 1983. *Renaissance Eloquence: Studies in the Theory and Practice of Renaissance Rhetoric.* Berkeley.

Myers, W. 1996. *"Poor Sinning Folk": Confession and Conscience in Counter-Reformation Germany.* Ithaca, NY.

Nagel, N. 1997. "Luther and the Priesthood of All Believers." *Concordia Theological Quarterly* 61:277–98.

Naphy, W. 1994. *Calvin and the Consolidation of the Genevan Reformation.* New York.

Nauert, C. 2006. *Humanism and the Culture of Renaissance Europe.* Cambridge.

Nauta, L. 2009. *In Defense of Common Sense: Lorenzo Valla's Critique of Scholastic Philosophy.* Cambridge.

Neal, J. 1972. *Conscience in the Reformation Period.* Cambridge.

Nelson, J. 1999. "'Solo Saluador': Printing the 1543 New Testament of Francisco de Enzinas (Dryander)," *Journal of Ecclesiastical History* 50:94–116.

New Catholic Encyclopedia. 15 vols. 2003. Detroit.

Newman, W., and A. Grafton, eds. 2001. *Secrets of Nature: Astrology and Alchemy in Early Modern Europe.* Cambridge.

Ngien, D. 2007. *Luther as a Spiritual Advisor: The Interface of Theology and Piety in Luther's Devotional Writings.* Bletchly, UK.

Nichols, A. 1991. *The Shape of Catholic Theology: An Introduction to Its Sources.* Collegeville, MN.

Nieto, J. 1970. *Juan de Valdés and the Origins of the Spanish and Italian Reformation.* Geneva.

Nimmo, D. 1987. *Reform and Division in the Medieval Franciscan Order: From Saint Francis to the Foundation of the Capuchins.* Rome.

Nobbs, D. 1938. *Theocracy and Toleration: A Study of the Disputes in Dutch Calvinism from 1600 to 1650.* Cambridge.

Noble, B. 2009. *Lucas Cranach the Elder: Art and Devotion of the German Reformation.* Lanham, MD.

Noll, M. 1991. *Confessions and Catechisms of the Reformation.* Vancouver.

Noreña, C. 1970. *Juan Luis Vives.* The Hague.

Norton, G. 1984. *The Ideology and Language of Translation in Renaissance*

France and Their Humanist Antecedents. Geneva.

Nugent, D. 1974. *Ecumenism in the Age of Reformation: The Colloquy of Poissy.* Cambridge.

Null, A. 2000. *Thomas Cranmer's Doctrine of Repentance.* Oxford.

O'Day, R. 1992. "Hugh Latimer: Prophet of the Kingdom." *Historical Research* 65:258–76.

O'Malley, J. 1993. *The First Jesuits.* Cambridge.

O'Malley, J. 2000. *Trent and All That: Renaming Catholicism in the Early Modern Era.* Cambridge.

Oakley, F. 1972. "Conciliarism at the Fifth Lateran Council?" *Church History* 41:55–78.

Oberman, H. 1963. *The Harvest of Medieval Theology.* Cambridge.

Oberman, H. 1981. *Forerunners of the Reformation.* Philadelphia.

Oberman, H. 1984. *The Roots of Anti-Semitism in the Age of Renaissance and Reformation.* Philadelphia.

Oberman, H. 1986. *The Dawn of the Reformation: Essays in Late Medieval and Early Reformation Thought.* Edinburgh.

Oberman, H. 1989. *Luther: Man between God and Devil.* Translated by E. Walliser-Schwarzbart. New Haven.

Oberman, H. 1992. "Europa Afflicta: The Reformation of the Refugees." *Archiv für Reformationsgeschichte* 83:91–111.

Oberman, H. 1999. "Calvin and Farel: The Dynamics of Legitimation in Early Calvinism." *Reformation and Renaissance Review* 1:7–40.

Oberman, H., and T. Brady, eds. 1975. *Itinerarium Italicum: The Profile of the Italian Renaissance in the Mirror of Its European Transformations.* Leiden.

Oberman, H.; F. James; and E. L. Saak, eds. 1991. *Via Augustini: Augustine in the Later Middle Ages, Renaissance and Reformation.* Leiden.

Old, H. 1992. *The Shaping of the Reformed Baptismal Rite in the Sixteenth Century.* Grand Rapids.

Old, H. 2002. *The Reading and Preaching of the Scriptures in the Worship of the Christian Church.* Vol. 4: *The Age of the Reformation.* Grand Rapids.

Olin, J. 1979. "The Pacifism of Erasmus." In *Six Essays on Erasmus and a Translation of Erasmus' Letter to Carondelet, 1523,* 17–32. New York.

Olin, J. 2000. *A Reformation Debate: Sadoleto's Letter to the Genevans and Calvin's Reply.* New ed. New York.

Olson, J. 1989. *Calvin and Social Welfare: Deacons and the Bourse Française.* Selinsgrove, PA.

Ong, W. 1958. *Ramus, Method, and the Decay of Dialogue: From the Art of Discourse to the Art of Reason.* Cambridge.

Opocenský, M., and P. Réamonn. 1999. *Justification and Sanctification in the Traditions of the Reformation: Prague V: The Fifth Consultation on the First and Second Reformations.* Geneva.

Osborne, K. 1990. *Reconciliation and Justification: The Sacrament and Its Theology.* New York.

Ozment, S. 1969. *Homo Spiritualis.* Leiden.

Ozment, S. 1980. *The Age of Reform 1250–1550: An Intellectual and Religious History of Late Medieval and Reformation Europe.* New Haven.

Ozment, S. 1983. *When Fathers Ruled: Family Life in Reformation Europe.* Cambridge.

Packer, J. 2008. *Keeping the Ten Commandments.* Wheaton, IL.

Packull, W. 1977. *Mysticism and the Early South German-Austrian Anabaptist Movement 1525–1531.* Scottdale, PA.

Packull, W. 1995. *Hutterite Beginnings: Communitarian Experiments during the Reformation.* Baltimore.

Parish, H. 2005. *Monks, Miracles, and Magic: Reformation Representations of the Medieval Church.* London.

Parish, H. and W. Naphy. 2002. *Religion and Superstition in Reformation Europe.* Manchester.

Parish, H., and P. Sullivan. 1992. *Bartolomé de las Casas.* Mahwah, NJ.

Parker, C. 1998. *The Reformation of Community: Social Welfare and Calvinist Charity in Holland, 1572–1620.* Cambridge.

Parker, G. 1997. *The Thirty Years War.* 2nd ed. New York.

Parker, G. 1998. *The Grand Strategy of Philip II.* New Haven.

Parker, K., and E. Carlson. 1998. *'Practical Divinity': The Works and Life of Revd Richard Greenham.* Aldershot, UK.

Parker, T. 1992. *Calvin's Preaching.* Louisville.

Parker, T. 1995. *Calvin: An Introduction to His Thought.* Louisville.

Partee, C. 2008. *The Theology of John Calvin.* Louisville.

Pastor, L. 1969. *The History of the Popes, from the Close of the Middle Ages.* Vol. 14. Edited by R. Kerr. Reprint, London.

Patterson, M. 2007. *Domesticating the Reformation: Protestant Best-sellers, Private Devotion, and the Revolution of English Piety.* Madison.

Pedersen, O. 1991. *Galileo and the Council of Trent.* New ed. Vatican City.

Pelikan, J. 1975–91. *The Christian Tradition: A History of the Development of Doctrine.* 5 vols. Chicago.

Pelikan, J. 1996. *The Reformation of the Bible: The Bible of the Reformation.* New Haven.

Pelikan, J., and V. Hotchkiss, eds. 2003. *Creeds and Confessions of Faith in the Christian Tradition.* Vol. 2, pt. 4: *Creeds and Confessions of the Reformation Era.* New Haven.

Pellistrandi, B. 1991. "The University of Alcalá de Henares from 1568 to 1618: Students and Graduates." In *History of Universities,* ed. L. Brockliss, 119–66. Oxford.

Pereira, J. 2007. *Suárez: Between Scholasticism and Modernity.* Milwaukee.

Perez, J. 2005. *The Spanish Inquisition: A History.* New Haven.

Perkins, P. 1994. *Peter: Apostle for the Whole Church.* Columbia, SC.

Peschke, K. 1967. *Naturrecht in der Kontroverse: Kritik evangelischer Theologie an der katholischen Lehre von Naturrecht und natürlicher Sittlichkeit.* Salzburg.

Peters, E. 1988. *Inquisition.* New York.

Peters, T. 2005. "The Heart of Reformation Faith." *Dialogue: A Journal of Theology* 44:6–14.

Peterson, R., and M. Williams. 2004. *Why I Am Not an Arminian.* Downers Grove, IL.

Pettegree, A. 1986. *Foreign Protestant Communities in Sixteenth-Century London.* Oxford.

Pettegree, A. 1987. "The London Exile Community and the Second Sacramentarian Controversy, 1553–1560." *Archiv für Reformationsgeschichte* 78: 223–52.

Pettegree, A., ed. 1993. *The Reformation of the Parishes. The Ministry and the Reformation in Town and Country.* New York.

Phillips, R. 1988. *Putting Asunder. A History of Divorce in Western Society.* Cambridge.

Pieper, J. 1960. *Scholasticism: Personalities and Problems of Medieval Philosophy.* London.

Pierson, P. 1975. *Philip II of Spain.* New York.

Pinson, J., ed. 2002. *Four Views of Eternal Security.* Grand Rapids.

Pitkin, B. 1999. *What Pure Eyes Could See: Calvin's Doctrine of Faith in Its Exegetical Context.* Oxford.

Pitts, V. 2009. *Henri IV of France: His Reign and Age.* Baltimore.

Placher, W. 1988. *Readings in the History of Christian Theology.* Louisville.

Placher, W., ed. 2005. *Callings: Twenty Centuries of Christian Wisdom on Vocation.* Grand Rapids.

Pocock, J., ed. 2009. *Political Thought and History: Essays on Theory and Method.* Cambridge.

Polišensky, J. 1978. *War and Society in Europe, 1618–1648.* Cambridge.

Posset, F. 2003. *The Front-Runner of the Catholic Reformation: The Life and Works of Johannes von Staupitz.* London.

Post, R. 1968. *The Modern Devotion.* Leiden.

Potter, G. 1976. *Zwingli.* Cambridge.

Prestwich, M., ed. 1985. *International Calvinism 1541–1715.* Oxford.

210   Secondary Bibliography

Preus, H. 1948. *Communion of Saints: A Study of the Origin and Development of Luther's Doctrine of the Church.* Minneapolis.

Preus, J. 1969. *From Shadow to Promise: Old Testament Interpretation from Augustine to the Young Luther.* Cambridge.

Preus, R. 1972. *The Theology of Post-Reformation Lutheranism.* 2 vols. St. Louis.

Proske, M. 2007. *Lucas Cranach the Elder.* New York.

Pujo, B. 2003. *Vincent de Paul: The Trailblazer.* Translated by G. Champe. Notre Dame, IN.

Quistorp, H. 1955. *Calvin's Doctrine of the Last Things.* London.

Rabil, A., ed. 1988. *Renaissance Humanism: Foundations, Forms, and Legacy.* Philadelphia.

Rahner, K. 1967. "Reflections on the Theology of Renunciation." In *Theological Investigations* 3:47–57. Baltimore.

Raitt, J., ed. 1987. *Christian Spirituality: High Middle Ages and Reformation.* New York.

Raitt, J. 1993. *The Colloquy of Montbeliard: Religion and Politics in the Sixteenth Century.* New York.

Rapley, E. 1990. *The Dévotes: Women and Church in Seventeenth-Century France.* Montreal.

Ravier, A. 1987. *Ignatius of Loyola and the Founding of the Jesuits.* Translated by M. Daly et al. San Francisco.

Ravier, A. 1988. *Francis de Sales. Sage and Saint.* Translated by J. Bowler. San Francisco.

Rawlings, H. 2006. *The Spanish Inquisition.* Malden, MA.

Reid, J. 2000. "France." In *The Reformation World*, ed. A. Pettegree, 211–24. London.

Reinhard, W. 1989. "Reformation, Counter-Reformation, and the Early Modern State: A Reassessment." *Catholic Historical Review* 75:383–404.

Rempel, J. 1993. *The Lord's Supper in Anabaptism: A Study in the Christology of Balthasar Hubmaier, Pilgrim Marpack, and Dirk Philips.* Waterloo, ON.

Renouard, A. 1843. *Annales de l'imprimerie des Estienne.* Paris.

Repcheck, J. 2007. *Copernicus' Secret: How the Scientific Revolution Began.* New York.

Rex, R. 1991. *The Theology of John Fisher.* Cambridge.

Rex, R. 1992. "Cardinal Wolsey," *Catholic Historical Review* 78:607–14.

Rex, R. 2006. *Henry VIII and the English Reformation.* 2nd ed. Basingstoke.

Rischar, K. 1968. *Johann Eck auf dem Reichstag zu Augsburg 1530.* Münster.

Rittgers, R. 2004. *The Reformation of the Keys: Confession, Conscience and Authority in Sixteenth-Century Germany.* Cambridge.

Robb, N. 1935. *Neoplatonism of the Italian Renaissance.* London.

Rodgers, D. 1994. *John à Lasco in England.* New York.

Rodríguez-Salgado, M. 1988. *The Changing Face of Empire: Charles V, Philip II, and Habsburg Authority, 1551–1559.* Cambridge.

Rohls, J. 1998. *Reformed Confessions: Theology from Zurich to Barmen.* Translated by John Hoffmeyer. Louisville.

Roldan-Figueroa, R. 2005. "'Justified Without the Works of the Law': Casiodoro de Reina on Romans 3:28." In *The Formation of Clerical and Confessional Identities in Early Modern Europe*, ed. W. Janse and B. Pitkin, 205–24. Leiden.

Roldan-Figueroa, R. 2006a. "Filius Perditionis: The Propagandistic Use of a Biblical Motif in Sixteenth-Century Spanish Evangelical Bible Translations." *Sixteenth Century Journal* 37:1027–55.

Roldan-Figueroa, R. 2006b. "Reina's Vision of the Reformed Ministry: A Reconstruction from the Fringes of the 1569 Spanish Translation of the Bible." In *Lay Bibles in Europe 1450–1800*, ed. M. Lamberigts and A. den Hollander, 159–81. Leuven.

Roldan-Figueroa, R. 2009. "Antonio del Corro and Paul as the Apostle of the Gospel of Universal Redemption." In

A Companion to Paul in the Reformation, ed. R. Holder, 387–425. Boston.

Rorem, P. 1988. "Calvin and Bullinger on the Lord's Supper, Part II: The Agreement." *Lutheran Quarterly* 2:357–90.

Rosemann, P. 2004. *Peter Lombard*. New York.

Roth, J., and J. Stayer. 2007. *A Companion to Anabaptism and Spiritualism, 1521–1700.* Leiden.

Routley, E. 1960. *English Religious Dissent.* Cambridge.

Rowell, G. 1993. "The Sacramental Use of Oil in Anglicanism and the Churches of the Reformation." In *The Oil of Gladness: Anointing in the Christian Tradition,* ed. M. Dudley and G. Rowell, 134–54. London.

Rubin, M. 1991. *Corpus Christi: The Eucharist in Late Medieval Culture.* Cambridge.

Ruderman, D., ed. 1992. *Essential Papers on Jewish Culture in Renaissance and Baroque Italy.* New York.

Rummel, E. 1986. *Erasmus' Annotations on the New Testament: From Philologist to Theologian.* Toronto.

Rummel, E. 1989. *Erasmus and His Catholic Critics.* Nieuwkoop.

Rummel, E. 1998. *The Humanist-Scholastic Debate in the Renaissance and the Reformation.* Cambridge.

Rummel, E. 1999. *Jiménez de Cisneros: On the Threshold of Spain's Golden Age.* Tempe.

Rummel, E. 2000. *The Confessionalization of Humanism in Reformation Germany.* Oxford.

Rummel, E. 2002. *The Case Against Johann Reuchlin: Religious and Social Controversy in Sixteenth-Century Germany.* Toronto.

Rummel, E., ed. 2008. *Biblical Humanism and Scholasticism in the Age of Erasmus.* Leiden.

Rummel, E., and M. Kooistra, eds. 2007. *Reformation Sources: The Letters of Wolfgang Capito and His Fellow Reformers in Alsace and Switzerland.* Toronto.

Rupp, G. 1969. *Patterns of Reformation.* London.

Russell, W. 2002. "Luther, Prayer, and the Reformation." *Word & World* 22:49–54.

Ryan, E. 1936. *The Historical Scholarship of Saint Bellarmine.* New York.

Ryan, J. 1998. *The Apostolic Conciliarism of Jean Gerson.* Atlanta.

Ryrie, A. 2006. *The Origins of the Scottish Reformation.* Manchester, UK.

Saak, E. 2002. *High Way to Heaven: The Augustinian Platform between Reform and Reformation, 1292–1524.* Leiden.

Saarinen, R. 1994. *Weakness of the Will in Medieval Thought: From Augustine to Buridan.* Leiden.

Safley, T. 1984. *Let No Man Put Asunder: The Control of Marriage in the German Southwest; A Comparative Study, 1550–1600.* Kirksville, MO.

Samuel-Scheyder, M. 1993. *Johannes Cochlaeus: Humaniste et adversaire de Luther.* Nancy, France.

Santoni, R., ed. 1968. *Religious Language and the Problem of Religious Knowledge.* Bloomington, IN.

Sasse, H. 1959. *This Is My Body: Luther's Contention for the Real Presence.* Minneapolis.

Sauter, G. 2004. "Luther on the Resurrection." In *Harvesting Martin Luther's Reflections on Theology, Ethics, and the Church,* ed. Timothy Wengert, 99–118. Grand Rapids.

Scarisbrick, J. 1968. *Henry VIII.* London.

Schade, W. 1980. *Cranach: A Family of Master Painters.* Translated by Helen Sebba. New York.

Scheible, H. 1966. *Die Entstehung der Magdeburger Zenturien.* Gütersloh.

Schilling, H. 1986. "The Reformation and the Rise of the Early Modern State." In *Luther and the Modern State in Germany,* ed. J. Tracy, 21–30. Kirksville, MO.

Schilling, H. 1987. "'History of Crime' or 'History of Sin'? Some Reflections on the Social History of Early Modern Church Discipline." In *Politics and Society in Reformation Europe.*

Essays for Sir Geoffrey Elton on his 65th Birthday, ed. E. Kouri and T. Scott, 289–310. New York.

Schlütter-Schindler, G. 1986. *Der Schmalkaldische Bund und das Problem der causa religionis*. Frankfurt am Main.

Schneider, J. 1990. *Philip Melanchthon's Rhetorical Construal of Biblical Authority: Oratio Sacra*. Lewiston, NY.

Schneider, J. 1999. "The Hermeneutics of Commentary: Origins of Melanchthon's Integration of Dialectic into Rhetoric." In *Philip Melanchthon (1497–1560) and the Commentary*, ed. T. Wengert and M. Graham, 20–47. Sheffield.

Schreiner, S. 1991. "*The Theater of His Glory*": Nature and the Natural Order in the Thought of John Calvin. Durham, NC.

Schreiner, S. 2010. *Are You Alone Wise? Debates about Certainty in the Early Modern Era*. Oxford.

Schurhammer, G. 1973–82. *Francis Xavier: His Life, His Times*. 4 vols. Translated by M. Costelloe. Rome.

Schwab, P. 1933. *The Attitude of Wolfgang Musculus toward Religious Tolerance*. Scottdale, PA.

Schwanke, J. 2004. "Luther on Creation." In *Harvesting Martin Luther's Reflections on Theology, Ethics, and the Church*, ed. T. Wengert, 78–98. Grand Rapids.

Schwöbel, C. 1989. "The Creature of the Word: Recovering the Ecclesiology of the Reformers." In *On Being the Church: Essays on the Christian Community*, ed. C. Gunton and D. Hardy. Edinburgh, UK.

Scott, T. 1989. *Thomas Müntzer: Theology and Revolution in the German Reformation*. Basingstoke.

Scribner, R. 1981. *For the Sake of Simple Folk*. Oxford.

Scribner, R., and G. Benecke, eds. 1979. *The German Peasant War 1525: New Viewpoints*. London.

Selderhuis, H. 1999. *Marriage and Divorce in the Thought of Martin Bucer*. Translated by J. Vriend and L. Bierma. Kirksville, MO.

Senn, F. 1997. *Christian Liturgy: Catholic and Evangelical*. Minneapolis.

Seymour, G. 1885. *The Reformation, Monasticism and Vows*. New York.

Shagan, E. 2003. *Popular Politics and the English Reformation*. Cambridge.

Sheridan, D. 2006. "The Catholic Case: The Index of Prohibited Books." *Journal of Hindu-Christian Studies* 19:22–26.

Shuger, D. 2008. "The Reformation of Penance." *Huntington Library Quarterly* 71:557–71.

Sider, R. 1974. *Andreas Bodenstein von Karlstadt: The Development of His Thought, 1517–1525*. Leiden.

Sider, R. 2001. "Karlstadt, Luther, and the Perennial Debate." In *Karlstadt's Battle with Luther: Documents in Liberal-Radical Debate*, ed. Sider, 157–61. Reprint, Eugene, OR.

Signorotto, G., and M. Visceglia. 2002. *Court and Politics in Papal Rome, 1492–1700*. Cambridge.

Simpson, J. 2007. *Burning to Read: English Fundamentalism and Its Reformation Opponents*. Cambridge.

Simpson, M. 1978. *Defender of the Faith, Etcetera: Elizabeth of England, Her Church and Parliament, 1558–59*. Edinburgh.

Slade, C. 1995. *St. Teresa of Avila: Author of a Heroic Life*. Berkeley.

Smalley, B. 1964. *The Study of the Bible in the Middle Ages*. Notre Dame, IN.

Smith, J., and J. Olthuis, eds. 2005. *Radical Orthodoxy and Reformed Tradition: Creation, Covenant, and Participation*. Grand Rapids.

Smith, T. 1985. *Petrine Controversies in Early Christianity: Attitudes towards Peter in Christian Writings of the First Two Centuries*. Tübingen.

Smith, W. 2008. *Reformation and the German Territorial State*. Rochester.

Smitt, C. 1983. *Aristotle and the Renaissance*. Cambridge.

Snyder, C. 1981. "Anabaptism and Revolution: The Case of Michael Sattler." *Church History* 50:276–87.

Snyder, C. 1984. *The Life and Thought of Michael Sattler*. Scottdale.

Snyder, C. 2003. *Anabaptist History and Theology: An Introduction.* Kitchener, ON.

Snyder, C. 2006. "The Birth and Evolution of Swiss Anabaptism, 1520–1530." *Mennonite Quarterly Review* 80:501–645.

Southern, R. 1990. *Western Society and the Church in the Middle Ages.* Reprint, London.

Southgate, W. 1962. *John Jewel and the Problem of Doctrinal Authority.* Cambridge.

Spade, P., ed. 1999. *The Cambridge Companion to Ockham.* Cambridge.

Spahn, M. 1964. *Johannes Cochläus: Ein Lebensbild aus der Zeit der Kirchenspaltung.* Reprint, Nieuwkoop.

Spierling, K. 2005. *Infant Baptism in Reformation Geneva: The Shaping of a Community, 1536–1564.* Aldershot, UK.

Spijker, W. 1996. *The Ecclesiastical Offices in the Thought of Martin Bucer.* Leiden.

Spijker, W., ed. 2009. *The Church's Book of Comfort.* Translated by Gerrit Bilkes. Grand Rapids.

Spinka, M. 1966. *John Hus's Concept of the Church.* Princeton.

Spinka, M. 1968. *John Hus: A Biography.* Princeton.

Spinks, B. 2006. *Reformation and Modern Rituals and Theologies of Baptism: From Luther to Contemporary Practices.* Aldershot, UK.

Spitz, L. 1963. *The Religious Renaissance of the German Humanists.* Cambridge.

Spitz, L. 1972. *The Northern Renaissance.* Englewood Cliffs, NJ.

Spitz, L., and B. Tinsley. 1995. *Johann Sturm on Education.* St. Louis.

Springer, M. 2007. *Restoring Christ's Church: John a Lasco and the forma ac ratio.* Aldershot, UK.

Sproul, R. 1997. *Willing to Believe: The Controversy over Free Will.* Grand Rapids.

Spykman, G. 1955. *Attrition and Contrition at the Council of Trent.* Kampen.

Stafford, W. 1985. "Repentance on the Eve of the English Reformation: John Fisher's Sermons of 1508 and 1509." *Historical Magazine of the Protestant Episcopal Church* 54:297–338.

Stanglin, K. 2007. *Arminius on the Assurance of Salvation: The Context, Roots and Shape of the Leiden Debate, 1603–1609.* Leiden.

Stayer, J. 1976. *Anabaptists and the Sword.* 2nd ed. Lawrence, KS.

Stayer, J. 1994. *The German Peasants' War and Anabaptist Community of Goods.* Montreal.

Steinmetz, D. 1980. *Luther and Staupitz: An Essay in the Intellectual Origins of the Protestant Reformation.* Durham, NC.

Steinmetz, D. 1993. "Calvin and the Monastic Ideal." In *Anticlericalism in Late Medieval and Early Modern Europe,* ed. P. Dykema and H. Oberman, 605–16. Leiden.

Steinmetz, D. 1996. *The Bible in the Sixteenth Century.* Durham, NC.

Steinmetz, D. 2001a. "Johannes Bugenhagen (1485–1558): Structures of the Church." In *Reformers in the Wings: From Geiler von Kaysersberg to Theodore Beza,* 76–82. Rev. ed. New York.

Steinmetz, D. 2001b. *Reformers in the Wings: From Geiler von Kaysersberg to Theodore Beza.* Rev. ed. New York.

Steinmetz, D. 2002a. "Luther Against Luther." In *Luther in Context,* 1–11. 2nd ed. Grand Rapids.

Steinmetz, D. 2002b. "Luther and Calvin on Church and Tradition." In *Luther in Context,* 85–97. Grand Rapids.

Steinmetz, D. 2002c. *Luther in Context.* 2nd ed. Reprint, Grand Rapids.

Stephens, W. 1986. *The Theology of Huldrych Zwingli.* Oxford.

Stephens, W. 1992. *Zwingli: An Introduction to His Thought.* Oxford.

Stephens, W. 2004. "Bullinger's Defence of the Old Faith." *Reformation and Renaissance Review* 6:36–55.

Stern, S. 1965. *Josel of Rosheim.* Philadelphia.

Stone, L. 1977. *The Family, Sex and Marriage in England, 1500–1800.* New York.

Stone, M. 2000. "The Origins of Probabilism in Late Scholastic Moral

Thought: A Prolegomenon to Further Study." *Recherches de théologie et philosophie médiévales* 58:114–57.

Strand, K. 1982. *Catholic German Bibles of the Reformation Era: The Versions of Emser, Dietenberger, Eck, and Others.* Novato, CA.

Strasser, U. 1995. "Brides of Christ, Daughters of Men: Nuremberg Poor Clares in Defense of Their Identity (1524–1529)." *Magistra* 1, no. 2:193–248.

Strauss, G. 1976. *Nuremberg in the Sixteenth Century: City Politics and Life between Middle Ages and Modern Times.* Bloomington, IN.

Strauss, G. 1978. *Luther's House of Learning: Indoctrination of the Young in the German Reformation.* Baltimore.

Strauss, G., and R. Gawthorp. 1984. "Protestantism and Literacy in Germany." *Past and Present* 104:31–55.

Strehle, S. 1988. *Calvinism, Federalism and Scholasticism.* Bern.

Strehle, S. 1995. *The Catholic Roots of the Protestant Gospel: Encounter between the Middle Ages and the Reformation.* Leiden.

Stump, P. 1994. *The Reforms of the Council of Constance 1414–1418.* Leiden.

Stupperich, R. 2006. *Melanchthon.* Translated by R. Fischer. Cambridge.

Sunshine, G. 1994. "Reformed Theology and the Origins of Synodical Polity: Calvin, Beza, and the Gallican Confession." In *Later Calvinism: International Perspectives,* ed. W. Graham, 141–58. Kirksville, MO.

Sunshine, G. 2003. *Reforming French Protestantism: The Development of Huguenot Ecclesiastical Institutions, 1557–1572.* Kirksville, MO.

Surtz, E. 1967. *The Works and Days of John Fisher: An Introduction to the Position of St. John Fisher (1469–1535), Bishop of Rochester, in the English Renaissance and the Reformation.* Cambridge.

Sutherland, N. 1980. *The Huguenot Struggle for Recognition.* New Haven.

Swanson, R. 2007. *Indulgences in Late Medieval England.* Cambridge.

Swietlicki, C. 1986. *Spanish Cristian Cabala: The Works of Luis de León, Santa Teresa de Jesús, and San Juan de la Cruz.* Columbia, MO.

Symington, W. 2006. *The Atonement and Intercession of Jesus Christ.* Grand Rapids.

Taplin, M. 2003. *The Italian Reformers and the Zurich Church, c. 1540–1620.* Aldershot, UK.

Taylor, L., ed. 2001. *Preachers and People in the Reformations and Early Modern Period.* Leiden.

Tentler, T. 1977. *Sin and Confession on the Eve of the Reformation.* Princeton.

Thayer, A. 2002. *Preaching, Penitence and the Coming of the Reformation.* Aldershot, UK.

Thayer, A., and K. Lualdi, eds. 2000. *Penitence in the Age of Reformation.* Burlington, VT.

Thompson, B. 1980. *Liturgies of the Western Church.* Reprint, Philadephia.

Thompson, N. 2005. *Eucharistic Sacrifice and Patristic Tradition in the Theology of Martin Bucer 1534–1546.* Leiden.

Thomson, J. 1980. *Popes and Princes, 1417–151: Politics and Polity in the Late Medieval Church.* Boston.

Thysell, C. 2000. *The Pleasure of Discernment: Marguerite de Navarre as Theologian.* New York.

Tierney, B. 1955. *Foundations of the Conciliar Theory: The Contribution of the Medieval Canonists from Gratian to the Great Schism.* Cambridge.

Tierney, B. 1971. *Ockham, the Conciliar Theory, and the Canonists.* Philadelphia.

Tierney, B. 1982. *Religion, Law, and the Growth of Constitutional Thought, 1150–1650.* Cambridge.

Tracy, J. 1996. *Erasmus of the Low Countries.* Berkeley.

Tracy, J. 2002. *Emperor Charles V, Impresario of War: Campaign Strategy, International Finance, and Domestic Politics.* Cambridge.

Tracy, J. 2006. *Europe's Reformations, 1450–1650: Doctrine, Politics, and Community.* Lanham, MD.

Trigg, J. 1994. *Baptism in the Theology of Martin Luther.* Leiden.

Trinkaus, C. 1970. *In Our Image and Likeness: Humanity and Divinity in Italian Humanist Thought.* Chicago.

Turner, D. 1995. *Eros and Allegory: Medieval Exegesis of the Song of Songs.* Kalamazoo, MI.

Turner, P. 1987. *The Meaning and Practice of Confirmation: Perspectives from a Sixteenth-Century Controversy.* New York.

Tylenda, J. 1974. "The Calvin-Westphal Exchange: The Genesis of Calvin's Treatises against Westphal." *Calvin Theological Journal* 9:182–209.

Tylenda, J. 1976. "Calvin's First Reformed Sermon? Nicholas Cop's Discourse—1 November 1533." *Westminster Theological Journal* 38:300–318. (Also contains translation of address.)

Tylenda, J. 1977. "The Warning That Went Unheeded: John Calvin on Giorgio Biandrata." *Calvin Theological Journal* 12, no. 1:24–62.

Tylenda, J. 1997. "Calvin and Westphal: Two Eucharistic Theologies in Conflict." In *Calvin's Books: Festschrift Dedicated to Peter De Klerk on the Occasion of His Seventieth Birthday,* ed. W. Neuser et al., 9–21. Heerenveen, The Netherlands.

Urry, J. 2006. *Mennonites, Politics and Peoplehood.* Winnipeg.

VanDrunen, D. 2006. "Medieval Natural Law and the Reformation: A Comparison of Aquinas and Calvin." *American Catholic Philosophical Quarterly* 80, no. 1:77–98.

Van Halsema, T. 1961. *Glorious Heretic: The Story of Guido de Brès, Author of the Belgic Confession. Told for the First Time in English.* Grand Rapids.

van Liere, K. 2004. "Catholic Reform of the Divine Office in the Sixteenth Century: The Breviary of Cardinal Francisco de Quiñones." *Worship in Medieval and Early Modern Europe: Change and Continuity in Religious Practice,* ed. K. Maag and J. Witvliet, 162–202. Notre Dame, IN.

Van Wyk, J. 2001. "John Calvin on the Kingdom of God and Eschatology." *Die Skriflig* 35, no. 2:191–205.

Vaughan, H. 1971. *The Medici Popes.* Reprint, Port Washington, NY.

Vedder, H. 1905. *Balthasar Hübmaier, the Leader of the Anabaptists.* New York.

Venema, C. 1994. *But for the Grace of God: An Exposition of the Canons of Dort.* Grand Rapids.

Venema, C. 2002. *Heinrich Bullinger and the Doctrine of Predestination: Authors of "the Other Resformed Tradition"?* Grand Rapids.

Venema, C. 2007. *Accepted and Renewed in Christ: The "Twofold Grace of God" and the Interpretation of Calvin's Theology.* Göttingen.

Verkamp, B. 1977. *The Indifferent Mean: Adiaphorism in the English Reformation to 1554.* Athens, OH.

Vignaux, P. 1971. "On Luther and Ockham." In *The Reformation in Medieval Perspective,* ed. S. Ozment, 107–18. Chicago.

Vodola, E. 1986. *Excommunication in the Middle Ages.* Berkeley.

Vollmann, W. 2006. *Uncentering the Earth: Copernicus and the Revolutions of the Heavenly Spheres.* New York.

von der Lippe, G., and V. Reck-Malleczewen, eds. 2008. *A History of the Münster Anabaptists: Inner Emigration and the Third Reich.* New York.

Voogt, G. 2000. *Constraint on Trial: Dirck Volckertsz Coornhert and Religious Freedom.* Kirksville, MO.

Voolstra, S. 1997. *Menno Simons: His Image and Message.* North Newton, KS.

Wabuda, S. 1998. "'Fruitful Preaching' in the Diocese of Worcester: Bishop Hugh Latimer and His Influence, 1535–1539." In *Religion and the English People, 1500–1640: New Voices, New Perspectives,* ed. E. Carlson, 49–74. Kirksville, MO.

Wagner, D., ed. 1983. *The Seven Liberal Arts in the Middle Ages.* Bloomington, IN.

Wainwright, G. 1988. "Perfect Salvation in the Teachings of Wesley and Calvin." *Reformed World* 40, no. 2:898–909.

Waite, G. 2007. *Eradicating the Devil's Minions: Anabaptists and Witches in Reformation Europe, 1535–1600.* Toronto.

Walker, D. 2000. *Spiritual and Demonic Magic: From Ficino to Campanella.* Reprint, University Park, PA.

Walsham, A. 1999. *Providence in Early Modern England.* Oxford.

Walters, B., V. Corrigan, and P. Ricketts. 2006. *The Feast of Corpus Christi.* University Park, PA.

Walton, K. 2007. *Catholic Queen, Protestant Patriarchy: Mary, Queen of Scots, and the Politics of Gender and Religion.* Basingstoke.

Walton, K. 2008. "Scotland's City on a Hill." In *Defining Community in Early Modern Europe,* ed. Karen E. Spierling and Michael Halvorson, 247–66. Aldershot, UK.

Wandel, L. 1995. *Voracious Idols and Violent Hands: Iconoclasm in Reformation Zurich, Strasbourg, and Basel.* Cambridge.

Wandel, L. 2006. *The Eucharist in the Reformation: Incarnation and Liturgy.* Cambridge.

Warnicke, R. 2006. *Mary, Queen of Scots.* New York.

Watt, J. 2001. "The Impact of the Reformation and Counter-Reformation." In *Family Life in Early Modern Times 1500–1789,* ed. D. Kertzer and M. Barbagli, 125–54. New Haven.

Watts, M. 1978. *The Dissenters.* Vol. 1: *From the Reformation to the French Revolution.* Oxford.

Wawrykow, J. P. 1992. "John Calvin and Condign Merit." *Archiv für Reformationsgeschichte* 83:73–90.

Weber, A. 2000. "Spiritual Administration: Gender and Discernment in the Carmelite Reform." *Sixteenth Century Journal* 31:123–46.

Wedgewood, C. 1938. *The Thirty Years War.* London.

Wendebourg, D. 2005. "Luther on Monasticism." *Lutheran Quarterly* n.s., 19:125–52.

Wendel, F. 1997. *Calvin: Origins and Development of His Religious Thought.* Translated by Philip Mairet. Reprint, Grand Rapids.

Wengert, T. 1997. *Law and Gospel: Philip Melanchthon's Debate with John Agricola of Eisleben over Poenitentia.* Grand Rapids.

Wengert, T. 1998. *Human Freedom, Christian Righteousness: Philip Melanchthon's Exegetical Dispute with Erasmus of Rotterdam.* Oxford.

Wengert, T. 2005. "Martin Luther's 'Priesthood of All Believers' and Other Pious Myths." http://www.valpo.edu/ils/assets/pdfs/05_wengert.pdf.

Wengert, T., and M. Graham, eds. 1999. *Philip Melanchthon (1497–1560) and the Commentary.* Sheffield.

Werrell, R. 2006. *The Theology of William Tyndale.* Cambridge.

White, K. 1997. *Hispanic Philosophy in the Age of Discovery.* Washington, D.C.

White, R. 2007. "An Early Doctrinal Handbook: Farel's *Summaire et briefve declaration.*" *Westminster Theological Journal* 69:21–38.

Whitford, D. 2001. *Tyranny and Resistance: The Magdeburg Confession and the Lutheran Tradition.* St. Louis.

Whitford, D. 2004. "*Cura Religionis* or Two Kingdoms: The Late Luther on Religion and the State." *Church History* 73, no. 1:41–62.

Wicks, J. 1977. "Thomism between Renaissance and Reformation: The Case of Cajetan." *Archiv für Reformationsgeschichte* 68:9–31.

Wicks, J. 1992. *Luther's Reform: Studies on Conversion and the Church.* Mainz.

Wiesner, M. 2008. *Women and Gender in Early Modern Europe.* 3rd ed. Cambridge.

Wiesner-Hanks, M. 2000. *Christianity and Sexuality in the Early Modern World: Regulating Desire, Reforming Practice.* London.

Wilcox, P. 1997. "Conversion in the Thought and Experience of John Calvin." *Anvil* 14:113–28.

Wiley, T. 2002. *Original Sin: Origins, Developments, Contemporary Meanings.* New York.

Williams, G. H. 1992. *The Radical Reformation.* 3rd ed. Kirksville, MO.

Williams, G. S., and C. Gunnoe Jr., eds. 2002. *Paracelsian Moments: Science, Medicine, and Astrology in Early Modern Europe.* Kirksville, MO.

Williams, T. 2003. *The Cambridge Companion to Duns Scotus.* Cambridge.

Willis, E. D. 1966. *Calvin's Catholic Christology: The Function of the So-called Extra Calvinisticum in Calvin's Theology.* Leiden.

Wilson, N. 1992. *From Byzantium to Italy: Greek Studies in the Italian Renaissance.* London.

Wilson, S. 2000. *The Magical Universe: Everyday Ritual and Magic in Premodern Europe.* New York.

Wingren, G. 1957. *Luther on Vocation.* Philadelphia.

Winter, E., ed. and trans. 2002. *Discourse on Free Will: Erasmus and Luther.* Reprint, New York.

Witte, J., Jr. 1997. *From Sacrament to Contract: Marriage, Religion, and Law in the Western Tradition.* Louisville.

Witte, J., Jr. 2002. *Law and Protestantism: The Legal Teachings of the Lutheran Reformation.* Cambridge.

Witte, J., Jr., and R. Kingdon. 2005. *Sex, Marriage, and Family in John Calvin's Geneva, Volume 1: Courtship, Engagement, and Marriage.* Grand Rapids.

Wolfe, M. 1993. *The Conversion of Henri IV: Politics, Power, and Religious Belief in Early Modern France.* Cambridge.

Wolter, A. 1990. *The Philosophical Theology of John Duns Scotus.* Ithaca, NY.

Wood, D., ed. 1993. *Martyrs and Martyrologies.* Oxford.

Wood, D., ed. 1994. *The Church and Childhood: Papers Read at the 1993 Summer Meeting and the 1994 Winter Meeting of the Ecclesiastical History Society.* Oxford.

Woodford, C. 2002. *Nuns as Historians in Early Modern Germany.* Oxford.

Wooding, L. 2008. *Henry VIII.* London.

Wright, A. 1982. *The Counter-Reformation: Catholic Europe and the Non-Christian World.* New York.

Wright, A. 2000. *The Early Modern Papacy: From the Council of Trent to the French Revolution, 1564–1789.* Essex.

Wright, D., ed. 1994. *Martin Bucer: Reforming Church and Community.* Cambridge.

Wright, D. 1997. "Calvin's Accomodating God." In *Calvinus Sincerioris Religionis Vindex,* ed. W. Neuser and B. Armstrong, 3–20. Kirksville, MO.

Wright, D. 2006. "Why Was Calvin So Severe a Critic of Nicodemism?" In *Calvin Evangelii Propugnator: Calvin, Champion of the Gospel; Papers from the International Congress on Calvin Research, Seoul, 1998,* ed. D. Wright, A. Lane, and J. Balserak, 66–90. Grand Rapids.

Wright, W. 1985a. *Bond of Perfection: Jeanne de Chantal and François de Sales.* New York.

Wright, W. 1985b. "Philip of Hesse's Vision of Protestant Unity and the Marburg Colloquy." In *Pietas et Societas: New Trends in Reformation History,* ed. K. Sessions and P. Bebb, 163–79. Kirksville, MO.

Wright, W. 2010. *Martin Luther's Understanding of God's Two Kingdoms.* Grand Rapids.

Wyatt, P. 1996. *Jesus Christ and Creation in the Theology of John Calvin.* Eugene, OR.

Yates, N. 2008. *Liturgical Space: Christian Worship and Church Buildings in Western Europe 1500–2000.* Aldershot, UK.

Young, F. 1991. *The Making of the Creeds.* Philadelphia.

Zachman, R. 1993. *The Assurance of Faith: Conscience in the Theology of Martin Luther and John Calvin.* Minneapolis.

Zachman, R. 2006. "Jesus Christ as the Image of God in Calvin's Theology." *Calvin Theological Journal* 25:45–62.

Zachman, R. 2007. *Image and Word in the Theology of John Calvin,* Notre Dame, IN.

Zeeden, E., and H. Moliter, eds. 1977. *Die Visitation im Dienst der kirchlichen Reform.* Münster.

Zeman, J. 1977. *The Hussite Movement and the Reformation in Bohemia, Moravia, and Slovakia (1350–1650): A Bibliographical Study Guide.* Ann Arbor, MI.

Zeumer, K. 1904. *Quellensammlung zur Geschichte der Deutschen Reichsverfassung.* Leipzig.

Ziegler, D., ed. 1969. *Great Debates of the Reformation.* New York.

Zorzin, A. 1990. *Karlstadt als Flugschriftenautor.* Göttingen.

Zweig, S. 1936. *The Right to Heresy: Castellio against Calvin.* New York.